GHOST, THUNDERBOLT, AND WIZARD

The Stackpole Military History Series

THE AMERICAN CIVIL WAR
Cavalry Raids of the Civil War
Ghost, Thunderbolt, and Wizard
Pickett's Charge
Witness to Gettysburg

WORLD WAR II
Armor Battles of the Waffen-SS, 1943–45
Army of the West
Australian Commandos
The B-24 in China
Backwater War
The Battle of Sicily
Beyond the Beachhead
The Brandenburger Commandos
The Brigade
Bringing the Thunder
Coast Watching in World War II
Colossal Cracks
D-Day to Berlin
Dive Bomber!
Eagles of the Third Reich
Exit Rommel
Fist from the Sky
Flying American Combat Aircraft
    of World War II
Forging the Thunderbolt
Fortress France
The German Defeat in the East, 1944–45
German Order of Battle, Vol. 1
German Order of Battle, Vol. 2
German Order of Battle, Vol. 3
Germany's Panzer Arm in World War II
GI Ingenuity
Grenadiers
Infantry Aces
Iron Arm
Iron Knights
Kampfgruppe Peiper at the
    Battle of the Bulge
Luftwaffe Aces
Massacre at Tobruk
Messerschmitts over Sicily

Michael Wittmann, Vol. 1
Michael Wittmann, Vol. 2
Mountain Warriors
The Nazi Rocketeers
On the Canal
Packs On!
Panzer Aces
Panzer Aces II
The Panzer Legions
Panzers in Winter
The Path to Blitzkrieg
Retreat to the Reich
Rommel's Desert War
The Savage Sky
A Soldier in the Cockpit
Soviet Blitzkrieg
Stalin's Keys to Victory
Surviving Bataan and Beyond
T-34 in Action
Tigers in the Mud
The 12th SS, Vol. 1
The 12th SS, Vol. 2
The War against Rommel's Supply Lines

THE COLD WAR / VIETNAM
Flying American Combat Aircraft:
    The Cold War
Here There Are Tigers
Land with No Sun
Street without Joy

WARS OF THE MIDDLE EAST
Never-Ending Conflict

GENERAL MILITARY HISTORY
Carriers in Combat
Desert Battles

GHOST, THUNDERBOLT, AND WIZARD

Mosby, Morgan, and Forrest in the Civil War

Col. Robert W. Black

STACKPOLE
BOOKS

Published by
STACKPOLE BOOKS
5067 Ritter Road
Mechanicsburg, PA 17055
www.stackpolebooks.com

Cover design by Tracy Patterson

Printed in the United States of America

10 9 8 7 6 5 4 3 2 1

FIRST EDITION

Library of Congress Cataloging-in-Publication Data

Black, Robert W.
    Ghost, thunderbolt, and wizard : Mosby, Morgan, and Forrest in the Civil War /
Robert W. Black. — 1st ed.
        p. cm. — (Stackpole military history series)
    Includes bibliographical references and index.
    ISBN-13: 978-0-8117-0203-4
    ISBN-10: 0-8117-0203-0
    1. Guerrillas—Confederate States of America—Biography. 2. Soldiers—
Confederate States of America—Biography. 3. Mosby, John Singleton, 1833–1916.
4. Morgan, John Hunt, 1825–1864. 5. Forrest, Nathan Bedford, 1821–1877.
6. United States—History—Civil War, 1861–1865—Underground movements.
7. United States—History—Civil War, 1861–1865—Cavalry operations. 8. United
States—History—Civil War, 1861–1865—Biography. 9. Confederate States of
America. Army—Biography. I. Title.
    E467358 2008
    973.7'84—dc22
                                                                                    2007037103

Table of Contents

In memory of my great-grandfathers,
Private 2nd Class William Henry Westervelt, Company E, 15th New York
Volunteer Engineers, who served the Union at Yorktown, Malvern Hill,
Fredericksburg, the Mud March, and Chancellorsville,

and

Sergeant John Wesley Black, Company I, 42nd North Carolina Infantry,
who served the Confederacy at Cold Harbor, Petersburg, and Bentonville;

and in memory of my great-granduncle,
Private Eli Black, Company C ("The Rip Van Winkles"), 2nd Regiment,
North Carolina Infantry, who was drafted into the Confederate Army on
July 8, 1862, died of disease near Richmond on February 17, 1863, and
left his widow an estate of $1.15 in Confederate currency

Prologue

A perfect instrument of death, the hawk circled watchfully in the leaden gray Virginia sky. The eyesight of a hawk is a miracle of nature, giving it the ability to see prey from a distance of three miles. The hawk saw many things, but only that which it could kill was of interest.

Below, not far from the twisting ribbon of steel that was a railroad, two cavalrymen in Union blue sat in silent misery, beating their arms against the onslaught of the bitter cold. Inspired by patriotism, they had answered Father Abraham's call and joined the army in the fall of 1862. They had been told they would have a good time in the cavalry, but now it was January 1863 and all they had known was work and discomfort. The men wanted to fight the Johnnies, but their regiment had the mission of guarding railroad tracks and bridges. These soldiers were called "Vedettes," the outer fringe of the outpost line, the forward edge of the defense system of Washington D.C., the capital of the United States. There was no satisfaction in the job. It was endless hours of misery and boredom, sitting in a cold leather saddle, staring through snow, sleet or rain, waiting for an enemy to come. Every now and then some damn bushwhacker would come sneaking up in the bushes with a rifle or shotgun and kill a soldier or shatter an arm or leg that the surgeons would saw off, maiming that man for life. On occasion guerrilla bands hit an outpost and the troopers there just disappeared. After that, there would be a period of heightened watchfulness, but it was so hard to always be alert.

One of the two cavalrymen looked up and saw blue sky in the distance. "It'll get better, Bill," he told his comrade.

"Yeah, but it'll be a damn long time coming," said Bill, then pointed upward at the hawk. "That's something to watch," he said, as he momentarily stopped shivering. "I'll bet we get to see a kill."

Across the clearing, concealed behind dense brush, ten horsemen looked with hungry eyes at the Union soldiers. Most of these Rangers were dressed in gray uniforms, but some of them wore captured Union blue overcoats as an outer garment. The leader, an undistinguished looking man about five feet seven and weighing 125 pounds, bent forward in the saddle as he heard the footfall of the eleventh rider. "Seven more behind these two," the returning scout said softly. "They're snugged up around a fire." The leader caressed the grips of the Colt .44 revolver he carried at his waist and lifted it from its holster; the other men followed the example of the leader. Most of them were armed with at least two revolvers and some carried three or four—the extras in saddle holsters or stuck down in a boot.

Overhead the hawk folded its wings and fell to the kill. "I told you he'd get him," said the cavalryman named Bill.

Across the clearing, the Ranger leader used his left hand to touch the rein to his horse's neck. With his right hand, he raised his pistol shoulder high. "Now boys!" he said grimly. "Let's go through them!"

September 17, 1863. The former superintendent and professor of engineering of what one day would be called Louisiana State University sat on a camp stool beneath a canvas roof penning a letter to Gen. Henry Halleck, general in chief of U.S. forces. Gen. William T. Sherman grinned as he thought of the words of South Carolina lawyer James L. Petigru who had observed South Carolina was "too small to be a Republic and too large for a lunatic asylum," but South Carolina had left the Union on December 20, 1860, and other Southern states quickly followed. At 4:20 on the morning of April 12, 1861, the fiery secessionist Edmund Ruffin pulled the lanyard on the first cannon to fire on U.S. soldiers, at Fort Sumter in Charleston Harbor. Five days later Virginia seceded and its governor, John Letcher, sent a message to Andrew Sweeney, the mayor of the city of Wheeling: "Seize the custom house, the post office, and all public buildings and documents in the name of the sovereign state of Virginia." Mayor Sweeney responded, "I have seized upon the custom house, the post office and all public buildings and documents in the name of Abraham Lincoln, President of the United States, whose property they are."

In Virginia the question was asked, "Will brother fight brother?" The answer was "Aye, when the mother is struck."[1]

As hot voices filled the air, women sewed uniforms and brightly colored banners, men sharpened sabers and practiced musketry. A man said he felt patriotic and when asked what that meant he replied, "I feel as if I wanted to kill somebody or steal something." [2]

The pounding of hooves as a dispatch rider reined his horse to halt outside the tent momentarily distracted Sherman. He heard the muffled voice of a staff officer receiving the message, then returned to his remembrance.

On April 25, 1862, the War Department of the Confederate States of America established and published "The Partisan Ranger Act" as General order No. 30. The orders spelled out the authorization by the Confederate Congress for the army to "form bands of partisan Rangers in companies, battalions or regiments, either as infantry or cavalry—the companies, battalions, or regiments to be composed, each of such numbers as the president may approve."

These same orders gave those partisan Rangers who were regularly received in the service the same pay, rations, quarters and status as members of the land forces of the Confederate States of America. This was important as it gave them legal protection under the rules of war. They were permitted to elect their officers.

Section 3 of the order would be controversial: "Be it further enacted, that for any arms and munitions of war captured from the enemy by any body of partisan Rangers, and delivered to any quartermaster at such place or places as may be designated by a commanding general, the Rangers shall be paid their full value, in such manner as the Secretary of War may prescribe."

Thus Section 3 introduced a profit motive into membership in these units. It set them apart from the line unit soldier who did not receive such reimbursement. The prospect of monetary gain would attract some undesirable men who were more interested in wealth than patriotism. When uncontrolled, it was only a small step to robbery and murder, not just of the enemy, but of their own citizens. When controlled it was the best recruiting tool the Rangers had. In most wars the manufacturers make money while the soldier gets nothing but misery but under the Partisan Ranger Act a fighting man could make a profit.

Virginia's initial effort to form local Ranger units failed due to lack of supervision. The officers in some of these units could not or would not control their men. Their criminal acts enraged both North and South and cast a shadow over future Ranger units and Ranger operations.

Many ruthless men sought to use the Partisan Ranger Act as a cover for their depredations. Even William Clark Quantrill, the butcher of Lawrence, Kansas, enrolled his men under its protection of legitimacy. The actions of these murderers detracted from the valuable service being done by authentic Rangers. There was intense jealousy on the part of generals who often did not have the knowledge to employ Rangers effectively, yet resented the idea of independent commands. Despite these problems, Sherman knew the Confederate Ranger performed a unique service to their cause. In Virginia alone, Rangers Mosby, McNeill, Gilmore and White—commanding fewer than 2,000 effectives—would tie down the equivalent of two Union corps by forcing the United States Army to guard everything. Some 30,000 to 35,000 Union soldiers would be kept from the battlefront by Ranger action.

Sherman put pen to paper and described the people of the South as being of four classes: The first was the large planters, the ruling class; the second was the small farmers and mechanics; the third was the Union men of the South and the fourth was the "young bloods." Sherman wrote of this

group, "War suits them, and the rascals are brave, fine riders, bold to rash-
ness and dangerous subjects in every sense. . . . This is a larger class than
most men suppose, and they are the most dangerous set of men that this war
has turned loose upon the world."[3] It was this class of "young bloods" that
produced the Rangers of the Confederacy.

No fighting force of the United States of America carries into battle a
heritage that equals that of the Army Ranger. With roots that reach deep
into the 1600s, the Rangers fought six American wars before the United
States was formed. The Rangers were citizen-soldiers, products of the American frontier. All volunteers who used a blend of Indian tactics and Euro-
pean discipline and weapons, the Rangers were experts at reconnaissance,
ambush and raid. The war was fought primarily in the South and the local
populace usually favored the cause of the Confederacy. These two factors
were critical to the frequent success of the Confederate Ranger.

Three Confederate Rangers occupy a special place in the history of the
Civil War. John Singleton Mosby became known as "The Gray Ghost," John
Hunt Morgan was called "The Thunderbolt of the Confederacy," and
Nathan Bedford Forrest was "The Wizard of the Saddle."

This is the story of the Ghost, the Thunderbolt, and the Wizard.

PART ONE

Ghost

CHAPTER ONE

The Gray Ghost

The man most closely linked to the word "Ranger" in the Civil War was Virginia-born John Singleton Mosby. In his work "The Scout toward Aldie," Herman Melville would write:

"As glides in seas the shark
Rides Mosby through green dark."

John Singleton Mosby was born December 6, 1833, at Edgemont, Powhatan County, Virginia, about 40 miles west of Richmond. His father, Alfred Mosby, was a farmer from Amherst County and his mother, Virginia, was the daughter of an Episcopal minister.[1] In 1838, the family moved to a farm near Charlottesville, where, from a nearby ridge, young Mosby could see Thomas Jefferson's home, Monticello.[2] In 1849 Mosby entered the University of Virginia. He was a good student, proficient in the classics and languages, but devoid of mathematical skills. His readings were wide ranging and his inquiring mind made him a good conversationalist and companion.

Mosby shot a bully named Turpin who threatened him. The wound was slight, but sufficient to bring a judgment of a year in prison and a $500 fine against Mosby. These were later rescinded when the facts became known. However, while young Mosby was spending time in jail, he became enamored of the law that consigned him there and decided to be a lawyer. When his studies were complete, he established his law practice in Howardsville, Albemarle County, Virginia. Mosby married Pauline Clarke, the daughter of a former congressman from Kentucky, on December 30, 1857, at Nashville and settled in Bristol, Virginia. Children came quickly, beginning with a daughter, May Virginia, and a son, Beverly, the name of Mosby's father-in-law.

By 1860, talk of secession was commonplace in Virginia, and militia units were forming throughout the counties. Mosby had grown up with the practice of slavery and, when a boy, had a slave as a personal servant. African slavery was an accepted practice of his time, but he was never known to speak in favor of it. He believed each state should have the right to decide if it would have slavery within its borders or not. He was a strong Union man, arguing against those who would tear the Union apart.

John S. Mosby, leader of Mosby's Rangers and the "ghost of the Confederacy," in full uniform. For the photograph, he poses with a saber, a weapon he described as "useful for cooking meat over a fire." In battle Mosby favored revolvers. USAMHI

It was a time when hot words by politicians and men of influence and financial power made secession seem a viable, indeed, the only choice. Robert Barnwell Rhett Sr. and William Lowndes Yancy of Alabama were not men known for battlefield accomplishment, but they were secessionist fire-brands who could stir up crowds and get the fight started. Confederate general Richard Taylor later noted that "a majority of the people of the South approved secession as the only remedy suggested by their leaders." Taylor wrote, "So travelers enter railway carriages and are dragged up grades and through tunnels with utter loss of volition, the motive power, generated by fierce heat, being far in advance and beyond their control."[3]

Had Virginia not left the United States, Mosby likely would have fought for the Stars and Stripes. Like Robert E. Lee, his primary loyalty lay with the state of Virginia. When Virginia seceded, so did John Singleton Mosby. Throughout his life, Mosby the lawyer felt that Lincoln had a legal precedent for calling out troops to suppress the Southern rebellion. He found it in the Pennsylvania Whiskey Rebellion of 1794 when Virginian George Washington had called up and dispatched troops to western Pennsylvania.[4] The man in command of the expedition in Pennsylvania was Virginian, "Light Horse" Harry Lee, the father of Gen. Robert E. Lee, with Virginian Dan Morgan leading advance troops.

Fearing war was coming, Mosby joined a militia unit to begin learning to be a soldier. In April 1861 he closed his law office and began military experience as a private under William E. "Grumble" Jones, the best cusser in the Confederate army. When the devout Stonewall Jackson was having difficulty with a subordinate, Grumble Jones offered to cuss out the man for him.[5] Jones was a U.S. Military Academy graduate, a tough fighter and strong disciplinarian. He drilled his "Washington Mounted Rifles" with colorful and profane commands.

Mosby was without friends in the cavalry company and requested a transfer to the infantry where he knew some people. The request disappeared in some administrative black hole, as both foot soldiers and horsemen were ordered to the defense of Richmond. The cavalry rode a distance Mosby called about 500 miles and the infantry went by train. Mosby would later write that at the time he was broken hearted his transfer did not go through.[6]

At Bunker Hill, a small community on the turnpike between Winchester and Martinsburg, The Washington Rifles[7] joined the 1st Regiment of Virginia cavalry commanded by 28-year-old Col. J.E.B. Stuart. Sharp's rifles were issued, and the good soldier Mosby was given one of them. His company had been issued sabers, but Mosby disliked them. In his memoirs he would write, "the only real use I ever heard of their being put to was to hold a piece of meat over the fire for frying."[8]

The young lawyer adapted well to campaigning. When Mosby heard that Col. J.J. Daniel was raising a unit of mounted Rangers in Gen. Henry Wise's brigade, the idea appealed to him. On Thursday, July 11, 1861, while on a scouting mission, Mosby's company captured two foraging Union soldiers from New York. Mosby got a zinc canteen that he treasured.[9] These men were the first of many prisoners he would take. But for the time being, the front was mostly quiet. For the first ninety days of the war, Mosby saw little action, but during that time he learned the routine of the soldier.

In July 1861, Stuart's command moved eastward from the Shenandoah and joined Beauregard's Confederate army to take part in the battle of Manassas (Bull Run). The Confederates were amazed at their own success in the battle. For the Union soldier there was little but scorn. Puffed up by their success at Manassas, many southerners thought the war would end quickly, and that northern men would sue for peace.

Mosby was proud of Virginia and wrote Pauline deriding South Carolina troops, "When we arrived on the field we met them running."[10] From a hilltop near Big Falls on the Potomac, the Confederates had a view of the capitol in Washington. Mosby wrote Pauline on Saturday, September 14, 1861, "We could see it distinctly with all their fortifications and the Stars and Stripes floating over it. I thought of the last time I had seen it, for you were there with me and I could not help but feel some regrets that it was no longer the capital of my country but that of a foreign, hostile foe."[11]

The character and spirit of the 125-pound Mosby soon caught the eye of senior officers. Six Colt pistols were secured for his company. Mosby was given one of the revolvers with the understanding that he and the other men who received them would serve as spearhead for the company when on raids. Doing picket duty along the Potomac River, Mosby and his comrades had frequent brushes with Union outposts. In these brief actions Mosby showed an aggressive spirit and a clear head. Nothing he experienced at this stage taught him respect for the enemy. In a September 17, 1861, letter to his sister Liz, Mosby wrote, "Nobody thinks the war will continue longer than a few months. We will clean them out in two more battles."[12] In November he killed a Union soldier from the Brooklyn Zouaves.

J. E. B Stuart liked what he heard about Mosby and began to take notice of this young lawyer serving as a private soldier. Stuart loved the company of beautiful women, and Private Mosby was selected to drive the carriage of some female friends home after a party. Mission completed on a snowy night, Mosby returned to Stuart's headquarters to get a pass back to his unit. Stuart, Gen. Joseph Johnston and G.W. Smith were at the headquarters by a fire and permitted Private Mosby not only to stay overnight, but also have dinner and breakfast with them. Mosby was in awe of their rank. He wrote, "I actually got into conversation with Joe Johnston, whom I would have regarded it as a great privilege the day before to view through a long range telescope."[13]

Though he was uncomfortable, Private Mosby must have impressed his seniors. The following day he was promoted from private to first lieutenant in the 1st Virginia Cavalry. He was appointed regimental adjutant, a position that gave him great difficulty as he had no experience in formal commands or dress parade procedures. It was Mosby's least-desired job as an officer. He would note, "I was never half as much frightened in any fight I was in as I was on that first dress parade I conducted."[14]

Stuart needed someone to go on a reconnaissance of Union forces. Mosby volunteered, asking only for a guide of the area. His mission was successful and brought recognition of his ability to move without discovery in enemy territory. Adjutant Mosby was in good position for promotion. His mentor Stuart was now a brigadier general, and his friend Grumble Jones had command of Stuart's former regiment. But command was determined by election, and Fitzhugh Lee was elected colonel, replacing Jones. Citizen-soldier Mosby was not sufficiently polished for Fitz Lee. Legend has it that when as Adjutant Mosby announced, "Colonel, the horn has blowed for dress parade," Lee was furious. "Sir!" he is said to have responded, " If I ever again hear you call that bugle a horn, I will put you under arrest." The sour relationship caused Mosby to resign as adjutant and with the resignation went his commission. He began to scout for Stuart as a private soldier. Mosby's relationship with Stuart was one of absolute admiration and loyalty.[15]

In June of 1862 on the Virginia peninsula, Union general McClellan's Army of the Potomac had taken position between the James and Pamunkey rivers. The right flank of the Union army was intended to be the Pamunkey and the left on the James. A creek named the Totopotomoy flowed into the Pamunkey and Stuart sent Mosby on a reconnaissance there to determine the accuracy of reports of enemy activity.

The 8th Illinois Cavalry, attached to Porter's corps, was providing men for a picket line of some eight to ten miles length, The efficient Hoosiers had passed warnings up the chain of command that there was an open area of several miles between their right flank and the Pamunkey River, but their warnings were disregarded. Mosby found the gap and reported that Confederate cavalry could pass easily through it.[16] Stuart was much impressed and ordered Mosby to write and sign the intelligence report that Stuart would take to General Lee.[17] Stuart wanted Lee to know of Mosby.

The results were orders from Lee that sent Stuart, Mosby and some 1,200 troopers and Pelham's artillery on the famed June 13–15, 1862, ride around McClellan's army. This was the first major raid of the war. The primary accomplishments of the raid were that it caused Union leadership to take men needed for the battle line to guard Washington D.C., and the impact it had on lowering morale in the North and raising it in the South. Mosby bragged to his wife about the raid in a Monday, June 16, 1862, letter: "I not only helped to execute, but was the first one who conceived and demonstrated that it was practicable."[18]

Mosby stood high in Stuart's favor and promotion seemed guaranteed. In early September 1862, the Confederate army moved north and into the bloody battle of Sharpsburg (Antietam). More of a spectator than participant at this horror that caused 28,000 casualties in a single day of battle, Mosby saw the dead and wounded and described the numbers of torn and bleeding bodies in his memoirs as "Like leaves of the forest when autumn hath blown."[19]

As cold weather set in, Mosby continued to lead small numbers of men on scouting operations. These missions made him keenly aware of the importance of knowing the terrain. He became adept at striking with the advantage of surprise. He began a tactic of vocal commands to imaginary Confederate units. On several occasions this created a panic that caused larger Union units to withdraw, leaving valuable equipment behind. Captured enemy materiel was his principal means of supply. Mosby wrote that he believed in the Napoleonic principle of making war support war.[20] It is not unusual in war to overestimate the number of the enemy. Mosby was a reasonably reliable scout, but in his writings home of the number of enemy he overcame in battle, there was a tendency to exaggerate. In a December 9, 1862, letter to his wife Pauline, he claimed that while on a scout to Manassas with nine men he "stampeded two or three thousand Yankees."[21]

Heading back to join Lee's army, Stuart made a temporary headquarters in Loudoun County. He choose the little community of Dover, located between Aldie and Middleburg. Mosby liked the area, describing it as "a land flowing with plenty."[22] As Stuart prepared to leave Loudoun, Mosby asked permission to remain behind for a few days with a squad of men. Stuart consented and gave Mosby nine men. Mosby claimed this was the start of his career as a Ranger.[23]

The Union defense of Washington was spread in a wide arc about the city. Since the spring of 1862, a combined force of Union artillery, cavalry and infantry had been headquartered at Fairfax Court House. The cavalry consisted of a brigade commanded by English volunteer Col. Percy Wyndham. The regiments of this brigade were the 1st Vermont, the 5th New York, the 18th Pennsylvania and the 1st Virginia (West Virginia). The men of

these cavalry regiments were scattered into forward outposts from Centreville to Dranesville and from there to the Potomac River; this was a line
extending some twenty miles.[24]

Much of the Union forward line consisted of small outposts backed up
by detachments large enough to provide at least two reliefs of the forward
outpost. The frontage covered was so large that in many cases the reserve
would require a half hour after notification to come to the assistance of an
outpost. The outpost duty was that of a weary guard watching for days, weeks
or months for an attack that might not come. The Reverend Louis N.
Boudrye, the historian of the 5th New York Cavalry, described the duty as,
"Mounted upon their shivering horses, the poor fellows with nothing cheer-
ing, but their courage, go out to sit in the saddle for two hours, facing the
biting wind, and peering through the storm of sleet, snow or rain which
pelts them in the face mercilessly. Happy if the guerrilla does not creep
through bushes impenetrable to the sight to inflict his cruel blows, the two
hours expired, relief comes and the Vedette [mounted guard] returns to
spend his four, six or eight hours off duty as best he may."[25]

With their companies scattered and deprived of their mobility by fixed
positioning, the morale of the Union cavalry suffered greatly. As expressed
in the history of the 1st Vermont Cavalry, "The arrangement of picket
stations could hardly have been better adapted to encourage the operations
of Mosby, and it is not surprising that these were often successful."[26]

At least one account has Mosby beginning independent operation on
January 2, 1863.[27] If not Mosby, someone was raiding his chosen area in early
January. The history of the 5th New York Cavalry recounts for Monday,
January 5, 1863:

> "At a post called Frying Pan, the pickets were attacked by guerrillas,
> and quite a number of the men were captured. The nature of
> the country is such as to afford the enemy the greatest possible
> advantage. Deep ravines, skirted by massive foliage summer and
> winter, give him shelter, while his knowledge of every road and foot-
> path gives him a fine opportunity to escape with his booty in case
> of pursuit."[28]

The next day the guerrillas struck the 5th New York again. A frustrated
Union officer wrote of Tuesday, January 6, 1863, " Several men were captured and one wounded on picket at Cub Run. The guerrillas are very
active. The utmost vigilance on our part cannot secure us perfectly from
their depredations. The only way to rid ourselves of this plague would be to
scour the entire country with a large force, arrest every male inhabitant able

to carry a musket, and burn to the ground every building, including houses, where these bushwhackers reside or find refuge. To so stern a punishment, falling upon the innocent and the guilty with like terror, the government is not willing to resort. If the war is to continue long this would prove to be true policy, saving the lives of many of our brave boys."[29] The officer's words were prophetic and in time would become U.S. government policy.

On Saturday January 10, 1863, Private John Mosby, carrying the honorary title of captain, began a documented ride into immortality. The objective was a picket post located at Herndon Station, a stop on the Alexandria, Loudoun and Hampshire Railroad in Loudoun County. Mosby had eleven men with him, the nine provided by Stuart, John Scott a volunteer from Fauquier County, and a remarkable guide by the name of John Underwood. Using his lawyer's analytical mind, Mosby had begun to formulate techniques of attack on Union outposts. He would attack at night, often in inclement weather, and would approach the outpost from the direction of Union supporting troops. The picket would be inclined to think it was a friendly patrol or relief coming into their positions. On his first independent operation, Mosby's objective was easily taken with one Union soldier wounded and a total of seven men captured with horses and equipment. No provisions were yet established for forwarding prisoners to Stuart. Mosby did not have the manpower to provide guards. Taking the prisoners some distance from their post, Mosby and his men "went through them," taking watches, wallets, weapons, horses and whatever else suited their fancy. Mosby then paroled the men and allowed them to begin walking back to their units.[30]

On the night of Monday, January 12, 1863, guide John Underwood led Mosby's men to another picket post. Not far from Herndon Station, Cub Run flowed across the Little River Turnpike. Here Underwood found five New York cavalrymen neglecting their duty. Instead of being on watch, the men were seated around a campfire playing cards. Mosby led his men close to the fire and, after watching the game for awhile, fired a pistol shot in the air. Mosby wrote that one man "was so frightened that he nearly jumped over the tops of the trees."[31] Five men with horses and equipment were taken prisoner. Not yet satisfied, the Ranger leader moved on to Frying Pan Church where a cavalry picket of ten men of the 1st Vermont Cavalry was located. Again Mosby approached the outpost from its rear, and it was not long before the remainder of the Union soldiers surrendered.[32] Again Mosby paroled the prisoners after taking horses, equipment and whatever else he could take. The equipment would be kept or sold under the provisions of the Partisan Ranger Act of April 1862.[33] The two raids had netted twenty-two horses, equipment and loot that were divided among all, except the leader. Mosby firmly believed in the rights of his men to legally profit under the law. He also knew that if he began to take personal profits, enemies both North and South would have a cause to pursue against him. He elected not to participate in the division of spoils.

Early in the war, prisoners who were paroled had hopes of furlough home until exchanged. Under the rules of gentlemen's war, they were on their honor not to fight again until an equal number of the enemy had been released. This romantic notion was observed by some but ignored by many on both sides. It would not last.

Mosby held his nine men on temporary loan and it was time to return them. On January 15, Mosby rejoined Stuart and asked for and received fifteen men and the authority to ride back to northern Virginia and begin operations on the border. Stuart liked what had been accomplished and provided fifteen men, primarily from Fitzhugh Lee's 1st Virginia Cavalry. Lee provided the men as ordered, but did not like having to do so. There remained bad feeling between Mosby and Fitzhugh Lee.

On Sunday, January 18,1863, Mosby made an attack on an outpost of the 18th Pennsylvania Cavalry near Chantilly Church and captured eleven men. The 18th Pennsylvania had been formed two months prior at Harrisburg and did not have sabers issued or its first mounted drill until twenty-one days prior to the capture. It did not arrive in the area until January 10. Its history shows for January 15, "Drill in the morning, mounted; in the afternoon target practice. Picket post captured by 'Mosby,' and nine men of the regiment taken prisoners."[34] In time, the 18th Pennsylvania would become a fine regiment. In January 1863, it was a collection of civilians in uniform, poorly equipped and armed. The regimental report for Thursday, January 29, 1863, reads, "Some of our captured men return to the regiment, paroled by Mosby who sent a verbal message to the lieutenant-colonel that unless the men were better armed and equipped it wouldn't pay to capture them."[35]

Mosby was building a reputation. On January 20, 1863, Companies E and G of the 5th New York Cavalry were sent to picket duty in the Frying Pan area. Disturbed by the loss of horses, their commanders sent them dismounted."[36]

The history of 5th New York Cavalry records that on Monday, January 26, "Mosby made an attack on the 18th PA on picket near Chantilly Church, capturing 11. A detachment of the 5th New York Cavalry under Maj. John Hammond was sent in pursuit of the guerrillas." The cavalry report stated, "Having reached Middleburg, Major Hammond [a future colonel and commander of the regiment] ordered a charge through town, which was executed handsomely and with entire success, resulting in the capture of 25 prisoners and the scattering of Mosby's men. The entire party save one man captured by the Confederates, returned safely to camp, after a journey of 34 miles. . . ."

Union cavalry commander Col. Percy Wyndham, the opponent of Turner Ashby, was captured at the time Ashby was killed. He later was exchanged. Wyndham was, according to some, a dashing soldier of fortune. Others thought him a pompous windbag. He had fought with Giuseppe Garibaldi in the effort to make the petty states of Italy a country. Wyndham was determined to capture Mosby and led 200 cavalry to Middleburg where, with his long handlebar mustache bristling, he threatened and frightened the civilians but did not get his man. In frustration, Wyndham sent Mosby a message calling him "Horse Thief." Mosby responded that all the horses he had stolen had riders, and the riders had sabers, carbines and pistols.[37] That was a bit of an exaggeration, but taking the opponents' transportation was necessary and routine. Mosby was just better at it than Wyndham.

Not all Confederates were happy with Mosby's efforts. The town fathers of Middleburg, Virginia, asked him to cease operations as Colonel Wyndham was threatening to burn Middleburg because of what Mosby was doing. In a Wednesday, February 4, 1863, response, Mosby wrote to them, " Not being yet prepared for any such degrading compromise with the Yankees, I unhesitatingly refuse to comply." Mosby defended his actions based on the "custom of war and the practice of the enemy."[38]

Fitzhugh Lee now called for the return of his fifteen men, an event that would put Mosby out of business. Fortunately a number of volunteers were coming in. Mosby even visited Confederate hospitals and recruited. As a result some of his raiders were on crutches. For a time the Mosby invalids evaded Union efforts to capture them; U.S. soldiers did not believe such men could have struck their outposts. Hospital recruiting fell off when one of the invalids was killed, but many more men were seeing that money could be made as Rangers and joined the command.[39]

The lush rolling countryside of Loudoun and Fauquier counties would be home turf for the new command. The area of Mosby's operations had been left largely to occupation by the Union army when Confederate general Johnston had determined he could not defend Harpers Ferry and had withdrawn in the summer of 1862. The loss of this territory left a deep wound in the Confederacy. Mosby believed that though behind enemy lines, the area was fertile soil for a Ranger. He wrote, "My idea was to make the Piedmont region of the country lying between the Rappahannock and Potomac Rivers the base of my operations. This embraces the upper portion of the counties of Fauquier and Loudoun."[40] This was a rich land that could supply him with food for his men and forage for his horses. He knew that the great majority of the people were devoted to the Southern cause. Initially, he did not plan to fight in his home area and bring retribution on his supporters, but to use it as a base of operations to range outward.

From the outset Mosby had a clear view of his purpose. He believed that "the most vulnerable part of every invading army is its rear."[41] His mission would be to draw enemy troops away from the front line to protect their rear areas. He told Stuart that he would "by incessant attacks, compel the enemy either greatly to contract his lines or to reinforce them; either of which would be of great advantage to the Southern side."[42] By striking successfully at one point in the enemy rear area he could force them to guard a hundred. Static guard positions are costly in manpower and supplies and are a drain on offensive action. Mosby clearly understood this. He believed, "It is just as legitimate to fight an enemy in the rear as in the front. . . . The military value of a partisan's work is not measured by the amount of property destroyed, or the number of men killed or captured, but by the number he keeps watching. Every soldier withdrawn from the front to guard the rear of an army is so much taken from its fighting strength."[43]

Mosby reaped the benefits of excellent guides and a friendly civilian community. His raids were a constant threat to the Union outposts and Northern reaction forces were established. Due to the slow communication of the period, word of a Mosby raid usually came too late and resulted in a long and tiring ride for the blue-coated cavalry. False alarms frequently kept the men in the saddle for long periods, tiring them and their horses. The news of Mosby's successful raids created a feeling of great pride in the Confederate ranks and lifted the spirits of the civilian community. The Rangers' success was a prime topic of conversation in the Union camps.

In this unusual war where men shared the same language and heritage, it was not uncommon for those who were dissatisfied to desert to the other side. Mosby would be plagued by two Rangers and a teamster who left his ranks and became guides for the enemy, but he struck gold when on February 10, 1863, Sergeant James F. Ames—a deserter from Company L of the 5th New York Cavalry[44]—walked into Middleburg and began telling people he had arrived to join Mosby's Rangers. Why a cavalryman would walk some thirty miles remains a mystery, but there were many things about Ames that were mysterious. He was described by one who knew him as "large and muscular, with determination stamped in every line of his face. His black eye is quick, clear, intelligent, while his bearing is manly and his manners and conversation are pleasing. Sergeant Ames had been a seafaring man ere he became a soldier and carries about him all the characteristics of that profession."[45]

Ames was carried twice in the records of New York, also being shown as "Aimes." The records are obviously of the same man:

AIMES, JAMES F. Age, 30 years, Enlisted, October 21, 1861, at New York; mustered in as sergeant, Co. L, October 31, 1861, to serve three years; deserted to the enemy, February 10, 1863.

AMES JAMES F. Age 30 years. Enlisted October 29, 1861, at New York; mustered in as corporal, Co. M, October 31, 1861, to serve three years; transferred to Co L————1862; deserted to the enemy, February 10, 1863.[46]

Sensing a plant, Mosby's men and the civilians of Middleburg cautioned Mosby about taking Ames into his command. Mosby instinctively trusted Ames and was rewarded when Ames became one of his best men and in time was promoted to lieutenant.

Following a habit of long term, Mosby stopped talking to his men, put a toothpick in his mouth and began chewing. The men knew he had been thinking, and it would not be long before they got orders. On March 8, 1863, twenty-nine Rangers gathered at Aldie in Loudoun County in response to Mosby's orders. As darkness came, a drizzling rain was falling and snow was melting on the ground, ideal conditions to keep the curious indoors and to conceal the sound of horses moving. Mosby led out, then called Ames (who was now known to all as "Big Yankee") to his side. He told Ames and Sgt. William Hunter that the destination was Fairfax Court House. This was scarcely two miles from the camp of the 5th New York Cavalry and not far from a brigade of infantry with artillery and cavalry at Centerville. Indeed the whole area featured scattered strong points that could interfere with the plan.

Both Stuart and Mosby had a personal dislike for Percy Wyndham. The temptation to let the air out of Wyndham's bubble of reputation intrigued them both. Wyndham's remarks about Mosby irked the Ranger leader. In the *Belford* magazine of 1892, Mosby would write that he had determined to make Wyndham pay for careless remarks. As the deserter, Ames knew both the Fairfax Court House area and the Union dispositions. Mosby had the best possible guide, but his information was incomplete. Mosby was not aware Wyndham was not alone at Fairfax. The youthful Union general Edwin Stoughton, who was the commander of the region, disdained to live with his troops. With a strong guard of some 200 men he established himself in the warmth and comfort of a home near the Fairfax Court House, several miles from his command.

The Rangers moved down the Little River Turnpike which passed by Fairfax Court House on its way to Alexandria and came near the courthouse. The Union password system was inefficient. In place of a daily sign and countersign it was necessary only to give the name of a unit that was in the area to pass guards. Whenever challenged, Ames would respond "Fifth New York Cavalry," and the column would move on, capturing the sentry as they passed. Telegraph wires were cut before they moved into the court house area.

In the Fairfax Court House square, surrounded by a Union encampment of several hundred officers and men, Mosby demonstrated his remarkable *sang-froid* in the face of danger by assembling his men and issuing his instructions. Mosby wrote "the men were detailed in squads; some were sent to the stables to collect the fine horses that I knew were there, others to different headquarters, where the officers were quartered. We were more anxious to capture Wyndham than any other."[47]

A sentry was walking his post in front of a hospital. Ames went to him, came close and held a pistol to his head and the sentry was silently removed. Ames then led a party to where Wyndham resided, only to learn that the Briton had been called to Washington. Wyndham's uniforms, his horses and several officers were captured by Ames. Among the officers was Capt. Augustus Barker who had been Ames commander. Mosby would have gone for Wyndham himself, but Ranger Joseph Nelson had captured the telegraph operator and another soldier who said he was part of the guard for Stoughton. On learning that Stoughton was in a nearby house, Mosby determined to capture the 25-year-old who graduated in the class of 1859 at West Point and, when made a brigadier general at age 24, was the youngest man of star rank in the Union army.

Taking Rangers Joseph Nelson, William Hunter, George Whitescarver, Welt Hatcher and Frank Williams, Mosby approached the door of Doctor Gunnell's two-story brick house where Stoughton was staying. Mosby rapped on the door and an upstairs window opened. Lt. Samuel Prentiss, a sleepy-eyed staff officer, inquired what was wanted. Mosby responded, "Fifth New York Cavalry, with a message for General Stoughton." When Prentiss came downstairs in shirt and underwear and opened the door, Mosby grabbed him by the collar and whispered who he was and who he wanted. Leaving Hatcher and Whitescarver to guard the horses, Mosby and three Rangers went up the stairs. Entering Stoughton's bedroom, he gave the sleeping general a slap on the back or backside to wake him. Stoughton naturally was nonplussed at this treatment. Mosby leaned close and asked, "General, did you ever hear of Mosby?"

"Yes," replied Stoughton. "Did you catch him?"

"No," was the response. "I am Mosby and I have caught you."

Mosby then took away any hope of rescue by saying that Stuart and his cavalry held the town.[48] In writing of the event, Mosby spoke of champagne bottles in the room and gave the impression that Stoughton had been carousing with women. Others reported Stoughton was being visited by his mother and sister. Whatever his female companionship, he was not with his troops as he should have been.

To Mosby's disgust, Colonel Wyndham was not in the prisoner bag, but General Stoughton, thirty-two prisoners and fifty-eight horses were rounded up and Mosby and his men started back to Confederate lines. At another house, an upstairs window opened and a man in his nightshirt called out to

John S. Mosby. NATIONAL ARCHIVES

ask what the riders were doing. The man was Lt. Col. Robert Johnstone, commander of the 5th New York Cavalry. Gleefully, the Rangers went after him. Deducing what was occurring, the 38-year-old Johnstone fled through the back door of the house, while his brave wife used tongue and nails to delay the Rangers at the front door. The story made the rounds that Johnstone's nightshirt tore free, leaving him naked as he hid under a barn or outhouse. Nude under an outhouse, immersed in feces, made the best story and laughter followed the unfortunate officer. Had he chosen to surrender, he would have gone into captivity, in time been exchanged and forgotten, or his career saved. Had he slept fully clothed, history might have spared this officer, but hiding nude under an outhouse made a good tale and his career was ruined. Johnston was cashiered from the service on December 5, 1863, by General Order No. 104, Army of the Potomac. Brave men go to great lengths to avoid capture. In 1865, Union officers reported Confederate President Jefferson Davis was wearing women's clothing when he was taken. Johnstone avoided capture and the hell of Libby prison, but could not avoid the ridicule of his opponents, fellows and present-day tour guides who have never been in his circumstance.

Mosby brought his Rangers back to Confederate lines before daylight. The captive Stoughton was anxious to see his West Point classmate, Fitzhugh Lee. Mosby was wet, tired and cold, but the warm reception Fitz Lee gave his defeated old school chum did not include the victor. While the two men chatted, Mosby was not even offered the opportunity to warm himself at the fireplace.

Far from being thankful, Fitz Lee soon tried to get the few men of his brigade that had been detailed to Mosby returned. Stuart put a stop to that. Always grateful to his mentor, Mosby sent Stuart the captured saddle of Stoughton. Yankee Ames's former company commander, Union Capt. Augustus Barker, was soon exchanged and returned to duty, only to be killed by guerrillas on September 14, 1863, at Kelly's Ford.

Mosby wrote, "I was never able to duplicate this adventure; it was one of those things a man can only do once in a lifetime. The Northern cavalry got too smart to allow the repetition."[49]

When President Lincoln heard of the raid, he managed to inject his ever-present wit into the calamity by remarking that he did not mind so much the loss of a general—for he could make another in five minutes—but he hated to lose the horses.[50]

Stoughton was exchanged, but his military career was finished, and he left the service to join his father's law firm. Ironically he would later serve as the defense counsel for a Confederate Ranger involved in the attempt to burn New York City. Stoughton fought hard to save his former foe but could not overcome the evidence. Edwin Stoughton died in Boston, Massachusetts, on Christmas Day 1869. He was 30 years old.

Mosby was now proclaimed a hero by newspapers throughout the Confederacy, but his status was unofficial. Governor Letcher of Virginia had offered him a commission in the Provisional Army of Virginia, but that organization was defunct and Mosby declined. Now President Jefferson Davis sent him a commission on orders dated March 23, 1863. Sent by General Lee's assistant adjutant general, Col. Walter H. Taylor, through General Stuart, the commission was accompanied by a letter whose wording is significant. It begins, "Captain: You will perceive from the copy of the order herewith inclosed that the President has appointed you a captain of partisan Rangers."

Mosby was delighted with the appointment. As a lawyer, Mosby knew what the Partisan Ranger Act of 1862 did for his men. Years later he pointed out in his reminiscences that the division of spoils provision of the act was merely maritime prize law carried over to land. He wrote that England did so in India and at Waterloo. He explained, "It will be seen how the peculiar privileges given to my men served to whet their zeal. I have often heard them disputing over the division of the horses before they were captured, and it was no uncommon thing for a man to remind me just as he was about going into a fight that he did not get a horse from the last one."

The fact that his commission came from the president of the Confederacy would prove to be significant to the Rangers. General Lee sent orders that Mosby should begin to organize his company, "With the understanding that it is to be placed on a footing with all troops of the line, and to be mustered into the Confederate service for and during the war." Mosby realized this instruction would cancel the provision of the Partisan Ranger Act whereby Rangers could keep or distribute the spoils of war they accumulated. This provision was critical to his recruiting. Mosby would later say "that his command resembled the Democratic party in at least one respect, that it was held together by the cohesive power of public plunder."[51]

Disturbed by Lee's order, Mosby wrote to Stuart requesting clarification. The letter included: "The men who have joined me have done so under the impression that they are to be entitled to the privileges allowed in the Partisan Ranger Act. If they are to be denied them I cannot accept the appointment. Please let me know." Stuart forward this to Lee who responded that Mosby had not been given authority to raise partisan troops, that his commission was limited to himself, and its provision did not extend to the troops he raised. These would be mustered into the regular service.[52]

Courage comes in many forms. His entire life would prove that when John Mosby believed he was right he would fight anybody. Mosby would not accept the decision of General Lee and appealed Lee's decision to the secretary of war. The powers in Richmond sided with Mosby's contention that his commission entitled him to recruit for partisan Ranger service. Lee was too much of a soldier to dispute the overturning of his decision and took it in good grace.[53]

Mosby's position as commander was secure, but the law stated that men were to be allowed to elect their lieutenants.[54] Mosby allowed elections to be held but told his men who they could elect. There were no secret ballots. Men were required to vote in the open and anyone who opposed Mosby's wish found himself quickly transferred to line units. Stuart urged Mosby not to allow his men to be called "partisan Rangers," thinking it would cause the unit to be looked upon as little more than pirates masquerading under a Letter of Marque. Stuart wrote Mosby on Wednesday, March 25, 1863. He suggested the unit be called "Mosby's Regulars" and cautioned Mosby about recruiting deserters or men too young or too old. Stuart wanted candidates tested in battle before they were accepted. Mosby practically worshiped Stuart, but he would not take chances on his men losing their benefits. His command would remain Rangers no matter what numerical or other designation higher authority would wish on them. He understood that war is fought by youth. He liked young recruits and tested them when possible. If conditions did not permit, the test period was waived. He had the authority and determination to rid himself of men who were not performing as he desired.

Greatly angered at the embarrassment of General Stoughton's capture, Union commanders took steps to prevent a recurrence. Col. Tom Kane of the Pennsylvania Bucktails was ordered to move his regiment of marksmen close to Fairfax Court House. The movement was done in secret, the cover story being that the hard-fighting Bucktails were being sent back to Harrisburg, for some rest and recuperation. The rumor brought hoots from the Union line infantry regiments being left behind.

While the Bucktails secretly guarded the headquarters after the general had been stolen, four of the top marksmen from each of the companies in this select unit were drawn off and formed into squads. On March 9, 1863, the Southern Unionist Yankee Davis led four covered wagons out from Fairfax village. Concealed in each of these wagons were the best shots the Bucktails had. The 1st Rhode Island Cavalry furnished a light escort that Mosby's men would not hesitate to attack. The small group of wagons traveled throughout the day and stopped for the night in a barn. On the morning of the tenth the march resumed and soon Mosby's men took the bait.

As gunfire erupted, the 1st Rhode Island Cavalry, with the Rangers in pursuit, came galloping back to the wagons. Hearing the horses, the overeager Bucktails threw aside their canvas covers. The marksmen found to their disgust that the Rangers had not yet come within effective range. They opened fire, but Mosby's men promptly shied off and the well-planned trap was a failure.[55] On March 23, Mosby led some fifty of his men from Rector's Cross Roads traveling the Turnpike until about six miles from Chantilly. There to avoid detection, he left the road and using cover and concealment continued traveling in the direction of Union forces. About a mile from the Chantilly Mansion, he exited a woods.[56] This put the Rangers close to a picket of the 5th New York Cavalry, which was posted by a small stream on the Little River Turnpike. Mosby opened the affair by shooting a New Yorker through the head.[57]

The Union soldiers fled as the Rangers advanced, but four or five were captured. Mosby knew the alarm would be given and that his horses were tired. As the reserve force of the 5th New York came out in pursuit, Mosby elected to withdraw. He had ridden about a mile when a force of some 200 Union cavalry was seen riding hard to catch the Rangers. Farther on Mosby's route was a woods that stretched across the road about a half mile. At two points within the woods, Union troops had previously felled trees across the road. Mosby withdrew to the second of these positions. The sight of the felled trees where they believed their enemy to be caused the Union cavalry to slow and make a cautious approach. When they were about 100 yards out, the Rangers suddenly charged them and the cavalry fled. Mosby wrote, "It was more of a chase than a fight for 4 or 5 miles." He reported five cavalrymen killed and a number wounded. One lieutenant and thirty-five enlisted men were taken prisoner.[58] The Union cavalry met with another force coming to its aid and both resumed the hunt. Mosby broke off the action and retreated until darkness when both sides discontinued the action. The 5th New York Cavalry history recorded the action as, "They escaped after inflicting upon us very serious injury. For some reason the regiment never acted with so little concert, and was never so badly beaten by so small a force, supposed to be about eighty strong. Every one felt mortified at the result of this day's work and resolved to retrieve our fortunes on some more fortunate occasion."[59]

Mosby was soon back in action. On Monday, March 31, 1863, he led seventy men toward Dranesville, intending to attack some outposts. He found that Union troops had pulled back on the road to Alexandria and, as darkness was falling, Mosby withdrew on the Leesburg Pike. The ground was covered with snow and the weather cold. They decided to camp at Miskel's farm, which was in the forks of Goose Creek and the Potomac on the north side of the Leesburg Pike and within a half mile of the Potomac River. The Rangers arrived there about 10 P.M., passing through the gate of a pasture fence that separated the turnpike from the Miskel farm.

There was forage for the horses at the Miskel farm, the family was friendly, the house was warm, and the barn had a well-filled hay mow that was a good place to bed down. As few of the men could be accommodated in the house, most of them slept in the barn. The barnyard had a high board-and-stone fence surrounding it, a fence too high for horses to jump. There was only one gate in the barnyard and that opened into a field and the dirt track that connected the farm to the turnpike. The tired men unsaddled, fed their animals and enjoyed the Miskel hospitality before settling in. There were no outposts, though Mosby would later claim he had left one of his men on the Leesburg Pike.[60] He admitted in his report to Stuart that he had not "taken sufficient precautions to guard against surprise," but excused that, when he wrote that he and his men had ridden through snow and mud some forty miles, his men and horses were exhausted and the enemy had fallen back some eighteen miles.[61] Mosby thought the enemy was distant. He would later quote Napier who wrote, "He who wars, walks in a mist through which the keenest eye cannot always discern the right path."[62]

Meanwhile, a local Unionist, who had seen Mosby's arrival at Miskel's, was riding through the cold night. He found Maj. Charles F. Taggart of the 2nd Pennsylvania Cavalry at Union Church, some two miles above Peach Grove. Taggart had command of detachments from various regiments that for a time were stationed at Dranesville. At this time they were some twelve miles away. The Unionist told Taggart that Mosby and some sixty-five men were at Miskel's farm. Taggert ordered Capt. Henry Flint, a courageous officer of the 1st Vermont Cavalry, to sound "Boots and Saddles" and lead some 150 men to attack the Rangers. Men of companies A, B, C, D, G and I of the 1st Vermont soon were on their way.

As it was the practice of Mosby's men to stay at private homes, Ranger Dick Moran had stopped for the night at the home of a friend named Green on the road between Dranesville and Miskel's. Flint's horsemen passed by Green's, and Moran hid while Flint stopped to question Green. As soon as the Vermont cavalry left, Moran ran to his horse and spurred cross-country to get a warning to Mosby.

It was now sunrise. The Rangers had breakfasted and were caring for their horses, all of which were tied in the fenced-in barnyard. Some of the men had saddles on their mounts, but all still had the bridles off and feeding was in progress. Mosby was in the Miskel house when one of the men entered and told him that Union troops on the other side of the Potomac River were making some kind of signals. Mosby left the house to see what was occurring. His attention was immediately drawn to Moran riding hard across the fields, waving his hat and shouting, "Mount your horses! The Yankees are coming!"[63]

Mosby could now see Flint's cavalry coming down the pike at a gallop. Hurrying to the barnyard, he shouted at his men to get mounted. Flint's column was in two sections, with Flint in the lead of the first and Capt. George H. Bean heading the second at an interval. As the Rangers hastily gathered equipment, bridled and saddled their horses, Flint and the lead section of Vermont cavalry came through the outer fence gate by the turnpike and drew up on line. Mosby's Rangers were outnumbered at least two to one and in a disadvantageous position, having to equip their horses, make it through the barnyard gate, and then pass through the gate by the road that Flint's cavalry now controlled. Flint's men closed the outer gate behind them, confident the trap was sealed. As Union troops on the other side of the Potomac began to cheer in anticipation of victory, Flint prepared to attack.

Flint was a brave man. Trained in Union cavalry tactics of the period, he was leading men armed primarily with rifle and saber. Flint divided his force, sending half the men to strike from the flank. He disdained a volley of rifle fire from his line and decided to lead a charge in the classic cavalry manner with sabers outstretched. Lt. Josiah Grout suggested Flint hold off on the charge until Bean's men were with them and deployed, but Flint was eager to engage and would not wait. Reports disagree on whether Flint decided to use a volley of rifle fire. If he did, it was from too great a range and was ineffective. The charge took Flint's men to the board-and-stone barnyard fence, but it was too high for the Union cavalry to leap and protected the Rangers who were still saddling. The charge resulted in milling confusion. Only those near the barnyard gate could engage, and there the revolvers of the Rangers were more effective than the cavalry sabers.

Still dismounted, Mosby threw open the barnyard gate, went through it, and ordered those of his men who could to charge. Ranger Harry Hatcher was on horseback but, seeing his leader on foot, leaped from the saddle. Mosby took Hatcher's horse, drew his pistols and led his men in a counter-charge. In most cases it was saber against revolvers and the Union troopers lost. Panicked, the Vermont cavalrymen fled toward the outer gate by the turnpike. It was a narrow gate, too narrow for a crowd of men to pass through together. Ranger Sam Chapman encountered a Vermonter armed with a revolver. Both men pointed their weapons at each other from a distance of one foot. The cavalryman pulled his trigger first, but his weapon misfired. Chapman killed him.

Seeing their comrades defeated, the other detachment of Vermont cavalry tried to get out the exterior gate. The fleeing cavalrymen jammed the opening with their horses and bodies, while others pressed upon them from the rear. Captain Flint was trying to bring his saber into play and rally his men. Flint died with six bullets in him. The death of their commander and the sudden charge of the Rangers sapped the fighting spirit of the Union cavalry. Lieutenant Grout was severely wounded but recovered and later would become speaker of the Vermont House of Representatives. As the trapped men were shot down, most surrendered. Those who made it through the gate were hotly pursued by the Rangers. Lt. Charles Woodbury tried to rally the Vermonters but was shot in the head and killed by Ames. Mosby estimated that fight occurred three miles from the initial fight, and he drove his opponents to Dranesville. A potential disaster was turned into Ranger victory by taking advantage of a mistake by the enemy and using fire-power and audacity. One Ranger was killed and three wounded.

The 1st Vermont Cavalry lost seven men, including Flint, and twenty-two wounded; eighty-two of the men were taken prisoner and ninety-five horses with equipment.[64] Only some forty men, primarily those at the rear of the column, were able to escape. Maj. Gen. Julius Stahel, commander of the Union cavalry division in the area, sent men of the 6th and 7th Michigan and 1st Virginia (West Virginia) cavalry in pursuit, but Mosby could not be located. Stahel in his report on the action attributed the defeat to "bad management on the part of the officers and the cowardice of the men."[65] Once again, a scapegoat was needed. Now Capt. George Bean was censured for failing to support Flint, and the unfortunate officer was dismissed from the service on April 28, 1863. He fought to clear his name, came back to duty and was killed in action on May 11, 1864.

Capt. John Singleton Mosby had been leading his Ranger band of brothers only two months, yet his reputation for military brilliance had flashed across both South and North. In forwarding the report of the action, General Stuart closed with the words, "Recommended for promotion." Confederate Secretary of War Seddon ordered that Mosby be promoted to major on Wednesday, April 22, 1863—the promotion was effected on April 26.

On Monday, April 27, 1863, Stahel's cavalry division was operating along the Orange and Alexandria Railroad. Stahel was a student of classical military history. He knew how Roman legions moved and believed what was good for the Romans was good for Stahel. Acting on false intelligence that Mosby had built a fort at Upperville, Stahel took two brigades of cavalry and four cannon, a force totaling some 2,500 men, and debouched for Upperville. Every military maxim that could be observed, was. Approaching a woods, he unlimbered his cannon and blasted the trees in a reconnaissance by fire. He then led his command forward and occupied the shattered trees. The one benefit of his effort would have been firewood, but though the night was bitter cold and rainy, Stahel would permit no fires, fearing these would reveal his position. Bits were taken from the horses' mouths only long enough for the animals to feed, and the troopers were required to sleep beside their saddled horses to be ready for instant action. Stahel's scouts had captured three of Mosby's Rangers who were on foot and trying to make off with the horses. Taking no chances of weakening his command, Stahel would not permit any of his men to escort the prisoners to the rear. The captives were required to march with the column. Meanwhile Stahel's mounted patrols rode through the night under strict orders to show results. The weary troopers, angry and knowing they had better not come back empty handed, raided houses and dragged the aged and infirm from their beds. A man named Hutchison, who was seventy years old and had always used crutches, was taken.[66] The barns were stripped of their horses. Next morning, the cavalry, who by this time likely hated Stahel more than Mosby, were again marching to attack the supposed fort at Upperville.

They had not gone far when a half dozen of Mosby's men under Tom Richards charged the advance guard and blazed away at the cavalry with pistols. Stahel acted with dispatch, deploying his command of more than 2,000 men for battle and bringing his artillery on line. The Rangers had vanished, but for more than an hour Stahel kept his men on line, ready to repulse an attack.

Uncertain of what lay ahead, Stahel determined to leave the nonexistent fort alone. He decided to turn south toward Salem (Marshall) and go back to Fairfax by Thoroughfare Gap. Meanwhile Mosby, who was setting out to attack a train, had passed through Salem en route to Thoroughfare Gap. As he neared the Gap, two of his Ranger scouts rode up with the information that 500 cavalry were on his trail. Mosby decided to attack them. He soon learned his information was incorrect. While Mosby was getting faulty information, Stahel was also. An informer had seen Mosby's riders and arrived at a wrong conclusion. Stahel was informed that Stuart's cavalry was waiting for him at Thoroughfare Gap. Stahel decided to avoid the trap and take another route to Fairfax through Hopewell Gap. Mosby's scouts correctly gauged Stahel's direction and both commanders now knew where they were going.

Mosby reached the road near Hopewell Gap where he encountered Stahel's scouts. These withdrew and informed Stahel that Stuart was in front of him and coming to the attack. Stahel promptly deployed for battle. From a hilltop, Mosby could see Stahel mounted on a splendid white charger, issuing orders to messengers who galloped away. His brigades of brave men were marshaled for battle, his artillery ready.

Mosby sat on the hilltop with his small number of men and greatly enjoyed the scene of several thousand soldiers busily occupied in preparations for defense. Darkness fell, giving Stahel the opportunity of escape. He determined on a night march and, taking all precautions, quietly slipped away. En route he had bridges destroyed, with trees cut and dropped across the roads to his rear. Meanwhile Mosby had enjoyed his laugh, dispersed his men and retired to the house of a friend at Middleburg. Mosby awoke the next morning to the sound of bugles and found that Stahel's night march had ended in a bivouac and he was right in the middle of it. Mosby slipped away. When he was asked later why he did not attack Stahel during the night march Mosby responded, "I knew nothing of it and I had no right to suppose that an idiot had been placed in command of two brigades of cavalry and four pieces of artillery."

Stahel made it back to his Fairfax headquarters, where he held a Roman triumph, wrote an article for the newspapers extolling his tactics, and paraded his aged captives as Mosby's band.[67]

The Stahel expedition amused Mosby as an example of rigid military thinking. He wrote of Stahel, "After shelling the woods in every direction so as to be sure of my extermination, and destroying many bats and owls, he took off as prisoners all the old men he could find. He had the idea that I was a myth and that these old farmers were the raiders."[68]

On Saturday, May 2, 1863, Mosby gathered what he estimated at seventy to eighty men.[69] He could hear the sound of battle from Chancellorsville and considered going in to attack Union general Hooker's wagon trains which were less than twenty miles away. Scouts brought word that Union cavalry was located nearby at Warrenton Junction. Mosby knew he could bypass this force and deal a significant blow by destroying the supply train of the Union army while the great struggle at Chancellorsville raged.[70] But the enemy cavalry was near, and Mosby had an independent command. To get too close to the main army might result in orders that would cost his freedom of action. Early on Sunday, Mosby and his Rangers moved out from Warrenton to attack the Union cavalry at the junction of the Orange and Alexandria and Manassas Gap railroads.

The Union cavalry was a 100-man detachment from the 1st Virginia (West Virginia). They had just returned from reconnaissance and their commander, Lt. Col. John S. Krepps, had not looked to their security. The cavalry horses were unsaddled, with many turned out to graze. Soldiers were taking their ease, some resting in a nearby building. Lulled by their belief that no enemy was about, the Union soldiers saw riders but thought a friendly force was approaching. In an effort to excuse lax security, they later reported that the front rank of Rangers were dressed in Union uniforms. The Rangers were soon among them with six-guns blazing. Many of the cavalrymen were caught in the open and promptly surrendered; others ran to nearby houses. Two of these were soon cleared, but most of the Union soldiers holed up in a house near the railroad tracks and commenced firing. Pressing their attack, the Rangers rode close to the house firing their revolvers through the windows. Mosby emptied his two Colt revolvers through a window, describing the house as "densely packed as a sardine box; and it was impossible to fire into it without hitting somebody."[71]

Seeing that his fusillade would not bring the defenders to surrender, Mosby determined to set fire to the house. While Ranger Glasscock was setting fire to a pile of hay, brush and straw beside the structure, a number of men, including Rangers John DeButts, Harry Sweeting and Samuel Chapman, kicked in the front door and went in firing. The Union soldiers in the house were out of ammunition and the house was burning. Mosby wrote that "the house was filled with smoke and the floor covered with blood."[72] The Union soldiers decided to surrender.

To this point, the operation had gone smoothly and Mosby and his men set about rounding up the prisoners and equipment in preparation to leave the area. The scales of war swing rapidly and Mosby's success vanished in the thundering sound of horses' hooves. Some seventy men of the 5th New York Cavalry under the command of Major Hammond had been in camp near Cedar Run Bridge, about a quarter-mile north of Warrenton Junction. Capt. Frank Munson of the 5th New York wrote that shortly after they heard the firing, the 1st Virginia Cavalry horses came stampeding through their camp and took many of the New Yorkers' horses with them. Those who could, about forty men, saddled and rode to the sound of the fight.[73] They were followed by the other cavalrymen as soon as the runaway horses were caught.

Now it was the Rangers who were taken by surprise. A running battle developed with the cavalry in hot pursuit of Mosby's men. Trying to break free, the Rangers managed to retain only seven prisoners and a small number of captured horses. The loss of Rangers and men from other units who accompanied them was significant. Dick Moran was among the wounded and captured. Among other Rangers captured were the scout Sam Underwood, Tom Richards and Capt. Samuel P. Ducheane. A man named Templeton, who had been one of Stonewall Jackson's best scouts and had volunteered for the day, was killed. Twenty-three Rangers were taken prisoner, sixteen of whom were wounded. The Union prize included forty horses taken from the Rangers.[74] Mosby suffered a major setback, losing men who were proven leaders. He consoled himself by overestimating the number of Union cavalry who attacked him and claimed he was driven off by ten times his number. Mosby knew he had made a mistake no matter what the outcome of this fight. He should have been going after Hooker's wagon train where he could have inflicted great harm on the Union main force.

Though the fight was a loss, Mosby was the wiser for the experience. His mission was to attack enemy lines of communication and supply in order to draw troops from the battlefront. He vowed to keep that mission in front of him. He also knew it was important for a small unit such as his to remain independent. Ranger units are small and specialized. When placed with the main army, they tend to be swallowed up and misused. An army is a traveling city and its size often bewilders the soldier and is beyond the comprehension of the civilian. At Chancellorsville, a woman came to Gen. John B. Gordon and asked, "Do you know William?"

"What William, Madam?"

"My son William."

Gordon replied: "Really I do not know whether I have ever met your son William or not. Can you tell me what regiment or brigade or division or corps he belongs to?"

She answered: "No, I can't, but I know he belongs to Gin'al Lee's company."[75]

Mosby had a tight knit organization and freedom of action. He had no desire to be in General Lee's company.

Union efforts to eliminate Mosby and his command continued with the establishment of an ambush using the 67th Pennsylvania Infantry and the 1st New York and 6th Maryland cavalry. On May 4, captured boats were used to move the infantry across the Shenandoah at Castleman's Ferry. Leaving guards at the boats, the infantry moved through Snicker's Gap and went into hiding between Bloomfield and Upperville.

About twenty cavalrymen and lieutenants William H. Boyd (later colonel) and Jesse F. Wyckoff of the 1st New York (Lincoln) Cavalry would serve as bait. With the infantry hidden in position, the two officers and their small party would ride toward Upperville to bring on an attack by Mosby. When Mosby attacked, the cavalry would turn and flee, drawing the pursuing Mosby into the ambush. The action began as planned. The cavalry point was attacked near Blakeley's Grove by Mosby's men, and the New Yorkers drew them along as they galloped back to the ambush site. One rider had gone to the front to tell the infantry the enemy would be coming soon. The plan fell apart when the infantry got excited and fired upon their own men, not only killing and wounding their comrades, but giving away the ambush. Only one of Mosby's men was wounded. The cavalry had two dead and six wounded, the latter including Boyd and Wyckoff.[76]

On Friday, May 6, 1863, some of Mosby's Rangers struck at a dispatch rider and his escort. One of the cavalry was killed, the rest scattered and the dispatch rider escaped. A reaction force was immediately sent out by the 1st New York Cavalry. Part of the cavalry caught sight of the Rangers and gave chase. In the advance party were 45-year-old George W. Peavey, his 21-year-old son George Peavey, and a trooper named Bernard Dougherty (also spelled Doherty). Moving at a gallop, these three crossed a hilltop and found themselves facing Mosby and some fifteen of his men. At a range of about fifty yards, both sides opened fire. Other Union cavalry came over the hill and Mosby's men began to think it was time to skedaddle.

Mosby did not think so. Yelling "Charge," he galloped at the lead three men. The younger Peavey kept his head, sighted his revolver on Mosby's chest and at a distance he estimated at three yards pulled the trigger. His revolver misfired.

Young Peavey later said, " I thought I was gone then. I still see that ugly smile that came over Mosby's face, which was as pale as death, his hat gone and his hair blown back, as he took deliberate aim and fired, the muzzle of his pistol almost touching me, the bullet passing through my right hand, striking me in the right breast and doubling me up in the saddle. He then dashed on exchanging shots with Charley Clark who was coming toward us and the next moment he met Father and exchanged shots with him, the bullet passing through the rubber coat and shelter tent strapped on the pommel of Father's saddle. He next met Dougherty and they also exchanged shots, but without effect on either side. Mosby seemed to think his men were following him and that every one of us he passed was a prisoner. On passing Dougherty he pulled up and, as he did so, Father, who had been pursuing him and had emptied his pistol in the chase, dashed past him. Mosby's pistol was now empty and he returned it and drew a fresh one. While he was doing this Dougherty got into a field close to the fence and fired, causing Mosby to crouch low in the saddle, and I thought he was 'gone'; but he was unhurt. He

Mosby in 1866. NATIONAL ARCHIVES

then made for me, pistol in hand shouting 'Surrender!' My pistol was empty; I thought I had my death wound; and my horse being much heavier than his, I charged right on him in order to ride him down. He jerked his horse aside however, and our boots just touched as I shot past him like a rocket. He then fired at Clark who was in rear of me, killing his horse. Then seeing the rest of our boys coming on a run, he rode for his life and escaped."[77]

Unfazed by close calls, Mosby put out another call for men to assemble and took some forty of them on a railroad bridge-burning raid near the Rappahannock. They found the guards sleeping and burned bridges over Broad Run and Kettle Run. The Union trains were getting harder to attack as they now were accompanied by considerable infantry escort. The Rangers were tired and the horses needed feeding, so they stopped at a farm. Security was posted and soon came rushing in to report Union cavalry coming fast. Mosby leaped into the saddle and as the cavalry charged, he met them with a counter charge. He described the fight as "they had drawn sabers, that hurt nobody and we used pistols."[78] The Rangers were trained to take out the leaders of the opposing force. The lieutenant who led the cavalry was shot from the saddle and his command broke and fled.

Knowing the cavalry would be hot on his trail, Mosby took his prisoners and left the area. He was finding the railroad strongly guarded and difficult to attack. He sent his friend and subordinate of long standing, Fountain "Fount" Beattie, to General Stuart, requesting a mountain howitzer for use on trains. Mosby had officer volunteers serving as privates and several of them were artillerymen. An artillery piece would be of great value in attacking trains.

The Union army needed vast quantities of supplies, and railroads were critical to this and the movement of troops. Three important railroads were within striking distance of Mosby's Rangers. The Baltimore and Ohio (B&O) ran on a generally east-west axis from Baltimore to Frederick to Harpers Ferry, Cumberland, Martinsburg and Wheeling. Part of the B&O route was along the Potomac River. At Harpers Ferry, the B&O began to leave the river trace and point toward Baltimore. Going southeast at this point the Chesapeake and Ohio Canal traveled to Washington; this canal was also an important logistics trail for the Union.

The Manassas Gap Railroad was farther south, but also traveled on an east-west axis. Coming from Mount Washington and Strasburg in the west, it crossed the Shenandoah River, passed through Manassas Gap following the trace of Goose Creek eastward to Rectortown, then dipping southward before continuing to Marshall, the Plains, through Thoroughfare Gap in the Bull Run Mountains and on to Gainesville and Manassas. Slightly east of Manassas at Manassas Junction, the Manassas Gap railroad connected with the Orange and Alexandria Railroad, a vital corridor that ran generally southeast to northeast, from Gordonsville to Alexandria. This railroad was like a dagger that could be used by either side to advance its aims. It connected at Gordonsville to the Virginia Central Railroad, a key link to Richmond and important railroads farther south.

CHAPTER TWO

Mosby and the Gun

By 1863 the Union controlled these Virginia railroads south to the Rappahannock River. The Orange and Alexandria Railroad was the key union supply route from Washington to troops along the Rappahannock River.

Because of the depth of Union penetration into Virginia, Mosby's horse-drawn cannon and limber had to be secreted through Union lines. It arrived on Friday, May 29,1863, and was placed in the care of the Baptist artillery-man Lt. Sam "the Reverend" Chapman and the former British officer Capt. Bradford S. Hoskins. The driver was Ranger George Tuberville and Rangers Richard Mountjoy and Fount Beattie formed the crew. Training began immediately. The gun, often described as a small bronze field-piece, had a $2^5/8$ bore and was made in 1862 at the Tredegar foundry in Richmond.[1]

Mosby led his men to Greenwich, halted for supper with friendly local people, and moved on before stopping for the night. Early the next morning, the Rangers rode to the railroad at Catlett's Station. Here they cut the telegraph wire, taking out a length of wire that would prove useful to them. Union patrols frequently made their way along the track. To remove a rail would leave something easily spotted by patrols or the engineer. By removing the spikes on a section of rail, the Rangers were able to tie the telegraph wire around the rail and conceal the wire as it ran off into the woods. As an unsuspecting train came along, men would pull the wire, thus throwing the rail out of alignment and causing the engine to derail. Posting a man to signal the arrival of a train, the Rangers concealed themselves. About 9 A.M., a heavily guarded train bound for Bealton came along and the rail was pulled, forcing the train to stop. The small bronze field piece fired a round into the engine, disabling it and terrifying the guards. A second shot from the gun went into the engine, sending steam escaping in hissing clouds. The Rangers charged in firing their revolvers and, though they outnumbered the attackers, the train guards fled into the woods.

Eleven boxcars filled with valuable supplies were taken. Men filled pockets and bags with oranges and foodstuffs. Fresh shad, which was now a luxury in the South, was taken along with a wide variety of sutler's supplies.

U.S. Mail bags were among the spoils. Within minutes, the Rangers had all they could carry, and the train was set on fire, sending a column of smoke into the air.

The success of the Rangers in drawing off soldiers to guard the rear area had resulted in more Union forces being available to pursue them. Col. William D. Mann of the 7th Michigan Cavalry had command of a brigade at Bristoe. He heard the cannon fire, but he and his officers thought it was Stuart's cavalry. Mann took quick action. He sent Capt. Abram H. Hasbrouck with part of the 5th New York Cavalry to cut across country and meet whatever Confederate force was attacking the train. Col. Addison W. Preston of the 1st Vermont was bivouacked at Kettle Run, some five or six miles from the train. Within ten minutes of the first shot being fired, Preston was galloping 125 of his cavalry along the tracks. Mann was leading a detachment of the 7th Michigan Cavalry Regiment along the railroad tracks toward the train.

Mosby had progressed only about a mile when he found the horsemen of the 5th New York in his path. Chapman unlimbered the cannon and put a shell into the New Yorkers that scattered them. Mosby faked a charge, but his real intent was to get free and save his precious gun. He could see Mann's and Preston's troopers approaching in numbers that Mosby described as "Clouds of cavalry."

Near Grapewood Farm, some two miles from Greenwich, Chapman found a narrow lane that had a high fence on each side. The terrain was such that the Union cavalry would likely come up that lane in pursuit. Chapman put the cannon into position there. Lt. Elmer Barker (later major) of the 5th New York Cavalry was tracking the Rangers by the fish and other loot they had dropped when he ran into the Ranger rear element. He and his two men found themselves facing Mosby, Hoskins and three other Rangers. Pistols blazed, Capt. Bradford Smith Hoskins and another of the Rangers were killed. Drawing his saber, Barker began cutting at the remaining Rangers and believed he hit Mosby. The fight swirled them apart and as soon as Barker broke free he led twenty-five men in a column four abreast up the lane directly into the mouth of the cannon. Chapman opened fire with grapeshot. The little gun killed three and wounded seven of the Union soldiers and forced a withdrawal.

Mosby charged with the rest of the men, but Barker, with two grapeshot from the cannon in his thigh, continued fighting and as more cavalry came up they counterattacked. Lt. John W. Hazelton led Companies H and C of the 1st Vermont in a charge and right behind them came Colonel Preston and the rest of the 1st Vermont detachment. A swirling fight broke out with the Rangers at times surrounded. Sgt. Job Corey of Company H, 1st Vermont was killed and his brother Stephen wounded.[2]

As Chapman fired his last round, Mosby charged again. Chapman kept the howitzer barking until he ran out of ammunition, and fighting around the gun was hand-to-hand. One of his shells had passed right through the horse of one of Preston's Vermonters. Though the Union cavalry had the numbers, many were trying to use sabers against the Ranger revolvers. Mosby was nearly unhorsed when struck in the shoulder by a blow from a cavalryman's saber. Reeling, Mosby shot the man. Sam Chapman was swinging the rammer of his gun when shot down beside the gun, and Fount Beattie and Richard Montjoy fought standing over him until captured. With the attention of the cavalry on the howitzer, Mosby and the rest of his men scattered and broke free. Six Rangers were killed and ten captured. Mosby made no estimate of the number of wounded Rangers—the cavalrymen claimed twenty. With the capture of Beattie and Montjoy and the badly wounded Chapman, the Rangers lost three of their best.[3]

Colonel Mann reported four Union soldiers dead and fifteen wounded. The blue-coated troopers were unable to keep up the pursuit as, in the initial effort to catch up, they exhausted their mounts. Mann claimed his men did use revolvers, calling it a "terrific fire," then followed with a saber charge that cut many Rangers severely.[4]

Mosby had been defeated in this engagement, but at the time the 6,000-man Union cavalry division under Major General Stahel was tied down trying to guard against the Rangers and to find and destroy Mosby. On Tuesday, June 9, 1863, the great cavalry battle between Stuart and Pleasanton was fought at Brandy Station. Ten thousand cavalrymen went into action on each side and both sides had reason to claim victory. One additional Union cavalry division may well have made it a decisive victory for the North.

On Saturday, June 6, some 100 bluecoats of the 1st New York (Lincoln) Cavalry came riding, searching for Mosby. Captain Boyd had intelligence that Mosby and his wife were at the house of James and Elizabeth Hathaway. The house was surrounded in darkness and demands made for entrance. Civility was followed, so delay occurred when there were objections from the ladies within and demands from without. When they got inside, the Union soldiers found Mrs. Mosby but no sign of her husband.

A uniform was there, there were good horses in the barn and military items, which were confiscated as the spoils of war. Sgt. Russell P. Forkey got Mosby's sorrel mare and named her Lady Mosby. Some twenty horses were taken, but there was no sign of Mosby so the frustrated cavalrymen rode away. Mosby left the tree limb where he was hiding and pulled himself back into the house. When Boyd's men had ridden into the yard, Mosby was asleep in an upstairs bedroom. He quickly opened a window, grabbed a nearby limb and swung himself into the tree. There he had remained, just a few feet from the searchers.[5]

Union officers frequently complained about the activities of partisan Rangers, and they were joined by some of the conventional West Pointers among the Confederate army. Taking out trains was considered a reprehensible act by men who would send hundreds of men to their deaths in fruitless charges. If derailing a train, "You might kill a woman or child," was a frequent complaint by Confederate officers who would fire their artillery into towns.

Mosby believed anyone riding railroads in a war zone should be prepared to accept risks. He wrote, "It does not hurt people any more to be killed in a railroad wreck than having their heads knocked off by a cannon shot."[6] There were always complaints that he did not fight fair. Mosby had a realistic view of war and was never taken in by the "You have the honor of the first shot" attitude that school-trained officers sometimes were wont to display. Mosby wrote, "I fought for success and not for display."[7]

The effort continued to make Rangers act like conventional units and put organizational numbers on them. On June 10, 1863, Mosby gathered his men for a meeting four miles west of Middleburg at Rector's Cross Roads. Under orders, he organized Company A of the 43rd Battalion, Partisan Rangers. Though the Rangers seldom used it, the designation became the formal name of Mosby's Rangers. His force would grow to two battalions by war's end. There was no doubt that Mosby would remain in command, but elections were held for the subordinate officers Mosby wanted elected. James W. Foster was chosen captain and Thomas Turner first lieutenant.

Mosby had been successful at drawing individuals to his raids. Increasingly he was getting entire units to come along under his leadership. Joined by Capt. John Brawner's company of the Prince William Rangers, Mosby rode for the Potomac River. His intent was to put a scare into Washington politicians. Any action near the capital would bring a great outcry for more guards. Chancellorsville, often called Lee's greatest battle, had recently been successfully concluded and conversation on the streets of Washington was filled with fear of an invasion by Lee's army. Mosby had heard that Company I, 6th Michigan Cavalry was at Seneca Mills, Maryland. He intended to cross the river at night, capture the outposts and charge in at daybreak. Plans often go astray and in this case Mosby's guide got lost, resulting in the Rangers having to make a daylight river crossing. Capt. Charles W. Deane, commanding the Michigan cavalry, learned Mosby was coming and prepared for the attack. Believing he was outnumbered, Deane planned to withdraw on successive defensive positions.

Mosby scouts Alfred Glasscock, Joe Nelson, and a third man identified only as Trunnell captured sixteen cavalrymen who were performing various patrol duties along the Potomac. The Rangers crossed over the river and

Mosby led the attack up a tow path. Deane's cavalry withdrew over a bridge beside the mill and creek, forcing the Rangers into a narrow front. Here the cavalry used their Spencer carbines to bring a withering fire on the Rangers. Spurs were put to horses and with whoops and yells the Rangers made a successful charge over the bridge. A vicious close-quarter fight occurred at Captain Deane's next position within the narrow confines of a deep cut though which the road passed. Capt. John Brawner and the newly appointed 3rd Lt. George S. Whitescarver were killed. As Deane withdrew from the cut to his next position, the Rangers broke off the attack, cleaned out Deane's camp and re-crossed the river. The cavalrymen lost four men killed, seventeen captured, twenty-three horses and five mules.[8]

In June 1863, the stage was set for John Singleton Mosby to play a critical role in a battle he did not fight. General Lee had faced and beaten an army that outnumbered him two to one at Chancellorsville. He now decided to take his army into Pennsylvania with options to capture the state capital of Harrisburg or threaten Washington. Lee's plan was to use the Blue Ridge Mountains as a screen for the Confederate movement; the passes through these mountains would be sealed by Stuart's cavalry to prevent General Hooker from knowledge of Lee's intention.

After the battle of Brandy Station on June 9, cavalry fights spread westward as Lee's army moved with Stuart's cavalry as a screen that Union horsemen sought to penetrate. Stuart was to keep his remaining horsemen east of the mountains, block the passes, and stay between Lee and Hooker. When Lee's infantry was well on the way, Stuart and his men, again continuing to stay between the two armies, would come north and join the main army. Mosby's Rangers were an important part of this plan. Mosby was in position to keep Stuart informed of the movement of Hooker's army. The Rangers could hear artillery fire from near Aldie. Riding to the top of a mountain they could see the great dust clouds raised by a marching army. Mosby rode to the Little River Turnpike. Hiding out until nightfall, he led his men under cover of darkness to a spot some four miles south of Aldie. The Rangers were now inside the encampments of Hooker's vast army, and tents and cookfires covered the hills around them. Heavy traffic still continued on the turnpike. Mosby decided to make a reconnaissance to determine Hooker's plans. Taking three of his Rangers, he boldly rode out onto the road and became part of the marching column. Darkness concealed his gray uniform.

As they were passing the house of a man named Birch, south of Aldie, Mosby saw three horses being held outside by an orderly. Mosby knew Birch originally was from New York and a Unionist. Again knowledge of terrain and his surroundings paid dividends. Mosby was suspicious and spurred close, asking the orderly who the horses belonged to. The soldier replied the horses were those of Maj. William R. Stirling and Captain Fisher and himself, and the three men were from General Hooker's headquarters. It was about 10 P.M. on June 18 when the two officers came out of the house and Mosby engaged them in conversation. The two unsuspecting men said they were on the way to the headquarters of cavalry commander General Pleasanton to deliver messages. All three men were made prisoner and Mosby took the dispatches from Stirling. They revealed General Hooker's intent and his order of battle. Mosby dispatched Ranger Norman Smith to carry the captured documents to General Stuart.[9] They showed that General Hooker did not have a grasp of Lee's intentions and was considering more cavalry action to get the answer. By June 21, 1863, Lee had passed behind the Blue Ridge Mountains, heading north.

Meanwhile Stuart was fighting a delay against Pleasonton's cavalry, keeping the blue-coated horsemen from penetrating Ashby's Gap in the Blue Ridge Mountains and learning the scope of Lee's movements. His defeat by Lee at Chancellorsville had put Joe Hooker under a cloud. Lee was on the move and, lacking firm information, the powers in Washington thought the Confederate army might be scattered and open to attack. By June 25 Stuart thought he could proceed north and join Lee. Mosby thought Stuart could go north, staying between Hooker and Lee, and Stuart acted on that advice.

Mosby was wrong. Hooker had gained some understanding of Lee's location and was moving his forces north. Stuart could not get between the two opposing armies and would be forced to ride around the Union army to get to Lee. Gettysburg was a battle unforseen. The detour Stuart had to take and the capture of much-needed wagons and supplies en route caused Stuart not to be at Gettysburg when Lee needed him most.

For the rest of his life Mosby would carry an uneasy feeling for his part in this affair. He was quick to rise in support of the reputation of J.E.B. Stuart. Mosby and Stuart knew Lee was not left without cavalry. Stuart had three brigades of cavalry consisting of some 5,000 men with him when he rode north, but two brigades of Stuart's horsemen under Beverly Robertson were at Lee's disposal. They were used to follow up the main army, blocking passes behind Lee. The Confederate leader also had Jenkins' and Imboden's horsemen. Indeed, Lee had some 8,000 horsemen available to him. In later years Mosby often would ask the legitimate question that if Lee was so blinded at Gettysburg by the absence of Stuart's three brigades of cavalry, why did the commanding general not make use of the two brigades of horsemen that were serving as an ad hoc rear guard and get them out in front of the army. Stuart would not live to defend himself, but the loyal Mosby made that defense a principal part of his post-war life. It was not politic to fault Lee, so Robertson got most of Mosby's criticism.

In late June, Mosby wanted to join in the Pennsylvania experience. On Sunday, June 28,1863, some fifty Rangers rallied at Glasscock's, four miles from Upperville. They started about noon for the Shenandoah Valley, passing through Snicker's Gap. Near Hancock they crossed over the Potomac River through Maryland and into Franklin County, Pennsylvania. They found Pennsylvania a land of milk, meat and bread, well stocked with cattle and horses. They helped themselves to the bounty of this land and were so occupied until Wednesday, July 1, 1863. Mosby and his Rangers were not aware the battle at Gettysburg was beginning, but being in Pennsylvania was different from their Virginia area of operation. Here they were not greeted with the warm smiles of home. They felt the scorn Union soldiers felt in the South. They did not know the country and did not have local guides willing to help them. Mosby did not know where Lee's army had gone and quickly decided to head back south. He took along twelve captured blacks to be sold back into slavery, 218 head of cattle and twelve horses he confiscated from farms along the way.

Back in Virginia, the Rangers and the South were plunged into gloom when they learned of the disastrous loss at Gettysburg, followed the next day by the surrender at Vicksburg. July 1863 would be a time of little rest as the Rangers operated not only behind Union lines but in the heart of the Union army. It was hard riding, and the replacement of horses was always a problem. Horse raids were critical to sustain the unit. By Tuesday, July 28, 1863, Mosby was reporting to Stuart the capture of 186 prisoners and 123 horses and mules with three wagons destroyed.[10] The hunting was so good that Mosby established his own prisoner-of-war camp just north of Hopewell Gap in the Bull Run Mountains. Much pleased by this activity, Stuart recommended Major Mosby be promoted.

Thanks to the freedom of action, being close to home and the chance for booty, there was no lack of volunteers for the Rangers. Company A was considerably over strength and would spawn Company B of the 43rd Battalion Virginia Partisan Rangers. Taking thirty men, Mosby rode to Fairfax Court House on Thursday, July 30, 1863. Operating in this area, he had great success capturing prisoners and twenty-nine wagons filled with supplies which the Confederate army badly needed. Mosby immediately sent the wagons and prisoners moving west on the Little River Turnpike toward Aldie. He was about to meet one of his primary adversaries.

Col. Charles Russell Lowell commanded the 2nd Massachusetts Cavalry Regiment operating out of Centerville. At age 28, Lowell's boyish, sensitive face concealed the heart of a warrior. He was a learned man, having graduated from Harvard with top honors, had a superb knowledge of mathematics and the ability to read or speak five languages. He was commissioned a captain in the 3rd U.S. Cavalry on May 14, 1861, joined the 6th U.S. Cavalry on August 3 of the same year, and became colonel of the 2nd Massachusetts Cavalry on May 10, 1863. Colonel Lowell's regiment was joined by a unit known in the west as the California Rangers. They were primarily men born in the East, men who removed to the West Coast. These highly touted California Rangers were justly proud they were the first unit from their area to come east to fight. Based on their initial number, they began to be known as the California Hundred. Traveling by ship around Cape Horn, they arrived on the East Coast in early January 1863. On April 16 several hundred more highly selected volunteers landed in New York. These contingents would comprise the 500-man California Battalion that became part of the 2nd Massachusetts Cavalry.

Around 8:30 P.M., Colonel Lowell led 150 men from Centerville, arriving at Aldie about 1 A.M. Moving to the sound of the firing, Lowell ordered a charge by his California and Massachusetts men. The Rangers immediately went into their dispersion tactic with four or five men reversing course on the road and the rest fleeing through the fields. Lowell sent troopers after those in the fields and pursued those on the road with his main force. After about three miles he came upon the captured wagons. Mosby had not had time to burn them and had wisely headed for the Bull Run Mountains with his prisoners. Lowell sent the wagons to Centreville under guard and started in pursuit of Mosby, tracking him into the Bull Run Mountains. Here he liberated nine prisoners and took some twenty of Mosby's horses.

Mosby reported the engagement through channels and included that he had only twenty-seven men with him on the raid. His report brought praise from Stuart and another recommendation for promotion. What Mosby received from General Lee was a contradiction. On August 18, 1863, Lee forwarded Mosby's report and Stuart's endorsement to the Confederate War Department with a mix of praise and criticism:

> I greatly commend Major Mosby for his boldness and good management. I fear he exercises but little control over his men. He has latterly carried but too few on his expeditions apparently, and his attention has been more attracted to the capture of wagons than military damage to the enemy. His attention has been called to this.
>
> R. E. Lee, General

After Gettysburg, wagons were a touchy subject with Lee.

Lee knew a lot more about running an army than Mosby, but Mosby knew more about living and raiding behind enemy lines than Lee. Mosby survived by dispersion, followed by quick assembly, hitting hard with small numbers of Rangers, quickly getting clear and dispersing again. If Mosby tried to slug it out with the big brigades of Union cavalry, he would be overwhelmed.

On Monday, August 24, 1863, Mosby's Rangers clashed again with Lowell's troopers. Mosby had about thirty-five Rangers with him when he encountered a horse herd being escorted by a detachment of cavalry. The Massachusetts men had stopped at Billy Goodling's tavern on the Little River Turnpike, about ten miles from Alexandria.[11] Mosby sent Lieutenant Turner and some Rangers to attack from the herd guard's rear while he hit the front. Though the attack routed most of the Massachusetts men, some took cover in the inn and opened fire on the Rangers. Lt. Norman Smith and 17-year-old Ranger Charles Shriver were killed. Smith was another of the skilled and experienced Ranger leaders who led from the front and were being shot off. Ranger Joseph Calvert was shot in the ankle, and Mosby was shot in the side and thigh. The Rangers got away with eighty-five horses, killed three of the cavalrymen, wounded three and took twelve prisoners. In his report to Stuart, Mosby wrote that his wounds had forced him to leave the fight. His men thought he was breaking off the action and followed him, thus many union soldiers got away.[12] The Rangers hid Mosby in heavy woods until the pursuit passed, then took him to where he could be treated by Dr. William L. Dunn, the battalion warrior surgeon.

Throughout his time in battle, Mosby was wounded at least seven times,[13] but he took little time off for recuperation. With the exception of jealousy and rivalry among subordinate leaders, the performance level of the Rangers continued to be high in his absence. Mosby had personally selected his lieutenants for election and, in or out of action, he directed objectives or areas to be raided. His trusted subordinates ably carried out the missions.

The frustration of Union commanders was expressed by Col. Horace Binney Sargent of the 1st Massachusetts Cavalry who wrote on September 2, 1863, "Tonight I might report that there is not an armed rebel within the circuit of country that the Colonel commanding expects me to clear. Tomorrow the woods may be full of them. A policy of extermination alone can achieve the end expected. . . . Attila, King of the Huns, adopted the only method that can exterminate these citizen soldiers. . . . I can clear this country with fire and sword, and no mortal can do it in any other way. The attempt to discriminate nicely between the just and the unjust is fatal to our safety; every house is a vedette post, and every hill a picket and signal station."[14]

On the night of September 28, 1863, Mosby and a half-dozen Rangers rode into Alexandria. His intention was to capture Union governor Francis Pierpont. The governor's house was reached without difficulty, but Pierpont had the good fortune to be in Washington. Accompanying Mosby on the raid was French Dulany, whose father was a Union colonel and the aide to the governor. With the aid of the son, Mosby captured the father and sent him to Richmond. On the way out the Rangers burned a bridge. On October 1, Mosby wrote to his wife Pauline about the raid in which Colonel Dulaney was captured. The colonel and his son were on opposite sides. The angry father had suggested in sarcasm that his son take an old pair of shoes from the house as he heard shoes were scarce in the Confederacy. The son held up his leg to show that he was wearing a fine pair of boots recently captured from a Union sutler.[15]

On September 30, 1863, Mosby wrote a report to General Stuart covering his actions from about August 20 until the time of the report. It is likely he was stung by Lee's critical words and knowing his reports were forwarded used this report as a teaching mechanism about Ranger operations. After describing his combat actions he included a paragraph that reveals both his object and his method. The report read, "The military value of the species of warfare I have waged is not measured by the number of prisoners and materiel of war captured from the enemy, but by the heavy detail it has already compelled him to make, and which I hope to make him increase, in order to guard his communications, and to that extent to diminishing his aggressive strength."[16]

It was now clear to Mosby that his command had to grow. In the Blue Ridge Mountains between Paris and Markham there was a quiet little hollow. The only buildings were a blacksmith shop, house and a wheelwright shop. This out-of-the-way place was called Scuffleburg and was a favorite meeting place of the Rangers as it was secluded and never visited by the U.S. cavalry. Scuffleburg was very near to the birthplace of Ranger Turner Ashby. It was a place of honeysuckle, sturdy chestnut trees and towering oaks.

Here on Thursday, October 1, 1863, the second company of Rangers was formed. Volunteers had continued to pour in, drawn by the freedom of action, better living conditions, freedom from army routine and, certainly for many, the prospect of loot. The formation of this additional unit and future units also was important to Mosby's career. No matter how heroic his actions or valuable his information and captures, many did not think he commanded enough men to be promoted to lieutenant colonel or colonel.

Mosby had participated in the liberation of goods during his ride with Stuart around McClellan's army. He did not take captain's share of loot on the raids of his men, and he refused money. He was capturing a great many horses, and some of them must have been his share. On October 1 he wrote Pauline a letter and added the postscript, "The horses that Aaron (his black servant) carried over I want sold. You can take the money. Perhaps you best invest it in tobacco. They ought to bring $2,000."[17]

The Union army was now a vast organization with a long supply train that offered many opportunities for the Rangers. The timing was right to expand. William R. Smith was chosen captain of Company B; Franklin Williams was first lieutenant.

On October 9, Mosby rode out from Rector's Cross Roads with forty men, heading toward Fairfax. They went to ground in a dense pine thicket near Frying Pan, staying there for two nights to make certain no one was aware of their movements. In the darkness of the early morning hours of October 11, they rode to and concealed themselves along the turnpike about six miles from Alexandria. Mosby and a scout moved to one observation point near the road and Captain Smith and John Munson took another some distance away. They stayed low as some 250 cavalry rode by escorting a long string of wagons, which Ranger Crawford estimated to number seventy-five.[18]

From Mosby's position he could see a large pothole in the side of the road that the wagoners were having difficulty avoiding. His hopes were fulfilled when the third wagon from the rear became mired in this muddy hole. Unaware of the trouble behind them, the Union column rode on. Mosby and Ranger Walter Whaley promptly rode out and at gunpoint commandeered the trapped wagons. The stuck wagon was freed and all three were driven into the woods. Meanwhile Capt. William Smith and Ranger John Munson saw another wagon that had straggled behind and was about a mile behind the rest. The wagon was quickly captured and found to contain a wealth of foodstuffs. This wagon also was concealed. The four wagons were horns of plenty to Mosby's men, being loaded with clothing, food and tobacco. One wagon had 175 pairs of new cavalry boots. There was nothing there that the South did not need. The men had a difficult time deciding what they should take. They loaded the sacks across the pommels of their saddles. Some men hid items they planned to retrieve later. The remainder was destroyed.

October 22 found Mosby leaving present-day Marshall, south of Rectortown, and riding for Warrenton with fifty men. Several miles south of Warrenton, the Rangers found a large wagon train under guard of two regiments of infantry. Both Union cavalry and infantry escorts tended to bunch up and not provide security throughout the wagon train. In this instance the infantry was out front and to the rear, but could not get to the scene of the action in time. Mosby divided his force. Capt. William Chapman stopped the wagon train, and the rest of the men provided security or unhitched the mules. The Rangers got away with 120 mules, twenty-seven horses and thirty-two prisoners. Union cavalry came up before the wagons could be burned, but the Rangers escaped.

The addition of some U.S. currency was always welcome. Crawford remembered a Ranger (it was Sam Alexander) yelling, "Give me your greenbacks! Surrender!"[19]

Mosby wearing the uniform he wore
when he captured General Stoughton.
USAMHI

Sam Alexander's never-ending efforts to collect money from his prisoners was a delight to his comrades who always sought to beat him to the cash.
Munson remembered a raid where Alexander leveled his pistol at a Union
soldier and yelled, "Give me your pocket book you blankety, blank, blank."
"I have not got any pocket book," the poor Union soldier replied. "Well
then, surrender," Alexander wailed in disgust.[20]

The war was changing. Gettysburg and Vicksburg had dampened Southern expectations. For many in the South it was plain the war would be lost. A
decline in discipline and patriotism accompanied the feeling of despair.
Men in Confederate uniforms—absent without leave or deserted from their
units—roamed the land, robbing people, claiming they were Mosby's men.
On Saturday, October 31, 1863, all of Mosby's men were issued certificates
to prove they were sanctioned by the Confederate States. Mosby was given
police power and could act as both judge and jury with the bandits. He
settled arguments and resolved administrative disputes; indeed he was lord
over his land.

Stuart forwarded Mosby's reports with the frequent recommendation
that he be promoted. Mosby had reached the rank where General Lee and
the army bureaucracy believed valor and results were not enough. Should a
man who commanded so few troops be promoted to lieutenant colonel,
they asked. General Lee did not think so. In forwarding a report on Mosby's
success to Richmond, he wrote, "I have hoped that he would have been able
to raise his command sufficiently for the command of a lieutenant colonel,
and to have it regularly mustered into the service. I am not aware that it
numbers over 4 companies."[21]

His opponents were more concerned with Mosby's actions than his rank. An extract from the diary of Capt. Harrison L. Newhall of the 3rd Pennsylvania Cavalry reads: "Returned last night from a raid to Middleburgh. It was reported that Mr. Mosby was in that neighborhood, but we had no luck. I came to the conclusion that hunting guerrillas with four regiments of cavalry and four pieces of artillery was very much like shooting mosquitoes with a rifle."[22]

Mosby had his Union deserter in Big Yankee Ames, but some of his men went over to the other side. One was Charlie Binns. While drunk, Binns had incurred Mosby's wrath and when the Ranger leader ordered him arrested, he promptly fled to the Union encampment at Fairfax. Binns knew Ranger hide-outs in the vicinity of Middleburg. Colonel Lowell of the 2nd Massachusetts Cavalry assembled some 300 men from his own unit and the 16th New York Cavalry and used Binns and the scout Yankee Davis to begin tracking down Rangers in their dispersed hide-outs. Colonel Lowell split his men into detachments of forty to fifty men led by capable officers. They rode at night and they had good intelligence. Sleeping men were rudely awakened to find themselves looking into gun barrels. The operation was a great success. Eighteen uniformed Confederate soldiers were captured who claimed to be with Mosby and had passes from the Ranger leader. Lowell believed some of these men were really from regular Confederate units. Lowell also reported the capture of eight men wanted for smuggling and horse theft and claimed one Ranger killed and thirty-five horses (thirteen with equipment) and twenty-five revolvers among the haul. As Mosby did with Ames, Lowell had high praise for deserter Charlie Binns, writing in his November 26, 1863, report: "I wish to employ him again on similar work, and as he shows no unwillingness to expose himself, I recommend that he be allowed the same pay as other Government Scouts while in my employ."[23]

Mosby had intelligence that all of General Meade's army was crossing the Rappahannock and that the Union army was on the march. If successful, they could turn the left flank of Lee's army. Messages of assembly went out and some 125 men came to the rally point at Rectortown. They rode south to Coon's Mill and stayed under cover while Mosby and three Rangers made a reconnaissance in the vicinity of Brandy Station. They found a large wagon train at this site of the vast cavalry battle. The wagon train had infantry guards but they were insufficient in number to preclude an attack. Mosby held one group of Rangers in reserve under Lieutenant Turner. He sent two detachments under Capt. William Smith and William Chapman to capture the mules, while a third under Richard Montjoy was to set fire to the wagons. Bored with their duty, the guards were unwary and were taken without sound as they had pistols held in their faces. Some of the mules were unhitched before the teamsters knew what was occurring. Terror reigned when these men found the Rangers among them. Many teamsters assisted in the unhitching of the mules and quickly obeyed any other order they were given.

One man walked away carrying a satchel. Thinking the man might be a paymaster, Ranger Charley Tyler rode after him, calling upon the man to stop. The man paid no attention to Tyler and kept walking. Tyler was right beside the man, pointed his pistol and threatened death. The man ignored him and kept walking away. Tyler could not handle this reaction and, unwilling to shoot what he called a "damned fool," gave it up and rejoined the Rangers.[24] The infantry guard finally began to rally, but their targets were widely dispersed among the teamsters and the wagons which were now burning brightly. The Rangers destroyed a large amount of supplies captured many teamsters, 160 mules, seven horses, and large quantities of harness.

More volunteers were pouring into the command. While Confederate infantry regiments watched desertion rates climb, Mosby was having his pick of men. On Tuesday, December 15, 1863, the Rangers assembled at Rectortown and organized Company C, 43rd Partisan Ranger Battalion. William H. Chapman, the devout Baptist gunman and head of the Ranger artillery, was elected captain. Adolphus E. Richards was elected first lieutenant. Richards was called "Dolly" by his comrades, but there was nothing girlish about this pure warrior. He came from Loudoun County and had come into the Rangers as a private after service with Turner Ashby. At the age of twenty, Dolly Richards would be a major and would take command of the Rangers and perform with brilliance when Mosby was seriously wounded. John Mosby continued to pick the officers the men then elected.

Mosby's gift to the Union, Charley Binns, was leading a cavalry search party on Christmas Day 1863 as it came up from Vienna heading for Fairfax. The Union horsemen were learning well. They moved only at night, and people scarcely knew they were about until a house was surrounded. Citizens were not harmed, but wanted men were picked up. Colonel Lowell of the 2nd Massachusetts Cavalry reported with contentment the capture of eight prisoners. Colonel Lowell's search party did have success bringing in men from their most-wanted list, but none of them were from Mosby's Rangers.

Col. Henry A. Cole's Maryland Cavalry (Union) had sent Capt. Albert M. Hunter and eighty men from Harpers Ferry in search of Mosby and his Rangers. Hunter's men were hoping to shoot someone, as one of their men had been killed at Upperville. The Rangers drifted in toward Rectorville singly or in small groups; they could be seen on every hilltop, watching Hunter's men and waiting.

Looking at the growing numbers of Rangers, Hunter pulled out of Rectorville heading south toward Salem (today Marshall). He was followed through and out of town by Capt. William Smith of Company B of the Rangers and thirty-two men. Hunter tried to shake off the Rangers by heading south on the Warrenton Road. A few miles out of town, the cavalry swung off the road to the left and changed direction, now going northeast past Five Forks, toward Middleburg. Smith rode cross-country to attack Union troopers in the flank at Five Forks. Closing on the Maryland horsemen, the Rangers executed their customary charge, firing their revolvers and concentrating on taking the enemy officers out of the fight as quickly as possible. Captain Hunter had his horse shot out from under him and was taken prisoner. Without their leader, the rest of his command fled toward Middleburg. Mosby had seen Smith's men in Rectorville, but from a distance he thought they were Hunter's troopers. Learning of his mistake, he led approximately fifteen Rangers toward Five Forks and arrived in time to take part in the tail end of the pursuit. For Cole's Union cavalry, the action was an embarrassing rout. The men divested themselves of loot, equipment, weapons and anything that would impede their flight. Some even jumped from their horses and tried to hide in the woods. Two Rangers were wounded. Four cavalrymen were killed, twelve wounded and forty-one captured along with fifty horses. Ranger Crawford wrote that "thirty fine army pistols were secured and distributed among the victors. The sabers and carbines we threw away as they were weapons we had no use for."[25] Four more of Hunter's men would be captured in the days that followed. They were lost and on foot in freezing cold.

This was Smith's fight. It was a decisive victory, but one that made Mosby furious. Northern newspapers credited the Southern cavalry brigade of Gen. Thomas Rosser with the victory instead of Capt. William R. Smith of the Rangers. Mosby gloried in the successes of his lieutenants.

Capt. Frank Stringfellow proposed to Mosby that an attack be made on Col. Henry A. Cole's Maryland cavalry camp at Loudoun Heights near Harpers Ferry. A recommendation by Stringfellow carried weight. One of General Stuart's top scouts, Stringfellow's reputation for daring was well known. It was said he had put on the uniform of a captured Union colonel and had entered the headquarters of Union corps commander Maj. Gen. John Sedgwick. Stringfellow stayed for dinner with the general, his staff and other officers while posing as the commander of a regiment from the far end of the line. He gained a good meal and valuable information which he brought back to Stuart.[26] Stringfellow had personally made a reconnaissance into Cole's camp and knew the troop disposition. On hearing the famed scout's information, Mosby agreed it would be an easy objective.

Cole's Maryland cavalry were experienced troopers, many having served since 1861. They were border state men. All knew the division of the war within their community—some knew it within their family. Christopher

Armour Newcomer had the experience of having family in arms against him and wrote, "Although connected by ties of birth and blood with the South, I loved my country and flag better than my state or section."[27] Cole's Maryland cavalry had patrolled along the Potomac in 1861 and 1862. They had fought in West Virginia and against Jackson in the Valley campaign and were accustomed to averaging twenty-five days a month in the saddle. It was not often the men got a good rest. Their position on Loudoun Heights was a good one, and there was the welcome opportunity to sleep with boots off, perhaps even remove outer clothing and have a good scratch.

In a chill wind on the afternoon of Saturday, January 9, 1864, Mosby rode out from Upperville with 106 men. By 8 P.M. the Rangers had reached Woodgrove, Loudoun County, and stopped to warm themselves and dine at the home of Ranger Henry Heaton. Two hours later, Mosby resumed the march. Two miles from Cole's encampment they were joined by Captain Stringfellow and ten men. They had scouted ahead and reported conditions favorable for the attack. The night was clear and starlit, but cold pierced men like a bayonet. Such cold quickly attacks the extremities, and feet in stirrups were particularly susceptible. Those men who had hooded, leather stirrups were grateful for the additional protection, but many men had to dismount and walk beside their horses to keep circulation going in their feet.

Ranger Williamson was affected by the sight of that snow-covered ground. He would write, "Fields, roads, trees and shrubs were alike clothed in the white robes of winter and it seemed almost a sacrilege against the beauty and holy stillness of the scene to stain those pure garments with the life blood of man, be he friend or foe."[28]

They passed Union campfires and heard the wailing whistle of a Union train crying in the night. The horses were climbing now, feeling their way on a narrow mountain path. Mosby's men were strung out in a long line, unable to maneuver to their flanks effectively, unable to do little but forge ahead. Capt. William Smith, commanding Company B, and Lt. Tom Turner, commanding Company A, were up front leading the column. Ranger Williamson described what followed: "Suddenly 'crack!' went the report of a pistol; then 'bang-bang-bang,' went the carbines from the camp in front, accompanied by loud shouts from Cole's camp. Above the din rang out the clear voices of Smith and Turner—'Charge them, boys! Charge them!' The rebel yell split the cold night air."[29]

Disaster was in the making. Mosby and Stringfellow were experienced, talented leaders who knew each other's reputation. Perhaps they knew those reputations too well and expected too much. A night attack requires that men fully know their assignments, coordinate their movements and, if time permits, rehearse the action. They need to know what the men on either side of them will do. Stringfellow's men were first up the mountain. Knowing the ground and eager to attack, they forged ahead, deciding to swing wide and strike Cole's first line of tents from the rear. Moving forward, a Ranger saw the figures coming through the darkness, thought they were Cole's troopers, and opened fire. The battle began with the Rangers charging Stringfellow's scouts, killing and wounding several, but they were soon into the cavalry's sleeping tents. Some thirty Rangers rode close and began to fire their revolvers into the first row of tents. Within the canvas, wounded were screaming and trapped men were begging for mercy and offering surrender.[30]

The attack on the first line of tents sent other Marylanders leaping from their blankets. It does not require clothing to fight and kill. Cole's nude or half-clothed men grabbed their weapons and boiled out of their tents. Trooper Newcomer would write, " During the fight every man was for himself. There was no time to wait for orders, the cry rang out on the frosty air 'shoot every soldier on horseback.' Many of the Confederates who were killed or wounded were burned with powder as Cole's men were using their carbines. It was hand to hand and so dark you could not see the face of the enemy you were shooting. It was perfect hell! Every man cursing and yelling and the horses were plunging and kicking in their mad efforts to get away."[31]

Cole had under his command an officer of quick mind and great courage, Capt. George Vernon of Maryland. Vernon's company was in the second line of tents. He reacted quickly to the gunfire and brought his men on line and firing. Vernon put a number of men in a nearby log cabin, and its windows and doors became the birthplace of a hail of lead. As Vernon fired the last round of his revolver, he was shot in the head, the bullet tearing out an eye. Though terribly wounded, Vernon would survive to become lieutenant colonel of the command. Williamson wrote that Lt. Tom Turner was going forward on horseback toward the Marylander's tents when he threw up his hands crying out, "I am shot!" Two Rangers guided Turner and his horse away. Ranger Paxson was shot from the saddle. Williamson wrote that Paxson cried out, "You are not going to leave me here on the field?" Capt. William Smith called out, "Fire the tents, shoot by the light."[32] Then as he rode toward Paxson's side, Smith was shot through the brain and killed. Honorary Confederate captain John Robinson was a Scot from the British army, serving with the Rangers as a volunteer. He was shot dead in the saddle and fell to the ground. Ranger Owens followed him in death. Dismounted and trying to rally the men, Ranger Colston, who like Turner was from Maryland, was killed. Mosby's friend and trusted lieutenant, Fountain Beatie, was shot in the thigh and his horse shot dead under him.

The scene was utter confusion, a madness in the dark where men stood firing at each other, sometimes at point blank range, screaming at each

other to surrender and refusing with vigor. The two Ranger company commanders were out of action. Smith was dead and Turner was dying. Control
was lost. Suddenly there came a sound that told the Rangers it was time to
skedaddle. A signal gun was fired at nearby Harpers Ferry. All the thousands
of Union troops in the area were now alerted and the Rangers were caught
up in a desperate fight on a mountaintop with only a narrow path as a route
of escape. By the force of his personality Mosby brought his men back under
control and broke contact.

The Rangers claimed they came off with seven prisoners and thirty-five
horses, but they did not return with all their men. The bodies of five dead
Rangers remained behind, Captains Smith and Robinson and Rangers Colston, Owens and Yates. Dying of their wounds were Lt. Tom Turner,[33]
William Turner (like Colston from Baltimore) and Charles Paxson. Rangers
Fountain Beattie, Henry Edmonds, and Boyd Smith were among the
wounded, and Leonard Brown was taken prisoner. Mosby claimed he made
an offer to exchange his prisoners for the bodies and his wounded and captured men. The ominous answer was that he could try to come back and get
them. Cole reported four men killed and sixteen wounded. He did not
report any of his men taken prisoner or horses lost.

Mosby's report of the action to General Stuart was dated February 1,
1864. Mosby claimed he had moved the command into position for a night
attack on the rear of Cole's encampment. He wrote that within 200 yards of
the camp he had sent Stringfellow forward to capture Colonel Cole and his
staff who were in a house about 100 yards from the camp. Mosby wrote, "All
my plans were on the eve of consummation, when suddenly the party sent
with Stringfellow came dashing over the hill toward the camp yelling and
shooting. They made no attempt to secure Cole. Mistaking them for the
enemy, I ordered my men to charge."[34]

Many of the Rangers felt the raid was compromised when some of the
men saw mules tethered in front of Cole's quarters and noisily broke formation to take them. Other men felt that some of Stringfellow's ten had broken
off from his party and made the personal assault that confused everyone.[35]

Mosby wrote, "My loss was severe; more so in the worth than the number
of the slain."[36] General Stuart again sought Mosby's promotion, writing
to Lee, "If Major Mosby has not won it, no more can daring deeds essay to
do it."[37]

It took Mosby time to recover from the shock of losing men whom he
loved and trusted so deeply. Capt. Richard Montjoy led fifteen men to a location between Warrenton and Warrenton junction near the Orange and
Alexandria Railroad. The mission was to attack the U.S. Mail and its twenty-
man cavalry guard.

Richard Montjoy was from Mississippi. A particular favorite of Mosby, he
was a handsome man who dressed with care, looked like a leader and lived

the part. Of this raid, Ranger Crawford wrote: "All his men wore the regular blue army overcoats to deceive the enemy."[38] When they reached the point where the ambush was to be established, they found the mail and its guard had passed the spot an hour before. It was not long before a sutler wagon came along and then a correspondent for the New York Tribune. Both men were relieved of their wallets. The Rangers learned the correspondent hoped to get to Richmond so they gave him their unwanted Confederate money with the admonishment that U.S. greenbacks were no good in Richmond, adding that they were doing him a good turn by swapping.[39]

Montjoy led his men onward. They saw the camp of a Union cavalry unit, and some 300 yards away a sergeant was putting out an outpost of ten men. Taking advantage of their blue overcoats, they rode up to the outpost detail and took them prisoner. Union commanders were furious that Confederate Rangers were wearing Union army blue uniform coats. General Pleasanton, Union cavalry commander, ordered that any Confederates caught in Union uniform were to be shot or hanged. Ranger Crawford wrote that many Rangers began to dye their overcoats black.[40]

The roving life of the Ranger was getting more difficult. The more Union soldiers the Rangers pulled off the line of battle, the more they were hunted. Large numbers of Union cavalry were riding around the clock seeking to kill or capture the raiders. Fighting Rangers with Ranger tactics, the Union sought to smother the countryside with combat patrols to keep pressure on Mosby's command. The effort had some results. Rangers were being captured at their hide-outs. The pursuit of the Rangers by the Union cavalry was relentless. Good intelligence of Union movements and eternal vigilance was necessary to elude being trapped by the regiments of horsemen. Each Ranger company was assigned an area it was responsible to outpost and patrol in order to provide early warning of Union raids. Three Union detachments, each of 150-300 men, were searching for them.

February 17 was a Wednesday and one of the coldest days of the year. Though water froze in canteens and a howling wind came through their camp, a detachment of 300 cavalrymen of the 1st New Jersey, 1st and 3rd Pennsylvania and 1st Massachusetts left their camp at Warrenton for a raid in northern Fauquier County. They were under the command of Lt. Col. John W. Kester and guided by one of Mosby's deserters, John Cornwall. After a dispute with Capt. William Chapman over an expense Chapman would not accept, Cornwall went over to the Union camp and was serving as a well-informed guide for the cavalry.

As the men left camp, the wind subsided but the cold was so intense that movement was misery. First Sgt. Henry Darris of the 1st New Jersey Cavalry saw a man dismount and moved to get him back in the saddle. The man begged to be permitted to lie down to sleep. The soldier was so cold he could not make his limbs move and merely wanted to die. In an unusual way to save a man's life, 1st Sgt. Darris took his saber and repeatedly hit the man's body to restore circulation. The technique worked and the horseman thanked his top sergeant for whipping him.[41]

The column passed through Salem and on to Manassas Gap and hill country. As night fell, the misery increased. The calvalry had to cross a mountain stream where the ice would not bear the weight of the horses. Wet, cold and tired men and horses were slipping and sliding. When they got across the stream, the guide, Cornwall, found he had made a mistake and they had to re-cross. At the height of their misery, the New Jersey troopers were divided into smaller detachments and sent off to search local houses where Cornwall said Mosby's men would be found.

Capt. James Hart kept his detachments moving rapidly from house to house before word of the raid could spread. The men with Hart caught two of Mosby's Rangers in bed—a third escaped into the cold night without boots or outer garments.

Lt. Samuel C. Lame found a house where there were an unusual number of women. As Lame searched room to room, he found a bedroom where six young women were in a state of undress. They were very upset that he would invade their privacy and told him there could not possibly be any men in the room. The lieutenant assured the ladies he was a married man and therefore was not embarrassed. He searched the room and found two of Mosby's men in the closet. The embarrassed women feigned surprise the men were there.

Lt. John Hobensack found one man hiding beneath the bed of an old rheumatic Negro; another was found hiding under a pile of hoop skirts. At still another house, a woman was in bed and furious at the notion she should be required to leave it. Hobensack was insistent and a Confederate was found under the mattress on which the woman had been lying.[42]

The Union cavalry took twenty-eight prisoners, who included Mosby Rangers, soldiers of the Regular army and deserters. Also taken were fifty horses and what was described as "a small arsenal of revolvers and sabers." Captains William Chapman and Montjoy assembled twenty-five men and harassed the columns, but did not have the strength to stop the raiders. It was charge and countercharge. Captain Hart took a bullet in the arm, but shot one of the Rangers from the saddle. The cavalry put their best marksmen armed with Spencer rifles in the rear. They would dismount and use aimed fire, then mount and gallop after the column until the Rangers charged again when the process would be repeated.[43]

About 9 P.M. on February 19, a detachment of Union cavalry rode out from Halltown. The horsemen, under the command of Maj. Nathanial Coles of the 13th New York Cavalry, included seventy-five men of the 15th New York under the command of Capt. Michael Auer and Lt. Burritt Hurd and

Lt. Charles G. Hampton; twenty-five from the 1st New York Veteran Cavalry
under Capt. William L. Morgan, and fifty from the 22nd Pennsylvania
Cavalry. About 2:30 on the morning of Saturday, February 20, 1864, the
detachment arrived in the vicinity of Uppersville, concealed itself in a
woods, and established outposts.[44] There was an air of anticipation in the
ranks. The men of the 15th New York Cavalry knew they would soon have
their first experience in combat.

The next morning, operations commenced in the vicinity of Upperville
resulting in several Confederates killed and nineteen prisoners being taken.
Of this number, one of those killed and four of the captured were from
Mosby's Rangers. Major Coles' party then rode in the direction of Front
Royal. The Union cavalry had barely passed through Upperville when it was
attacked by Mosby. The prisoners were put toward the front of the Union
column, and a rear guard formed under the experienced forty-eight-year-old
Capt. William Morgan. Capt. Richard. P. Montjoy led the Rangers in an
attack on the rear guard, killed Morgan, and drove the rest of the rear guard
into the main body of Union horsemen. In a situation of charge and countercharge, the Union column found itself moving on a narrow, steep and icy
road that had stone walls on either side. The horses had difficulty keeping
their footing and progress was slow.

At the foot of the hill, the road turned to the right. The Rangers rode
cross-country, trying to cut off the head of the column and rescue the
prisoners. Captain Auer of the 15th New York had taken over the rear guard
and led a charge of that group to frustrate the Ranger intent. Fighting was
fierce and, at close range, Captain Auer and Lieutenant Hampton had their
horses shot. Auer leaped into a vacant saddle and continued fighting.
Hampton had been shot in the shoulder, and some Rangers who carried
sabers knocked him out with a blow to the head. The Rangers took him
prisoner. The Rangers reached the wall but the prisoners had gone past.
Now the remaining members of the 15th New York Cavalry had to run a
Ranger gauntlet. The Rangers leaned over the wall pointing their pistols and
yelling, "Surrender, you ————." Some of the cavalry rode through, but
others were shot down or captured. Lt. Burritt Hurd was one of the last to
make the run. He laid on the side of his horse opposite the Rangers, but
they shot the horse which fell mortally wounded. Hurd was trying to get his
feet from the stirrups when his spurs jabbed the horse. The animal sprang to
its feet and ran on, carrying Hurd to safety before it died.[45]

Williamson claimed the Rangers killed seven and captured eight of the
cavalry.[46]

When they could, the Rangers held funeral services for their men, an
event that would have amazed soldiers in line infantry regiments. On Sunday, February 21, 1864, such a service was being held for Ranger McCobb

who had been killed by Coles' men. A scout came in with a report that a column of Union cavalry totaling about 150 men was on the march in the vicinity of Rector's Cross Roads. About two miles from Dranesville, Mosby found an ambush site that would allow him to sweep down on the column from all sides. Though he seldom used shoulder-fired weapons, Mosby directed that carabineers under Montjoy would fire the first volley, which would serve as the signal for a general assault on the horsemen.

The Union troops were of the 2nd Massachusetts and included the California contingent. Capt. J. Sewell Read of San Francisco was in command. Read was a valiant officer of proven reputation, but the Union column was taken by surprise. At the first fire by Montjoy, Mosby blew a whistle to signal the attack.

Mosby came in from the front leading Companies A and part of Company B. Companies C and the remainder of B struck from the flanks and rear. The 2nd Massachusetts column was overwhelmed. Captain Read wounded Mosby's Prussian volunteer, Baron Robert von Massow. The Rangers claimed Read fired after he surrendered. True or not, Read was killed by Capt. William Chapman. Breaking contact, the survivors fled. The 2nd Massachusetts had thirteen men killed, and the California contingent considered this fight "the most disastrous affair of the war to the Californians."[47] The Rangers also claimed some twenty-five of the cavalry as wounded, seventy-two prisoners and ninety horses captured.[48]

Though the Rangers were having success, the war was getting beyond the reach of the South. As the weather warmed, the Union army began to flex its considerable muscle. U.S. Grant was now wearing the three stars of a lieutenant general and in command on the Union army. Lincoln said that once Grant got hold of a piece of territory, it was like he inherited it. He never let go. Union recruiting was reaching for numbers which the South could not match. Goals were 200,000 men in February and 200,000 in March; another 500,000 were called for in July.

The year 1863 had been the turning point for the Union cavalry. It had ceased to be the whipping boy of the battlefield and was being welded into a mighty force. Brandy Station and Buford's and Gregg's handling of the blue-coated horsemen at Gettysburg showed the emergence of a giant.

In April 1864, while the Confederate cavalry was struggling to replace mounts, the Union army bought or captured some 210,000 horses.[49] By the time of Appomattox, Sheridan had 15,000 cavalrymen under his command.

Mosby believed the South squandered its advantage by not conserving its cavalry during the first winter of the war. He wrote of Southern cavalry in the early periods of the war, "It was largely consumed in work which the infantry might have done."[50] He added, "When the Southern army retired in March 1862, three-fourths of the horses had been broken down by the hard work of the winter, and the men had been furloughed to go home for new ones. The Confederate government did not furnish horses for the cavalry, but paid the men forty cents a day for the use of them. This vicious policy was the source of continual depletion of the cavalry."

In addition to his responsibilities as a military commander, Mosby was expected to maintain civil control on behalf of the Confederate government; this was done in spite of the area being occupied by the Union army. The Richmond bureaucrats expected the old men, boys and women who were left on the farms to supply food to keep the army going. It was a hard life for these civilians as the bacon, corn and other foodstuff were taken by one army or the other, and Confederate money was a poor substitute. All across the Southern battle fronts, the civilians suffered the loss of anything edible.

Even their pets were not safe. One of the South Carolina Iron Scouts wrote, "Our orderly sergeant, a Frenchman of many accomplishments, is said to have called on the widow Hancock in Dinwiddie County and on taking his leave also took her gray cat. His mess ate her in a stew smothered with garlic the next day."[51]

Patriotism was sorely tested. Nothing could stand in the way of the war. Fighting men needed bacon, bread and milk. Corn, oats and hay were essential food for Ranger horses. A permanent detail led by Ranger quartermaster Capt. J. Wright James searched for corn and that which interfered with the supply had to be prevented, which meant the elimination of home distilleries. Mosby's Rangers not only fought the Union, but they were a prohibition force that hunted for stills, smashed the equipment and poured out the liquor. Mosby would not tolerate a drunken man in his command and that, combined with the critical need for grain, caused some local anger. The destruction of the Downey family still along the Potomac River in Loudoun resulted in the Downeys inviting a Union ambush party who captured quartermaster James and two other Rangers who had come to confiscate corn.

Sgt. Artemis Weatherbee and Cpl. James Simpson were members of Company H of the Griswold Light Cavalry, numerically named the 21st New York Cavalry. On Friday, March 25, 1864, these noncommissioned officers and two others with their horses had been captured by Mosby and six Rangers. It seemed the Union soldiers were destined for the discomforts of a prisoner-of-war camp. The weather was terrible, a day of storm with wind and blinding snow. Mosby loved coffee, genuine coffee, and was insistent on having sugar with it. In 1864 both coffee and sugar were luxuries in the South. A few miles south of Paris, Mosby stopped at a house and went inside in search of coffee and information, his favorite combination. Ranger James W. Wrenn, the second sergeant of Company B, was left outside to guard the prisoners. Corporal Simpson watched as Mosby dismounted from his beauti-

Lt. Col. William Chapman, Mosby's second in command.
Mosby said Chapman went into battle "with his hat in one hand
and banging away with his revolver in the other." USAMHI

ful gray horse and saw that Mosby, who loved revolvers, had a holstered pistol fixed on his saddle. While the unsuspecting Wrenn watched, Simpson dismounted as though to tie his horse at the steps to the house. Suddenly, Simpson leaped for Mosby's horse and into the saddle. Without hesitation, Simpson drew Mosby's pistol and fired at Wrenn. The shot missed, but before the startled Ranger sergeant could respond, Corporal Simpson and Sergeant Weatherbee galloped off into the snowstorm and escaped. Corporal Simpson was a brave man, the only one to take Mosby's horse and pistol.

The Ranger command continued to grow. At Paris, on Monday, March 28, 1864, Company D of the 43th Battalion of Virginia Partisan Rangers was organized. The men were well aware they had been given the privilege of electing their officers by General Lee. A movement had begun to overturn Mosby's practice of making the selection. This was a rebellion which Mosby would not tolerate. He reiterated that anyone who resisted his selections would be stricken from the Ranger rolls and sent to regular units. Ranger John Scott wrote that line service was considered by the Rangers the equivalent of being sent to the Australian penal colony at Botany Bay.[52] The vote for Mosby's candidates was naturally unanimous. Richard P. Montjoy of Mississippi was elected captain.

On Monday, April 13, 1864, Ranger M. W. Flannery of Company A was killed because of a gust of wind. Flannery was wearing a Union overcoat and approached a Union guard on outpost with the intent of deceiving and capturing him. The guard was alert and kept his weapon trained on Flannery while he halted and began to question the Ranger. Flannery's deception came apart when a sudden gust of wind blew open his blue overcoat and revealed the Confederate uniform beneath. The guard immediately put a bullet into Flannery's chest.

Both sides fought a war of bullets and a war of nerves. Rumors began to spread among the Rangers that the Union army planned to send a massive force to crush them. Twice Mosby assembled the maximum number of Rangers he could rally in preparation to ambush an attack that did not come. Wearying of this, Mosby went back on the offensive, taking thirty men into Fairfax County to attack an outpost near Hunter's Mill. Though uncharacteristic, Mosby followed Turner Ashby's favorite tactic, dismounting his men and attacking on foot. The Rangers killed one Union soldier, took three prisoners and nine horses. Mosby was continuing the scout and sent the prisoners and all but two of the Rangers back under the command of Lt. Joseph Nelson. It was not long before riders of the Union California Battalion were riding from their camp at Vienna in pursuit of Nelson.

About ten miles from Aldie, the Union riders caught up with Nelson and his men, who turned on the cavalry and charged. In the melee that followed, the Union soldiers recaptured two horses and shot and captured Lt. William L. Hunter of Company A. Lieutenant Nelson tried to aid his friend and was shot in the hip and badly wounded, but escaped. Ranger Henry Hatcher was slightly wounded.

Union efforts in Mosby's Confederacy grew in scope. The enterprising Col. Charles Russell Lowell Jr. of the 2nd Massachusetts Cavalry rode out from Vienna in Fairfax County on Friday, April 29, 1864. Lowell would have twelve horses killed under him and in six months would be killed at the battle of Cedar Creek. But as he left Vienna, he had reason for optimism. At his back was a brigade of cavalry; another brigade, this one of infantry under General Tyler, would be coming from Fairfax Court House to join him. A third force of Union cavalry was moving from Leesburg to Middleburg, and at Leesburg these riders found good hunting. Lowell's objective was to show the flag, destroy a wool factory, seize stores of tobacco and capture any of Mosby's men or Confederate stragglers.

Ranger security failed at Leesburg. A group of Mosby's Rangers was having an impromptu party at a hotel. Their horses had been left in the street and some of the men were relaxing on the veranda or refreshing themselves in the bar room. Lowell's cavalry was within 200 yards when it was spotted. It came like a whirlwind. "Skeddadle" was the cry, and all who could raced for their horses and rode as though the devil were after them. Rangers Thomas Flack and Ewell Atwell made it to the edge of town. Flack of Company D was killed there. Ewell Atwell of Company C, finding his horse not moving fast enough, jumped off and escaped through a thick hedge. Ranger John DeButts was one of Mosby's most experienced men. He was shot in the chest and captured. Elsewhere, the cavalry killed Ranger Edward Smith and wounded Ranger Felix Ware. Mosby's men did not have the strength to meet Lowell's force head on. They hung on the flanks, harassing and looking for stragglers they could attack. Colonel Lowell had light casualties and stated in his report that one of his three men killed and the three who were taken prisoner were lost because of straggling.[53]

Friday, May 1, 1864, saw little celebration of the rites of spring in the Confederacy. U.S. Grant's orders were that all of his commands should attack. In Richmond, President Davis was bewailing the barbarism of the Union army with the plundering and burning of buildings. Chewing on his cigar, Grant was likely thinking, "You ain't seen nothing yet."

Like Mosby, Grant did not live under the delusion that this was a polite and chivalrous fight. He intended to end this war, and if that meant taking casualties or making the South howl, it would also mean the saving of thousands, likely hundreds of thousands, of lives on both sides that would be lost if the war continued for years.

Sherman was in Georgia in preparation for a march on Atlanta. Butler was on the James and Meade was preparing to fight Lee in that section of Virginia known as the Wilderness. Grant knew he was in for a hard fight, but it was not his nature to shrink from a battle.

On Friday, May 8, 1864, Mosby returned from a scout and met his command at Rectortown. He ordered Dolly Richards of Company B and William Chapman of Company C to take small detachments of some fifteen men each and operate in the Shenandoah Valley. A foraging party was sent on a confiscation ride to get corn from the farmers. Mosby took fifty select men and rode with the intent of disrupting the rear of Meade's army.

Mosby and his men rode southeast from Salem (Marshall) to Warrenton where they stopped after dark for a late meal, then rode on to war-torn Rappahannock Station. There they went into an assembly area near the railroad and organized for the attack. Mosby took some thirty-five men and headed toward Fredericksburg. The remainder of the Rangers under Sgt. Horace Johnson were to burn two bridges close to Bealton Station. The heavy fighting had laid waste to the area. The landscape and landmark structures were so changed that a local guide born and raised in the area could barely find his way. This part of the mission failed.

Mosby again split his men, sending some twelve Rangers to destroy bridges toward Culpeper Court House. Near Belle Plain, a wagon train was found moving toward the Potomac. Both night and drizzling rain were falling. The wagon train was taking a fork in the road. Mosby ordered Grogan to count back ten wagons, go to the driver of the tenth and, posing as an officer, tell the teamster the wrong road was being taken by the lead. The tenth wagon and those that followed were instructed to turn off on the left fork. Lacking any semblance of wit, the driver of the tenth wagon did as told and the wagons behind him followed.

Mosby sent Palmer to the front to stop the rest of the train. Palmer met an angry Union officer coming back along the line of wagons. Williamson wrote that the conversation went as follows: "Who in the hell has stopped these wagons and turned the off the road?" demanded the officer. "Major Mosby," answered Palmer, covering him with his pistol.[54]

Palmer had to exchange some shots with a few reluctant teamsters, but in the end the train was taken in its entirety. The haul was twenty-five prisoners, forty-five horses, and fifteen mules, plus supplies from the wagons.

Monday, May 11, brought gloom to the South and a sense of deep personal tragedy to John Singleton Mosby. On that date, the Confederate cavalry leader Gen. James Ewell Brown Stuart was mortally wounded while engaged in a battle with Phil Sheridan's cavalry at Yellow Tavern, Virginia. Stuart was Mosby's guiding star, his patron, his defender and his friend.

Mounted patrols were scouring the countryside looking for the bolt holes that Mosby and his Rangers used to avoid capture. In a letter dated May 11, 1864, Maj. Henry Alvord of the 2nd Massachusetts Cavalry wrote home about finding one such hideout:

"A bedroom on the ground floor formed a wing to the house, under this there appeared to be no cellar. All the furniture was removed, the carpet taken up but no opening nor loose boards appeared in the floor. A stone chimney stood at the end of the wing, jutting into the room. Each side of this, filling the niche were drawers and shelves with a small cupboard at the bottom. The floor appeared tight and O.K.

"I finally tried the little threshold to the cupboard door and found it was easily removed. That covered a crack in the matched boards and at once showed the whole floor of the cupboard to be a trap door. This I removed and letting myself through the aperture, I stood in a fine underground apartment filled with uniforms both Federal and Rebel, arms, equipments and Mosby's personal effects. On the wall hung a satchel containing his private papers, and among them his two commissions as captain and 'major of Partisan Rangers' signed by the Rebel secretary of war.

"This was quite a find and I got the credit for it. I knew there must be a hole for this fox somewhere and I stuck to it till I found it."[55]

The placid community of Waterford, Virginia, was home to many Quakers and Germans. It was a rallying place for those who did not like slavery and were strongly pro-Union. This was the home of the Loudoun Rangers (Union). This once happy hamlet found itself a Union island in a Confederate sea. It did what it could to stand by the United States. A band of Union Rangers came together here and had little but themselves to rely on. They were hated by their one-time neighbors who surrounded them, and being a small force they were hit repeatedly and hard.

Mosby sent out word for an assembly. On Saturday, May 28, 1864, 144 Rangers gathered at Rectortown. With hard riding ahead, the men were appreciative to see that the delightful character called Major Hibbs had brought in a wagon load of impressed corn. It was feast time for their steeds, and the Rangers enjoyed a day of companionship. It is easier for men to get along when they do not see each other every day.

On Sunday, May 29, 1864, Mosby led out a column of Rangers, crossing the Shenandoah River, moving toward Strasburg. They went to ground near the village, with scouts watching the roads for a slow-moving wagon train. The success of their campaign was demonstrated by the heavy guard that accompanied each supply column that passed.

Maj. Gen. David Hunter was in command of Union troops in the Valley and the signs of his handiwork were visible everywhere. When U.S. wagons were burned or a Union soldier bushwhacked, Hunter sent out his burners. Every family within five miles of the burning or death that could not prove loyalty to the Union saw their homes, barns and outbuildings go up in flames. He then taxed the people ten miles out for five times the value of the U.S. property destroyed. David Hunter was the most hated man in the Shenandoah Valley. There was no indication the hatred bothered him.

Riding between Middletown and Newtown, Mosby and his men saw proof they were in the hunting territory of another Ranger. The smoking wreckage of a Union wagon train gave proof that the Maryland Cavalier Maj. Harry Gilmor was in the area. A burning barn nearby was David Hunter's response.

Mosby's command had now grown to the point where its commander was testing the limits of his span of control. Superb fighting men were in the Rangers. Most of them were also good soldiers, but some were there for the opportunity to rob and a few went home when they pleased. It was time to exercise the iron fist of discipline in the velvet glove of organization. It was time to set boundaries on Mosby's military turf.

On Wednesday, June 22, 1864, 200 well-uniformed Rangers assembled at Rectortown. Mosby published orders that put limits on where the men could travel when not participating in unit operations. The area would be called Mosby's Confederacy.[56] The western boundary began in Snickersville (now Bluemont vicinity) in Loudoun County, then ran southeast along the Blue Ridge Mountains near Paris, crossed over into Fauquier County, and then continued to Linden. From Linden the boundary went generally eastward through Salem (now Marshall), then through the plains to the Bull Run Mountains. The eastern boundary ran northeast along the Bull Run Mountains to Aldie. It then followed the Snickersville Pike generally northwest back to Snickersville. The instructions were concise and clear. No member of Mosby's Rangers was permitted to leave this area without permission. When Mosby called for the men to be assembled, the roll would be called. Being absent for two assemblies without just cause would result in the individual being dismissed from the Rangers and sent to a line unit.

As established, Mosby's Confederacy was not the limits of an operational area. The activities of the command would continue to be wide ranging. Mosby would always be a leader, but as the size of his organization grew he became a commander. During the existence of Mosby's Rangers, he would form seven lettered companies designated A through G, with G being formed only a few days before the war ended. Despite his victories, his promotions hinged in large part on the size of his command. General Lee remained disinclined to promote to colonel a man who commanded two companies, even if he did more than many generals. In part, Mosby's promotion to colonel was achieved by calling Company A, the 1st Battalion, with William Chapman commanding and Company B the 2nd Battalion, with Dolly Richards commanding.

From Rectortown, Mosby led out Companies A, B, C and D and a howitzer to the Plains. They rode to Thoroughfare Gap where they stopped for the night and then passed beyond Haymarket, the Manassas battlefield and Manassas Gap Junction. About midnight, they halted and spent the remainder of the second night near Union Mills. On the following day, Friday, June 24, 1864, they rode toward Centerville. Ranger Walter Whaley brought in information that a small detachment of the 16th New York Cavalry was there. Mosby sent Company A to make the attack, but the Rangers found the Union horsemen had moved on. The scouts traced them, moving on the road to Chantilly. Company A attacked and captured these few men who were the scouts of a forty-man patrol under Lt. Nathan Tuck. As men of the other companies rode along, a few climbed trees along the road to pick some cherries. They had the good fortune to see Union soldiers also picking cherries. These were from the remainder of Tuck's cavalry patrol who were dismounted and feeding their horses in a nearby field. Bridles and bits were off the horses and Union troopers were lolling about, taking their ease or sleeping. The only guard was sitting on a fence rail. It was an ideal target and the Rangers hit hard, riding in shooting, surprising and killing the lone guard and wounding five others. Pausing only to round up thirty-one prisoners and thirty-eight horses with equipment, the Rangers rode back to the newly named Mosby's Confederacy.

Under the new system of rallying, larger numbers of men came in for each raid. On Tuesday, June 28, four companies assembled, again with Mosby's one-gun artillery. As darkness fell, they met at Upperville then rode westward through Ashby Gap, turned north and crossed the Shenandoah at Shepard's Mill. There the column split, with Company A continuing on to Charlestown. Though Company A was operating independently, the remainder of the command was following the same general trace and close enough to provide support if needed. Company A was under the command of Lt. Joseph Nelson who led his men through the streets of Charlestown and allowed them to enjoy the admiration of the women of the town—it is good to be a hero. When Nelson halted his command outside of town, the women brought their charm and accompanied it with a wide variety of baked goods and refreshments. Rangers James Williamson and William Walston were posted as security on the road to Harpers Ferry and saw a dust cloud that became a column of Union cavalry approaching. Leaving Walston to keep the enemy under observation, Williamson rode to his commander. Nelson started the assemblage of his men and went forward to see the enemy for himself. When he returned, he briefed those men he could find that there were about sixty cavalrymen. He felt confident they could be surprised and beaten.

The physical and culinary attractions of the females of Charlestown had drawn off a number of the Rangers who had disappeared into houses both in town and the outskirts. Nelson was reduced to twenty-three men but not deterred. He sent two Rangers forward to show themselves to the Union cavalry and lead them on. The ruse went as planned. On seeing the two men, the Union horsemen galloped after them. Nelson then organized his men into a column of twos, seeking to make his force look larger. When the Union cavalry came over a hill, they saw the Rangers below them, halted and attempted to engage at long range with their carbines. They fired high and caused no injury. As soon as the cavalry fired carbines and before they could draw pistols, Nelson said, "Now boys, charge them!"[57]

The sudden assault carried the Rangers within pistol range before the cavalry could respond. Panic ensued and the priority of the Union soldiers was to escape. Inevitably this makes a fertile hunting ground for the attacker. It was a good road, one well suited to a hot pursuit, and the Rangers made the most of it, routing their enemy. Ranger Williamson saw a wounded Union cavalryman fall from his horse which then galloped away. The horse was kicking the soldier while it fled and the man's head was being dashed against the roadway. Williamson tried to get two captured Union cavalrymen to help their comrade, but their minds were locked on surrendering and they did not understand until the man was kicked and dragged to his death.

Meanwhile, Mosby used the rest of the command to seize Duffield Depot, its military stores and garrison of forty-five soldiers. Mosby had the telegraph wires cut, isolating the depot from calling for help. He then put the one-gun Ranger artillery into position. The Union soldiers at the depot had no artillery to respond and surrendered. Mosby's men took what they wanted from the extensive stores and burned the remainder. Mosby then rode on to see if Nelson was being attacked. When he heard of Nelson's victory, he exhibited his customary delight at the success of a subordinate. Brig. Gen. Max Weber, who commanded at Harpers Ferry, blamed poor security and a shortage of Union cavalry for the loss of men and materiel.[58]

CHAPTER THREE

The Sweet Taste of Victory

Time and again when Mosby's Rangers returned from a raid, the procession into his Confederacy took on the aspects of a Roman triumph. The Rangers came mounted on high-spirited horses and dressed in fine-looking uniforms. Many wore jaunty plumes in their broad-brimmed hats. If they captured musical instruments, some led the way playing banjos, fiddles or jew's-harps. The Rangers might be singing. There would be dusty lines of prisoners marching into captivity. The captive horses would follow, and they or captive mules would be laden with captured weapons and equipment. Now and then a captured cavalry guidon, regimental or U.S. flag would appear. They received the heroes' welcome. In the admiring throng were old men, politicians, wounded veterans, and slaves who had grown up with and knew these men better than they knew the men in blue. There were women of all ages, many showering their affection on the Rangers. The eyes of the onlookers would stray to the sacks the Rangers had tied over their saddles. In these sacks were goods that were rarely seen in the South in 1864. There were real coffee and sugar, spices, bacon and hams. There were good quality cloth, needles and thread, overcoats and boots. On some raids, Rangers visited stores, showed pistols, and brought back hoop skirts, shawls, women's shoes and hats and ribbon for their wives and girlfriends. Then there were the other items prisoners and others parted with. There were watches and jewelry, and many a Ranger had a nice roll of greenbacks. The return from the Duffield Depot raid resembled this, but there were even bigger processionals to come.

It was inevitable that the Rangers would be loved by the people and despised or envied by the Confederate soldier in the trenches. What soldier would want to stay in the hell of a trench at Petersburg when he could live in a warm house, get home cooking, have one or more girlfriends, fight with an all-volunteer outfit, and make big money doing it? Ranger life was rewarding but hazardous. Ranger Munson wrote that the command never numbered more than 350 men available for active service at any one time. He discussed casualties as follows: "During our career of a little over two years death was making its unceasing subtractions. In that time we had seventy of our best men killed and nearly 100 wounded. We had nine of our commissioned officers killed and nineteen of them were seriously wounded. Colonel Mosby was honey-combed with bullets."[1]

The hurt of losing friends in war is carried by a man throughout his life, but in the carnage of the Civil War Munson's estimate of 198 casualties might have brought a shrug from a veteran infantryman of many a Confederate or Union regiment. In the slightly more than two years Mosby's Rangers fought, some 2,000 men probably passed through Mosby's command. To have the impact Mosby's Rangers had on the war with his unit suffering only 198 casualties was a remarkable achievement.

The Fourth of July still held fond memories for many Rangers. In 1864 it was celebrated by a raid at Point of Rocks, Maryland, southeast of Frederick. Gen. Jubal Early, with about 25,000 men, was attacking north up the Shenandoah Valley and had reached Winchester by July 2. The Fourth found Early near Harpers Ferry preparing to cross the Potomac into Maryland. Mosby's raid was intended to help General Early by attacking the Union line of communication from Harpers Ferry and Washington.

Two hundred and fifty Rangers supported by their one-gun artillery were on the raid. Leaving the assembly area at Upperville on Sunday, July 3, 1864, some of them must have thought back on events of the past year and the Southern hopes and despair of just one year prior at Gettysburg. With scouts in advance, the Rangers rode through Bloomfield and Purcellville to Wheatland, which was on the North Fork of Catoctin Creek and west of Waterford, the home of the Union Loudoun Rangers. Early on July 4 they continued toward the Potomac, finding a ford approximately one mile from Point of Rocks. The Potomac ford was defended by Companies A and B of the Loudoun Rangers under Capt. Daniel M. Keyes and Capt. James W. Grubb. Two companies of Maryland troops were present, bringing the Union strength to about 225 men, but the U.S. soldiers did not have artillery.

About two o'clock in the afternoon of July 4, Mosby brought his cannon into play, quieting Union rifles across the river. Anticipating the need for long-range fire, some of Mosby's Rangers were supplementing their pistols with carbines. These, added to the cannon, allowed the Confederates to drive off the guards and occupy an island in the center of the Potomac. From there they could push on. There was a canal at this point whose depth was an obstacle. The planks of a crossover bridge had been removed by the Union soldiers and while under hot fire the Confederates tore the boards from a nearby building to use as planking. With the bridge floor laid, Capt. Dolly Richards led a dismounted charge that swept into the town. One civilian, a woman named Hester Fisher, was hit by a ball fired from the Confederate side and killed instantly.[2] The Maryland troops and the Loudoun

Rangers withdrew from Point of Rocks. Captain Keyes was wounded in the foot, but the Loudoun Rangers suffered no other casualties and withdrew safely.

Maryland would have been an important acquisition had it gone to the Southern side. In retrospect, Virginia would have been eternally grateful if the majority of the battles had been fought farther north. But Maryland hung on the border, furnishing men to both sides, with the greater number supporting the Union. Jubal Early, who had a fixed-price ransom, would not help the reputation of the South with Maryland when he ransomed Hagerstown for $20,000, Boonsboro for $20,000, and demanded $20,000 from Middletown. Ranger Goodhart wrote that while this was going on, the Confederates were riding along singing the Confederate song "Maryland My Maryland."[3]

Mosby's Rangers were greatly taken by the appearance of the land. The place they came from was wrecked by more than three years of war. Here just over the Potomac was a land of plenty where barns were full and crops were growing. They saw many horses. Local farmers were trying to drive their horses into the woods to hide them, but acquiring horses was practiced work for Mosby's Rangers and they gathered a sizable herd.

Mission accomplished, the Rangers prepared to depart for home. They were inspired to movement by reports that Lt. Col. David R. Clendennin, who had taken command of the 8th Illinois Cavalry on October 16, 1864, was coming after them. The Rangers did not fear the 8th Illinois, but they had a great deal of respect for this large and experienced regiment. The Illinois troopers were not an outfit to tangle with when driving a horse herd and carrying sacks of goods the people back home needed.

Re-crossing the Potomac, the Rangers bypassed Leesburg while sending scouts into the town to gather intelligence. They spent the night near Waterford. When the scouts returned, they reported that about 250 men of the 2nd Massachusetts and 13th New York Cavalry were at Leesburg and planned to move south, heading for Oatlands on Goose Creek. The Rangers had started dispersion and some 175 men were left with the main body. On the morning of July 6, 1864, Mosby marched. He hoped to cut the cavalry off near Oatlands, but it had moved on heading toward Mount Zion on the Aldie turnpike east of Aldie.

The cavalry was under the command of Maj. William H. Forbes of the 2nd Massachusetts Cavalry. Forbes was known as Colonel Lowell's fighting major.[4] The troop estimate obtained by the scouts was based on civilian reports that were inflated. Forbes actually had 150 men, 100 from the 2nd Massachusetts and fifty from the 13th New York. Forbes had heard Mosby had sent four or five wagons of plunder and a guard of sixty men. It was these Rangers and their loot the Union force was trying to catch.

Forbes had his men getting ready to move after resting and feeding their horses when the Rangers came in view. The Union leader was not caught napping and quickly formed his men for battle. The Ranger cannon fired a shot that was way off the mark, and both sides put the artillery out of their minds. The Rangers charged and a hard-fought battle ensued. Three times Forbes' cavalry fell back, but each time the major rallied his men.

Forbes emptied his revolver at the first stage of the fight and went to the saber. Ranger Munson wrote, "Major Forbes occupied the center of the action, standing in his stirrups with saber drawn fighting desperately."[5] Union soldiers reported that he lunged and pierced Mosby's coat in the swirling action. He engaged in a hand-to-hand fight with Dolly Richards' brother, Capt. Tom Richards. Richards was severely wounded in the shoulder by Forbes' saber but pointed his revolver in Forbes face and pulled the trigger. The weapon failed to fire. Just then, Forbes' horse was killed and fell on him. Forbes was forced to surrender. According to Ranger Williamson, seventeen of the cavalry died on the field and another fifteen of wounds; twenty-five were wounded, and fifty-seven taken prisoner. More than 100 horses were taken. The Rangers had seven men wounded, one of whom, Henry Salmwood, died.[6]

The Rangers and the cavalry were fighting so intermixed that the cavalrymen carrying carbines could not fire without hitting one another; they used carbine stocks and butts to club Ranger Willie Martin unconscious.[7] When Forbes went down, the fight went out of the cavalry and the chase began. Munson wrote that the "flight and pursuit were strung out from the scene of the first engagement to old Dudley Church, a distance of ten miles." Colonel Lowell in his report of Wednesday, July 8, 1864, wrote, " I have only to report a perfect rout..." Lowell reported the courage of Forbes but did not have a good understanding of the fight; he believed that Forbes should have given the order to draw sabers and charge. The inability to see the superiority of the revolver over the saber cost the U.S. Army many lives.

Jubal Early's July 1864 move north put a scare into the U.S. capital. Gen. Lew Wallace led a makeshift collection of inexperienced men who offered their bodies for a delay. As a result, when Early's troops reached the outskirts of Washington, there had been time to pull two divisions of veteran soldiers of the Union VI Corps from Grant's effort at Petersburg and entrain them north.

President Abraham Lincoln left the White House and on July 11 witnessed Early's attack at Fort Stevens. Lincoln stood calmly on a parapet while bullets sang by him. An officer was killed and another wounded within a few feet of the president. Legend has it that an unimpressed sergeant yelled at his commander in chief, "Get down from there you damn fool, before you get shot!"

Mosby and a group of his Rangers. Mosby is in the center in light trousers with right leg crossed over left. USAMHI

By the Monday, July 13, 1864, the situation had changed. Early found he did not have sufficient force, beat a hurried retreat toward the Potomac, and headed into the Shenandoah Valley with the forces of Indian fighter Maj. Gen. George Crook and combined Union armies moving after him.

Crook's march gave Mosby the opportunity to harass the Union rear area. Detachments of Rangers under Mosby's lieutenants went raiding and did such damage that an appreciative Jubal Early gave Mosby the present of a small rifled cannon that was ideal for Ranger artillery.

More men came to Mosby, eager to join his command. On Tuesday, July 28,1864, Company E, 43rd Battalion Partisan Rangers was organized. Mosby allowed the men to elect Samuel F. Chapman as captain. Fountain Beattie, his comrade from the beginning, was made first lieutenant.

Sam Chapman had been double-hatted, his first job as adjutant and his second as commander of artillery. Now heading Company E, he gave up both his jobs. Artillery command passed to Capt. Peter A. Franklin. John Mosby's younger brother, William, took over Sam Chapman's former work as battalion adjutant. At the time, William Mosby was a fire-eating, mouthy youth who thought he could whip a Yankee regiment single handed.

On Thursday, July 30, 1864, Union forces at Petersburg exploded a giant mine under the Confederate works.[8] The attack failed because of the combination of a drunken Union officer, lack of scaling ladders to get out of the thirty-foot deep hole, and poor coordination of the attack.

The makeshift hospitals of Petersburg were crowded with men of both armies whose bodies were torn and broken by shot and shell. Brave women frequently served as volunteer nurses and did what they could to help the wounded and dying. One beautiful daughter of the South stopped at the pallet of a badly wounded soldier and asked if she could do anything for him. He told her that it was too late because he had not long to live. The girl said, "Will you not let me pray for you? I hope that I am one of the Lord's daughters, and I would ask him to help you." The sight of the lovely face over him made the soldier briefly forget his pain, "Yes, pray at once," he responded, "and ask the Lord to let me be his son-in-law."[9]

Seeking to take pressure off of Lee's army, Jubal Early pushed north again, crossing the Potomac. Sending troops into Chambersburg, Pennsylvania, Mosby now had three pieces of artillery. With 200 men, the Ranger leader moved on Tuesday, July 28, 1864, in support of Early's northern effort. The Rangers headed for Purcellville, then to Morrisonville, and crossed the Potomac River. Whenever they crossed rivers, the Rangers made use of those men who now included carbines in their armament. These sharpshooters covered the river crossing from the opposite shore or, if the ford was shallow but wide, would wade on the flanks. Their purpose was to cover the horsemen until they could get within revolver range of an enemy.

The Rangers crossed the river at Nolan's Ferry and then rode to Adamstown. Here they chopped down telegraph poles or cut the wires. Later, they visited a store and, as Ranger Alexander would write, "we proceeded to provide for our families and appropriated to our own use, with liberal hand and joyous hearts . . ."[10] In the midst of their collections, Lt. Joseph Nelson of Company A arrived and told them to put the material back or pay for it. The store owner had claimed to be a Southern supporter. Ranger John Munson had what was estimated at $300 worth of goods loaded on his horse and without Nelson seeing him promptly laid $5 of Confederate money on the counter and left. The young Rangers were disappointed they were called off, but they had eaten as much as they could of the shopkeepers' groceries and later they came to another store before the owner could hang out a Confederate flag. Store owners on the border learned to hurriedly change allegiance, hang out the right flag, and speak English with the proper accent in order to stay in business.

At Adamstown, the command split. Company B moved down toward Monocacy, found nothing, returned and re-crossed the Potomac. Com-

panies A and D pushed on toward Barnesville, then on by the Sugar Loaf to
the mouth of the Monocacy River. There was an eighteen-man outpost there
manned by the 8th Illinois Cavalry and that offered a chance to hurt this
pesky adversary.

The position of the 8th Illinois outpost was well chosen. From a high
bluff they could overlook and cover with fire both the road and the ford.
Lieutenant Nelson sent Lt. Harry Hatcher and twenty-five men to circle
around the outpost while he made a demonstration to attract the attention
of the Hoosier horsemen. Nelson then rode forward by himself in front of
the outpost. Not willing to see his officer alone, Ranger Alexander rode after
him. The demonstration brought forth well-directed fire from the hilltop
and as Alexander related, " I felt a sharp tap on the side of my head, and the
next thing I knew I was lying behind a wood pile with a handkerchief tied
around my head."[11] Just in time, Hatcher and his men hit the outpost from
the rear. The 8th Illinois lost one man killed; one officer and fifteen men
were captured. Censure is among the many things that flow downhill. The
blame fell on Lt. Henry A. Van Ness of Company F of the 3rd New Jersey
Infantry, who had overall charge of the outpost line. The official report of
July 31, 1864, included: "Colonel Clendennin reports the conduct of the
lieutenant as cowardly in a superlative degree."[12]

Every military unit has its characters. One of the best known in Mosby's
Rangers was a boy named Cab Maddux. His was perhaps the most unusual
entry into the Rangers. Munson remembered a day when the Rangers were
in hot pursuit of some of Coles' Maryland cavalry and were chasing them
through the streets of Upperville. The riders thundered by a boys' school
that was in the process of dismissing class. Seeing the action, a fat schoolboy
leaped on his pony and joined the charge armed only with a McGuffy third
reader that he waved about. Cab Maddux was that boy and he did not go
back to school. He traded his books for a horse and pistols.[13]

Boys often make good soldiers. They don't know any better. They often
have a feeling of immortality that makes them take chances from which a
mature, experienced man would step back. Cab was usually found in the
thick of the fighting. He had a great wit and an irrepressible nature that
sometimes got him in trouble.

As the Rangers were making their withdrawal from the Adamstown raid,
they had to again cross the river at Noland's Ford. Union cavalry was riding
hard after them. Moving with Cab Maddux was William Hibbs, an older
private who was jokingly called Major. As they crossed the Potomac River,
Union soldiers began shooting at Maddux, and their bullets were splashing
water about him. Hibbs was some distance off, and Maddux felt Hibbs was
not getting a just share of attention from the Union soldiers. "Hurry up,

Major Hibbs! Come along, *Major!*" yelled Maddux. Believing it more useful to shoot an officer, the Union soldiers immediately transferred their fire to Private Hibbs, who cried out that Maddux was "respectful all at once."[14]

Jubal Early had been traveling up and down the Shenandoah Valley against a series of Union generals. Now as August 1864 began, Early stopped his retreat at Strasburg, Virginia, faced his pursuers, and attacked north. Meanwhile, Early's cavalry commander, General McCausland, was fighting Union troops at Cumberland, Maryland. These constant threats from Early were a distraction to General Grant who was trying to cork the bottle of Petersburg with Lee and his army inside. Grant could not afford the frequent dispatching of combat units to the west. He needed someone who could send him a dispatch about "the late Jubal Early." Grant decided on Maj. Gen. Phil Sheridan and on August 1, 1864, the flamboyant, hard-hitting, egocentric Sheridan became commander of the Middle Department with headquarters at Harpers Ferry. Sheridan promptly attacked and Early withdrew.

On August 8, Mosby planned a trap. He anticipated that Union horsemen would come after him and planned to ambush them when they did. The soldiers in blue had the same intention. En route to the site he had selected to waylay the Union troopers, Mosby ran into an ambush. The trap was established in a pine wood by a detachment of the 13th New York Cavalry. The Union horsemen were impatient and fired too soon on the Rangers who were riding on point. What could and should have been a successful ambush ended with the wounding of Ranger George Slater and his horse. The men from the 13th New York then withdrew toward Fairfax Station and linked up with men of the 16th New York whose captain, James H. Flemming, assumed command. The two cavalry parties each numbered thirty men; these waited for the Ranger attack that was not long in coming.

Mosby brought his men close and heard Captain Flemming give the standard commands used by the Union cavalry. The order was to fire a volley and charge with the saber. Mosby did not wait for these instructions to be carried out, but ordered a charge that hurried the cavalry aim. Only one Ranger was hit before the Rangers were at close quarters firing their revolvers into the blue-uniformed horsemen. They concentrated fire on the Union officers. Captain Flemming was killed and John McMenamin of the 13th New York was hit in the knee and had three bullets rip his uniform. The New Yorkers broke and the roundup began. The cavalry had six killed, twenty-seven men taken prisoner and thirty-seven horses secured.

On Friday, August 12, 1864, Mosby assembled 330 men and two howitzers at Rectortown—the largest force he had ever assembled.[15] The Rangers rode northwest past Upperville, through Snicker's Gap (Bluemont), and crossed the Shenandoah River. Mosby was acting on good intelligence that a large supply train for General Sheridan's army was en route to Winchester from Harpers Ferry. About midnight, the Rangers settled into an assembly area in a woods not far from Berryville. Ranger scouts were sent out and soon returned telling Mosby that a large wagon train was on the pike close to Berryville. Ranger Munson was trying to find a soft spot on the ground to spread his blanket while John Russell, who was lead scout in the area, briefed Mosby. Munson's hope for a good sleep passed when Mosby ordered him and some other Rangers to saddle up then follow Russell to the wagon train. The wagons were moving by night and in the darkness it was not difficult for the Rangers to blend into the convoy. Mosby, Munson and other members of the reconnaissance party rode among the drivers and guards. They talked casually with them, learning of their strengths and objectives and gathering other valuable information. Munson asked a cavalryman for a match to light his pipe and in the glow looked at the face he would soon be chasing. Munson listened as Mosby learned that this convoy included 150 wagons and more than one thousand head of livestock. There were one Maryland and two Ohio infantry regiments plus cavalry totaling nearly 2,000 men traveling with the wagon train, and Union Brig. Gen. John Reese Kenly was in command.[16] Kenly's weak spot was that his horsemen were a Maryland brigade of hundred-day men, short-time soldiers eager to get home.

Mosby pulled his scouts out of the Union column, then sent Munson back to tell Capt. William Chapman to bring up the command. Meanwhile, Mosby rode on the flanks of the wagon train and waited for daylight to pick his terrain. The morning of August 13 came with fog that hugged the ground and helped conceal movement.

Mosby was close enough to see that some of the teamsters had stopped to care for their teams. The train was well guarded by cavalry and infantry. One of the two howitzers had damaged a wheel and was out of action, the other was placed on a high hill that dominated the roadway. The plan for attack nearly came apart when the howitzer was positioned over a nest of yellow-jackets. The wasps came swarming out, and the gun crew ran for cover. One brave soul went back and pulled off the light gun.[17]

Mosby sent Dolly Richards and two companies to attack the head of the column; William Chapman and Alfred Glasscock took two more to hit the rear. Mosby kept Sam Chapman near him on the hill that held the howitzer.[18] The ground fog provided excellent cover, allowing the Rangers to move close to the train. As the sun warmed and dissipated the mist, Mosby's men were on a high knoll and had closed to within 100 yards. Below them they could see the wagon train, looking like a long serpent winding its way toward Berryville. Capt. James C. Mann, the quartermaster of the 1st

Division, XIX Army Corps, later told a board of inquiry that the wagon train took about two and a half hours to pass a given point.[19] Mosby estimated the number of wagons at 325.[20]

The trains were those of the VI Army Corps, XIX Army Corps, the Army of West Virginia, the cavalry corps, and Brig. Gen. John R. Kenly's brigade. Kenly had numbers of 100-day men, inexperienced soldiers, to guard these critical supplies.

The Rangers were seen, but no threat registered until the first shot from the howitzer struck in their midst; a second caused a panic among the teamsters. Many unhitched a mule and fled. On the third shot, the Rangers charged into the train.

Munson wrote, "Then we rushed them, the whole Command charging from the slope, not in columns but spread out all over creation, each man doing his best to out-yell his comrade.[21] The Cavalry escort did not know where the attack was coming from and rode to and fro emptying revolvers, when we got among them, right and left."

They were followed by the infantry who did not go far, only taking cover in woods, in buildings and behind stone fences. The mountain howitzer played a vital role in shelling these threatening positions. There was no cannon with the wagon train that could respond. The scene on the road was pandemonium. Men shouted and cursed and fired at each other at close range. Wagons collided as teamsters struggled to move their teams. Loose horses, mules and cattle ran in panic among the contestants. The Rangers were unhitching teams at gunpoint, setting wagons on fire.

Williamson wrote, "Teams running off at a furious pace, which it was impossible to check, would attract the notice of some of our men, who riding alongside would set fire to the wagon, and as the smoke curled up the frightened mules rushed frantically along until they fell exhausted or were released by dashing the wagon against a tree or some obstacle in the road."[22]

Rangers were breaking into the contents of wagons. One contained musical instruments and fiddles were confiscated. Mosby was hurrying his men, rounding up horses, mules and cattle, burning wagons and assembling prisoners. Mosby threw out a screen of riders to cover the withdrawal, then, pushing themselves and their captives, the Rangers crossed over the Shenandoah River and back to Mosby's Confederacy. Their losses were Welby H. Rector and Lewis Aldie killed, and three other Rangers wounded.

The Berryville raid netted more than 500 horses and mules. There were 200 beef cattle and 208 prisoners, including seven officers, taken. Seventy-five wagons and their contents were destroyed. Unknown to the Rangers, one of the boxes hurriedly thrown from a wagon was a paymaster's chest

that contained $125,000. The homecomings of the Rangers were tri-
umphs—this one especially so. It would become the subject of an artist's
painting entitled "Return from the Raid."

This was a battalion raid that accomplished what divisions could not.
Sheridan was stung by the loss of supplies and the baggage of his cavalry
corps. Until he could sort out how badly his supply system was damaged, he
cancelled his attack orders and withdrew to his former position.

Sheridan also was embarrassed. Newspaper correspondents with the
army sent back stories that his leadership might have failed. In hot rage
Sheridan ordered all newspaper correspondents from his department. As
they had authorization from the secretary of war, they protested. Sheridan
told the writers to "go to hell." It did not help matters when one newsman
said, "But General, I believe that place is in your department too." When the
displaced correspondent returned to Washington, he related the story to the
stone-faced Secretary of War Stanton who laughed until he cried. Stanton
then overrode Sheridan and provided the press credentials for all depart-
ments.[23]

Encouraged by his success, Mosby decided to attack Sheridan's rear
areas by a series of pin-prick raids. Small parties of Rangers led by Mosby's
capable lieutenants would strike at varying locations, forcing Sheridan to use
large numbers of troops for rear area security and busy himself trying to
guard everything and defend everywhere. Message traffic filled with alarms
flashed back and forth across Union telegraph wires.

An entire regiment was ordered to stand ready to guard a high-level
courier traveling from Washington to Sheridan's headquarters. Union
patrols wired they could not get through Mosby's men to get to Sheridan.
Even small wagon trains required escorts. Mosby's men were believed to be
in U.S. uniform reconnoitering a Union camp.

Grant and other Union commanders did not see Mosby as a soldier but
as a bushwhacking criminal. Grant felt that to break the enemy will and
eliminate the support base of Mosby's men, he needed to sweep the rear of
battle areas clean of those who could resist the Union army and the food
that sustained them. The policy of destroying enemy habitations to break
the will of the people was worldwide. Prior to the Civil War, Americans of
both North and South destroyed Indian villages and crops creating famine
and, long after the Civil War, the burned out cities of Germany and Japan in
1945 were testimony that Americans can practice total war.

On August 16, 1864, Grant telegraphed Sheridan twice from his headquarters at City Point. At 1:30 P.M. the message included: "The families of
most of Mosby's men are known and can be collected. I think they should be
taken and kept at Fort McHenry, or some secure place, as hostages for the

good conduct of Mosby and his men. Where any of Mosby's men are caught hang them without trial." The second message sent at 3:30 P.M. read: "If you can possibly spare a division of cavalry, send them through Loudoun County to destroy and carry off the crops, animals, Negroes, and all men under fifty years of age capable of bearing arms. In this way you will get many of Mosby's men. All male prisoners under fifty years of age can be fairly held as prisoners of war, and not as citizen prisoners. If not already soldiers, they will be made so the moment the rebel army gets hold of them."[24] The second message has often been interpreted as removing the instruction to hang Mosby's men, but if Grant wanted to rescind his first message he had only to say "disregard the instruction to hang."

Sheridan moved quickly and published the following order to his subordinates:

> Headquarters Middle Military Division
> Cedar Creek, Virginia, August 16, 1864
>
> In compliance with instructions of the Lieutenant-general commanding, you will make the necessary arrangements and give the necessary orders for the destruction of the wheat and hay south of a line from Millwood to Winchester and Petticoat Gap. You will seize all mules, horses and cattle that may be useful to our army. Loyal citizens can bring in their claims against the government for this necessary destruction.
>
> P. H. Sheridan
> Major-general Commanding[25]

On August 17, Sheridan sent a message to Grant that read, "Mosby has annoyed me and captured a few wagons. We hung one and shot 6 of his men yesterday."[26]

None of the dead were Mosby's men, but they were not the only Confederate Ranger threat. Harry Gilmore, John and Jesse McNeill, and a host of freelance bushwhackers were involved in attacks on Union soldiers.

Mosby had Capt. William Chapman with Companies C, D, and E active around Berrysville. Dolly Richards and Company A were at work near Charlestown and Mosby, who often preferred to go hunting with smaller numbers of companions, joined Company A to harass traffic on the heavily traveled road between Charlestown and Harpers Ferry.

On August 18, 1864, a small party of Rangers under James G. Wiltshire struck a four-man outpost near Castleman's Ferry. They killed a picket of the

5th Michigan Cavalry, wounded one and captured two who later escaped. The event, reported in the August 25, 1864, *New York Times*, was that men in civilian clothes rode up to 5th Michigan Cavalry pickets near the Snicker's Gap Road, and fired into them, killing Cpl. Adolphus Day of Company E. A short time later, Pvt. John Connell of Company G was fired at by men dressed in the uniform of U.S. soldiers. Connell was wounded in the hand. In a war in which thousands would die in a day, the killing of the lonely soldier walking his guard post by a guerrilla became a very personal thing. It seemed more like murder than the mowing down of a regiment. The *New York Times* article included "Men were everywhere fired at, even within sight of the camp, while foraging and several wanton murders were reported." Union commanders knew the local populace was supportive of Confederate activities by guerrilla forces.

In retaliation for what was viewed as the murder of Corporal Day, the commander of the Michigan brigade, Brig. Gen. George Armstrong Custer, ordered Col. Russell A. Alger, commanding officer of the 5th Michigan Cavalry, to burn the houses of four men: Col. Josiah Ware, Province McCormick, William Sowers and Col. Benjamin Morgan. There were five members of the Sowers' clan, two Morgans and one Ware riding with Mosby's Rangers. All were homes believed to belong to prominent secessionists. A detachment of fifty men under Capt. George Drake and Lt. Franklin Allen of Company H and Lieutenants Milo P. Bibbens and George W. Lounsberry of Company M were ordered to do the burning. They rode first to the Ware home of Springfield. Josiah Ware was sixty-two years old, a former militia colonel who in the early stages of the war had been recruiting a command when he was captured by Union troops and, because of his age, paroled. Ware had been arrested as a spy and was in prison in Washington at the time Custer gave Alger the burning order. Springfield house had been used as headquarters by Custer's division commander, Gen. Wesley Merritt, who had verbally informed Mrs. Edmonina Ware that the house was under his protection. According to a brief family history written by a son, Josiah William Ware Jr., Mrs. Ware bravely stood her ground before the burning party and informed its officer that the house had Merritt's protection. The officer asked to see the order. Mrs. Ware replied that the order was verbal, but she would send someone to Merritt's camp. The officer replied that "the word of a lady was sufficient" and led his men on to McCormick home which was set ablaze. Springfield would in time burn, but not until 1899.[27]

In the morning light of Friday, August 19, 1864, Capt. William Chapman with Ranger Companies C, D, and E saw the home of Province McCormick burning and was told by the weeping family what had occurred. The Rangers rode on to find Mrs. William Sowers holding her children and sobbing as they watched their home in flames. A grim fury swept the Rangers, who rode on rapidly toward the residence of Col. Benjamin Morgan on the Shepard's Mill Road close to the Berryville and the Snicker's Gap Pike. The Morgan house dated to 1750. Along with its barn and outbuildings, the house was set back from the road and reached by a lane approximately one-quarter mile long. As it neared the house, the lane sloped downward so that much of the area surrounding the house, barn, outbuildings and stone fences were at a lower elevation. The terrain is such that as the Union soldiers were setting fire to the barn, haystacks and the house, an attacking force could suddenly ride over the higher ground and take them by surprise.

The 5th Michigan officers had failed to put out security. Captain Drake had left Lieutenant Allen and a party to destroy Morgan's property while Drake took others of the detachment to burn a nearby building. At this point Chapman's Rangers swept into view, charging down over the ridgeline on Lieutenant Allen and his men. The men of the 5th Michigan had no time to organize a defense. The Rangers charged into them and the killing began. A few cavalrymen managed to jump the stone fences of the lane and barnyard with their horses, but most were dismounted or found the fences too high. The single gate was blocked and the cavalrymen could find no exit. The dismounted Michigan soldiers who ran along the fence were soon trapped and threw up their hands in surrender.

Now pent-up passion and rage was with the Rangers. At such a time it did not matter that these soldiers did not give the orders to burn the houses. It did not matter that numbers of men had been lynched or shot or had their property destroyed in the South merely because they believed in the United States. There was no rational thought. Pleas to surrender were ignored, and the cavalrymen were assembled and shot down as they begged for their lives. Men lying wounded on the ground were mercilessly killed. According to the *New York Times*, when Privates John Lutz and Samuel K. Davis surrendered, Lutz was shot down. Davis surrendered his pistol and was attempting to hand over his carbine when one of Chapman's men said, "I will pay you for this right now," and fired into the face of Davis. The bullet went into the right nostril and lodged under the right eye. Davis went down bleeding profusely.

The *Times* reported, "Ten men were murdered on the ground after surrendering, nearly all of whom were shot through the head. Four have since died and two more cannot live. Some of the fiends, appalled at the bloody agonies, did not shoot their prisoners until ordered to 'shoot the d-n Yankee son of a b——' by their officers.

Pvt. Samuel Davis, Company L, age thirty-four, feigned death. When found, he said that in a short time some of the Rangers came back and killed wounded men who survived the initial shooting. A Ranger thought Davis was too close to death to waste a bullet, but he survived.

The dead of the 5th Michigan Cavalry included:

Sgt. Squire E Skeels, Company M, age twenty-five
Cpl. Charles C. Craft, Company M, age thirty-three
Cpl. Hiram A Withington, Company M, age twenty-one
Pvt. Alphonso Chart (or Chant), Company G, age nineteen
Pvt. Charles B Clyde, Company M, age eighteen
Pvt. Oliver M. Warner, Company C, age twenty-four
Pvt. Alfred A. Henry, Company C, age eighteen
Pvt. Isaac C Osborn, Company M, age twenty
Pvt. Samuel K. Epler, Company C, age unknown
Pvt. Eaton Lewis, Company M, age nineteen
Pvt. John G. Lutz, Company C, age twenty-two
Pvt. James C. Kennicut, Company L, age twenty-five
Pvt. Peter Talmadge Caston, Company M, age twenty
Pvt. Absolom B. Shaffer, Company C, age fifty

Cpl. Francis M. Wright, Company M, age 20, was shot in the face. He would die of his wounds on September 10, 1864. Believed mortally wounded but surviving were Samuel G. Eldred, Company C, age 19. A sergeant, E.S. Field, a member of another organization also was reported killed.

In his report to Lee's assistant adjutant general Lieutenant Colonel Taylor, Mosby wrote, "About 25 of them were shot to death for their villainy."[28] In actuality, sixteen Union soldiers were shot down. No prisoners were taken, but thirty horses were secured.

Rage at the burning of the houses resulted in the murder of men who had surrendered. News of the killings swept throughout the Union cavalry. As the *New York Times* reported, "The soldiers, naturally are indignant at the bloody outrages perpetrated upon their companions, and whenever the opportunity occurs, will no doubt retaliate."[29]

On Tuesday, August 23, 1864, 300 Rangers assembled at Rectortown and headed east across the Bull Run Mountains, riding by night until they reached a Union camp at Annandale. They had two cannon with them, but the Ranger artillery had not been shooting well and this raid would give the gunners a chance to redeem themselves. The commander of the Union camp was Capt. Joseph Schneider of the 16th New York Cavalry. He was assisted by Capt. Philo D. Mickels Jr. Schneider's three-man picket was taken captive, but he was ready for the Rangers when they rode up, and the Union soldiers delivered a volley of fire that caused them to sheer off.

Disregarding the niceties of war, the Rangers sent in a flag of truce carried by Capt. Richard P. Montjoy. While Montjoy talked to one of the captains, the Confederate guns were moved forward. Montjoy returned and the guns fired. Because the result was unsatisfactory, the Rangers attempted the same trick, moving the guns forward while a flag of truce was sent in with Lt. Harry Hatcher. Schneider saw the guns being shifted and looked with anger at Hatcher and his flag. "I have a mind to burn that rag and if you send anymore they will not be respected," growled the Union captain.

"Don't burn that," begged Hatcher, "It's the only handkerchief I've got!"[30]

Unable to dent Schneider's resolve or his defense, Mosby's Rangers went hunting elsewhere. The Union report noted, "No damage was done by him (Mosby) except the wounding of one horse."[31]

On August 28, Sheridan ordered Maj. John M. Waite, commander of the 8th Illinois Cavalry, to move to Aldie and to link up with Major Horton and the 16th N.Y. Cavalry. With Waite in command, the two regiments were to move with speed on Upperville and Middleburg to hunt guerrillas. The order included, "The special object of your scout is to destroy as far as practicable, the sources from which Mosby draws men, horses and support. To this end you will arrest and bring in all males capable of bearing arms or conveying information, between the ages of eighteen and fifty . . . impress all wagons and bring them in loaded with forage; destroy all crops of hay, oats, corn and wheat which you cannot bring in . . ."[32]

There were many hunting for Mosby, and the Rangers were about to encounter a new adversary. On September 3, Mosby and some ninety Rangers rode via Bloomfield to Snicker's Gap. A steady rain had turned the road to a quagmire, so the Rangers rode to the mountaintop and spent the night where there was good drainage. On the morning of September 4, 1864, they went westward to Myer's Ford on the Shenandoah River. Mosby took fifteen men and crossed the river to go in search of the enemy. Dolly Richards and a small patrol scouted in another direction.

Lt. Joseph Nelson was left in charge. Nelson concealed his men in the woods, put out security and the men concerned themselves with rest. Suddenly Union horsemen were on them. The Rangers were caught as they had caught many Union troops. Bridles and bits had been removed from some horses and saddles were off or the girths were loosened. The men were sleeping or at their ease. Rangers were running to get their horses or trying to escape on foot.

Lieutenant Nelson was wounded as were Rangers Frank M. Woolf, William S. Flynn, William R. Stone and Francis M. Yates. Ranger Allan McKim's horse fell beneath him, and the young man broke his neck in the fall and died. General Sheridan reported to General Halleck that two officers and eleven men were killed and six other men were taken prisoner.[33]

The Union unit which hit the Rangers was tailor-made for the job. Called Blazer's Scouts, they were an all-volunteer outfit. Their patron was Brig. Gen. George Crook whose experience as an Indian fighter gave him an understanding of guerrilla warfare. Crook persuaded Sheridan to give the experiment a try and on August 20, 1864, Sheridan had written General Auger: "I have 100 men who will take the contract to clean out Mosby's gang. I want 100 Spencer rifles for them. Send them to me if they can be found in Washington."[34] Sheridan got the Spencers, but commanders are reluctant to give up good men. Blazer usually operated with fifty to sixty-five men. Selected from nine regiments, they began by working together in anti-guerrilla operations in West Virginia fighting the Thurmond brothers.

While Lt. Joseph Nelson's men were being hit, Mosby was taking prisoners in Sheridan's rear. The hunting was good, and he sent a messenger for Nelson to bring the men forward, which would now take some reorganization. When Mosby rejoined those who had been surprised, he offered ridicule in place of consolation. Shamed, the Rangers involved now had a personal reason to look forward to the next meeting with Blazer's men.

General Grant's resolve to take away the Confederate support base in Loudoun was hardening. From his City Point, Virginia, headquarters, on Sunday, September 4, 1864, he wrote General Sheridan:

> Major-General Sheridan
> *Charlestown, Virginia:*
>
> In clearing out the arms-bearing community of Loudoun
> County, and the subsistence for armies, exercise your own judge-
> ment as to who should be exempt from arrest, and as to who
> should receive pay for their stock, grain &c. It is in our interest that
> the county should not be capable of subsisting a hostile army, and
> at the same time we want to inflict as little hardship upon Union
> men as possible.
>
> U.S. Grant
> *Lieutenant General*[35]

The more Union force that made its way into Mosby's land, the more his force of Rangers grew. On Tuesday, September 13, 1864, Company F was

Gen. J. E. B. Stuart, a friend and supporter of Mosby. USAMHI

organized at Piedmont. Mosby followed his routine of allowing the men to elect the slate of hand-picked officers he chose. Walter Frankland was captain, and James F. "Big Yankee" Ames, the Union deserter who was now a trusted companion, was first lieutenant.

A company when formed might number sixty men, but there was no table of organization and equipment (TO&E) that specified strength and equipment. Three or five men might go out on a raid, or thirty men, the 43rd Virginia Partisan Ranger Battalion might launch 300 men in the attack. Mosby silently chewed his toothpick, thought for awhile, then led or sent them to action. After the organization of his newest company, Mosby in characteristic fashion took two men and went off on a personal reconnaissance to locate units or installations to attack.

The 13th New York Cavalry was on a sweep operation looking for Rangers. They had been to Aldie and now were into Fairfax County. Col. Henry S. Gansevoort, commander of the 13th New York, had heard Mosby was in the area and had passed Fairfax Court House with two men heading toward Centreville. Gansevoort feared a large force might alert Mosby, so he sent what seemed a tempting target, five men (likely volunteers) on the road to meet Mosby. Predictably, Mosby was not deterred from coming on, and the two groups rode to within pistol range of each other and opened fire simultaneously. Two of the horses of the Union soldiers were killed, and their riders were thrown to the ground. Mosby thought the two men were under their horses. The 13th N.Y. made no report of casualties and say they ran to the security of the woods. Pvt. Henry Smith of Company H, 13th New York Cavalry fired a shot that shattered the grip of Mosby's pistol and another that tore into Mosby's groin. Both sides broke off the action. The cavalrymen thought, but were not certain at the time, that it was Mosby who was wounded. In his September 15 report, Gansevoort wrote, "he or the person in question was seen, before riding off, to throw up his hands and give signs of pain." Gansevoort sent a squadron of cavalry to the scene, but rain and violent storms slowed movement, and they could not find the Rangers.[36] Rangers Thomas R. Love and Guy Broadwater were with Mosby. They helped him stay in the saddle until they could get a light wagon from a farm. Mosby was taken back to his father's farm at Lynchburg. It was Wednesday, September 14, 1864; Mosby would be out of action for 15 days.

Union leaders and soldiers looked upon Mosby's Rangers as bushwhacking murderers. Grant's "hang them" order, the stories of isolated pickets being gunned down, and the execution of the men of the 5th Michigan Cavalry had both officers and men eager to extract revenge. That opportunity was coming.

CHAPTER FOUR

Hang Them High

Though General Phil Sheridan and his troops won the battle of Winchester, the army of Confederate Jubal Early was not destroyed. Early counterattacked, but by September 20, 1864, was again beaten and retreated on the Valley Pike to establish a defensive position at Fisher's Hill, southwest of Strasburg and west of Massanutten Mountain.

Massanutten is an approximately fifty mile long mountain in the center of and dividing the Shenandoah Valley. Sheridan planned to attack Jubal Early west of the mountain at Fisher's Hill using his infantry and a primarily West Virginia cavalry force consisting of the 2nd Cavalry Division under General Averell. Sheridan's main cavalry move would be in the Luray Valley to the east and therefore screened by Massanutten Mountain. Sheridan wanted his chief of cavalry, Brevet Maj. Gen. Alfred Thomas Archimedes Torbert, to attack down the Luray, using Wesley Merritt's 1st Cavalry Division and James Wilson's 3rd Cavalry Division to come in behind and strike at Early's rear.

Sheridan began his attack on Jubal Early on September 22, 1864, and routed him. If Torbert accomplished his mission, Early's army would be trapped and the Shenandoah Valley secured for the Union. Torbert was not aware that Sheridan had succeeded. South of Front Royal at Milford Creek, Torbert encountered strong Confederate defenses and decided to withdraw northward through Front Royal.

Wesley Merritt's 1st and 3rd brigades of the 1st Division were ordered to move through Front Royal to Cedarville.[1] En route, Merritt's ambulance train carried the wounded from the previous engagement. The ambulances were at the front of the column. Escorting the ambulances was a detachment of the 2nd U.S. Cavalry under the command of newly promoted (September 19) 1st Lt. Charles McMaster. A popular officer, McMaster was born in Ireland. He had enlisted in the U.S. Army in 1858 and rose through the ranks from private, corporal, sergeant and first sergeant with the 4th U.S. Cavalry. He was commissioned as a second lieutenant in the 2nd U.S. Cavalry on August 10, 1863.[2]

Trailing McMaster's detachment, somewhat behind the ambulances, was the remainder of the 2nd U.S. Cavalry Regiment. The regiment had seen heavy action at the Winchester fighting only a few days before. Its primary commander, Capt. Theodore Rhodenbough, had his horse shot from under him within a few yards of the Confederate entrenchments, but his life was saved by the heroic action of 1st Sgt. Conrad Schmidt of Company K who rode to the assistance of his commander, dragged Rhodenbough up on the rear of his powerful gray horse and brought him to safety in a hail of gunfire. The horse took five wounds and the pommel of the saddle and Schmidt's canteen were pierced. In a following charge Rhodenbough had his right arm shattered by three shots, causing the loss of the arm. The seriously under-strength 2nd U.S. Cavalry Regiment was now commanded by Capt. Robert S. Smith. Lieutenants McMaster, Cahill and Wells were the only three troop officers available for duty.[3] Behind the 2nd Cavalry was its parent, the 3rd (Reserve) Brigade of the 1st Cavalry Division. Under the command of Col. Charles R. Lowell of the 2nd Massachusetts Cavalry and down to a strength of 600 men, the 3rd Brigade consisted of the 1st, 2nd and 5th U.S. and Lowell's 2nd Massachusetts Cavalry regiments. It was called the Reserve Brigade as it contained the Regular army cavalry regiments.

Thus four regiments of cavalry preceded the next brigade in line. This trailing force was George Armstrong Custer's 1st Brigade, consisting of the 1st, 5th and 7th Michigan and the 25th New York Cavalry regiments.

The stage was now set for one of the great controversies of the Civil War.

Thursday, September 22, 1864, found Capt. William Chapman and some 120 Rangers just south of Front Royal where they bivouacked for the night. One of the Rangers was newly joined seventeen-year-old Henry C Rhodes, whose mother lived in the town. In the early morning light, scouts reported an ambulance train coming toward Front Royal. Chapman rode up Browntown Road to take a look for himself. In 1864 the road south of Front Royal narrowed between the Shenandoah River on the west and a high bluff in the east. After observing the oncoming ambulances from a high bluff, Chapman concluded these narrows would be a good spot to launch an attack. Capt. Walter Frankland and forty-five men were sent to approach over Prospect Hill and launch a sudden surprise attack on the front of the train. Chapman planned to approach from the east on Criser Lane to attack the rear of what was Wesley Merritt's 1st Cavalry Division ambulances and wagons. A Civil War ambulance looked considerably different from a wagon that hauled supplies. There is no record of their justification, but Union and Confederate reports of the action show Chapman knew he was attacking ambulances.

As Frankland made his attack, the light security forces of the 2nd U.S. Cavalry under McMaster rode to head off the Rangers. Some cavalrymen, including Lieutenant McMaster and Sergeant Schmidt, were overwhelmed and captured. Charles Uber, Harvey D. Haynes and James Tryon (Trion) were killed. First Sergeant Conrad Schmidt and Sergeants James Hogg and William Murphy were hit, with Schmidt being severely wounded. Lt. Charles McMaster was shot down. The McMaster casualty report reads: "Many wounds through body." Privates Rodney M. Powers and James Sullivan also received wounds.[4] The casualty reports for the dead Union enlisted men read "buried on the battlefield."

Frankland did not know that the remainder of the 2nd U.S. Cavalry was close at hand, riding through a cut with banks estimated by Capt. Robert Smith to be ten feet high. These banks hid them from low-level observation. When the firing began, the remaining cavalrymen put spurs to their horses and climbed the bank. From higher ground Chapman suddenly saw the rest of the 2nd U.S. Cavalry followed by the other four regiments of Lowell's brigade. Chapman hurriedly told his men to break contact and ride for Chester's Gap. Chapman rode to Frankland to call off his attack. The Rangers did a skedaddle eastward over primarily low ground owned by Perry Criser and called Criser Bottom. The cavalry was in hot pursuit.

There were varying reports of how Charles McMaster was shot down. Staff officer Captain Bean would write that McMaster's bridle broke and he had a runaway horse that took him into the Rangers. The commander of the 2nd U.S. Cavalry, Capt. Robert S. Smith, wrote that McMaster was trying to defend the ambulances and head off the Rangers. Captain Smith was in the best position to know what occurred. The mortally wounded McMaster told his men that he was shot after surrendering.[5] McMaster would be taken to Winchester where he died.

The Rangers would claim that they were on the run, shooting down anything in their path in a fair fight. Williamson wrote, "McMaster's horse was killed and he, a brave dashing fellow, fell riddled with bullets from our rough-riders who rode over him in their flight."[6] Mosby's men and John Mosby used the "fair fight" version of events for years and it became ingrained in history.

In a request for pension upgrade letter dated March 13, 1895, Sergeant Schmidt wrote, "Lt McMaster, myself and three other enlisted men, were captured, robbed and shot by the robbing, murderous gang of Col. Mosby's."[7] Schmidt was shot through the face, the ball entering the upper lip on the left side, breaking off four teeth and passing diagonally in a downward direction and exiting through the neck on the right side. The angle would indicate that the shooter was at a higher elevation, such as a mounted man shooting down at one dismounted. The mother of Pvt. James Tryon filed for the $8-a-month pension awarded to needy mothers of Union soldiers killed. While giving an incorrect date of death, the records of the Department of the Interior read: "Killed while a prisoner at Front Royal Virginia."[8]

During the Ranger skedaddle, cavalrymen captured Rangers Anderson, Carter, Overby, Love, and Rhodes. The shooting of McMaster, Schmidt and other troopers after surrender was murder in the eyes of their comrades and there was more. There are claims that wounded men in the ambulances were robbed. The men of the 2nd U.S. Cavalry were livid with rage at these murders and they wanted revenge.

Capt. Robert Smith, commander of the 2nd Cavalry, claimed McMaster was first robbed, then gunned down. Smith wrote: "The circumstances of this dastardly murder were such to justify, in the opinion of his comrades, the severest reprisal. To a short shrift and a strong rope were the cruel bandits justly entitled."[9]

Brevet Lt. Col. Bean wrote:

This unwarrantable act (shooting of Lt. McMaster) incensed his fellow officers and volunteers were called for, who quickly responded, to ride down a number of the partisan band and revenge the death of this young and gallant officer. The volunteers numbered about twenty-five men, well mounted. They pursued the scattered squads of Mosby's men, who having been deprived of their booty, now sought the sheltering hills as was their wont. But before they reached the "bush" six of them were overhauled; three were shot on the highways and three were brought back to town. One of these three, one quite a youth, was surrounded by the Michigan Brigade on the outskirts of town and shot down. The remaining two were hung in a small grove between the town and the river Shenandoah. I witnessed the execution of these two men; it took place within two hours after their capture. The troops present and on duty at this time were Companies E and L of the Seventeenth Pennsylvania Cavalry, and Lieutenant McMaster's troop of the Second United States Cavalry. The latter's non-commissioned officers and enlisted men, being eyewitness to the brutal conduct of Mosby's men, requested the privilege of executing the order of General Torbert to hang them, which was granted. It is due to these men of Mosby's command to say, they met their cruel fate bravely. Both declared their unqualified loyalty to the Confederacy and their willingness to die for it, if necessary assuring their executioners, however, that they might expect retaliation in kind. Both were hung at the same moment, side by side, to the projecting limb of a large oak tree, within sight of the town, and a card with their full names on it; and below, "Such is the fate of Mosby's men."

At some point, Rangers Thomas E. Anderson, David L. Jones and Lucien Love were summarily executed by gunfire. Another killed by gunfire was Henry C. Rhodes of Front Royal, a youth who had been on his first mission. There are varying accounts of when, where and by whom these Rangers were shot. The fleeing Rangers had scattered and were not all captured by men of the 2nd U.S. Cavalry. Young Henry Rhodes sought to escape along a streambed in Harmony Hollow. He was captured by an element of Custer's Michigan brigade. Rhodes was then lashed between two riders so that he had to run between them. He was taken into Front Royal passing on East Main Street before the house of his mother. She ran to the young Ranger but was brushed aside. Rhodes was then dragged between the two horsemen north on Chester Street.

The 5th Michigan Cavalry whose men had been shot down after surrendering at Morgan's farm were in Custer's brigade and now under the command of Maj. Smith Hastings. James Henry Avery, a member of 5th Michigan, had just rejoined the command on September 20. In his memoirs Avery wrote, "We made a move up above Front Royal, capturing a few of Mosby's men at Front Royal. They were recognized as a part of a band that had recently captured a lieutenant and some of the men of our advance guard and murdered them. Being caught and recognized by the lieutenant before he died, they were sentenced without court or jury, and two of them were given over to our regiment. Being brought in front of us, the colonel (obviously Hastings, as Custer had been a brigadier general since June 1863) said; if any of the Fifth had a spite against Mosby's men to ride out. This was wrong, we all had a spite against them, but did not feel like murdering them in cold blood. The only proper way would have been to detail a firing party, under orders. Only two men rode out; one was a man who had just had a brother killed by them at Berryville; the other was the bugler of the regiment who had nothing but his own spleen to vent.

"The boys, one about sixteen and the other about eighteen years old, were to be shot. They begged of the chaplain a chance to run for their lives, but no such boon was allowed them. They were placed a short distance away, and the two men began firing at them. The first shot killed the younger, but the other received two or three balls before he fell."[10]

Eric J. Whittenberg, who edited the Avery memoir, believes the personnel listing of the 5th Michigan makes it likely that the man who rode out to avenge his brother's death was George Warner of Company C. Oliver Warner, also of Company C, had been shot down by Mosby's men during the Morgan farm executions. The bugler is unknown.[11]

A February 1896 article in the *Warrenton Virginian* was written by a Southern eyewitness who chose to identify himself only as "B." This witness wrote, "Rhodes was lashed with ropes between two horses and dragged in plain sight of his agonized relatives to the open field of our town, where one man volunteered to do the killing, and ordered the helpless, dazed prisoner to stand up in front of him, while he emptied his pistol upon him. Anderson and Love were shot in a lot behind the court house. Overby and Carter were carried to a large walnut tree upon the hill between Front Royal and Riverton and were hanged."[12]

There were many things wrong with B's report. He obviously did not know General Torbett, General Merritt or Colonel Lowell. He incorrectly claimed Custer was in charge of the Union column and that he had set an ambush for Mosby's men. He did not see or hear Custer issue an order but wrote, "General Custer, at the head of his division, rode by. He was dressed in a splendid suit of silk velvet, his saddle bow trimmed in silver or gold. In his hand he had a large branch of damsons (plums) which he picked and ate as he rode along. He was a distinguished looking man with his yellow locks resting upon his shoulders." Custer did not have a division but a brigade, and there was no ambush by Union troops. There are photographs of Custer taken on August 8 and October 23, 1864, at which time his hair did not rest upon his shoulders.[13] Of course, Custer was at Front Royal, his brigade was heading north behind Lowell's reserve brigade, and he would naturally have been riding through the town with his men.

Conflicting statements between witnesses is commonplace, but the evidence is that Henry Rhodes was executed by Michigan cavalrymen, and the brother of a Michigan soldier executed by Mosby's men at Morgan's farm may well have pulled the trigger.

It is clear that William T. Overby and a Ranger apparently newly joined, whose name may or may not have been Carter, were hanged by the troopers of the 2nd U.S. Cavalry; this was done on the order of Maj. Gen. Alfred T. A. Torbert with Captain Bean, a staff officer of the 17th Pennsylvania, ordered to supervise the hanging.

Mosby was not involved in the attack on Merritt's ambulances, but he blamed George Armstrong Custer for the executions. In his memoirs, Mosby wrote that his information that Custer was responsible came from a Confederate newspaper. That report closed with, "It is said that Torbert and Merritt turned the prisoners over to Custer for the purpose of their execution."[14] To his dying day Mosby hated Custer and accused him of the murder of these Rangers. Because Mosby believed Custer was responsible, many who have written about the incident accept that view, but the accusation lacks proof and disregards the eyewitness account of Lt. Robert Craig Wallace (later lieutenant colonel) who was Torbert's aide and heard him give the order and then Captain Bean of the 17th Pennsylvania Cavalry who was present and heard General Torbert give the order. According to Wallace, Bean was the man to whom the order was given to supervise the execution. Colonel Bean saw the men of Lieutenant McMaster's Company L of the 2nd U.S. Cavalry hang the two men.

Mosby ignored the misdeeds of his own men. By his own admission, Mosby's men shot down Union soldiers who had surrendered at Morgan's farm. He felt it was justified because they had been burning houses. The soldiers of Colonel Lowell's 3rd Brigade saw Mosby's men shooting into a train that included ambulances. The men of the 2nd U.S. Cavalry believed their officer had been shot after surrendering. First Sgt Conrad Smith lived to say that he, McMaster and two other men had been shot after they had surrendered. The men of the 2nd U.S. Cavalry felt their reprisal was justified.

Three other Union officers wrote about the hangings: Lt. Charles Veil of the 1st U.S. Cavalry wrote in his memoirs that he saw Custer and a crowd of men at the hangings. Veil did not accuse Custer of ordering the hangings, but does not mention any other senior officer being present. Torbert's aide Wallace wrote that Mosby's men had attacked the ambulances and robbed the wounded. Wallace wrote that McMaster had led his men in a charge and driven off the Rangers, but McMaster got ahead of his men, was cut off, and captured when the Rangers were unable to get away with their prisoner, "they shot him in cold blood using his own pistol." Wallace did not claim he was an eyewitness to the death of McMaster but he was an eyewitness to Torbert giving the order for the hangings. According to Wallace the order was given to Captain Bean who did not relish the assignment. Bean took the two men aside and asked them to provide information that would help in the capture of Mosby, but the men refused and Torbert's order was carried out. Wallace wrote that McMaster was a friend of General Torbert. Both men were part of the small Regular army prior to the Civil War.[15]

Officers report on actions in which they are involved. The report of the action is found in that of Generals Torbert and Merritt and Colonel Lowell. The attack on the wagons is not recorded in Custer's after-action report. None of the Union senior officers wrote about the hangings, which could have been an omission for posterity in that they were following Grant's orders or that by September 1864 shooting and hanging prisoners by both sides was so routine that the manner of death was not significant in a report.

Torbert's report reads: "Brigadier-General Merritt's division went through Front Royal, crossing the Shenandoah and stopping at Cedarville, in the meantime having a skirmish with Mosby's guerrillas at Front Royal, killing two officers and nine men . . ."[16]

Merritt reported, "and the command the following day returned to Front Royal. Near this town the advance of the Reserve Brigade encountered a body of guerrillas, under a Captain Chapman, who were in the act of capturing an ambulance train of our wounded. The gang was quickly dispersed with a loss of eighteen killed. Lieutenant McMaster, of the Second U.S. Cavalry, was mortally wounded in this affair, being shot after he was taken prisoner and robbed."[17]

Colonel Lowell, the 3rd (Reserve) Brigade commander wrote, "September 23, marched to near Cedarville, dispersing en route a detachment of Mosby, under Captain Montjoy, killing thirteen."[18] In a letter of October 5, 1864, Lowell wrote to his wife Effie, "I was sorry enough the other day that my brigade should have had a part in the hanging and shooting of some of Mosby's men who were taken—I believe that some punishment was deserved—but I hardly think we were within the laws of war, and any violation of them opens the doors to all sorts of barbarity, it was all by the order of the Division Commander however."[19] The division commander was Wesley Merritt who was on the scene and left no record of objecting to his commander General Torbert's order.

Mosby saw nothing wrong in the murders of the 5th Michigan men at Morgan's farm or that Chapman's men had been firing into ambulances at Front Royal. If Mosby knew that his men had shot McMaster, Schmidt and other men after capture, he said nothing. Because Mosby believed Custer guilty of executing his men and, in particular, hanging two of them, his accusation carried weight and has been presented as truth by a number of historians who should have done better research, but found it easier to accept a lie and trash a reputation.

The evidence for Mosby's accusation is provided by people who did not know the Union commanders involved, while Union officers, who served under them even as members of their personal staffs, were present and said General Albert Torbert gave the order to hang the two Rangers. In doing so, Torbert was carrying out the orders of U.S. Grant.

Some commanders have a charisma that exceeds their rank. John Mosby and George Custer were of that breed. No matter if it was done by Harry Gilmore, or Elijah White, or John and Jesse McNeill, or a host of freelance operators, most actions that involved guerrilla warfare in Virginia were attributed by Union newspapers and troops to John Singleton Mosby. For the Union cavalry, the name George Armstrong Custer was a shining star. He was incredibly brave, beloved by his troops, and a colorful personality known on both sides of the lines.

A few local civilians who did not know the commanders and were not privy to the passage of orders blamed Custer, and the big lie grew. Mosby would later find himself in a similar circumstance when he was falsely accused of being involved in the assassination of President Lincoln and members of the Lincoln cabinet. The tragedy is that the big lie has been permitted to exist throughout the years. Many historians who should have done more thorough research have simply copied what was written before.

Despite the fact that they executed Union prisoners, when word of the execution of Mosby's men reached the Rangers, there was a wave of outrage. Some men wanted to execute prisoners that were on hand. Capt. William Chapman and his officers kept a tight rein on these emotions, telling the men to wait until Colonel Mosby returned. Mosby was still on crutches and in pain and had to be lifted onto a horse. But on Thursday, September 29, 1864, he returned to duty and ordered a Ranger rendezvous for Sunday, October 2, 1864, at Piedmont. He intended to strike at Sheridan's long supply line in the Shenandoah Valley. His scouts reported that Sheridan was withdrawing. The withdrawal was temporary, as within a week the Union cavalry divisions of Merritt and the newly promoted Custer would send the Confederate cavalry under Rosser and Lomax fleeing for miles. Not expecting this, Mosby had turned his eyes eastward. An intelligence report was received that Union troops were assembling in Fairfax to move against Fauquier and Loudoun counties. The purpose was to restore the Manassas Gap Railroad. Mosby felt such a restoration would result in the fall of Richmond.

On Monday, October 3, 1864, Lt. John R. Meigs, an engineer and mapmaker on Phil Sheridan's staff, was shot down by Confederate guerrillas wearing Union uniforms. The shooting occurred behind Union lines and within a few miles of Sheridan's headquarters. Sheridan thought highly of the young officer and his anger seethed. On the same day, Mosby with 300 men and two pieces of artillery marched from Piedmont traveling by way of Plains to Thoroughfare Gap in the Bull Run Mountains. Darkness had fallen when they passed through the mountains. Shortly beyond, Ranger scouts were fired upon by Union soldiers. Mosby turned north along the mountains to Craven Kings and bivouacked the command. Questioning his scouts, he learned that Union infantry was coming along the Manassas Gap Railroad westward to Thoroughfare Gap. Mosby led his men to about two miles east of Gainesville. Here they found the construction train with an infantry and cavalry guard. A line of Union static defense was being established along the bed of the Manassas Gap Railroad which was being repaired westward as far as Rectorville.

The 201st Pennsylvania was at Manassas Junction (with the Orange and Alexandria Railroad), at Gainesville the 202nd Pennsylvania was at Thoroughfare Gap and Plains, and the 5th Pennsylvania Heavy Artillery (now Infantry) guarded from Salem to Rectortown. A cavalry escort was with the

Union general Alfred Thomas
Archimedes Torbert, who ordered the
hanging of several of Mosby's Rangers at
the request of the men of the 2nd U.S.
Cavalry after Mosby's Rangers shot
down several
prisoners from that unit. USAMHI

construction train and numbered forty men from the 13th New York Cavalry
under 1st Lt. Hugh F. Pugh.

On October 5, Mosby took 200 men, one howitzer and one gun and
marched on Salem (Marshall). He sent men armed with carbines forward
and put the artillery south of Salem on Stevenson's Hill overlooking the
Union camp. When he opened fire, the guards broke and ran toward Rectortown, leaving all tentage and equipment behind. Eighty men were sent in
pursuit while the remainder destroyed the camp and wrecked the repair
work that had been done on the railroad. A line of blue-coated infantry
briefly checked the Rangers' pursuit force, killing two of Mosby's men. The
Union troops then retreated toward Rectortown. Two Union lieutenants
and forty enlisted men were taken prisoner.[20]

The Rangers spent the night of October 5 in a hayloft between Salem
and Rectortown, while Ranger Grogan was sent to see if the infantry was still
at Rectortown. Grogan returned with a prisoner whom Mosby questioned.
The next morning, the Rangers were back at Salem tearing up track. A train
arrived from Plains, but the Ranger artillery caused it to withdraw. Another
train loaded with infantry appeared, and it was taken under artillery fire.
Though the infantry dismounted, they soon boarded the train and returned
to Thoroughfare Gap. The Rangers rode to Rectortown, where they shelled
and harassed the infantry dug in there. Some good food and rest was

needed, so the command dispersed across the countryside, staying at farm houses. They reassembled the next morning at Blackwell's near Piedmont.

Messages were flying to Gen. Daniel C. McCallum. He was informed by Mr. M. J. McCrickett, assistant superintendent of the road, that the 600-man railroad guard at Salem had fallen back to Plains. An accidental train wreck at Thoroughfare Gap had an engine and twelve cars thoroughly smashed. The railroad men wanted to advance the track, but the infantry wanted to go forward by another route. Meanwhile, Mosby had brought all four of his artillery pieces together and began to shell Rectortown and tear up track. The Rangers forced the Union troops at Rectortown to retreat to Salem where they dug in on the high ground at Stevenson's Hill and would not be moved.

Enough was enough. On October 7, seven companies of the 8th Illinois Cavalry rode through Middletown on the way to Rectortown. Colonel Gansevoort led 625 men of the 13th New York Cavalry to the same location. By October 8, the infantry was moving up the railroad line, strongly supported by cavalry. Mosby decided it was best to let railroad activities cool. He sent the four artillery pieces to a hiding place, then split the command into three elements.

Mosby split his rival subordinates. Dolly Richards took a force into the Shenandoah Valley. William Chapman was assigned to raid south of the Manassas Gap Railroad while Mosby operated to the north.

The Manassas Gap Railroad had been completed to Piedmont (now Delaplane). The work was being guarded by one-year men of the Pennsylvania Volunteers. Among these was the 204th Regiment, recruited as the 5th Artillery but serving as infantry. They had been mustered into service at the end of August 1864.

James F. "Big Yankee" Ames, formerly a sergeant in Company L of the 5th New York Cavalry, deserter and traitor, had risen to be first lieutenant of Company F, 43rd Battalion, Virginia Partisan Rangers. He had become a beloved member of Mosby's command. On Monday, October 10, 1864, he was riding near Yew Hill, the home of Miss Kitty Sacklett, near Piedmont. How Ames was killed is unknown. His death was not part of a general engagement. Ranger Ludwell Lake claimed he happened by and killed the Union soldier who had shot Ames and was "going through him."[21]

However, Lake did not see Ames killed, merely a man going through his clothes. Cornelius Raver, a private in Battery E of the 204th (5th Artillery), was from Cavettsville in Westmoreland County, Pennsylvania.[22] Raver proved that poor spelling is not a bar to expression when he wrote his wife on Sunday, October 16, 1864, "We had the pleasure of bering Mosbeys first lieutenant he went by the name of yankey Ames One of our Boys shot him on last Monday throu the hart he was the sunofa bitch that cut so many of ower mens throats so he is gone up the spout at last..."[23]

Mosby was deeply saddened by the loss of Ames. He later wrote, "The Emancipation Proclamation which had been put in operation was the reason he gave for deserting the cause of the Union, but I always suspected it was some personal wrong he had suffered. He seemed to be animated by the most vindictive hatred for his former comrades. I felt an instinctive confidence in his sincerity which he never betrayed."[24]

The Union railroaders kept pushing the Manassas Gap Railroad westward, but it was difficult to guard the long line of track. Trains often moved slowly with infantry marching on both sides. Lt. Alfred Glasscock led an ambush of a train near Plains. Glasscock had his men remove rails to stop the train. When the Rangers opened fire into the cars, the engineer gave full throttle. His effort ran afoul of the displaced tracks and derailed the train. There were a number of casualties. Mr. McCrickett, the able assistant superintendent of the railroad, was reported among the dead.[25] Gen. Christopher Augur wrote to Gen. Henry Halleck in Washington, "Simply patrolling the track and guarding the bridges is not going to be sufficient on this road; it must be literally guarded the whole way."[26]

While Glasscock was wrecking the train, Lieutenant Grogan and a twenty-man patrol found a foraging force of some 100 Union cavalry getting hay from Glen Welby, the farm of Maj. Richard H. Carter. The hay had been bundled and each cavalryman was carrying a large bundle. They were caught totally by surprise when Grogan charged them in the narrow lane of the farm. Burdened with the bundles, the cavalry fled, scattering hay. One Union soldier was killed and ten horses captured. In a gunfight with Union cavalry, Mosby's horse was shot by a trooper and fell, pinning the Ranger leader beneath him. His men hurried to his assistance, pulled the dead horse off him, and he galloped away behind one of the Rangers. A sprained ankle was his only injury. Six Union soldiers were wounded or killed.

Acting on the orders of General Torbert, Col. William Henry Powell moved the 2nd Cavalry Division through Chester Gap, Flint Hill, Gaines' Cross Roads, and Little Washington to Sperryville. Powell had taken command of the 2nd Division when Sheridan relieved William Averell. Welshborn William Powell had been in the iron business before the war, and he was as hard as his product. He had cut his warrior teeth in the bushwhack campaigns of western Virginia, was wounded, and spent months in Libby prison before being exchanged. He had no reason to be kind to Confederates, and Powell had a particular hate for guerrillas, whom he was quick to suspend from a rope.

Powell captured and executed one of Mosby's men, his report reading as follows: "October 13, having learned of the willful and cold-blooded murder of a U.S. soldier by two men (Chancellor and Myers, members of Mosby's gang of cut-throats and robbers), some two miles from my camp a few days previous, I ordered the execution of one of Mosby's gang whom I had captured the day previous at Gaines' Cross-Roads, and placing the placard on his breast with the following inscription: 'A.C. Willis, member of Company C, Mosby's command, hanged by the neck in retaliation for the murder of a U.S. soldier by Messrs. Chancellor and Myers.' I also sent a detachment of cavalry, under the command of Captain Howe, First West Virginia Cavalry, with orders to destroy the residence, barn and all buildings and forage on the premises of Mr. Chancellor, and to drive off all stock of every description, which orders were promptly carried out."[27]

The Confederates claimed the U.S. soldier they killed was a Union scout dressed in Confederate uniform. When they found him at the Chancellor residence, they took him outside and shot him.[28]

Nineteen-year-old Albert Gallatin Willis had been captured the night of October 13 at Gaines Cross Roads. Powell's division was then camped on the Marlow farm in Rappahannock County by a graded road leading to Chester Gap. At about 11 A.M. Friday, October 14, 1864, he was hanged at Flint Hill from a large poplar tree that stood by the road of the Marlow farm. He is buried at the right rear of the Baptist church in the town of Flint Hill.

Near Upperville, some of Mosby's men captured Francis Marion White, a soldier of the 22nd Pennsylvania (Ringgold) Cavalry. With Mosby's Rangers were a number of men from McNeill's Rangers. McNeill's men and the Ringgolds had fought each other extensively in western Virginia. The Ringgolds protected the homes and families of the Confederate Rangers, and McNeill's men refused to allow the hanging to take place. A stormy argument occurred, and a shootout between the two groups of Rangers was narrowly averted when they recognized the folly of Confederate fighting Confederate. White was spared hanging.[29] He would spend ten months in Andersonville and suffered so greatly that he died soon after release.[30] The relationship of mutual respect between the Confederate McNeill Rangers and the Union Ringgold Cavalry led to friendship and visits in the latter years of life.

Mosby was well served by his scouts. He was delighted when Jim Wiltshire found a way through the string of encampments that guarded the steel ribbon of tracks of the vital Baltimore and Ohio Railroad. On October 13, 1864, Mosby called for a gathering of Rangers at Bloomfield, a small village in Loudoun County about five miles from Snicker's Gap. Seventy men responded. Mosby led his men across the mountains at Snicker's Gap and the Shenandoah River at Castleman's Ferry. They moved through Cabletown and took a rest break in Jefferson County near the home of the friendly Doctor Williams. At 9 P.M., they mounted and slipped through the Union guard posts to a point west of Harpers Ferry near Kearneysville at

Duffield Station.[31] Railroads prided themselves on "running on the adver-
tised," and throughout the war published their timetables in newspapers
Mosby had the B&O railroad schedule and selected a passenger train, as its
burning would create a greater sensation and thereby greater alarm in the
North. He chose to derail the train while it was in a cut, rather than choose
a place where the train would run off an embankment and cause greater
death and injury to passengers.[32]

The derailing threw the engine off the track where it exploded in a furious burst of steam and fire. Even the Rangers, many of whom had been
sleeping, were stunned by the force of the crash. There were shouts from
the male passengers, children crying and women screaming. Concerned
that Union patrols would hear the noise, Mosby hurried his men in, got the
passengers off and burned the train. One passenger car was filled with
German immigrants heading west. They spoke no English and did not
understand what was happening. Sensing no danger to their car, they
remained in their seats, unable to understand the threatening gestures of
the Rangers. Mosby did not hesitate, "Set fire to the coach and burn the
Dutch, if they won't come out." Making torches of copies of the *New York
Herald* that were intended for the Union army, the Rangers set fire to the
cars. The Germans now understood and hurried outside.

Though Mosby did not participate, robbery of passengers did occur
when trains were wrecked. In this instance Ranger John Alexander described
relieving a fat civilian of his gold watch and chain. He also inquired about the
man's money case as well, but another Ranger reached over his shoulder and
snatched the fat purse as it was being handed over.[33] Alexander described
what transpired in the car as looting.[34] Ranger Crawford wrote, "Some of the
men commenced 'going through' the passengers." Crawford described
$5,000 taken from a man who sold hogs to the federal government. Over-
coats, gloves and hats were coerced from the passengers. Ranger John Horn
was robbing a Union officer who seized Horn by the throat and choked him
"till his tongue hung out." Ranger Puryear "dispatched" the officer.[35]

Ranger Cab Maddux had been left in the woods to hold the horses.
Upset at being denied his chance at profit, he came riding in, claiming that
Union cavalry was coming. Everything was confusion as men tried to burn
cars, loot passengers and get to their horses. Mosby ordered his men
mounted and sent another scout to check on the enemy. No enemy was in
sight. A furious Mosby vocally considered having Maddux shot. The chas-
tened Ranger wisely kept quiet and was spared. Years later, Maddux embel-
lished the story by claiming that Mosby said Maddux would be shot at
sunrise and Maddux replied he hoped it would be a foggy day. According to
Maddux, Mosby laughed and spared him.[36]

Alexander related that Union officers and soldiers were among the passengers on the train. When Ranger Charley Dear attempted to take a satchel from him, Maj. Edwin Moore, a Union paymaster, refused. Dear waved a pistol and warned him not to resist. Moore handed over the satchel, telling Dear to be careful as it contained greenbacks.

On opening the case, Dear was beside himself with excitement when he found rolls of uncut U.S. currency. Meanwhile Ranger West Aldridge had located another Union paymaster, Maj. David Ruggles, who was trying to conceal something. Aldridge hurried his prisoner from the car, then being suspicious, returned to find a tin box also filled with money. A man of low repute attempted to talk Alexander into deserting with the money, but the young Ranger took it to Mosby.

More than $173,000 had been taken. The men met at Bloomfield in Loudoun County the next day. In accordance with the law established by the Confederate Partisan Ranger Act of 1862, the money was distributed among the men, with each man getting more than $2,000. Ranger Alexander wrote that he received $2,200 and could hardly believe his good fortune.[37] Ranger Mumford remembered getting more than $2,200 and wrote that everyone was buying gold braid and ostrich plumes for their hats. If they could not get what they wanted locally, they sent north for it through line-crossing smugglers, and they paid in U.S. currency. Mumford ordered a beautiful gray uniform, but it was torn in a fight with another Ranger.[38] Ranger Grogan said the money was "circulated so freely in Loudoun County that never afterwards was there a pie or a blooded horse sold in that section for Confederate money."[39]

Mosby denied his men had robbed passengers. He must have chosen to ignore it, as the writings of his men show robbery was commonplace. In a later report of the action to Lee, Mosby complained that reports in Northern newspapers were inaccurate; he had told his command that this would not be tolerated. Mosby claimed his men must have been under threat from the enemy, otherwise they would have saved the passenger baggage. He further explained to the passengers that they took a known risk by traveling on a railroad that was actively involved in the war.[40] Mosby may not have personally witnessed the thefts. Crawford said one man who took a watch was ordered to give it back.

Union Brig. Gen. John Stevenson, commanding at Harpers Ferry, reported to Secretary Stanton that from the time of the derailing of the train, the whole affair did not last more than an hour.[41] Pursuit was ineffectual, as the Rangers had a head start.

The loss of the payroll thoroughly alarmed Union commanders and other paymasters. On October 14, Jonathan Ladd, paymaster at Martinsburg reported, "I have my funds in the parlor of the United States Hotel here, guarded by a regiment."[42]

Meanwhile in the Shenandoah Valley, things were not going as well for the Confederates. In the words of Southerner Henry Kyd Douglas, it became the Confederate Valley of Humiliation. Custer faced his West Point classmate, Tom Rosser. Near Woodstock, the dashing, young Union general rode in front of his troops, made a mocking bow to the Confederate cavalry, then charged. Wesley Merritt's other riders came in at the same time. The Confederate cavalry of Rosser and Lomax were beaten, then chased for twenty-four miles, losing twelve guns, fifty wagons and 300 prisoners. The gray- and butternut-coated men of the Laurel Brigade were shamed; their own civilians called the action the "Woodstock Races." Gen. Jubal Early said, "The Laurel is a running vine."[43] The delightful Southern belle, Tee Evens, confided to her diary a telling remark about General Early, "They ran him out of his hat."[44]

With not much of an army remaining, Early took Henry Kyd Douglas and went to church. The preacher spoke of the dead of centuries and dramatically asked his listeners what they would do if the dead came marching back to earth. "I'd conscript every damn one of them," muttered Early.[45]

The four guns Mosby had managed to assemble through gift and capture were hidden at an out-of-the-way location at Emory's on Cobbler Mountain. The guns were guarded by Sergeant Babcock and a few Rangers. For reasons unknown, John H. Lunzeford, one of the guards, decided to desert and took his information to Col. Henry Gansevoort, commander of the 13th New York Cavalry. What story Lunzeford told Babcock or why the guns were not moved when Lunzeford left is not known. Lunzeford led Gansevoort, his 13th and two squadrons of the 16th New York Cavalry, plus two companies of the 5th Pennsylvania Artillery to the hiding place. Mosby's four guns, Babcock and five Rangers were captured.

Perhaps in an effort to conceal the source, Gansevoort reported the information was received from a prisoner. He did not claim he was led to the specific location of the guns, but reported he captured Mosby's men, including Babcock, at the base of the mountain. In the interest of security, very few of Mosby's men had been told where the guns were. Gansevoort deployed skirmishers up the mountainside in search of the artillery. This may well have proved fruitless as the Cobbler Mountains, which are some four miles west of Salem (Marshall) in Fauquier County, are north to south four and a half miles long. Gansevoort claimed "intimidation" was used on the prisoners. He claimed that just as the search looked hopeless, an unnamed driver of the artillery teams, who knew the trail, broke and revealed the secret.

The guns were in a dense thicket on a precipitous side of the stony mountain. Gansevoort reported the capture of one 3-inch ordnance gun, a

12-pound howitzer and two small mountain howitzers. Mosby reported the loss of the guns to Lee and assigned the blame to an unnamed deserter. Lee's response commiserated on the loss but told Mosby in gentle terms that Lee had no guns to spare and Mosby would have to capture more. Lee also cautioned Mosby about the character of men he enlisted.[46]

On Sunday, October 16, 1864, Mosby assembled his companies at Bloomfield. Mosby took Companies A, B and D to attack a train of 100 wagons reported moving between Burke's Station and Fairfax. Companies C, E, and F were ordered to continue operations to disrupt the Manassas Gap Railroad. Word of Mosby's movements were received by Union commanders who put a heavy guard on the train and held it in camp. Mosby's effort was fruitless. Captain Montjoy and Company D moved to Falls Church Village, where they broke open Mr. Sines barn and appropriated five quality horses. They then headed for Vienna on the Alexandria and Lewinsville pike. A four-man outpost of the 16th New York Cavalry was captured and a Negro member of the home guard, who tried to help the New Yorkers, was killed. Montjoy's Rangers then heard a horn blow. Initially, they thought a coon hunt was in progress but then came to believe the horn was a warning to Union soldiers. They attributed the sound to the Reverend John D. Read (or Reed), the minister of First Baptist Church at Falls Church.[47] Reed was taken into the woods and shot. The Union report makes no mention of Mr. Reed being a spy or giving warning but tells of him being murdered in a dense pine wood by Mosby's men. Reed's skull was shattered and contained the powder that indicated the gun was held close to his skull. In Confederate belief, Reed's execution was justified. It was murder in the eyes of the Union and contributed to the impression that Mosby's men operated under the black flag.

On Wednesday, October 19, 1864, Jubal Early launched an attack on Sheridan in the Shenandoah Valley at Cedar Creek near Belle Grove Plantation. The Confederates were initially successful, driving back the VIII and XIX Corps and taking many Union soldiers prisoners.

In the Shenandoah, the Union VI Corps was executing a fighting withdrawal when Sheridan arrived. Sheridan had just returned by train from a meeting in Washington. He rallied his troops. The Union soldiers counterattacked and routed Early's Confederates. The defeat was so decisive that the Confederate army ceased to be a serious contender for the Shenandoah Valley. Sheridan's army would be free to move eastward to assist Grant. When that happened, the Manassas Gap Railroad would lose much of its significance. All of these events would have an impact on Ranger operations.

To a soldier, victory is the only acceptable end to a battle or a war. Sheridan's troops enjoyed themselves. Some who had been printers in civilian life went into the print shops of Virginia towns and printed their own newspapers. Under prior ownership there had been advertising for the return of captured slaves. The soldier-printers took these brochures but placed the names of Confederate generals Jubal Early and Thomas Rosser in place of that of a slave. The advertising offered rewards for "My boy Jube," and "My man Rosser."[48]

The Rangers remained a constant threat to Union communications and supply lines. The havoc being wreaked by Mosby, White, McNeill and other Rangers fighting a guerrilla war led the U.S. political leaders to condone and U.S. Army officers to institute ever more stringent measures. They let it be known that secessionist leaders and some of Mosby's captured Rangers were being positioned on trains so that, if the train were wrecked, they likely would be killed. Any house or building within five miles of the railroad that was not owned by a Unionist was to be burned. Any civilian found within five miles of the railroad tracks was subject to being treated as a robber or bushwhacker. Mosby was furious about this directive but would not cease his attacks.

Ranger Williamson heard Mosby say, "The Yankees are worse than the Chinese, but no matter what they do, I will not swerve one inch from my path of duty. They might as well place women and children in front of their lines of battle. My mode of warfare is just as legitimate as that of the army fighting in their front. I am placed here to annoy them and interrupt their communication as much as possible. This I intend doing, and should I again have the opportunity of throwing off a train I will do it, even if I knew my own family were upon it."[49]

On October 29, 1864, Mosby wrote Lee telling him of the use of citizen hostages on the Manassas Railroad and also the hanging of his men, accusing Custer of the crime. He proposed to hang an equal number of Custer's men when he captured them. Mosby pointed out that the U.S. Congress had passed a bill of punishments for men found to be guerrillas and suggested contact with representatives of the United States to come to an understanding. He reiterated that he would not be deterred from his mission.[50]

Lee had no inclination or time to cause an investigation to be made. He accepted Mosby's incorrect view that Custer was responsible. Lee forwarded Mosby's report to Secretary of War Seddon. He told the secretary that he had sent orders to Mosby to hang an equal number of Custer's men in retaliation. Seddon approved and ordered that whenever Southerners were used as hostages on U.S. trains, the "signal vengeance" should be taken on conductors and officers of those trains when captured, and all males should be treated as prisoners.

Retaliation was unending. The soldiers understood this—being captured was now even more to be avoided. Young John Stuart, a member of the 1st New York (Lincoln) Cavalry, was captured by some of Mosby's men. He pretended to be an idiot in blue, so stupid that he was not worth watching. It worked. The men guarding him became careless and Stuart escaped.[51]

Mosby called for an assembly at Bloomfield on Monday, October 24, 1864. Nearly 400 voices answered the roll call. Mosby led out heading west, crossed the Shenandoah at Castleman's Ferry and bivouacked near Summit Point. The next morning the riders moved to within six miles of Winchester, halting near the turnpike to Martinsburg. Taking several Rangers, Mosby went to see what traffic was on the pike. A two-horse light-spring wagon was moving from Winchester under a ten-man cavalry escort. Behind at about a mile and a half distance was a long wagon train. Mosby sent back for the rest of his command, then unleashed the small party of Rangers upon the wagon. The Union soldiers saw them coming, whipped their horses, and tried to make it to the safety of the wagon train. Concerned that the conveyance would make the safety of the train, Ranger Smith shot one of the two horses; then he and Ranger Dickson rode to the wagon and found they had captured Brig. Gen. Alfred Duffie and Captain Roome, an officer who was convalescing from a wound. Duffie was a Frenchman, a cavalry brigade commander when the 1st New York was part of his organization. He had shown courage on the battlefield but was a martinet. Prior to one attack he told his troops, "You all have got to die sometime anyway. If you die now, you won't have to die again. Forward!" The men thought unfavorably of Duffie's logic and French army discipline. "Frogeater" was one of the more respectful names he was called.[52]

On October 13, Duffie had been ordered from his post at Cumberland, Maryland, to proceed to Martinsburg, West Virginia, gather all the officers and men of the 2nd Cavalry Division department of West Virginia, and then move to Hagerstown, Maryland, to establish a remount camp.[53]

According to the October 25 report of Colonel Edwards at Winchester, Duffie was traveling with the wagon train and an escort of fifty men, most of whom were from the 22nd Pennsylvania (Ringgold) Cavalry and under the command of Lt. Benjamin F. Hasson, Company F. After five miles of travel, Duffie took ten men of the escort and went ahead of the train.

Sheridan was furious. He wrote General Halleck, "Brigadier General Duffie was captured between Winchester and Martinsburg. I respectfully request his dismissal from the service. I think him a trifling man and a poor soldier. He was captured by his own stupidity."[54]

As soon as the pursuit of Duffie started, a courier galloped back from the wagon train to Winchester. Col. Oliver Edwards immediately started the 17th Pennsylvania Cavalry and the 49th Pennsylvania Volunteer Infantry on the march to the wagon train. Mosby could not tempt them from the train which they gathered to protect, and he would not risk an attack on such numbers.

On Saturday, October 29, 1864, Mosby learned that some 200 men of the 8th Illinois Cavalry were on a raid near Snickersville. Mosby believed the cavalry would be returning to its base in Rectortown. Looking to attack the cavalry on its return trip, he assembled Capt. William Frankland and some 100 Rangers. He sent them to ambush the cavalry at a point between Rectortown and Upperville. Mosby continued his efforts to gather more men. Frankland tracked the cavalry and dispatched messengers to Mosby and other Ranger scouting parties. The Hoosier cavalry stopped at Hatcher's Mill to water and feed their horses. Frankland stayed under cover in a nearby woods. According to Ranger Williamson, Frankland was soon joined by Mosby, Hatcher and other Rangers. Williamson related that in this action Mosby decided to serve as scout for his subordinate, saying, "I want you to make this a second Dranesville. I will do the scouting and will keep you informed of the enemy's movements." Mosby does not mention the fight in his memoirs.[55]

The Winchester to Alexandria Turnpike ran east and west through Upperville. About a mile east of Upperville, the road southeast to Rectortown joined the pike. Finishing the search at Upperville, the 8th Illinois rode to the Rectortown Road. Approximately one mile from town, they entered a broad open field near the home of a Mr. Henry Dulaney. The property sat on rising ground, a slight hill that would conceal the Rangers in an ambush position.

Over strong protests from some of the men, Walter Frankland ignored his orders to establish an ambush. He decided to charge the cavalry while it was in the open and to strike his enemy simultaneously in the front and flank. Frankland ordered Lt. Albert Wrenn to make a frontal attack from the direction of the Dulaney house. Lt. Charles Grogan would lead the charge from the right flank. Williamson wrote that Frankland rode with Wrenn's element.

Frankland and Wrenn led their men down the hill toward the cavalry, moving at a trot in preparation for the charge. On seeing this force, the men of the 8th Illinois immediately moved with precision. Company F, Lt. Joseph Clap commanding, was in the lead. He began withdrawing slowly, opening a lane of fire for the remainder of the cavalry. As a result, Frankland and Wrenn's attack would meet the combined fire of Company K and Companies G and H under Capt. Malcomb H. Wing and Lt. John W. DeLaney. Capt. James F. Berry and Company L came in from the flank. Alexander was with Wrenn's party of approximately fifty Rangers whose avenue of approach was on a lane past the Dulaney barn. They passed through the lane gates and used the barn to conceal their movements as they came up over the crest of the hill.

At 300 yards, the opponents saw each other. Wrenn looked back quickly and reined in his horse. There were only seven men with him. Someone in

Union colonel Percy Wyndham, the
flamboyant British commander of the
1st and 5th New Jersey Cavalry. He
called Mosby a horse thief. Mosby was
attempting to capture him when he
instead nabbed Union general
Stoughton at Fairfax, Virginia. After the
war, Wyndham died in a ballooning
accident. NATIONAL ARCHIVES

the rear had determined this was not an attack that offered success and had
taken the remainder of Wrenn's men toward the Dulaney barn. While the
eight Rangers stared at their departing comrades in disbelief, the cavalry
opened fire with Spencer rifles. Three of the eight Rangers were shot in the
first volley and, while gathering their wits, two additional men were hit.
Wrenn, Alexander and another Ranger spurred their horses forward, each
emptying a revolver toward the cavalry to give them pause, then raced
toward the barnyard gate. The cavalry was in hot pursuit. This was the
reverse of the Miskel farm fight. Now it was the Rangers who were caught
trying to get through a gate.

The cavalry moved in around the house and barn, keeping up hot long-
range fire. Wrenn's small group was being soundly whipped, and those who
could were trying their best to skedaddle. Frankland's whereabouts are not
clear. It quickly became evident that Lieutenant Grogan had not attacked
from the flank. It is questionable if Mosby was on the battlefield. He did not
claim to be present. But if he was and agreed to scout the terrain, he did a
poor job. When Grogan attempted to attack the Illinois right flank, he
found his way barred. His assault was interrupted by a deep ditch and fence
and he stopped cold. Finding a gate in the fence, Grogan's men passed
through, but they lost time and momentum. His attack did not come until
the 8th Illinois had beaten Wrenn. Now Grogan drew the attention of the
cavalry and at least one company was on his flank with Spencer rifles. Grogan's men turned and rode for their lives.

The 8th Illinois let an excellent opportunity pass when it did not press a pursuit of the Rangers. Rangers Luther Carrington and George Gulick were killed on the battlefield. John Atkins, a volunteer from Ireland, and Edgar Davis would die of wounds. Rangers Maddux and Bryan were wounded and Chancellor, Darden, Munson, McIntosh and J .J. Williams were taken prisoner. Ranger Alexander wrote, "The cold, sad record is, we were whipped in detail; and the Eighth Illinois did it. And I will add that they were worthy of their laurels."[56]

Ranger John Munson was among the captives. Munson said when his time to be captured came that he threw up his hands "with that same alacrity with which other hands had been thrown up to me."[57] Munson now experienced another aspect of captivity of which he had seen only one side. The young Ranger wrote, "Before I got a hundred yards from the wall they pounced on me and made the most complete capture of a rebel ever witnessed. About twenty men made as many passes at me, and the baubles and splendors of guerrilla life disappeared. They got my hat and plumes, my gloves and pistols, my watch and belt, and all my personal belongings. Before I had time to make the slightest protest, one fellow set me down abruptly, put his foot on me and relieved me of my boots in a most startling and finished manner. Talk about Mosby's men going through a man! There was not a man in our Command who could swoop down and capture a pair of boots like the man who took mine! It was my initial touch at the game of retaliation, and the Yankees trimmed me well."[58]

Ranger John Munson felt any "Poor Private" could be condoned for looting a prisoner. He feigned shock that officers would do it. Munson claimed it was the major of the 8th Illinois Cavalry (the hard-charging John Waite) who set the example by robbing him of his pipe and silk tobacco bag.[59]

For some time Mosby had been looking for prisoners from Gen. George Armstrong Custer's command. In his mind, the actions of his men in shooting the wounded and surrendered men at Morgan's farm and the attack on the ambulances and the killing of Lieutenant McMaster were justified. Convinced that the hanging and shooting of the Rangers at Front Royal was unjustified and had been done on Custer's orders, he was determined to execute men from Michigan in retaliation. On November 5, 1864, Dolly Richards entered with fourteen prisoners; these and others on hand made what the Confederates believed was a total of twenty-seven of Custer's men who had been captured.

One of the prisoners was Lt. Charles Brewster who served as commissary of subsistence for the Michigan brigade. Early in November, Brewster had been ordered from the supply base at Winchester to join the brigade at

Cedar Creek. On the morning of November 4, Brewster rode up the Valley accompanied by privates Mathew J Crothers, Company C, 6th Michigan Cavalry and George Soule of Company G, 5th Michigan, Cavalry,[60] and a former officer, now a civilian lawyer, who had business with Sheridan. They were joined by the saddler-sergeant of the 1st Vermont Cavalry who was on his way to get his discharge papers. The weather was cloudy, damp and cool and the men wore overcoats and rubber ponchos. As they were approaching a crossroads near Newtown (Stephens City), they saw on another road to their right approximately fifteen riders. This group of men rode toward them. Brewster was uncertain what to do as the oncoming men wore blue overcoats or ponchos and yellow hatbands, as Union cavalry would. When these men came close, they drew pistols and Brewster's party was captured and relieved of their arms and their wallets. Brewster had $30 of his own money in the wallet that was taken and $1,700 in government funds hidden inside his overcoat. He was later able to pass the larger sum to the civilian lawyer. The captors, who were Mosby's Rangers, then split into two groups with three Rangers led by James R. "Doctor" Sowers leading the prisoners away by a difficult route. Brewster saw the Confederates take off Union blue overcoats and hang them over their saddles, revealing their gray uniforms.

The captives were taken across the Shenandoah River by way of the ford leading to Ashby's Gap. In the gap they met another column of men wearing blue overcoats. John Mosby was riding at the rear of the column and questioned the prisoners. Brewster said Mosby accused Custer of being responsible for the hangings and shootings at Front Royal. He said nothing about the hanging of Ranger Willis by Col. Powell but told Brewster, "I have got a little account to settle with General Custer." Other prisoners were added to the group and one of them, a youth from Michigan, related that Mosby had told him he intended to hang him.

Another prisoner Brewster identified as Private Prouty of the 7th Michigan Cavalry Regiment approached and, greatly dispirited, told Brewster that Mosby said he intended to hang him. The prisoners were taken to the town of Paris where they were kept overnight in grain bins in a barn. That night the captives divided the $1,700; it might prove useful in the event of an escape. Brewster kept $300 on his person. The next morning, the Rangers divided the prisoners' horses and gear under the eyes of the captives. Dolly Richards took Brewster's excellent steed. Brewster had recognized one of the Rangers as a man he had met in Minnesota and whose family he knew well. Brewster asked the man if his name was Magner. The man was Ranger Matthew F. Magner who had been born in Ireland and moved to Minnesota in 1852. Brewster knew Magner's family well. Magner's brother was a captain in the 28th Massachusetts Infantry. Matthew Magner told Brewster he had removed to Missouri where Union forces (Jayhawkers) had destroyed his property and in revenge he joined Mosby.

The prisoners were next taken to an empty storeroom with shuttered windows in another part of Paris. Other prisoners joined them here. There were about thirty, some of whom were civilian. The door was left open. Brewster wrote, "Here we conversed most with these men and listened to their recitals of deeds of butchery of Union soldiers, wanton cruelty and heartlessness to 'prisoners and other captives' to their fellow men of the same nationality."[61] Using a few secreted pocket knives, the prisoners tried to cut through the thick oak planks in the floor but before they could succeed, they were moved again. They were required to walk from Paris to Rectortown, where they were put in a corncrib or granary. En route, Brewster saw the rallying system of the Rangers in effect. Whenever parties of Rangers met, they would exchange information on where and when Mosby's command would next meet. Corncribs had spaced gaps between boards to permit air to reach the corn. While in the corncrib, the prisoner could watch Mosby's men ride in from various parts of the country, coming alone or by twos and threes until Brewster estimated 500 or 600 had arrived. Brewster heard the Rangers speaking of where they stayed and the Union belief that the critical support base of the Rangers was the local populace was proven true. Brewster noted, "We learned that these valiant men boarded at Mrs. Smith's, Mrs. Jones', Auntie Plimpton's, Cousin Jamison's, Granny Longnecker's, etc." While the names he used were examples, the principle was true. Brewster added, "these men belonged to the invisible part of the enemy's forces and the assembly was to us at this time a decided curiosity."[62]

Mosby was now prepared to carry out the recommendation he had made and that General Lee and the Confederate secretary of war had approved. In retaliation for what the men of the 2nd U.S. Cavalry believed to be the murder of Lieutenant McMaster, two Rangers had been hanged at Front Royal by order of General Torbert, with four others executed by gunfire. On October 13, Ranger Willis had been hanged by Col. William Powell at Gaines Cross Roads in retaliation for the gunning down of a Union soldier. On the basis of incorrect information, Mosby placed the blame on George Armstrong Custer.

It was Sunday, November 6, 1864. The weather had cleared and the sun shone brightly when the drawing for death began. The twenty-seven Union captives, two of whom were officers, were formed in a line. Military courtesy was observed with Lt. Charles Brewster positioned on the right. Though Mosby thought all those he selected were Michigan men, there were a number who were not. The officer to the left of Brewster was Lt. Israel C. Disosway of the 5th New York Heavy Artillery. Disosway was twenty-four years old; he had joined the service from Baltimore, Maryland, in 1862 and served with the 83rd New York Infantry before becoming a member of the 5th New York Artillery.[63]

The prisoners were told that seven of their number would be selected by lot and hanged in retaliation for men hanged and shot by General Custer. Twenty-seven pieces of paper were put in a hat, seven of which supposedly had numbers on them. The remainder were blank.[64]

Brewster later related that three men conducted the drawing. A tall man used his hat as a receptacle for the slips of paper. He would pause in front of a man and require a slip of paper to be drawn which would then be examined by the other two. Those who drew blank slips remained in line to be taken to Libby Prison in Richmond. Those selected for execution were immediately placed under a special guard.

When the drawing was concluded it was found that Ranger mathematics were faulty. Only five Union soldiers had been selected. Among them were Privates Soule and Prouty, both of whom had expressed a premonition of their deaths. An excess of blank slips had been placed in the hat and as a result there remained slips with numbers in the hat. The death lottery committee revised the number of slips to conform to the number of men and the drawing had to be repeated. One and possibly two of the twenty-seven captives were youthful drummer boys. One had drawn a death number and he now began to weep and wail. On the basis of his youth and that he had not carried arms, Mosby excused him. Years later, a man named James A. Daley gave the aging Mosby a cane and claimed that he had been captured in April 1864 near Newtown and was the drummer boy who was spared. No confirmation of the legitimacy of Daley's claim has yet been found. It is questionable why and how Mosby's men would have held a drummer boy or any prisoner for seven months. In the second drawing, four men were to be selected for death and the hat, this time with the correct number of slips, was passed again.

A Confederate Brewster described as a "a red-headed man, with bushy untrimmed red beard" was among those who passed down the line with the hat and the slips of paper. As the slips were drawn, he would say, "We'll give you a chance to stretch hemp. You can shake the dust off your feet." Brewster remembered that the final draw for death came down to the two Union officers. Disosway drew the marked slip, passed his hand across his forehead and said to Brewster, "This is tough."

Brewster wrote, "Had we been the same men who had carried out the orders for executing their comrades, for which revenge was to be taken, there would perhaps be some ground for justification, from their standpoint, by this scum of the rebellion, but we were all innocent of any irregular warfare."[65]

As is customary for those who order executions, Mosby passed the gruesome work to someone else. By choice or by command Lt. Edward F. "Ned" Thomson of Company H became chief executioner. Lt. James R. Sower was another of a hanging party reported as consisting of four Ranger officers and three enlisted men. Thompson was ordered to take the prisoners on the Valley Pike as near to Sheridan's Winchester headquarters as possible before killing them. Rain fell heavily and travel through the night was difficult. By the time they reached Berryville, Capt. Richard Montjoy had joined the group with some prisoners. Brewster later wrote that Disosway had served as assistant provost marshal at Fort McHenry and was recognized by a Ranger who had been in captivity there. The Ranger, whom Brewster called Leslie, and Disosway were both Freemasons, and Disosway had treated the man kindly. Brewster thought Leslie was returning the fraternal kindness. It is more likely that Montjoy was wearing a Masonic pin that Disosway saw, thus enabling him to give a Masonic distress signal to the Ranger officer. Montjoy ranked Thomson and took the responsibility for changing the selection. He spared Disosway and another of the condemned men (believed to be from Vermont) who was also a Mason and substituted two of his prisoners to be hanged in their place. Disosway was sent to Libby prison, would survive the war, and end it as a captain. He would die in 1889, no doubt a fervent Mason to the end.[66] When Montjoy later told his leader that he had made the switch, Mosby responded that his "command was no Masonic lodge."[67]

The two substitutes were twenty-one-year-old Cpl. (acting sergeant) Charles E. Marvin and twenty-four-year-old Cpl. James Bennett of the 2nd New York Cavalry. The day prior, their regiment had been moving eastward from Newtown toward the Shenandoah. They had been separated from their command when Marvin's horse lost a shoe and the two headed for base camp and the farrier. En route, they met a group of riders wearing blue overcoats and black hats and appearing as Union cavalry. Two of these men came close and asked to what regiment Marvin and Bates belonged. Marvin replied, "Second New York Cavalry the Harris Light," and asked what unit the riders belonged to. The stRangers identified themselves as belonging to the 19th Pennsylvania Cavalry, then rode close, raised pistols they had been holding shielded by their hands on their saddles, and captured Marvin and Bates. The two captives were then disarmed, and taken to join the main body of Confederates commanded by Captain Montjoy, where their overcoats, money, watches, pipes and tobacco were taken. Marvin had some pistol caps in his pocket that had become water-soaked. The Rangers did not know they were defective so the caps were avidly seized and distributed.

Montjoy continued on his route until meeting Thomson and the execution party. Montjoy had other prisoners, but when the unknowing Marvin and Bates said their unit was a part of Custer's division, Montjoy selected them for the exchange.

When he recognized he was selected to die, Marvin protested the switch. When a captor asked if he was a Mason, Marvin replied that he was too young but hoped to be as soon as he was old enough.[68] Intent was not sufficient and Marvin was put in the death line.

The prisoners were roped in single file and as the march proceeded, Pvt. George Soule loosened his bond. Taking advantage of the darkness and rain, Soule dropped into a ditch along the side of the column unnoticed by the Confederates. He safely made his way to Winchester. Mosby's men were uneasy. Winchester was Union general Phil Sheridan's headquarters a short distance away. Union cavalry patrols would likely be about.

An ancient white oak tree stood on Grindstone Hill beside the road to Winchester, approximately one mile from the center of Berryville (present day business Route 7). Tall and stately, the tree was used in deeds to designate a limit of the Bonham family property. Ranger Charles Russell later identified this as the hanging tree.[69] When the prisoners were place in line, Charles Marvin was farthest from the tree. The first man was gotten up, his hands tied behind him, and a bed cord doubled around his neck. The guards lifted the man into the air beneath the limb and the loose end of the rope was taken by one of the men on horseback and tied to the limb. Then the man was left to fall and strangle. Three U.S. soldiers, one being Pvt. Wallace Prouty of the 5th Michigan Cavalry, and two unidentified infantrymen Soule believed to be from the 4th West Virginia and 23rd Ohio regiments were killed in such fashion. Death was not swift. The bed cords stretched and from the dig marks on the ground and position of the bodies, those who found them could tell that their toes had touched the ground, and they suffered in a torturous macabre dance of death. Soule reported hearing the sounds of the deaths. Men who had not yet been hanged were pleading to be shot.

The hangings were going poorly. One of the Mosby's men grumbled "this hanging is too damn slow work."[70] The Confederates decided to shoot the remaining four men.

When the captives were forced to stand, the Confederates saw that one was missing and grew excited. The three union soldiers were stood in line. Pvt. Melchior H. Hoffnagle, age twenty-three of the 153rd New York Infantry was on the left, Marvin in the center and James Bennett on the right.

Though he had little hope of escape, Marvin had managed to loosen the rope on his wrist. Three Confederates stood in front of the three Union soldiers with pistols raised. Marvin heard the pistol to his left fire and the pistol to his right fire, but the one facing him fell on a defective cap and failed to explode. Marvin described the click of the hammer as an "electric shock." He went up on the balls of his feet, brushed the revolver aside and hit the man in front of him with his fist, knocking the man prone. Leaping over the fallen Ranger and running for his life Marvin heard a Confederate yell, "There goes that big Yankee ———." Marvin was running from the direction of the road into Beemer's Woods. He ran "like a streak of lighting" about 100 yards then, though he always had difficulty climbing, went up a tree "faster than a squirrel." Concealing himself in the darkness, he stayed there until he heard the executioners ride away.

Despite firing at point blank range, excitement and darkness combined to affect the aim of the executioners. Hoffnagle took a bullet in his arm which shattered his elbow. He fell to the ground and feigned death. Mosby's men kicked him in the ribs and rolled him over, but thought he had been killed. The first bullet struck Bennett in the shoulder and he exclaimed "For God's sake, kill me if you are going to! Do not torture me to death!" The Confederate placed a pistol close to the left side of Bennett's head and pulled the trigger. The bullet entered at the top of the cheekbone, about a half-inch behind his eye which it ripped out, and passed completely through his head. The force of the explosion knocked Bennett to the ground.

The grisly work was done. Another occurrence in the endless cycle of retaliation was now complete. Of the six prisoners who were hanged or shot so Mosby could mistakenly have revenge on George Custer, only Wallace Prouty may have been at Front Royal on September 23, 1864, and Prouty did not shoot any of Mosby's men.

When Mosby's men left the scene Marvin came down from the tree and began to walk through the woods toward Winchester. In daylight he took to the road and about two miles from the execution site found the wounded Hoffnagle, weak from loss of blood. They moved toward Winchester, but Hoffnagle could not continue. Marvin took a chance and knocked at the door of a house by the road. An elderly lady who cared more about humanity than North or South took them in and cared for them until they could be taken to Winchester in a wagon. At the execution site, James Bennett dragged himself against a tree and lay in misery until the next morning when traffic on the road began. A man with a little girl found him and he was taken to the house of a former Confederate surgeon who treated his wounds and made arrangements to have him taken to the Union hospital at Winchester.[71]

Charles E. Marvin would become a first sergeant, gain a commission and end the war as a lieutenant. In 1891, when he told of his experience, he was in the jewelry and auction business in New York City. James Bennett was cared for at the U.S.A. General Hospital in Pittsburgh, was promoted to sergeant and discharged on April 16, 1865. He lost an eye and the use of his left arm. Bennett had great difficulty securing a pension, having to make application three times. Supporting the claim, a disgusted Marvin at length told a clerk to write down anything it would take to get approval and he would sign it. Melchior Hoffnagle lost an arm. He would be discharged for disability on May 6, 1865. For his service he was breveted to second lieutenant.[72]

Mosby had scout John Russell take a message to General Sheridan.

November 11, 1864

Major-General P. H. Sheridan
Commanding U.S. Forces in the Valley:
GENERAL:

Some time in the month of September, during my absence from my command, six of my men who had been captured by your forces, were hung and shot in the streets of Front-Royal, by the order of and in the immediate presence of Brigadier-General Custer. Since then another (captured by a Colonel Powell on a plundering expedition into Rappahannock) shared a similar fate. A label affixed to the coat of one of the murdered men declared that: this would be the fate of Mosby and his men.

Since the murder of my men, not less than 700 prisoners, including many officers of high rank, captured from your army by this command, have been forwarded to Richmond, but the execution of my purpose of retaliation was deferred in order, in so far as possible to confine its operation to the men of Custer and Powell. Accordingly on the 6th instant, seven of your men were by my order executed on the Valley pike, your highway of travel.

Hereafter any prisoners falling into my hands will be treated with the kindness due their condition, unless some new act of barbarity shall compel me reluctantly to adopt a new line of Policy repugnant to humanity.

Very respectfully, your obedient servant,
JOHN S. MOSBY
Lieutenant-Colonel.

Mosby wrote, "No further 'acts of barbarity' were committed on my men."

The murder of the Confederate soldiers at Front Royal has been frequently reported on, a monument was raised to the men in Prospect Hill Cemetery and the dead, with Albert Gallatin Willis included, are called "The

Seven Martyrs." The Commonwealth of Virginia has erected historical markers about the town that incorrectly blames George Armstrong Custer. There are no historical markers to the Union soldiers who were murdered or maimed on Grindstone Hill at Berryville, Virginia. Indeed in the repetition of murder that occurred, the death of Union prisoners is frequently dismissed as "Oh, they were burners" or "our retaliation was justified."

The war fought by the men of John Singleton Mosby was a guerrilla war, a war of ambush, raid and robbery, where men walking guard posts or riding in rear areas often were shot down. Some of Mosby's men boasted of shooting prisoners.

The people of the once rich area of the Shenandoah Valley did not think the situation was resolved. The war had become a bare-knuckles, no-holds-barred brawl. The Valley was put to the torch, and the sky blackened with smoke as barns, outbuildings and houses were destroyed and the Confederate base of support and supply was eliminated. Retaliation followed retaliation. Confederate John O. Caslar wrote, "Our cavalry followed close after the burners and dealt out vengeance with a vengeful hand. Whenever they caught a party burning they would take no prisoners, but shot them down; and often threw them in the fire alive when they caught them burning their own homes."[73]

In retaliation, many Confederate prisoners did not reach the gates of a prison camp. Neither Torbert nor Mosby's executions stopped the brutality that was done by both sides and justified by the word retaliation.

The controversy over the hangings of the Rangers in Front Royal and that of Ranger Albert Willis by the order of Colonel Powell and the hangings of the Michigan soldiers by Mosby continued throughout the years. On September 23, 1899, some 150 of Mosby's Rangers gathered in front of a large crowd at Front Royal, Virginia, to dedicate a monument to the Confederate Rangers who were killed after capture. Mosby was not present at the memorial service. The keynote speaker was Maj. Adolphus "Dolly" Richards, who had become a lawyer and judge. Richards spoke of the events of the September 23, 1864, and he noted that the Ranger attack was made on an ambulance train. Richards said the Rangers retreated "back to the foot of the mountain where they found a detachment of 2nd United States regulars under command of Lieutenant McMaster directly across their path. Clustering together for a final rally, they charged through this obstacle, killing a number of Federals, among them the officer in command. In these various encounters, six of Chapman's men were unhorsed and captured. After the fight was ended, four were shot and two were hung, with a label pinned upon them bearing the ominous words, 'Such is the fate of all of Mosby's men.'"[74]

Dolly Richards mentioned the attack on the ambulances but had no comment on any of the Union complaints of atrocities, such as gunning down prisoners and wounded at Morgan's farm, or the Union view that Lieutenant McMaster and other men were shot down at Front Royal after they surrendered. Richards stated that in his opinion Gen. George A. Custer had nothing to do with the executions and as a soldier based that on the positioning of the units. Richards believed it was clearly men of Lowell's brigade, not Custer's, that was engaged and spoke of the August 16, 1864, order of General Grant, "When any of Mosby's men are caught, hang them without trial."

Mosby was clearly disturbed when he read of Dolly Richards' speech. He responded with a detailed defense of the hanging of what he thought were all Michigan soldiers, excusing Grant, with whom he now had a special relationship. Mosby wrote, "Custer's brigade was not engaged in the fight, and of course he made no mention of it. But that is no evidence that he had nothing to do with the hanging—he was on the ground. As none of the reports speak of the hanging, they would equally prove the innocence of Torbert, Merritt and Lowell—in fact of everybody." Mosby wrote that he based his retaliation on the fact that the people of Front Royal felt Custer was the most conspicuous actor in the event and that Custer never denied it. Custer had no reason to deny anything to Mosby and certainly not to accuse Torbert, who Custer in an 1864 letter to his wife Libbie described as "an old and intimate friend of mine and a very worthy gentleman."[75] Mosby used the *New York Times* August 25, 1864, article as a reference that Custer performed acts that justified his men being hung. Ironically, the title of the article was: "More About the Massacre by Mosby—Rebel Treachery—Cowardly Cruelty."

Dolly Richards did not back away from the anger of his former commander. He responded with a step-by-step sequence from the official records of the war. Richards used the exchange of messages between Grant and Sheridan to show Sheridan had and understood Grant's order to execute any of Mosby's men who were captured. Richardson pointed out that in the official records the reports of Colonel Lowell and General Merritt stated it was Colonel Lowell's troops who "killed" the men in the Front Royal action. Richards also wrote to Confederate general Thomas Rosser, who had known and been friends with Custer before and after the war. Rosser's response read:

CHARLOTTESVILLE,
November 23 1899.
Major E. A. Richards, *Louisville, Ky,:*

MY DEAR MAJOR,—I saw a great deal of Custer while I was constructing the Northern Pacific R.R. in the Northwest, in the seventies, and had many talks over the war with him; and he often stated that he was in no way responsible for the execution or murder of those men.

I have no doubt of Custer's innocence, for he was not in command, and his superior officer was present; and it is not probable that such a matter would have been turned over to Custer under the circumstances.

Yours most truly,
Thos. L. Rosser

Rosser and Richards understood the ways of the military. Richards wrote, "it would have violated all military rules for one brigade commander to have taken the prisoners from another brigade commander and ordered their execution, especially when the division commander was in reach."

In conclusion, Richards wrote, "This statement of General Rosser, supported as it is by the official record, seems to me to be conclusive, and the future historian must exonerate General Custer from the responsibility of the Front Royal tragedy."

It is time that historians do just that and tell both sides of the event.

Mosby had clearly ordered that the Union soldiers who were to be hung were to be Michigan men. Mosby would not accept Custer's innocence. To admit he was wrong would harm his reputation and his feeling for U.S. Grant who saved him from a noose.

Union general Alfred N. Duffie, a French officer serving in the United
States. He was captured by Mosby. NATIONAL ARCHIVES

CHAPTER FIVE

End of a Dream

The dashing Mississippian, Capt. Richard Paul Montjoy, was a particular favorite of Mosby's, and Montjoy earned his commander's favor with the elan he wore like a cloak. On Tuesday, November 16, Montjoy led Company D through Ashby's Gap and crossed the Shenandoah at Island Ford within a mile of Berry's Ferry. They took advantage of concealed routes as they rode. Close to Winchester they hid, resting for the remainder of the night in a woods, with security posted. At first light the men were mounted, while Montjoy scouted activity on the Winchester-Newtown road.

Blissfully unaware of the Rangers, a detachment of Union cavalry was on the road riding without point men in advance or flankers. A hill located beside the road offered concealment for Company D. The Rangers waited until the unsuspecting Union cavalry rode by, then charged into their flank, coming at them from only a few yards and with pistols blazing. Those of the cavalry who could, fled—a number were killed or wounded and seventeen prisoners with horses were taken.

Montjoy led his men through Berryville and began dispersing them. Those who lived in Loudoun crossed the Shenandoah at Castlemen's Ferry. Montjoy with some thirty men and the prisoners rode southwest toward Berry's Ferry, intending to cross into Fauquier County. Some two miles short of the ferry near a house owned by Mr. Frank Whiting, Montjoy and his men were ambushed by Richard Blazer and his independent scouts. Ranger Edward Bredell was killed by one of Blazer's Spencer rifles. Montjoy's men attempted to make it to the river. Captain Montjoy and Lieutenant Grogan attempted to rally the men near Vineyard, the home of John Cooke, but Blazer pushed his advantage, freeing the prisoners and taking back the captured horses. Five of Montjoy's men were wounded and the Rangers broke contact as quickly as possible.

Mosby's men had varying views of Capt. Richard Blazer. Williamson wrote, "Captain Blazer was not only a brave man and a hard fighter, but by his humane and kindly treatment . . . he had so disarmed our citizens that instead of fleeing on his approach and notifying all soldiers, thus giving them a chance to escape, but little notice was taken of him."[1] Ranger Craw-ford thought the Union officer's name was Brasher. He did not have a high regard for the fighting ability of the Union scouts but praised their con-duct.[2] Doctor Monteiro named the Union officer "Blaizor"and promoted him to major. Monteiro, who gained his impressions of Blazer through Mosby's younger brother and adjutant William Mosby, called the officer a desperado and had the impression that Blaizor "must be one of the most uncouth bipeds that ever aspired to military honors."[3] John Mosby said his men named their adversary Old Blaze and were eager for a fight with him. Mosby described Blazer as "a bold, but cautious commander."[4]

Though the Union army occupied the country, it could control only that portion where its troops were present in large numbers. Although there were exceptions, the population generally supported the Confederacy. Cap-tain Blazer's scouts were a small band of Union Rangers operating inde-pendently in a hostile environment where their movements were frequently under the eyes of Confederate sympathizers. Small parties of five to ten men were frequently detached on patrol or ambush duty. While performing this duty, Lieutenant Ewing and five men were attacked and only Ewing got away. Sergeant Fuller and ten men were located and attacked by guerrillas; only three Union Rangers escaped. The dispatching of small parties to cover his large area of operations and a lack of replacements was whittling away at Blazer's numbers, leaving him with a functional strength of about fifty men.

Mosby ordered Dolly Richards to take Companies A and B in pursuit of Blazer. Ranger Williamson wrote that 110 men made the November 17 roll call at Bloomfield; other sources place the number at 300. The Rangers had a strong numerical advantage of skilled fighters, important in battle. Scouts picked up Blazer's trail at Snickersville, but Blazer was gone when the Rangers arrived. The Rangers knew Blazer made his headquarters at Kable-town on the west side of the Shenandoah, so Richards and his men crossed the river below Castleman's Ferry and bivouacked in Castleman's Woods, putting them in position to attack the following day.

A heavy fog lay on the land when, early on November 18, Rangers Puryear and McDonough were sent forward to scout. Puryear was a young and brash man. McDonough was an able soldier, but a ruthless killer and robber who was hardly a credit to the Rangers. Unable to see clearly, the two scouts stumbled upon to one of Blazer's outposts. McDonough escaped, but Puryear was taken prisoner and hustled to Blazer's camp where he was roughly interrogated by Lt. Thomas K. Coles, Blazer's second in command. The Confederates claimed that when Puryear refused to give information, Coles had a rope put around Puryear's neck and twice hoisted him off the ground, once leaving him hang to the point of unconsciousness. Unable to secure information, Coles released Puryear from the ropes and placed him with four other Confederate prisoners.

Blazer was unaware his enemy was in significant numbers. Both commands began to search for each other as the fog started to lift. Richards located Blazer's camp, and the Confederate Rangers charged in with pistols drawn—to no avail. The camp was empty. Blazer had gone toward the Shenandoah searching for Richards.

Near Myerstown, the opponents came into contact. Richards was in the open, but Blazer had a wood line to offer some concealment. It was to the Union advantage to fight the battle at long range, pitting seven-shot Spencer rifles against the six-shooter handguns of the Rangers. Richards recognized this disadvantage. Leaving Company B to form a line, Richards withdrew Company A, simulating a withdrawal of his command. Blazer's caution failed him. Not able to see the full strength of his opponent and observing what he believed to be a Ranger withdrawal, Blazer ordered his men to attack.

Company A had disappeared from the view of the Union soldiers. Now as Blazer's men clashed with Company B, Richards led Company A in a slashing assault on Blazer's flank. The Union Rangers threw down their Spencers and drew revolvers. A furious but brief fight ensued. Richards was a skilled leader who knew how to use his advantages. He had superiority of numbers and brought his command into a favorable tactical position where its firepower could be employed.

Despite Blazer's efforts, his men began to waver, then break. Riders on both sides were well mounted, and the flight and pursuit lasted for several miles. Though he had emptied his pistols, Ranger Sydnor Ferguson of Company B had a fast horse. He managed to ride abreast of Captain Blazer and strike the Union officer with an empty weapon, knocking him from his saddle.[5]

McDonough saw with Blazer's scouts a man named Harrell, whom he recognized as deserter from a Confederate regiment in which they both had served. The two men exchanged shots and McDonough was wounded. Harrell's horse was hit and fell, pinning him under it. McDonough had emptied his revolver and borrowed one from another Ranger. Standing over Harrell, he pulled the trigger three times, only to have the weapon misfire. On the fourth pull, a bullet shattered the skull of the helpless man.[6]

Ranger Alexander pursued and captured a wounded Union officer who had holstered his pistols. As he began to take the officer's weapons, Puryear rode up in a state of agitation. He had taken a pistol from a Union soldier and was now after this officer, who was his former captor, Lieutenant Coles. Alexander said, "Don't shoot this man: he has surrendered."

Puryear cursed and said, "The rascal tried to hang me this morning."

Alexander asked Lieutenant Coles if that was true. Coles was bleeding profusely from a chest wound and made no response. Puryear then shot and killed Coles. The officer fell between Coles' and Alexander's horses and gave Alexander a dying look that seared itself on the Ranger's brain. Torn with mixed emotion, Alexander dismounted and unbuckled Cole's holsters. Both pistols had all chambers fired. Lt. Thomas K. Coles had fought as long as he could. Blazer's scouts were finished. Twenty-two of Blazer's men were killed, the same number of prisoners taken, and a large number of wounded. Fifty horses were captured. Dolly Richards had one man killed and at least five men wounded.

On Sunday, November 27, Montjoy with thirty-eight men tangled with thirty-nine men of the Loudoun Rangers under Lieutenants Graham and Rhodes. Montjoy was galloping after Ranger M. H. Best when the Union Ranger turned in his saddle and fired his revolver. The ball struck Montjoy in the brain, killing him instantly. Four Confederate Rangers were wounded. Montjoy's loss was a heavy blow to Mosby's command. Lt. Alfred Glascock assumed command of Company D.[7]

The use of artillery had given a new dimension to Mosby's operations and the loss of the guns was a serious blow. His hopes that they would be replaced were dashed when Secretary of War Seddon ordered the artillery company disbanded and its men formed into another unit. It became Company G on Monday, November 28, 1864. Thomas Richards, the brother of Dolly Richards, was elected captain.

John Singleton Mosby was not good for the reputation of Philip Henry Sheridan. To the commander of the Middle Department, Mosby was like a hornet buzzing around his ears, seemingly stinging at will. Mosby could not stop Sheridan, but he could make life difficult. Since the burning of his wagon train and the embarrassment with the news correspondents, Sheridan had been keeping in mind Grant's August 16 orders to burn and hang and was laying waste to the Valley. Carl Sandburg would describe Sheridan as "a destroyer with a system."[8] Tearing the support base out from under the Confederates was U.S. Grant's system, and Sheridan and Sherman were his disciples.

Now Sheridan had won his Valley campaign. Early was finished. The defeated commander who could not keep his guns had lost more than fifty in a month. When he was resupplied with artillery from Richmond, Confederate jokesters tagged them with, "To General Sheridan, care of Jubal Early."[9] The remnants of Early's troops were sent to Lee and, allowing some time for courtesy, Lee would relieve Early.

Sheridan was mopping up. His VI Corps could be sent to join Grant and he looked forward to taking the Cavalry Corps east to strike Lee. Of this time, he would write in his memoirs: "During the entire campaign I had been annoyed by guerrilla bands under such partisan chiefs as Mosby, White, Gilmor, McNeill and others, and this had considerably depleted my line-of-battle strength, necessitating as it did large escorts for my supply trains. The most redoubtable of these was Mosby, whose force was made up from the country around Upperville, east of the Blue Ridge, to which section he always fled for a hiding place when he scented danger. I had not directed any special operations against these partisans while the campaign was active, but as Mosby's men had lately killed within my lines my Chief Quartermaster Colonel Tolles and Medical Inspector Ohlenchlager, I concluded to devote particular attention to these 'Irregulars.'"

On Saturday, November 26, 1864, Gen. Phil Sheridan sent a telegram to General Halleck, who was buried like a mole in Washington. Sheridan wrote:

I will soon commence work on Mosby. Heretofore I have made no attempt to break him up as I would have employed ten men to his one, and for the reason that I have made a scapegoat of him for the destruction of private rights. Now there is going to be an intense hatred of him in that portion of the valley which is nearly a desert. I will soon commence on Loudoun County, and let them know there is a God in Israel. Mosby has annoyed me considerably; but the people are beginning to see that he does not injure me a great deal, but causes a loss to them of all that they have spent their lives accumulating. Those people who live in the vicinity of Harpers Ferry are the most villainous in this valley, and have not yet been hurt much. If the railroad is interfered with, I will make some of them poor. Those who live at home in peace and plenty want the duello part of this war to go on; but when they have to bear the burden by loss of property and comforts they will cry for peace.[10]

One day later Sheridan issued the following orders to Maj. Gen. Wesley Merritt, commander of the 1st Cavalry Division:

You are directed to proceed tomorrow morning with two brigades now in camp to the east side of the Blue Ridge, via Ashby's Gap, and operate against the guerrillas in the district of country bounded on the south by the line of the Manassas Gap Railroad as far east as White Plains, on the east by the Bull Run range on the west by Shenandoah River, and on the north by the Potomac.

This section has been the hotbed of lawless bands, who have from time to time depredated upon small parties on the line of army communications, on safeguards left at houses and on all small parties of our troops. Their real object is plunder and highway robbery. To clear the country of these parties that are bringing destruction upon the innocent as well as their guilty supporters by their cowardly acts, you will consume and destroy all forage and subsistence, burn all barns and mills and their contents, and drive off all stock in the region the boundaries of which are above described.

This order must be literally executed, bearing in mind, however, that no dwellings are to be burned and that no personal violence be offered to the citizens. The ultimate results of the guerrilla system of warfare is the total destruction of all private rights in the country occupied by such parties. This destruction may as well commence at once, and the responsibility of it must rest upon the authorities of Richmond, who have acknowledged the legitimacy of guerrilla bands. The injury done this army by them is very slight. The injury they have indirectly inflicted upon the people and upon the Rebel army may be counted in the millions . . . You will return to your present camp, via Snickers Gap, on the fifth day.[11]

Merritt had been commander of the 1st Cavalry Division. Sheridan had recently relieved Maj. Gen. Alfred T. A. Torbert as chief of cavalry and put Merritt in the job. Wesley Merritt fell upon Loudoun and upper Fauquier like a bolt of lightning. It was not that Merritt could expect to kill or capture many of the elusive Rangers. It was more like the man the *Chicago Times* reported on who climbed trees to capture woodpeckers. He knew he couldn't catch them in that manner, but he sure could "worry them like hell."

Merritt's raid began on Monday, November 28, 1864, a foggy day according to Ranger Crawford.[12] Merritt's 1st and 2nd brigades came through Ashby's Gap where two regiments of the 1st Brigade turned south into Fauquier County and two regiments of the 2nd Brigade did a left wheel northward along the Blue Ridge, some six miles to Bloomfield. The remainder of the troopers covered the center area. Returning in a burning arc, Merritt's men assembled at Upperville for the night. It was not only cavalry at work. One infantry regiment was prowling the crest of the Blue Ridge Mountains, another was marching through Ashby's Gap to Paris. Two more infantry regiments were heading for Millville and Middleburg. The infantry would ensure that anything the cavalry missed was destroyed. They would also assist in the roundup and movement of livestock.[13]

On November 29, 1864, the march continued, with the 1st Brigade moving in Fauquier County through Mosby's haunts of Rectortown, Salem (Marshall) and Plains. Like the fingers of a hand, columns rode eastward, some toward Centreville and another toward Fairfax County. Two columns rode northeast, crossing the line of the Loudoun and Hampshire Railroad, then swinging back toward Middleburg. The two brigades now fanned out and burned out the countryside some seven miles north to Philomont, spending the night there. Merritt's 3rd (Reserve) Brigade commanded by Lt. Col. Casper Crowninshield had been not been involved in the operation; now they were moved into the Snickersville Gap.

On Wednesday, November 30, 1864, the 1st Brigade burned in the south. The 3rd Brigade turned left from Snickersville, keeping the Blue Ridge and Short Hill mountains to its left, where it spread out and torched its way to the Potomac. The 2nd Brigade burned northeast past Hamilton and Waterford, then followed Catoctin Creek westward toward the Short Hill Mountains where it linked up with the 2nd Brigade. Ranger Crawford wrote, "they burnt every mill . . . barn, stable, hay and straw-rick and wheat-stack and even shocks of corn in the field; every cow, horse, sheep and hog they could see was driven off . . . when hogs had been killed by the farmers and hung up to cool off, these men would take an axe, chop the hams off and drop the remainder in the mud."[14] Ranger Scott wrote, "As soon as night invested the scene, blazing fires were visible in all directions, lighting up with their lucid glare the whole of the vast circumference, while columns of dense black smoke mounted up from the burning piles."[15]

December 1, 1864, was a Thursday. Merritt's 1st Brigade passed over scorched earth traveling to Middleburg, Millville and Philomont, then on to Snickersville. The 2nd and 3rd brigades torched their way southward to Pur-cellville and then west to Snickersville, the point of concentration for the attack. Vast herds of livestock were driven before them.

The next day Merritt's troopers passed westward through Snickersville Gap, leaving charred ashes, tears and broken dreams behind them. They had stripped the once rich land, taking some 700 horses, 3,000 to 4,000 sheep, and 5,000 to 6,000 head of sheep. Poultry too numerous to count were destroyed and more than 1,000 hogs were slaughtered. It is likely that nearly 700 barns were burned.

The Ranger attacks could do little to stop the destruction. Ranger Williamson wrote, "Colonel Mosby did not call the command together, therefore there was no organized resistance."[16]

There are few actions that better demonstrate Mosby's sagacity as a leader than the fact that he did not do something foolish at a time when he must have been consumed with rage. To bring his command together at this time would have been the end of it. Merritt could have brought forces against him from all points of the compass. This was not the isolated out-post, wagon train or a detachment of horsemen. Merritt had a highly trained and experienced division of cavalry.

The Rangers did what they could to retrieve livestock for farmers. Williamson said they took these to areas that had already been burned over. They also harassed the cavalry, hovering about them, then swooping in to empty a revolver and gallop away. General Merritt did not feel Mosby's men hindered him in the slightest. In his report to Sheridan he wrote: "the orders from army headquarters were most fully carried out . . . The guerrillas were exceedingly careful to avoid any encounter with any of the parties, even the smallest, that were out on this duty." Casper Crowninshield reported his brigade as having two men slightly wounded.[17]

In his memoirs, Mosby devotes little space to "The Burning." He does not explain his actions or lack of action. In the few lines in which it is mentioned, the stress would have no effect on his operations and serve only to sharpen the appetite of his men for vengeance.[18] Sheridan noted "Merritt carried out his instructions with his usual sagacity and thoroughness."[19]

Recruits kept coming to Mosby's command. In the dispersed conditions under which he operated, he felt control slipping from his grasp. The command would function more effectively if organized into two battalions. William Coleman and Dolly Richards were deserving of promotion and command, and so was Mosby. There was no lieutenant colonel in the Confederate army who was tying down the number of Union troops which Mosby was. Under traditional military thinking, his command was not large enough to have a colonel in command. Yet colonels were commonplace on the Confederate army staff.

On Tuesday, December 6, 1864, Mosby wrote a letter to James A. Seddon, the Confederate secretary of war, outlining his plans for reorganization and the promotions of Chapman and Richards.[20] The letter was not addressed through channels. It was not that Mosby did not respect, indeed, admire General Lee, but Mosby held his appointment through President Davis.

Mosby wanted to discuss future operations and the planned reorganization with General Lee, so he turned the command over to William Chapman and departed for army headquarters. When he left the train at Chester, he recognized a face in the crowd as his former friend from college days, Dr. Aristides Monteiro. The doctor was returning to the trenches of Petersburg after taking a trainload of wounded to Richmond.[21] Dr. Will Dunn was Mosby's Ranger surgeon, but Dunn had a mercenary lust for loot. As Mosby said, "I wanted a surgeon that took more pride in curing than killing."[22]

Monteiro was agreeable to coming with Mosby but was assigned to Gen. Henry Wise's command, which required clearance. Mosby then visited with General Lee, discussed plans of reorganization and got approval to promote William Chapman and Dolly Richards. Mosby's promotion to colonel would not be long in coming. Mosby took Monteiro along when he asked Lee to permit his assignment to his command. Lee agreed, provided that it met with the approval of the medical director, Doctor Guild.

Tired from his exertions, Guild was asleep. When awakened, he refused the request. Mosby was not tolerant of those who crossed him. Monteiro described Mosby's reaction as follows: "This is infamous red tape," said the irate colonel. " This is the devil's work in all military matters. This red tape is the halter of stupidity and indolence that has strangled General Lee and starved the armies of the South. I shall not submit to it. You shall at once grant what I ask, or I will get an order from the secretary of war this very night and have it delivered in the morning."[23] Now jarred fully awake, the senior medical man in the Lee's army gave way and approved the transfer.

Monteiro's brigade commander, Gen. Henry Wise, took it with less grace, saying with heat, "Are you going to leave the 26th Regiment, sir; my brigade sir? Do you know that Mosby fights under the black flag, sir? Do you desire to be captured and hung, sir?" Unwilling or unable to cease his tirade, Wise continued, "you will be hung, sir; hung by the neck like a dog, sir; hung to a tree, sir, as certain as you leave my brigade sir, and join that band of pirates. The worst part is that you will deserve to suffer, sir for leaving my poor 26th regiment sir."[24]

Monteiro wrote that General Wise concluded his tirade by asking that he be sent the best pair of boots of his size that were captured from the Yankees and to do it before Monteiro was hanged.[25]

Mosby returned to his command via Richmond and, on Wednesday, December 21, went to the home of his friend, Joe Blackwell, to attend the wedding of a sergeant. Mosby was dressed in his finest gray uniform, newly purchased in Richmond. Warned that a Union cavalry patrol was approaching, Mosby and Ranger Tom Love rode cross-country to investigate. They encountered and engaged a few cavalrymen whom Mosby reasoned were flank security for the main body. Mosby and Love used their fleet horses to ride out of harm's way, then sat on a hill and watched the enemy move to Rectortown. It was a cold, miserable day. The rain changed to sleet and the trees and ground had an icy coating. The cavalry stopped and began to build fires. It appeared they had settled in for the night.

Mosby determined this group of cavalry was a suitable target to attack the next morning. As it was always Mosby's practice to disperse his men between operations, they now had to be assembled. Mosby and Love turned their horses to begin the alert network that would assemble the Rangers. It was dusk. The two riders were cold, wet and hungry. As they rode past the home of Mosby's friend, Ludwell Lake, Mosby was hungry. When he saw candlelight shining through the window, he decided to stop at Lake's for dinner. As they prepared to dismount and tie their horses, the combat-experienced Tom

Love suggested that he stay outside and keep watch. It was a difficult choice for a commander. Experience said someone should keep watch, but it seemed unfair. Mosby decided the cavalry would not be out on such a night, and there was no danger. Mosby told Love to come into the house with him.

The Lake family was at dinner, and Mosby and Love were soon chewing on spareribs and hot biscuits and washing it down with coffee. The dinner conversation was suddenly interrupted by the sound of horses' hooves in goodly number around the house. Mosby sprang to his feet and opened the back door to the house only to find cavalrymen in the back yard. He turned back to the room just as the front door opened. Several Union officers and enlisted men entered. Mosby put his hand to his collar to conceal his rank. The dining room table was jarred and some of the candles went out.

The cavalrymen were of the 1st, 13th and 16th New York under the command of Maj. Douglas Frazer of the 13th New York. They had captured Ranger Willie Cocke and Sgt. Hugh McIlhany of Mosby's command near Salem. Rangers Richard Buckner and Robert Parrott at Rectortown, after a short break, were on their way to Middleburg to link up with Lt. Col. David R. Clendennin's 8th Illinois when they stopped at Lake's.[26]

Through a window, Capt. John Kane of the 1st New York Cavalry saw the lights suddenly dimming and a man in uniform crossing the room. Without hesitation, the quick-thinking corporal put a bullet through the glass and into Mosby's body. Mosby cried out, "I am shot." Sarah, one of Lud Lake's daughters, screamed. Lake's other daughter, Mrs. Landonia Skinner, Tom Love and the cavalry at the front door ducked for cover. Even the ponderous Lud Lake, who was as broad as he was tall, found the energy to move. Fearing being killed by their own men, the Union officers retreated. Mosby was bleeding heavily, but managed to stagger from the dining room to a bedroom. While doing so, he stripped off his uniform coat with its rank insignia, hid it under a bureau, and then fell on the floor.[27]

Now the cavalrymen returned. It was a time of candles. Night meant poor visibility and shadows. As the cavalrymen burst into the bedroom, the flickering light did not reveal clearly the figure on the floor. They turned to Mrs. Skinner, whose brother was serving with Mosby. When the cavalrymen asked who the wounded man was, she replied she did not know, that the man was a stRanger. They asked if it was one of Mosby's men and Landonia Skinner said it was not.

An officer bent over and asked his identity. Mosby in the voice of a dying man responded that he was Lieutenant Johnson of the 6th Virginia Cavalry. Major Frazer, commanding the Union cavalry, had been warming himself by drinking from his flask, and his reason was clouded by alcohol. He did not search the house or question other people there. They opened Mosby's

Mosby at age eighty in 1915. USAMHI

trousers and pulled up his blood soaked shirt. Mosby believed that he was examined by a doctor, who thought the wound was mortal. It was not a doctor but Major Frazer, who thought, because the ball had entered below and about two inches to the left of the navel, that the wound must be fatal. Frazer decided not to carry away the dying man. In his report, Frazer said that as he ordered his men from the room he remarked, "He will die in twenty-four hours."[28] Mosby wrote that he thought the doctor who examined him did not know much about the human body. He thought he overheard an Irish cavalryman say, "He is worth several dead men yet."[29] Mosby's cloak, plumed hat and boots were taken. With daylight and sobriety, questions began to be asked, but the carelessness of an inebriated officer ruined the chances of a Union success. The cavalry took Love prisoner, but he would not betray Mosby.

By the next morning, an examination of the captured cloak and hat led a sobered Major Frazer to conclude that a senior officer, and likely Mosby, had been shot. A massive search was initiated, but Mosby was gone, hauled to safety on Lake's ox cart. Taken to his father's home by his men, Mosby welcomed the arrival of his doctor. Though wounded six times previously, this was the most serious. He had been shot below the heart, the bullet coursing around his body and coming to rest beneath the skin on the right side. Mosby was still able to issue orders, but would not return to combat until February 1865.

Lee's army had lost mobility. It was pinned by Grant into holding Petersburg and defense of Richmond. Now in that vast area of Virginia that lay to the west, only the Rangers remained. Lee's troops were short on equipment, supplies, food and ammunition—all the needs of an army. Desertions were increasing. Men on both sides of the line had found that war was not a glorious adventure. Men sought to stay out of the army and, once in service many tried to get out. There was the story of the soldier who would tie a string on his bayonet and drop the string in rain puddles. When questioned, he replied that he was fishing. Authorities came to the conclusion the man was insane and discharged him. He said, "That's what I was fishing for."

The Rangers were the best-equipped fighting force in the South and likely the North as well. Their many successful raids had netted them the best equipment and horseflesh the North had to offer, and they had it in quantity. Time and again, Mosby's Rangers had proved their horses could outrun any cavalry unit. Many men rode horses that had once been the pride and joy of a Union lieutenant, captain or top-ranking noncommissioned officer. They had money from their raids. When Union cavalry went through one of Mosby's privates who had been captured, they found he was carrying more than $1,000 in greenbacks. The Rangers bought the best horses in the South. Most Rangers did not use the standard McClellan saddle. They had the brass-trimmed, enamel, leather saddles used by Union officers.[30] Their revolvers were tested and selected from the many that had been taken. There were so many that some men had collections. Their uniforms were of the best cloth greenbacks could buy and were tailor made.

Mosby's Rangers was an all volunteer unit. A number of the privates and noncommissioned officers had been commissioned officers with Lee or Early. They had resigned or been wounded and discharged and chose to come back as Rangers. Mosby did not tolerate deserters from other units. Unlike the rest of the Confederate army, Mosby's Rangers grew ever stronger as the war went on.

Mosby was now a colonel. On Tuesday, January 3, 1865, the two-battalion plan went into effect. William Chapman had been promoted from captain to lieutenant colonel. As second-in-command under Mosby and battalion commander, he took Companies C, E, F, and G into the northern neck of Virginia. According to Doctor Monteiro, Chapman had about 600 Rangers.[31] Dolly Richards had been promoted to major. He controlled the original area of operations with Companies A, B and D. Dolly Richards, who was the Lancelot of Mosby's Rangers, was responsible for the counties of Fairfax, Loudoun, Fauquier, Culpeper and Clarke.

This system had many advantages. The burning had made it difficult for the farmers of Loudoun and Fauquier counties to logistically support the Rangers. By spreading out the command, the food, forage, shelter and security which the Rangers needed would be available. The new system meant the enemy would be forced to defend a greater area, taking more Union troops away from the line facing Lee. More profitable targets would be available. The last, but certainly a consideration, would allow Chapman and Richards to compete with each other in a manner that would not be destructive to the command.

The Ranger life had grown increasingly hazardous. The Union cavalry was now such a vast and potent arm that, while it provided many targets of opportunity, its pursuit was relentless. Carpentry was a major aspect of Ranger survival as they constructed trapdoors and secret compartments in the houses in which they stayed. Frequently, an oilcloth would cover the trap door. A bed, bureau or piano would be rolled over that. At any hour of the day or night, a cavalry patrol might ride up. Now they came in the worst kind of weather and at the most unreasonable hour. There had been a time when they would knock, but now frequently the door was broken open.

The delightful Doctor Monteiro described one such call by the Union cavalry. The doctor was at Glen Welby, a beautiful plantation home near Rectortown. With him was Col. Welby Carter, whose relatives owned the property; Col. Joseph Blackwell, a great barrel of a man; and an unknown youth. These three shared an upper room. Monteiro shared a room with his patient, the wounded Lt. Charles Grogan and Mosby's younger brother, the exuberant Lt. William Mosby, adjutant of the Rangers. Feeling secure, they all went to bed without an escape plan. The sound of horses' hooves and the thudding of carbine butts jarred Monteiro from his slumbers. No sooner did he say the word "Yankees!" than young Mosby was gone from the room. Lieutenant Grogan recommended Monteiro head for the roof, and the doctor grabbed his clothes, pistols and boots and fled. Monterio wrote that one of the little Negro girls of the household staff showed him the way through the attic to the roof. In days gone by, the attic or garret was the last repository of any furniture or clothes which a family cast off. It was much like a storage bank for old items that might someday be useful.

Monteiro struggled to a small window that he found unlocked. He threw his clothing and gear onto a flat roof and climbed after it. There was an adjacent slanting roof but no opportunity to make for it. Much to his surprise, he found the roof already occupied by Willie Mosby. There was little space on the roof that could not be observed from the window, and Willie Mosby occupied that. He had little in the way of clothing with or on him. The roof was partially covered in snow, and Willie Mosby was lying with half his scantily clad body in the snow and half on the icy-cold tin of the roof. There was no room for Monteiro to hide, so he threw himself on top of Willie and dragged his overcoat over them. Monteiro thus had the advantage of an overcoat on top and Willie's body beneath. The young officer could not complain as they both could hear the uproar coming from the house beneath them as the cavalry made a thorough search. They could hear the sound of axes being used and doors giving way. It was not long before the cavalry was in the attic and one of its members at the window. The Yank was possessed of a colorful vocabulary which he used freely as he vowed his intent to find every Rebel in the house. Monteiro could hear another soldier out front yelling about how much he liked a horse he had just found. It was Monteiro's.

Willie Mosby was freezing and, as his body shook, his toes were beating on the roof. Monteiro had greater concerns. He knew that if someone leaned out the window they would see his cavalry boots with their big brass spurs. He determined to reach out and draw them back. He could hear Willie Mosby trying to pray, but the young warrior had not much experience at it. Monterio was reminded of the old sailor whose ship was sinking and was asked to lead the prayer. He said he did not know how to lead a prayer, but offered to take up the collection.

Monterio was trying to draw his boots toward him over the roof, which made a noise that disturbed Willie Mosby at his prayers.

"Good Lord," Willie would say with energetic though whispered unction. "We have done many things we ought not to have done and there is mighty little help in us . . . (Stop that damn noise, they will hear you.) We have left undone many things that we ought to have done (let them damn boots alone), and have mercy upon us dear Lord! (If those damn scoundrels catch us it will be your fault, damn you.) Have mercy on all the sick women and children in the perils of . . . (them damn boots will be the death of us. Stop that noise, by God, stop it!)"[32]

Downstairs, the cavalry had captured Colonel Carter. The unknown youth had climbed to the top of a wardrobe. The wardrobe interior was searched; it was moved and a search made underneath, but no one looked on top. Joe Blackwell was a short, rotund man. He was a great friend to Mosby and often had given him shelter. In reprisal, the Union horseman had burned his house, barn and outbuildings. Blackwell felt he had nothing left to give the Yanks but his neck, and he wanted to keep that. Having no place to hide his corpulent frame, Blackwell leaped from a second story window to the ground and raced away. His flight was more akin to a rolling cannon ball than a speeding bullet. Some of the cavalry were firing at Black-well, some were laughing, and some pursued. From his rooftop perch, Mon-teiro saw Blackwell crash through two fences, race across an open field, leap a stone wall and disappear into the gloom. All this occurred within the space of a half hour.

Monteiro and William Mosby dreaded the coming of the dawn as it likely would reveal their hiding place. They were unaware that three of their Ranger friends had learned of their predicament and were determined to help. Despite being vastly outnumbered, these three Rangers came gallop-ing up to the house and fired into the cavalry, then turned their horses and galloped away. The cavalry immediately stopped its search and rode after them. When the sun was high, Blackwell returned looking much the worse for wear from his flight and the elements. He was proud of his feat, however, and said to Monterio, "Ah! Doctor, I beat them running, but I am mighty cold. Help me for God's sake and give me a drink!"[33]

General Hancock was now heading the Union effort in much of Virginia. He was known as Hancock the superb, a hero of Gettysburg who as he rode slowly back and forth behind his men on Cemetery Ridge was begged to take shelter from the rain of bullets and hail of shrapnel. Hancock had replied, "There are times when a corps commander's life does not count."[34] Hancock wanted to clean out Mosby and sent two regiments to accomplish the task.

Col. Marcus Reno, who years later would be part of the Custer saga in the West, had assumed command of the 12th Pennsylvania Cavalry on Janu-ary 1, 1865. On Monday, March 20, 1865, Reno took five companies of his regiment, eight companies of the 1st U.S. Veteran Infantry under Lt. Col. Charles Bird, Companies A and B of the Loudoun Rangers under Capt. Charles Grubb, and two pieces of artillery on a raid to remove Mosby from Loudoun County.[35] The Union column moved from Harpers Ferry about 1 P.M., crossed the Shenandoah and marched to Hillsborough at the Short Hill Mountains. Here they took five Confederates prisoner. The column bivouacked for the night near Wood Grove. The night was restless with Union pickets being fired upon. When the march resumed the next morn-ing, they found themselves under constant harassment by Mosby's men who hung on the flanks, riding in to empty a revolver and then speed away.

The resilient Mosby had returned to command at the end of February. Now on March 21, he decided to establish an ambush position in the Quaker country at Hamilton (Harmony), some six miles southeast of the Hillsboro. He was not at his chosen site long before Reno and Bird moved their troops toward Hamilton in search of the Rangers.

About a mile south of Hamilton on the road to Silcott Springs, Mosby established a baited ambush. Capt. Alfred Glascock with Company D and part of Company A were concealed in a wood to the left of the road. The bait put before the Union horsemen was twenty-five Rangers led by the rising star Charles Wiltshire. These select few all were mounted on fleet horses that could outrun the cavalry mounts. Their mission was to ride forward and charge Reno's point element, then turn and gallop away at just enough speed to draw the cavalry after them. The ruse worked. Wiltshire's men feigned surprise at meeting the cavalry, fired and fled. Lt. John Black of the 12th Pennsylvania Cavalry promptly led a detachment in pursuit with the remainder of the Union cavalry coming on. Wiltshire was in the rear of his men and as they passed the ambush location, Wiltshire wheeled and killed the closest man in pursuit. With saber drawn, Lieutenant Black was close behind. Wiltshire claimed he disarmed and knocked Black to the ground, stunning him,[36] but Black had been shot in the back during the melee and as he lay on ground paralyzed he was gone through and stripped of his personal possessions.

Reno's lead units had been following Lieutenant Black. Mosby wanted to wait a little longer and called to his men to better conceal themselves. Some of the men misunderstood and began to move forward. Glascock did not allow his men to become confused. He urged his horse out of the woods and yelled, "Come on Company A! Come on Company D!" and charged.[37]

The cavalry was stunned by this sudden turn of events. They tried to rally, but the Rangers were on them with six-guns blazing. The blue-coated horsemen turned and fled with the Rangers in hot pursuit. The Union path to the rear led through a narrow lane with steep banks on either side. The inevitable jam occurred as many men and horses tried to escape through a small opening at the same time. The Rangers poured fire into what had become a mob. Mosby sat on a bank above the fray, a black plume in his hat and his horse prancing as he waved his men on. Away went the cavalry, with the Rangers staying with them. The road was narrow, giving only those Rangers at the head of the column the chance to fire. The faster horses of Rangers permitted them to close, even intermingle, with the cavalry. Ranger John Chew was intermixed with the cavalry and was shot by a cavalryman behind him. Chew would live twenty-five years in pain from the wound. Capt. Robert Walker, Rangers Charles Deer and Robert Chew all reported Charles Wiltshire's horse becoming caught up in the fighting and attacking cavalry horses. The horse "reared upon the backs of the enemy horses, walking upon his hind feet."[38] The Union men reached a woods near Hamilton and attempted to rally, but there was no time to establish a line. Fighting was at point-blank range. Lt. Delose Chase and eight troopers of the 12th Pennsylvania were killed. Soon the cavalry broke and ran again.

Colonel Bird's infantry took a position near the road and opened a hot fire on the Rangers. Mosby saw the danger and called off the attack. Some men rode on through the infantry line, the deafening gunfire or the excitement of the chase keeping them from obeying the order. Rangers James

Keith and Wirt Binford were killed and at least six Rangers wounded. Nine cavalrymen were killed, twenty wounded (two of whom would die) and five were taken prisoner.[39]

Surprise magnifies numbers. Reno obviously believed he faced a large force. His column pulled away from Mosby's sixty men and marched toward Bloomfield. The next morning, Union troops moved before first light, heading for Upperville. Meanwhile additional men were coming into Mosby's ranks, giving him about 200 men to continue the pursuit. The Union troopers next rode for Middleburg, doing a tour of Mosby's Confederacy. They then turned north, linking up with 8th Illinois Cavalry on Little River Pike. From there they moved back to Hamilton, then to Waterford and Harpers Ferry.[40] The Rangers stayed close, always just one hill behind. The best that could be done was hit-and-run harassment, and the pursuit was discontinued when Reno was obviously finishing his tour of Mosby land.

The Union cavalry was not cowering in its camps. Each day men rode out searching houses for guerrillas. Some days were not favorable for the Rangers. On Thursday, March 30, 1865, Union cavalry patrols coming across the Potomac River captured seven of Mosby's men.

Mosby kept his eye on the fighting men who rode the crest of battle; Charles Wiltshire was one of these. Mosby planned to make Wiltshire a lieutenant and ordered him to lead a reconnaissance to Sevenson's depot on the Winchester and Potomac Railroad. Wiltshire set out with Rangers John Orrick, George Gill and Bartlett Bolling. On the way they were joined by Ranger Robert Eastham. On Saturday, April 1, 1865, they were riding near Berryville when Eastman and Bolling stopped at a house for refreshment and information. When they rode to rejoin the patrol, they came to the crest of a hill and saw their three companions riding to attack something at the home of Col. Daniel Bonham. The two Rangers came on rapidly to join in the fun. Two Union soldiers could be seen running toward the stable. One was 1st Lt. Eugene W. Ferris from Springfield, Vermont. Ferris was the twenty-three-year-old adjutant of the 30th Massachusetts Infantry, and he was combat experienced and had been wounded twice. The other man was his orderly, Pvt. James McLaughlin. McLaughlin previously had been a prisoner of war and was wounded in 1863 and 1864.[41] The 30th Massachusetts had been in service since 1862, spent time in New Orleans under Gen. Ben Butler, served at Vicksburg and moved north in time to participate in the battle of Cedar Creek. From January through March 1865, the regiment had been scattered about guarding bridges and other vital points. On April 1, it was ordered to move eastward and officers were gathering their men.[42]

Ranger Charles Wiltshire was riding in the lead and, not bothering to draw his pistol, demanded that Ferris surrender. Ferris replied, "Not with life," and the two men reached for their revolvers. Ferris was a crack shot and before Wiltshire had his pistol from his holster, he was shot in the left breast. Ranger Gill fired but missed. Ferris turned and fired at Gill, inflicting a severe neck wound. Lieutenant Ferris made his shots count. He wounded Orrick, whose terrified horse bolted and threw him from the saddle. Ferris ran to the fallen Wiltshire, took his pistols and swung into the saddle of Wiltshire's horse. He then shouted to McLaughlin who was in the barn getting the horses and the two men galloped away. Orrick had remounted and Eastman had come up firing. Ferris was slightly wounded, but sent two bullets whizzing in their direction and sped for his camp.[43] In the flight McLaughlin was separated from Ferris and captured.[44] He would escape that evening. Rangers Charles Wiltshire and George Gill would die of their wounds.

Ferris was promoted to captain on April 21, 1865. Both he and orderly McLaughlin were mustered out of service on July 5, 1866. He received the congressional medal for his courageous action.

It was Palm Sunday, April 9, 1865, when Gen. Robert E. Lee surrendered the Army of Northern Virginia. Disbelief, gloom and a desperate clinging to rumor swept through the ranks of Mosby's Rangers. President Jefferson Davis had long predicted that General Sherman's army would be cut off in the heart of the South and would be eliminated. Now the rumor was that Gen. Joe Johnston had accomplished that and Southern hopes rebounded. Mosby sent Capt. Robert Walker to Gordonsville to learn the truth of the state of the Confederacy.[45]

Doctor Monterio wrote that he first learned of the surrender of Lee and the fall of Richmond by reading a copy of the *Baltimore American*. He showed the newspaper to Mosby, who was heartbroken and spoke words of sadness, which had no effect on Monteiro's avaricious assistant, Dr. William L. Dunn. The assistant surgeon had just participated in a small raid in Maryland and had robbed a storekeeper of several hundred dollars. Monterio related that on learning of the surrender, Dunn cried out, "This is just like all the rest of my damned luck. If the world had been a cow I would have been its infernal tail, I expect. Now I have been fighting for several years in bad luck—not making a cent—and just as I was getting in a good way of making money for the first time in my life, the damned thing busted up."[46]

The contrast between the patriotism of Mosby and the greed of Dunn struck Monterio. He and other Rangers began to wonder how they would fit into this surrender. The 43rd Battalion of Virginia Partisan Rangers was a regularly constituted part of the Confederate army, but what if the victors did not see it that way? The North had a massive army that could go where it would and do as it wished. What if it saw the Rangers as bushwhackers, thieves and robbers. Would the Rangers be treated like other soldiers or would they become hunted, destined for prison cells and the noose?

General Lee assigned missions to Colonel Mosby and gave him responsibility for the defense of a large part of Virginia, yet no mention of Mosby and his men was made by Lee or his staff during surrender negotiations with Union officers. No dispatch riders were sent by Lee telling him that the Army of Northern Virginia had surrendered. Either Lee forgot about Mosby in the great stress of his surrender or he now considered the Rangers a unit directly under the command of the government which was fleeing Richmond.

Mosby was not willing to submit as long as he could participate in a meaningful fashion. He believed General Johnston's army was still in the field against General Sherman and the opportunity was there to continue the fight.

On Monday, April 10, 1865, Major General Halleck, chief of staff of the Union army, passed a message from Secretary of War Stanton to Major General Hancock, commander of the Middle Military District. The message directed Hancock to inform those under the control of his army of the arrangements between Grant and Lee and included the statement, "The guerrilla chief Mosby will not be paroled."

General Hancock sent a circular from his headquarters of the Middle Military District to be distributed to the citizens in the area. Hancock announced the generous terms that had been given to Lee and his army. Hancock stated that deserters and stragglers from the Confederate army would be allowed to go to their homes in peace and reminded people that those who did not obey would be arrested and be prisoners of war.

Hancock continued with words that reached into the heart of every member of the Rangers. Hancock wrote, "The guerrilla chief Mosby is not included in the parole," and continued, "It is for you to determine the amount of freedom you are to enjoy. The marauding bands which have so long infested this section, subsisting on the plunder of the defenseless, effecting no great military purpose, and bringing upon you the devastation of your homes, must no longer find shelter and concealment among you. Every outrage committed by them will be followed by the severest infliction, and it is the purpose of the Major General commanding to destroy utterly the haunts of these bands if their depredations are continued."

This was sufficient to cause concern to any logical human being. Without a war going on, the full resources of the United States could be put to hunting down the guerrilla bands. The populace that had been so supportive no longer was a reliable base. They had suffered enough in what was being called the Lost Cause. Reasonable Southerners might still resent the North, even hate it, but those who still had houses or barns did not want them burned over something that was lost.

Mosby was more knowing of guerrilla war than to think he could hide out in the mountains and conduct a protracted campaign. The terrain may have been suitable and some volunteers may have been willing, but Mosby's Rangers depended upon the support of the population. Mosby's base of operations was burned out. The food and forage he needed did not exist and he would now have the full attention of the Union army. Those Southern civilians still willing to support him likely would have found themselves transported. In his corncrib jail, the captive Lieutenant Brewster had, while awaiting Mosby's lottery of death, heard the Rangers talking of where they stayed, places Brewster remembered as Mrs. Smith's, Mrs. Jones', Auntie Plimpton's, Cousin Jamison's and Granny Longnecker's. The Civil War was not a television war. Had guerrilla tactics continued, the Union likely would have taken a page from Gen. William Sherman's Atlanta campaign and put Auntie Plimpton and Granny Longnecker on railroad cars and shipped them south, perhaps to the Florida Everglades, then burned anything they left behind. There were more than 10,000 Union cavalry available to hunt those who choose to continue and many thousands of Confederate deserters and civilians ready for a return to the old flag and willing to inform. Mosby continuing in guerrilla warfare against the United States was fantasy, and he was wise enough to know it.

As Mosby looked at the shadows of the evening, they looked like the shape of a gallows. He was rescued by a surprising source. Ulysses S. Grant was the man who ordered Sheridan to hang Mosby's men and to burn out the Shenandoah Valley. But Grant was also a reluctant soldier, a man whose father forced him to go to West Point, a man who despised the conqueror Napoleon and would tell the Duke of Cambridge, "all I did was try to make myself useful."[47]

Grant and Lincoln were of one mind and that mind was geared to reconciliation not revenge. Lincoln put it best when he said, "Let 'em up easy." Both Lincoln and Grant considered the Confederates their countrymen.

So great was the prestige of Gen. U.S. Grant in April of 1865 that not even the secretary of war could deny him. On April 12, Major General Hancock sent a message to Major General Halleck. The message began, "In accordance with the instructions of General Grant, I yesterday sent a communication to Mosby offering to receive the surrender of his command on the same terms as indicated in General Grant's dispatch to General Lee."

Hancock went on to say he thought Mosby was more likely to disband than surrender. Hancock believed that as the Rangers had fine horses and arms they would try to hold on as long as possible. Hancock was prepared to hunt them down with his cavalry.

Hancock used the form of having a subordinate send the letter to Mosby. It went out over the signature of Brevet Brig. Gen. Charles H. Morgan, Hancock's chief of staff. Mosby was offered the same terms as Lee, and an officer of his rank to discuss the surrender with him. He was allowed to select the time and place of the meeting and was urged to follow the example of General Lee.

April 14, 1865, was Good Friday to Christians. For evening entertainment, Mary Todd Lincoln wanted the president to attend a play. It was a comedy called "Our American Cousin." The president did not want to go but gave in to the pressure of his wife. General and Mrs. Grant were invited to attend in the President's box, but Mrs. Lincoln had turned her temper on the wives of several generals, including Mrs. Grant, and Julia Grant did not want to be in her company. It was during this play that assassin John Wilkes Booth, aided by the dereliction of duty by the police officer assigned to guard the door to the president's box, killed President Lincoln with tragic results to the reconciliation of the nation.

Mosby was not aware of the murder, but this was a time of great unease for the Ranger leader. His face bore the look of determination, but inside was a turmoil of doubt. His command was intact, well armed and equipped with the supplies required to continue the struggle. If he fought as a guerrilla without being in concert with a Confederate army, he would bring a wave of devastation on the countryside. If he was to continue fighting, it would have to be with Johnston's army in an unfamiliar land. Many of his command would not go south with him. He had no information of Johnston's intention or ability to continue the fight. Perhaps he had already surrendered. A few days prior, Hancock's message had told him he was an outlaw. Now he was being treated like a soldier, but could that be relied upon?

In response to Hancock, Mosby decided to stall and on Saturday, April 15, 1865, sent a party consisting of Doctor Monteiro, adjutant William Mosby, Capt. Walter B. Frankland and Lt. Col. William Chapman under a flag of truce. The men brought a letter in which Mosby wrote that other than the copies of surrender documents provided him with General Morgan's letter, he had received no notice of that action. Mosby wrote he did not feel events justified the surrender of his command, but he had no desire to see a useless waste of blood. He wrote that he was ready for a short suspension of hostilities to enable him to contact his authorities.[48]

Mosby's second in command, Lt. Col. William Chapman, was the logical man to conduct negotiations on Mosby's behalf, but Chapman had not been present when the letter from General Morgan arrived. Monteiro was dispatched to the Chapman residence where, despite the protest and fainting of Chapman's wife, Colonel Chapman saddled his horse and accompanied the party.[49]

The ride to Hancock's headquarters at Winchester was made in weather that fit the mood. Cold, rain and gloom surrounded them as they swam their horses across the Shenandoah. They stopped for the night at a house about four miles from the town. It was here they learned of President Lincoln's assassination and that Mosby was accused of the murder.[50]

The Confederates were treated with the utmost courtesy by everyone they met. When General Hancock took Monteiro's hand and treated him with every kindness, Monteiro felt like the prodigal son and was inspired to write, "I for the first time encountered a doubt as to the righteousness of our cause."

General Hancock was pleased to see Mosby's delegation. His courtesy and kindness were genuine, but Hancock's intent on the ending of opposition was overriding. Hancock told Chapman that the war was over, and those who did not understand would pay a heavy price. Hancock had ordered 10,000 men into Loudoun and Fauquier counties to burn every house that gave refuge to Mosby and his men. This was not an idle threat. To the great relief of Chapman and Monteiro, Hancock said that because the delegation had arrived, he was rescinding the burning order.[51]

Much to the surprise of the Confederates, General Hancock said he would be pleased if they would dine with him. Montiero was quick to accept. He wrote that on the way to General Hancock's mess tent, they had to pass through throngs of Union soldiers who understood that Mosby was in the camp. When asked who was Mosby, Monterio and Chapman would point to each other. Montiero was much taken by the comments of the Union soldiers and reported them as follows: "Many were the comments made, and some not of a decidedly complimentary character as to our appearance. Some of the men expressed great surprise that 'sich an onery man should have made such a fuss in the worl'." Others said they thought "he must hav' bin an ugly cuss from the way he behaved heself, but he wuz re'ly wus lookin' than we had spozen he wuz.' 'Lor! what a hard-lookin feller! No wonder he fout so, frum his looks. He looks like a foutin' man he do.' I ain't never seen no wus lookin' man, I ain't; he looks like he wuz bought outen a drove of wild men, he do. He don't look like he tame yet, he don't . . .'" The remarks continued, being summed up with, " I didn't think he looked like that, I didn't."[52]

Hancock dictated his desires to his chief of staff, General Morgan, and the delegation was sent back to Mosby carrying a letter signed by that officer. Hancock was not interested in an armistice with Mosby but was willing to give him three days to make up his mind, provided there was no conflict. At noon on Tuesday, April 18, 1865, a Union colonel would be waiting at Mill-wood for Mosby's response.

On Monday, April 17, Union general Sherman and Confederate general Johnston met at Durham Station, North Carolina. The process of the surrender of Johnston's force began and continued the next day. Fighting ended in North Carolina.

On April 18, Mosby arrived at Millwood and met with Union Brig. Gen. George Chapman. Subject to the approval of Hancock, a cessation of hostilities was agreed "to be in force for ten days, commencing on the Thursday April 20 at 12 M., and ending on the 30th at 12 M." Hancock knew Mosby had exercised governmental as well as military control in his area of operations. He wanted Mosby to use his influence to end guerrilla warfare by other bands or individuals.

The agreement concluded that during the cessation of hostilities if the Confederate army opposing General Sherman would capitulate or be dispersed, "Colonel Mosby will disband his organization [the 43rd Virginia Battalion]."[53]

Johnston had surrendered and Mosby had given his word that on that surrender the existence of his Rangers would end. The agreement made with General Chapman and approved by General Hancock did not call for Mosby to formally surrender his command, but to disband the organization. On Friday, April 21, 1865, the morning began with rain followed by fog. It was gloomy weather befitting the spirits of the men who assembled at Salem (Marshall) in Fauquier County on Mosby's call.[54] He rode among his men and greeted them as they came in.

There were 600 Rangers at the final roll call; another hundred were absent, languishing in federal prisons. They were well uniformed, riding the finest horses, and carrying tested weapons. Gloom hung heavy on them, and the black plumes many sported in their hats were wilted in the morning wet. Still there was an aura of quiet pride. What they and their comrades of Gilmor's, White's, and McNeill's Rangers had accomplished was a military miracle. These few, comprising less than 2,000 men, had taken some 35,000 Union soldiers from the front and forced their usage as rear area guards. At least the equivalent of two Union corps had been kept from the fight.

The command was formed. It was too large for Mosby's speaking voice to carry to the rear ranks, so each squadron leader read Mosby's remarks to his men.

SOLDIERS,—— I have summoned you together for the last time. The vision we cherished of a free and independent country has vanished, and that country is now the spoil of a conqueror. I disband your organization in preference to surrendering to our enemies. I am no longer your commander. After an association of more than two eventful years, I part from you with a just pride in the fame of your achievements, and grateful recollections of your generous kindness to myself. And now at this moment of bidding you a final adieu, accept the assurances of my unchanging confidence and regard. Farewell! John S. Mosby, Colonel.[55]

In a play on words some writers point out that Mosby did not surrender his men as a unit but disbanded them. In truth, Mosby and all of his men were required to seek their parole. It was surrender or be hunted down and shot or hanged. There were many in the North who wrongly considered John Singleton Mosby to be no different than Quantrill or Champ Ferguson and wanted him at the end of a rope. The Northern belief that he was a bandit grew to a howl of outrage when the rumor continued to spread that Mosby had been involved in the assassination of President Lincoln. Secretary of War Stanton sent a message to that effect to General Hancock at Winchester. As Mosby was in negotiations for surrender of his unit with General Hancock at the time, the falseness of the accusation was easily proved.[56] Still the old cry of pirate, combined with assassin, created problems for him. One of the plotters in the killing of Lincoln and the attempted murder of Secretary Seward was a former member of Mosby's command. Unfounded rumor would tar Mosby with the same brush he would persist in using with George Armstrong Custer in the false allegation that Custer order the hanging of his Rangers at Front Royal. To be obstinate is on occasion useful to a soldier in war but it can be a disservice to a man's character in peace.

Mosby's wife tried pleading his case with President Andrew Johnson but was rebuffed. She tried General Grant and gained his sympathy. Mosby was paroled as of February 2, 1866. He settled in Warrenton, Virginia, resumed a law practice and raced horses. Gratitude was a hallmark of Mosby's character. His appreciation drew him to support of U.S. Grant, who became president of the United States. Mosby clearly understood what Grant had done for him. He would write that when General Lee surrendered at Appomattox, he and his Rangers were in northern Virginia, 100 miles away. U.S. Secretary of War Stanton applied the same terms of surrender to all Confederate soldiers in Virginia, except Mosby and his men. It was General Grant who overrode his political senior and extended the same courtesy to Mosby and his Rangers.[57] Mosby would never forget that.

When Grant became president, Mosby visited the White House, and there was immediate rapport between the two former enemies. Despite the anger of many in the South and even an attempt on his life, Mosby was outspoken in his support of Grant. A feeling of mutual respect grew. In his memoirs, U.S. Grant wrote of the man he was once willing to hang, "Since the close of the war I have come to know Colonel Mosby personally, and somewhat intimately. He is a different man entirely from what I had supposed. He is slender, not tall, wiry, and looks as if he could endure any amount of physical exercise. He is able, and thoroughly honest and truthful. There were probably but few men in the South who could have commanded successfully a separate detachment in the rear of an opposing army, and so near the border of hostilities, as long as he did without losing his entire command."[58]

The price of friendship with Grant was painful. Gen. Jubal Early and his "South will rise again" clique reviled Mosby, as they did Confederate general James Longstreet who also recognized that prolonging the hatred served no useful cause.

Mosby felt that the greatest compliment he and his Rangers ever received was from Union general Phil Sheridan, who knew from experience what Ranger action could do. Sheridan wrote that, in his 1864 Shenandoah Valley campaign against Early, he had 94,000 Union soldiers against not quite 20,000 Confederates. Sheridan penned, "The difference of strength between the two armies at this date was considerably in my favor, but the conditions attending my situation in a hostile region necessitated so much detached service to protect trains, and to protect Maryland and Pennsylvania from raids, that my excess of numbers was almost canceled by these incidental demands."[59]

Grant was a good friend. To spare Mosby facing the daily hatred of people he had so well served, Grant made Mosby the U.S. counsel to Hong Kong, where he served for seven years. Even in his last days, Grant did not forget Mosby. He arranged a lucrative job for Mosby as an attorney with the Southern Pacific Railroad. More success came to the Ranger leader as a lecturer and military historian. Mosby wrote he felt he had lost his best friend when Grant died.[60]

As the years advanced against him, Mosby became absent-minded and quick to anger at the changes in society. His body was in the present, but his mind was in the past and he could not change. He always believed the big lie that Custer was responsible for the hanging of his two men and ignored the misdeeds of his own soldiers. He wished he had died in the war. Death chose its time on May 30, 1916. He was buried in Warrenton, Virginia. His Rangers never forgot him, but at death, most of his praise came from the North.

Ranger John S. Mosby is buried in grave G-26 in the old cemetery in Warrenton, Virginia. Located on a rise near the monument and mass grave of 600 Confederate soldiers, the headstone is in the company of others, including the brave Capt. Richard Paul Montjoy. The simple inscription of this unique Ranger leader reads:

Col. John S. Mosby
43rd Battalion Virginia Cavalry
Born Dec 6 1833
Died May 30 1916

PART TWO

Thunderbolt

CHAPTER SIX

The Thunderbolt
of the Confederacy

John Hunt Morgan was born at Huntsville, Alabama, on June 1, 1825. His father Calvin Morgan was a merchant, a transplant from Virginia and a distant relative of the famed Revolutionary War Ranger Daniel Morgan. His mother Henrietta Hunt was the daughter of John Hunt, a wealthy businessman in Lexington, Kentucky.[1] The opportunities offered them by Henrietta's father resulted in the family moving to near Lexington, when John Hunt Morgan was four years old. Young Morgan received a good education for the time and grew up in comfortable fashion in Kentucky's beautiful bluegrass country, where fine horses and horsemanship were a way of life. In 1846, at age nineteen, Morgan enlisted for the Mexican War and was elected first lieutenant of Captain Beard's company of Colonel Marshall's regiment of cavalry.[2] His unit experienced heavy fighting at the battle of Buena Vista.

As his father and grandfather were businessmen, John Hunt Morgan had good training in business techniques and received financial support. He quickly acquired property and became a clothing manufacturer. Morgan lived in a time when a man's honor was rigorously defended. When a young man, Morgan fought several duels and was seriously wounded in one encounter. Militia service of the period was both patriotic and social. Morgan enjoyed military activities and in 1857 organized a militia unit called the Lexington Rifles. His men were proud of his leadership and adopted the motto "Our laws, the commands of our captain."[3]

When the Civil War began, Morgan was doing well financially, but his young and frail wife Rebecca Bruce was ill and would die in July 1861. Weighed down with sorrow, Morgan found the call to battle a better path out of sadness than the accumulation of money. At age thirty-six, he was the oldest of six brothers, five of which were of age when the Civil War began. At the beginning of the war Morgan was six feet tall and weighed 185 pounds. His gray-blue eyes seemed sleepless to his friends, and his tireless nature and perhaps the inner grief kept him going when others fell by the wayside.

John Hunt Morgan, the "thunderbolt of the Confederacy." He
led his men through a series of
stunning victories until his bold-
ness produced rash decisions.
USAMHI

A Union regiment was stationed near Lexington and it was feared it
would seize the weapons there. Gathering together several dozen of his like-
minded friends, on the night of September 20, 1861, Morgan used the guise
of holding a drill to take all the weapons from the armory. The next morning the removal of the weapons sparked a conflict between those who supported the Union and those in favor of secession. An order was issued for
the arrest of Morgan, who rode out of town at the head of some 200
Lexington men who wanted to fight for the South. On the evening of Monday, September 30, 1861, Morgan and his companions linked up with the
Confederate army assembling on the Green River. They then split up, joining various Confederate units.

The war was opportunity for a man shedding sorrow to find release in
adventure. Kentucky was a border state wooed by both sides as its men met
on the field of battle. The vacillation was annoying to both sides, but
Kentucky was accessible to invasion from North and South and wished it
from neither. Kentucky had no desire to emulate Virginia and be a battle-
ground. In the end, much to the disgust of Southerners and native sons who
supported the Confederacy, life under the Stars and Stripes seemed a better
option and Kentucky stayed with the Union. Tennessee was divided. Most of
the slaveholders were in western Tennessee and strongly for the Confeder-

ates. East Tennessee included small farms and mountain people of the Appalachians. They were strong for the Union. There were many fights, and raid and ambush took a steady toll of men from both sides.

Morgan was a superb leader. He had a quick and decisive mind, and his manner and voice were those of a man accustomed to command. He was elected captain of those who stayed with him, and as he and his volunteers were skilled riders and well mounted they were assigned the Ranger role of scouting for the army.

Morgan had as friend, brother-in-law and second-in-command Basil Duke, who like Morgan had an aptitude for the life of a Ranger. Duke noted that Morgan "was a capital judge of information." Duke felt that Morgan could infallibly detect the true from the false, and determine the precise value of what he heard and that Morgan also had "a good eye for the country."[4] There were those who believed it was Basil Duke who was the wiser officer. The history of the 7th Pennsylvania Cavalry recorded "Colonel Duke was Morgan's adjutant, and the general opinion of Union officers, who had the honor of meeting this command in battle, was that Prentice, of the *Louisville Journal,* told the truth when he said; someone might hit Duke on the head and knock Morgan's brains out."[5]

Morgan went on overnight scouts four or five times a week, usually leaving just after dark. He and his men performed intelligence-gathering to determine location and disposition of Union forces and sought to capture prisoners. On several occasions Morgan posed as a Union officer, but his face quickly became known.

These expeditions were a training ground. On at least one occasion the riders covered sixty-eight miles in twenty-four hours. Getting accustomed to rapid movement over long hours in the saddle hardened the men. Many mistakes were made during this learning period, but on each effort Morgan, his officers and men became a better unit. Their attacks on Union pickets created an anger on the Union side who saw this as bushwhacking. In response Basil Duke noted:

> There are certain rules of war whose observance humanity and the spirit of the age demand. Prisoners ought not to be killed or mistreated, unless in retaliation; the terms of capitulations and surrenders ought to be honorably fulfilled and observed; war ought not to be made on non-combatants. But the soldier ought to be content to take his chance. It is more soldierly to teach pickets to fight when attacked, than to complain of it, and a picket who will allow himself to be surprised on his post ought to be shot.[6]

Each time he made a night attack on a picket, Morgan caused a response. Union commanders had to assume that a full-scale attack was coming and turn out their men. This created a constant tension and was wearing on the soldiers of the United States.

Serving as the eyes and ears of some general was not sufficient to hold Morgan's interest. He was a man accustomed to thinking for himself, to doing what he believed was correct. Under that philosophy, he would rise and fall as a military leader. From the onset, the raid was the specialty of John Hunt Morgan and his Rangers. He used the mobility of select horses and skilled riders to move rapidly and hit hard. Duke noted that when on the attack Morgan threw detachments right and left, confusing the enemy and thereby paralyzing their vigor. Not knowing which objective was being attacked, the enemy would scatter his forces in defense. Morgan would quickly reassemble and strike. When withdrawing, Morgan sought to avoid any contact that would delay his movement or pin his force in position.

In civilian life Morgan had enjoyed the many advantages given Kentucky and Tennessee by the Louisville and Nashville Railroad. The steel wheels on steel rails were a vital part of family and commercial life in the two states. Now the L&N was a vital artery carrying the lifeblood of Union effort in the region. The Louisville and Nashville Railroad became a prime target for John Hunt Morgan. He would give its directors many sleepless nights.

Starting with nine select companions, Morgan began to roam behind enemy lines. He displayed the reasoned audacity that is the hallmark of a successful raider. Rapid concentration of force, speed and surprise were hallmarks of his raids. One of his earliest raids was on a railroad bridge under construction at Bacon Creek. Morgan led his men from Bowling Green, moved rapidly and reached his objective to find that the bridge guard felt the night was for sleeping. Morgan burned the bridge and learned from the experience how careless men in rear areas can be. Taking only two men, Morgan went into Union lines and burned the railroad depot at Rowlett's Station. In January 1862 Morgan and five men rode sixty miles to the town of Lebanon. Getting inside a Union encampment, he burned stores, and captured nine prisoners and a large flag. He escaped, despite the pursuit of two companies of cavalry.

As Morgan was aggressive, always eager for action, men sought to enlist under his leadership and his command grew quickly. No matter the number, Morgan seemed at home in command. One of his early recruits was George Ellsworth, a man so skilled as a rapid telegrapher that he was known as Lightning. Ellsworth carried a revolver, but his best weapons were a portable electric battery and telegraph key. The telegraph had become a vital part of military communication, but few men had thought of its vulnerability to interception over miles of unguarded wires. Morgan operated behind Union lines and using Ellsworth's skills he became privy to the communications of Union commanders and even influenced their actions.

An early and friendly relationship was established with Terry's Texas Rangers, who like Morgan's command were serving under Gen. Thomas C. Hindman. The two units shared the Ranger philosophy of war and were closely allied in camp and in battle. They patrolled the Green River country of Kentucky, conducting ambush and raid operations and enjoying the game. Union armies were on the march and Fort Henry and Fort Donaldson fell to the soldiers in blue. It was with anger and great sadness that Morgan and his men learned the Confederate army was withdrawing from Kentucky. On February 14, 1862, the pullout began. At Nashville, the withdrawing Confederates found a city of rumor and panic. Small groups of soldiers, often without leaders, had escaped the fall of Fort Donaldson and contributed to the confusion. Nathan Bedford Forrest, who had refused to surrender, led his horseman into town. General Floyd was in command of the city and knowing the city must fall began to transport what supplies could be taken in the eighty to ninety wagons he had at his disposal. The rest of the supplies were to be destroyed or distributed to civilians. Constantly harassed by civilians and officers making demands, looting and drunkenness, Morgan and his men camped at La Vergne, a railroad station about midway between Nashville and Murfreesboro. Within visual distance was the camp of the Union 4th Ohio Cavalry and the two units skirmished frequently. Morgan led a patrol into the Ohio camp and killed an officer. Taking fifteen men he rode to Nashville, penetrated Union defenses and burned a Union steamboat. A Union brigade now occupied the location of the 4th Ohio Cavalry. Morgan led his men through the lines and hid them in thickets along the road. Unsuspecting Union officers and soldiers who came along the road were captured. Disguised in a blue overcoat, Morgan approached a detail of ten Union soldiers led by a sergeant. The men were lounging with their arms stacked. Morgan posed as a Union officer and, placing himself between the Union soldiers and their weapons, began to berate the sergeant and his men for allowing Morgan to penetrate the camp. Drawing his pistol Morgan informed the sergeant that he and his men were under arrest for dereliction of duty. The Union soldiers thought they were being marched to the guardhouse, but they were marched into Confederate captivity. Thirty-eight prisoners were brought back. Sixty more Union soldiers were captured, but escaped when smoke from burning wagons attracted the attention of the 4th Ohio Cavalry. The Union horsemen killed one of Morgan's men, wounded two or three and captured the same number.

The success of these raids began to build a reputation for Morgan on both sides of the lines. Freelance Confederate partisan Rangers were operating in the Nashville area and Union soldiers were being killed in ambush. These actions were widespread. Though Morgan was now raiding with fewer than 300 men, soldiers and newspapers of both North and South began to attribute any ambush or raid in the area to him. A legend grew and Union commanders began to believe his force consisted of many thousands of men.

Some thirty miles from Nashville, to the north of the Cumberland River, was the small Tennessee town of Gallatin. Its importance was that it was located on the line of communication between Louisville and Nashville. The juncture of roads, railroad and telegraph brought Gallatin to Morgan's attention. Leaving Murfreesboro, he passed his command through Lebanon, camping nearby, then crossed the Cumberland River and Canoe Branch ferry and moved on to Gallatin. Once in town Morgan tricked the Unionist telegraph operator into getting him the latest news. He then took a locomotive that was on a siding and ran it for several miles to see if a nearby railroad tunnel could be destroyed. He found that wrecking the tunnel would consume too much time. Staying around Gallatin for several days, he destroyed the locomotive and railroad supplies, the telegraph and other military stores. After returning to Murfreesboro and a short rest, Morgan marched his command toward the Confederate army at Shelbyville. They crossed the Tennessee River at Decatur and reached Byrnesville near Corinth.

It was now April 3, 1862, and the Confederate army under Gen. Albert Sidney Johnston was preparing for an attack. The Union forces had reached Pittsburgh Landing, on the southern bank of the Tennessee River some twenty miles from Corinth. There was a little church there called Shiloh. Over the objections of many of his officers, including his subordinate General Beauregard, Johnston meant to use about 45,000 men to surprise the Union army under U.S. Grant. Pittsburgh Landing was the only suitable place on the river to bring large numbers of men ashore for a considerable distance. Grant had moved his army, also of about 45,000, into what amounted to a riverside assembly area. From here he intended to attack south. Marching to join Grant was another Union army of 50,000 men under Don Carlos Buell. Johnston meant to defeat Grant's army before Buell arrived.

On April 4, 1862, Morgan was promoted to colonel. Although promotion was gratifying, Basil Duke noted that Morgan put a higher value on the information that when this campaign was over he would again be allowed to act independently.

Flush from the victory at Fort Donaldson, neither Grant nor his subordinate William T. Sherman expected an attack. Few men in either army were combat experienced; they were in the early stages of learning to be soldiers. Most of the Union commanders had not established outposts. The scouts of Confederate Albert Sidney Johnston informed him of this. Johnston was a superb general who understood this was a great opportunity for the South and was not cowed by Union numbers. He told his aide Col. William Preston, "I would fight them if they were a million."[7] On forming for the attack, the Confederate army was dispersed in three forward lines with the 6,000-man division of General Breckinridge as the reserve and Morgan's horsemen to the left of Breckinridge.

Heavy rains and the late arrival of General Polk's corps delayed the Confederate attack, but on the morning of April 6, 1862, the Confederates caught most of the Union troops unprepared. Most, not all.

Union general Benjamin Prentiss of Illinois had sent patrols to his front and they made contact with the advancing Confederates. As the Rebel attack came home routing his other units, Prentiss held his ground with such vigor that the Confederates called the area the hornet's nest. Sixty Confederate guns were lined up to pound his 2,000 men and Confederate troops concentrated on this small force. All about him, Union troops fled for the river, but Prentiss held, buying precious hours until Grant had time to regroup. Of critical importance to the battle was one bullet fired by a Union soldier from the hornet's nest. That shot pierced the leg of General Johnston, cut an artery and the skilled Confederate general, thinking it a minor wound, bled to death.

Morgan, augmented by the Texas Rangers, was trying to ride down a Union regiment in a thick woods and having difficulty doing so. A number of Texas Rangers were shot from the saddle and their riderless horses galloped about in panic. By late afternoon the Union lines were holding. Buell's army arrived and was ferried across the river by steamboat. On the death of General Johnston, General Beauregard, who had not had his heart set on the attack, was in command. Beauregard decided to withdraw the Confederate army to Corinth. Tactically, Shiloh was a draw. In strategic terms the North came out on top. This battle was a golden opportunity for the South that likely died with Albert Sidney Johnston. Shiloh was a horrendous battle, one of the bloodiest of the Civil War. Basil Duke, who was seriously wounded at Shiloh, noted that "many who seek military distinction, will obtain it posthumously, if they get it at all."[8]

Eager to get away from the restrictions of the main army, Morgan got permission to make a raid into Tennessee and strike Union forces in the rear. On April 23, 1862, he assembled 325 men from various units at Brynesville where three days were spent readying horses and packing mules with rations, ammunition and equipment. They marched on April 26,

passed through Iuka, Mississippi, and the following day made a difficult
high-water crossing of the Tennessee River.

On April 30, Morgan and his men reached Lawrenceburg and camped.
The following day's march took them near Pulaski. Here, Morgan learned
that 400 Union troops had passed through, moving toward Columbia. They
were convalescents, men who had been wounded or were sick. Now they
were on light duty and putting up a telegraph line. Morgan went after them.
The Union soldiers learned that Morgan was coming and tried to throw up
a breastworks, but Morgan's charge collapsed the Union defense and the
Union soldiers were taken prisoner. They were sent back to Pulaski under
guard and their twenty wagons burned.

The night was spent in a village of Union sentiment. Morgan told his
men to act as though they were Union troops. The result was good food for
both men and horses. The townspeople even provided horses and money as
they were assured they would be reimbursed by Union paymasters at
Nashville. On May 3 the column was at Harrington, about fifteen miles from
Shelbyville. They burned cotton to keep it from use by Union forces, tapped
into the telegraph line and sent false messages. At the close of a busy day,
they had reached the town of Lebanon in Wilson County. Here the entire
command was billeted in town with Morgan's headquarters at the hotel.
Orders were issued for the command to be formed up at four in the morning. Outposts were established on roads leading into town, but the night
rains were uncomfortable. The outpost on the Murfreesboro road took
advantage of a nearby house to get out of the weather.

In the early morning darkness of May 5, a Union force under Gen.
Ebenezer Dumont came down the road and an entire regiment had passed
the pickets before the Confederates were aware of their presence. Pleasant
Whitlow, one of the men on outpost, quickly mounted and raced cross-
country to get ahead of the Union troops. Whitlow reached the hotel just as
Union soldiers did and was shot dead as he shouted warning.

In the town the sleepy-eyed Confederates were trying desperately to get
to their horses and escape. They were driven like chaff before the wind.
Many were captured. Men of Morgan's Company A made a brief stand at the
edge of town. They killed some Union troops and captured seven officers
who rode into their position by mistake. Morgan had lost some 225 men and
was trying to get away with the hundred he had left. Union cavalry charged
them with sabers swinging and Morgan's men scattered. Morgan's magnifi-
cent horse Black Bess was terrified by the confusion and broke the restraint
of her bridle. Morgan was unable to control the animal who ran away with
him. The chase continued for thirteen miles to the town of Rome. There
those Confederates who remained were able to break free. Twenty-one miles

from Lebanon they found a ferry over the river. A skilled rider, Morgan had managed to regain control over Black Bess. Now the men had to choose between taking the time to bring their horses or leaving their mounts and being ferried quickly across the river. Despite the pleadings of his men, Morgan would not risk leaving soldiers behind if the enemy made another sudden appearance. All horses, including his own, were left behind and Morgan crossed the river and made a getaway. He found to his dismay that he had only about twenty men left. Morgan cried that night, but other men straggled in and when he reached Sparta, he found that about 150 had escaped. Though many of his men were poorly armed, Morgan felt he had sufficient force to continue the attack. He lived by the principle that audacity is a vital ingredient of a raid.

Morgan reasoned that word of his defeat would have Union garrisons less watchful. If he could strike smaller positions he could rearm and re-equip his men from the enemy. With this in mind, he marched toward Bowling Green. This was terrain he and his guides knew well.

Morgan and his men were careful to travel by forest paths and little-known roads. Normally his approach would have been unobserved, but there were many in Tennessee who favored the Union. These men had organized as home guard units and they had a curious but effective communications system. Wherever Morgan rode he could hear the blowing of conch shells and horns. The sound was a notification that Confederates were in the area. No matter how he pressed forward, Morgan could not beat the speed of sound.

He also was being mocked. Union pianos were tinkling out a song and voices were raised in a song called "Kentucky! O Kentucky!" that was sung to the tune of the Confederate ditty "Maryland My Maryland."

John Morgan's foot is on thy shore
Kentucky ! O Kentucky!
His hand is on thy stable door
Kentucky ! O Kentucky!
You'll see your good gray mare no more;
He'll ride her till her back is sore
And leave her at some stRanger's door
Kentucky! O Kentucky!

Near Glasgow, Morgan halted his men for rest and sent local scout John Hines to Bowling Green to determine if it was feasible to attack the town. Hines reported 500 enemy troops were present and the plan was scrapped. Morgan believed the garrison would remain in the town to defend it. He therefore decided to cut the Louisville and Nashville Railroad and begin capturing trains. On May 11, Morgan and five Rangers rode the twelve miles to Cave City, Kentucky, with the main body of his command following. While he watched the railroad tracks, a long train came into view. As his command came up, Morgan stopped the train, destroyed the engine and forty-four cars and took captive a large force of railroad repairmen. A passenger train was soon stopped by blocking the train tracks with timber and as the train slowed, blocking it in the rear in the same fashion.

A Union major named Coffee opened fire with two pistols, blazing away until the chambers were empty. Duke wrote that with bullets smashing woodwork and glass around him, the Union major then stepped out on the platform and called "Stop firing, boys! I'm out of ammunition and have concluded to quit."[9] Morgan was the soul of courtesy, charming the female passengers. When one lady begged that the Union officer who was her husband not be taken away, Morgan gave the man back to her. Carried away by his own courtesy to the fair sex, he even gave the ladies the train instead of burning it. There was the matter of $8,000 that was taken, but Duke excused that as government funds. Others believed all greenbacks fit that description. Nonetheless it was a fine raid, an experience that added zest to life. The train had been going to the Cave City Hotel near Mammoth Cave and a fine meal had been prepared for the passengers. Morgan and his men greatly enjoyed the repast.

Morgan now marched for the Cumberland River. At the close of a long day of hard riding, an incident happened that Basil Duke felt was indicative of Morgan's approach to command. In the past twenty-four hours, Ben Drake, a Ranger on point, had been in the saddle far longer than Morgan. Yet at the close of the march, Morgan ordered Drake to take care of his horse. Drake was angry, but complied. When Drake returned to the house where Morgan had his quarters, Morgan had made a place for Drake to sleep before the fire. The next morning Morgan awoke Drake and told him to eat breakfast as the command was ready to move. Drake complained that he had not had time to care for his horse. Morgan responded that he had fed, groomed and saddled Drake's horse himself as he wanted Private Drake to be able to sleep longer.[10]

Morgan passed through Burkesville and twelve miles on forded the Cumberland River. From there he marched to Sparta where his Tennessee troops went home. He continued on to Chattanooga and there he left his command and personally proceeded to Corinth to obtain permission to again raid in Kentucky. While he was absent, his primarily Kentucky Rangers were joined by two companies of Texas Rangers who were commanded by Kentucky-born officers. At Chattanooga, the recovered Basil Duke rejoined Morgan as second in command and brought with him thirty more men.

Morgan and Duke set about the process of reorganizing the three companies of men they had into the foundation of a regiment. They were joined by 300 men of the 1st Kentucky Infantry whose enlistments had expired.

Now, with the command numbering nearly 400, they were organized into seven companies. It was named the 2nd Kentucky with the Texans preferring to retain their own identity. Morgan's men were a ragtag bunch with torn shirts and the seats of their pants worn through. Men were greatly embarrassed as they marched before women, knowing their buttocks were showing. Despite their appearance, they were all bred to the saddle, skilled riders who were becoming increasingly well-trained in tactics and could maneuver as one on command. They frequently would fight dismounted, forming a long line with the two ends curving forward like the horns of a bull. Duke wrote that men could be controlled better on foot. He did not think of Morgan's command as cavalry, but as mounted riflemen who would use the horse as transportation to the battle and then fight on foot, backed up by a small reserve of hard-charging horsemen. As Rangers they fought away from the main army, often separated from friendly troops by hundreds of miles.

Morgan understood the use of combined arms. Had he been given the men and equipment to do so, his command would have been made up of hard-hitting, self-contained battalions of infantry-cavalry-artillery. Organizing based on what he had, Morgan trained his men to attack mounted or dismounted. In the early going men carried whatever weapons they could find. The rifle was critical to them and the Enfield was their weapon of choice. The short version of the rifle did not have the range and accuracy, and the long version was too cumbersome for use on horseback, so a medium length was most desired. Morgan wanted carefully aimed fire, so the single shot rifled musket was the choice. Morgan's Rangers sought revolvers and at the height of their raiding each man normally carried two Colt six-shooters. In artillery, the lightweight mountain howitzers were preferred. When General Bragg's ordnance officer took them from Morgan, Basil Duke said it nearly caused a mutiny and he himself would have gladly tied the officer to the muzzle of a howitzer and shot (him) off.

Morgan was joined by Lt. Col. George St. Ledger Grenfell, an English officer who roamed the world looking for any war in which he could fight. He fought with the French in Africa and then against them. He took part in the Sepoy Rebellion, the Crimean War and was with Garibaldi in South America. Duke said of Grenfell that he "may have encountered something early in life that he feared, but if so, it had ceased to exist."[11] Grenfell became Morgan's adjutant general. He drove the Confederate War Department to distraction by making up all reports in the manner of the English army. Grenfell was sixty years old when he joined Morgan, but he had lost none of his fighting spirit. Duke described Grenfell jumping his horse over a stone wall at Union troops and slashing left and right with his saber. Grenfell liked to fight with his fists, but was suffering from an injured finger that was not healing fast enough to suit him. He wanted the surgeon to amputate the finger, but the doctor said it would heal. Grenfell took a knife and cut off his own finger. The next day he beat up his landlord and thrashed another British volunteer in an argument over a mule.[12]

Toward the end of June 1862 a 300- to 400-man Georgia regiment of partisan Rangers under Colonel Hunt arrived to take part in the raid Morgan was planning. Now Morgan was a brigade commander with some 876 men. With this force, Morgan departed from near Knoxville, on July 4, 1862, for a thousand-mile raid into Kentucky. Some 200 of the men were without weapons and many others were poorly armed and mounted. Still Morgan was confident they could equip themselves from the enemy.

They rode to Sparta, where they met Champ Ferguson—a scout, bushwhacker and ruthless man who was considered a hero by secessionists and murderer by Unionists. Even Ferguson's own brother sought to kill him. Ferguson and his Union counterpart Tinker Dave Beatty of Fentress County engaged in frequent raids against each other's holdings and supporters. Their combat ranged the Cumberland Mountains between Tennessee and Kentucky and was a deadly struggle between men who knew each other. The raid and the ambush was the specialty of these adversaries and it was war devoid of mercy. If Ferguson was a hammer, Beatty was a viper. Both were deadly. As often happens in war, the two mortal enemies had a deep respect for each other's ability. Champ Ferguson's side lost the war and he would be tried by military court on twenty-three specifications, accused of murdering more than fifty men. Tinker Dave Beatty was a reluctant witness against his old foe, one the prosecution was not sorry to see leave the stand.

At his trial, Ferguson's defense revealed the mindset of a bushwhacker. He stated that he was a Confederate officer in Kirby Smith's and Morgan's command. He denied that he had personally performed all the killing attributed to him, but freely confessed to numerous executions of individuals who were unarmed, indeed helpless, at the time he killed them. He admitted that he killed William Frogg while Frogg was sick in bed, saying "He was lying on a bed, and on seeing me pulled the cover over his face. I then shot him twice." He admitted killing sixteen-year-old Fount Zachery saying "I shot the lad . . . and stabbed him after he fell to the ground." Ferguson and his men entered a Confederate hospital where he murdered Lieutenant Smith of the 13th Kentucky Cavalry (Union), a relative of Ferguson's first wife, while Smith was wounded and in bed. He admitted killing Reuben Wood, Joseph Stover, Elisha Kogier, Peter Zachery, John Crabtree, Offey Williams, Boswell Taber and men he did not know personally. On

October 20, 1865, Champ Ferguson was hanged in Nashville. Ferguson was unrepentant to the end, telling a reporter, "I was a Southern man at the start. I am yet and will die a Rebel. I believe I was right in all I did."[13]

Ferguson's fate was in the future as he and his companions guided Morgan from middle to east Tennessee, with the column facing a 110-mile march to Knoxville. The route was covered by Union bushwhackers, including Tinker Dave Beatty whose sniping was a constant threat.

In the vicinity of Tomkinsville, Morgan came upon a battalion of the 9th Pennsylvania Cavalry under Maj. Thomas J. Jordan. Vastly outnumbering Jordan's cavalry, Morgan's men pinned them on a high hill and overran the Pennsylvanians, getting a rich haul of supplies and capturing Jordan. Colonel Hunt of the Georgia partisan Rangers was wounded and would die a few days later.

The command then moved on to Glasgow where some of the men had been recruited. "Lightning" George Ellsworth tapped into the telegraph lines and gathered information about the whereabouts of Northern units. Morgan also had Ellsworth send false reports about his location and one that Nathan Bedford Forrest had taken Murfreesboro and captured the garrison. Morgan's fantasy became reality when some time later Forrest did just that. The column pressed on through the night, getting within fifteen miles of Lebanon. Company B was sent to cut the rail line between Lebanon and Lebanon Junction. The rest of the command rested until late afternoon, then pressed onward around six miles from Lebanon. It was now dark. At the bridge over Rolling Fork River they were fired upon and Morgan's hat was shot off. The opposition was soon dispersed by a shot from a howitzer and the attack went on. They moved into Lebanon and took nearly 200 prisoners as the town surrendered.

Having been hurt by a previous lack of security, Morgan put out pickets that were carefully instructed. Company B had stopped a train from coming into Lebanon with reinforcements. The train quickly backed up and escaped, but Lebanon was found to be a Union storehouse. Good weapons and ammunition were abundant and the command was soon well armed. All Union supplies that could be taken by Morgan's men were gathered up and the rest given to civilians or destroyed. Once again the column was on the road. A carefully selected body of twenty-five Rangers under the command of Lt. Charles W. Rodgers of Kentucky served as point. They moved 300 to 400 yards in front of the column with three messengers posted at hundred-yard intervals between the Rangers and the head of the main body. Scouting parties were also sent to front, flanks and rear. When action began, these parties would rally and form the reserve.

They rode through Springfield to Macksville, where one of the scouting parties had a brush with the home guard and some of Morgan's men were wounded and captured. Morgan had taken prisoners and an exchange was made. They continued to Harrodsberg, a friendly community where tired men were treated to home-cooked meals and forage for their horses. Some twenty-eight miles from Harrodsberg was Lexington, the headquarters of the Union forces in the area and Morgan's objective. He sent out parties to destroy bridges and cut rail lines around Lexington to isolate the town. At the same time, Morgan sent scouting parties toward Frankfort to fake an attack on that town.

At a little railroad town between Lexington and Frankfort, appropriately named Midway, the Rangers captured the telegraph operator and his key. "Lightning" George Ellsworth had the operator send several trifling messages while he studied the style of the operator. Then Morgan and Ellsworth sat down together and began to send messages designed to mislead their Union opponents. The gist of the false reports was the Morgan was on his way to Frankfort with a large force. The final message was:

Frankfort to Lexington:

Tell General Ward our pickets just driven in. Great excitement. Pickets say the force of the enemy must be two thousand.

Operator[14]

Ellsworth rendered the telegraph equipment inoperable, leaving Union commanders to believe that the operator had fled or the raiders had destroyed the line. Brushing aside home guards, Morgan headed for Georgetown, some twelve miles from Lexington and eighteen from Frankfort. From here Morgan could watch the developing moves by Union commands. As was Morgan's practice, detachments were thrown out over a large area, burning bridges, attacking home guards and destroying supplies. Georgetown was firmly for the Confederacy and Morgan's men were sheltered, fed and provided with all the information the townspeople had. Those few who supported the Union were confused by the entrance of the troops. One Union man seeing Captain Gano expressed delight as Gano was a school chum from earlier days. Brimming with excitement, he handed over dispatches from the home guard headquarters. After reading the document, Gano shocked his former friend by telling him the troops were not Union, but "Morgan's Texas Rangers."[15]

Union forces in Lexington remained strong and Morgan recognized he had to clear out of enemy-controlled territory before he was trapped. He delighted in taunting Union commanders and had Ellsworth sending off messages designed to ridicule his opponents, generals Jeremiah Boyle and George Prentiss.

Somerset
July 22 1862
George D. Prentiss, Louisville

Good morning George D. I am quietly watching the complete destruction of all Uncle Sam's Property in this little burg. I regret exceedingly that this is the last that comes under my supervision on this route. I expect in a short time to pay you a visit and wish to know if you will be home. All well in Dixie.

John H. Morgan
Commanding Brigade

General J. T. Boyle, Louisville

Good Morning Jerry. This telegraph is a great institution. You should destroy it as it keeps you too well posted. My friend Ellsworth has all your dispatches since the 10th of July on file. Do you wish copies?

John H. Morgan
Commanding Brigade[16]

Morgan next marched for Cynthiana, twenty-two miles from George-town and thirty-two miles from Lexington. Strong detachments were sent to drive Union reconnaissance parties back into Lexington and prevent them from determining his intention. At Cynthiana the Confederate Rangers met a mixed, but determined force of Union infantry and home guards, all under the command of Lt. Col. John J. Landrum. This group had one cannon, a 12-pounder, and used it well.

To get into town Morgan had to cross a bridge over the Licking River and the single gun of the defenders covered the bridge. Houses lined the banks of the opposite side of the river and these were filled with marksmen. When Morgan sought to bring up his howitzers the gunners were driven off by good shooting. A Confederate gunner named Talbot stood the heat as long as he could, single-handedly loading and firing several shots while rifle balls were striking the cannon and its wheels around him.

Fords were found about a mile distant both above and below the town. Morgan sent Capt. Richard Gano and the Texas Rangers above the town and the Georgia partisan Rangers below the town to cross the fords and close on both sides of the town. Morgan's Kentuckians would storm the bridge when the flanks closed in.

In furious fighting the defenders were driven from position. The English warrior Grenfell charged the depot and had eleven bullets strike his clothes, horse and body, but came away with only slight wounds. Some ninety of the Union soldiers and civilians were killed or wounded and 420 captured. Morgan had forty casualties. The Union commander, Landrum had a fast horse and despite a hard chase, he escaped capture.

Morgan's men moved on to the little town of Paris which quickly surrendered. The Rangers were now hotly pursued by blue-coated soldiers. A force of some 2,500 men under Gen. Green Clay Smith was marching fast from Lexington. Rapid movement by the Rangers was hindered as it was Morgan's policy to not leave behind wounded who could be safely moved. Wagons were rounded up for the injured and the command pressed on. Reaching Winchester, south of Lexington, they rested briefly then crossed the Kentucky River on a night march and headed to the small community of Richmond, arriving there around 4 A.M.

At Richmond, townspeople told Morgan that Union troops were converging from various points of the compass to catch him. The officers and men were exhausted, but there was no respite. The march continued south through the communities of Crab Orchard and Somerset. En route Morgan burned any wagons and captured artillery that would slow him down. These included 130 Union wagons and considerable amounts of weapons, ammunition and supplies. From Somerset the command marched to Stagall's Ferry and crossed over the Cumberland River where it was greeted by Confederate pickets. On July 22 they continued twenty-one miles to Monticello, Kentucky, then on to a base camp at Livingston, Tennessee, where they rested. Morgan reported the raid had taken twenty-four days. His command had traveled more than 1,000 miles. They had captured seventeen towns, scattered 1,500 home guard troops and captured some 1,200 Regular troops. Vast amounts of Union supplies were destroyed.

While they were at Livingston rations were scarce and the men were hungry. One of the men decided he no longer wished to be part of an effort that treated him so and asked to quit. Basil Duke described his punishment:

He was deprived of his horse, arms and equipments, and "blown out" of the regiment; that is, upon dress parade, he was marched down in front of the regiment (after his offense and the nature of the punishment had been read by the Adjutant), with the bugler blowing the "Skedaddle" behind him amid the hisses of the men, who were thoroughly disgusted with him; he was then driven away from the camp.[17]

In August 1862, Confederate general Braxton Bragg was at Chattanooga, pondering an advance on east Tennessee and Kentucky. Morgan's men had moved northwest of Chattanooga to Sparta, Tennessee. Morgan's Rangers numbering about 700 men went into the routine of camp life. The days were filled with drill, followed by drill, followed by drill as there was drill at company and regimental level and on foot and in the saddle. Caring for equipment and horses consumed many hours. Morgan's Rangers were a unit whose young leaders achieved rank through performance in combat, thus there was trust and confidence between officers and men. Morgan's reputation was constantly growing and honors were coming his way. Newspapers reported that the Confederate ordnance department was giving Morgan the pistols of Gen. Barnard E. Bee, the officer killed in action at Bull Run who had given Stonewall Jackson his nickname.

Morgan, Duke and Nathan Bedford Forrest knew that the army of Union general Don Carlos Buell was scattered guarding various parts of Tennessee. Confederate Braxton Bragg had 30,000 men at Chattanooga and it was expected that he would move on Buell. Bragg was cautious. Buell was a capable general, but his ability was better understood by his opponents than his seniors, who were badgering him to attack. Buell was assembling transport at Nashville to facilitate an offensive move. To disrupt Buell's preparations, Morgan took 110 men on a raid to cut the railroad between Louisville and Nashville and to strike the Union post at Gallatin. General Bragg hoped Morgan's moves would draw off Union cavalry in pursuit, and movement by the Confederate army could be better concealed.

On August 12, 1862, Morgan's men rode out from Sparta and the next day crossed the Cumberland River at Sand Shoals ford, three miles from Carthage, then moved to Dixon, about eight miles from Gallatin, Tennessee. They were traveling through secessionist country and were well treated. Some thirty men under Capt. Joseph Desha of the 1st Kentucky Infantry (Confederate) joined them with a few opting to become a permanent part of Morgan's command. With guides who knew the countryside, they bypassed the Union outposts with Rangers dropping off to take these pickets from the rear. Captain Boone, the Union commander at Gallatin, was captured at a house in town and agreed to write a surrender note to his command. Thus 200 Union infantry fell into captivity. Now, without senior

Union commanders knowing it, Morgan was in control of Gallatin. It was not long before a train arrived and eighty fine horses, several hundred new Springfield rifles and other stores were captured.

George Ellsworth was a wizard at the telegraph key but usually unsuccessful at other matters. Ellsworth decided to go hunting for a noted Union bushwhacker named Captain King. For reasons known only to himself, Ellsworth took Lieutenant Colonel Grenfell's horse. On the Englishman's horse was his favorite saddle, tied to that was his favorite coat and inside the coat was concealed all the gold he had brought from England in order to live in the comfortable style to which he was accustomed.

Ellsworth and a companion found Captain King and soon wished they hadn't. King, being unafraid of two men, opened fire on them with shotgun and revolvers. Ellsworth's companion was wounded and the two Confederates fled. Grenfell's horse, saddle, coat and gold were lost in the process. For three days Ellsworth had to be hidden to keep the Englishman from killing him.

Once back at the telegraph key, Ellsworth proceeded to fool Union operators into believing his messages were authentic. Ellsworth sent a false request for a special train of supplies. The train was sent and all was in readiness to effect the capture. When the train was within six miles of Gallatin a courageous black man warned the engineer that he was steaming into a trap and the plan fell through. Ellsworth spread the word that Morgan had 4,000 men and that among them were 400 Indians who were ready to lift scalps. The word spread quickly and towns began begging for Union troops to protect them. Morgan left a small detachment at Gallatin while his main body moved to Hartsville, about twenty-six miles away.

The Louisville and Nashville Railroad now became the recipient of Morgan's attention. L&N directors screamed for protection as machine shops and bridges were burned and depots laid waste. Morgan destroyed property valued at $10 million and throttled the supply line of General Buell by wrecking an 800-foot tunnel north of Gallatin and a railroad bridge between Gallatin and Nashville. Railroad cars were run into the tunnel and set ablaze. The fire burned out the wooden supports and this and the heat caused rock slides into the opening. The tunnel was closed for many weeks. This was a critical supply route for Buell's army. The superintendent of the railroad estimated Morgan kept the line closed nearly five months of the year. Morgan's destruction of this supply line was a key factor in General Buell retreating to Louisville.

At various places along the railroad, Union troops had built stockades that were log fortresses. These fortifications were built of thick timbers, more than ten feet high, buried in an upright position, loopholed for rifles and surrounded by ditches. Normally artillery was needed to defeat these defenses. But the Confederates did not have artillery with them on the raid. Lacking guns, Morgan had to resort to other means. Though he lost some key men, Morgan was able to trap part of a stockade garrison outside the walls and follow them closely into the enclosure, which then was captured.

Buell was furious. He put all his cavalry under the command of Gen. Richard W. Johnson and told Johnson to find Morgan and kill him. A series of small unit actions were fought between the advance of the Union cavalry and Morgan's scouts, but Morgan had the advantage of operating in friendly territory and locals told him of Johnson's route of approach. When Johnson's cavalry came in pursuit, Morgan was waiting in ambush near Hartsville, Tennessee. The long line of dismounted Rangers had carefully selected firing positions. They waited as the cavalry charged with drawn sabers, then at thirty yards opened fire and sent the Union horsemen reeling back with many saddles empty. Johnson reformed and charged again only to have more men shot down. As the Union survivors withdrew, Morgan's men leaped to their horses and followed. Some 200 Union horses had been killed and the dismounted cavalry was quickly rounded up. Morgan sent three columns after the remainder. After a pursuit of three miles, Basil Duke's men found Johnson and what was left of his command attempting to make a stand. The Rangers dismounted and charged. After a brief but stiff fight, General Johnson and about five officers and thirty enlisted men surrendered. The result of this engagement was sixty-four known Union dead and many wounded. Some 200 Union prisoners were taken. Morgan lost seven men killed and eighteen wounded. He led the rest of his men back to Hartsville, knowing he was in control of the area.

Nathan Bedford Forrest had heard Morgan was in danger of being trapped and rode to be of assistance. When Forrest arrived on August 22, 1862, he saw the situation was well in hand and hurried off on a destructive sweep around Nashville. To have both Forrest and Morgan in their area of operations was a nightmare to Union commanders. Morgan and Forrest captured so many Union prisoners that their raids were being hindered. They would parole these captives on their honor not to fight again until properly exchanged for a Confederate prisoner. The Union troops would then be sent off in a direction that would have them roaming the countryside, but not meeting their own troops and commanders. It had a demoralizing effect.

On August 28, Braxton Bragg made his long-awaited move. Bragg's objective was to take eastern Tennessee and Kentucky, and if possible strike north. Throughout the first week of September 1862 the drive went forward, bypassing Buell's army at Murfreesboro and Nashville and heading toward

Cincinnati. For a time, it appeared that city would fall to the Confederates, but Buell was marching to head off Bragg.

Morgan and his men rested at Hartsville for a few days until Morgan received orders summoning him to meet with Gen. Kirby Smith at Lexington on September 2, 1862. Warmed by the praise of the South, Morgan and his men rode to Scottsville in Allen County, Kentucky, near where they spent the night. They then continued on to Glasgow and Columbia the next day. Morgan's two mountain howitzers had been taken by Bragg and Morgan wanted them back. Morgan sent his brother, Captain C.H. Morgan, and a seventy-five-man escort to bring the guns back and was traveling slowly as he awaited their arrival.

A Union cavalry regiment also was after the guns and in its pursuit rode within twenty yards of the Confederate detachment hidden in the woods. The two guns were in position and manned but the Confederates did not risk their loss and refrained from firing. After a two-day wait by Morgan at Columbia, the guns joined the main body. Possessing artillery, Morgan could now deal with any blockhouses he should locate.

Morgan's Rangers now moved on toward Liberty, in Casey County, southeast of Louisville and northeast of Nashville. This was Union country, mountainous and wooded. Union bushwhackers took full advantage of the opportunity and it seemed to Basil Duke that they were fired at from behind every fourth or fifth tree. The ambush war was one of no quarter; prisoners were killed by both sides. Duke noted that Confederate colonel Clarence Prentice wrote in an official report, "It is a gratifying reflection that many of them will whack no more."[18]

The Rangers rode on to Hustonville, southwest of Lexington, where they learned that Bragg's invasion of Kentucky was under way. Kirby Smith had opened the Southern effort with a victory near Lexington and had driven Buell's blue-coated soldiers north toward Louisville. On September 4, 1862, Morgan and his men rode into Lexington, enjoying the cheers of its citizens. Confederate fervor was at a high point and recruiting progressed rapidly. Morgan's command was used to pursue the withdrawing Union troops northward toward Ohio and an invasion of that northern state appeared imminent. The Rangers searched the mountains to locate and capture disorganized groups of Northern soldiers. Learning that a recently recruited Union infantry regiment and cavalry were near Walton, south of Cincinnati, Lt. Col. Basil Duke led a force against them. The Union pickets were captured, but the infantry regiment had learned its lesson and formed quickly with the cavalry behind it. Duke and his men got some eighty prisoners and left while the enemy stood in formation. Duke then took 450 men and the two howitzers and attacked the town of Augusta on the Ohio River southwest of Cincinnati. Two armed steamboats and home guards were the defense of the town. Duke put his two howitzers on a high hill and they dropped some shells on the steamboats. The boats quickly slipped their moorings and steamed out of range. House-to-house fighting erupted as the men of the town fought the Confederate column. The fighting was hand-to-hand with men being shot, knifed and bludgeoned. Any house from which the Confederates were fired upon was set ablaze by Morgan's men. The battle raged only for twenty minutes, but was so intense that Duke had twenty-one men, including some of his best officers, killed and eighteen wounded. Duke had intended to continue the raid into Ohio, but he was out of howitzer ammunition and had 200 prisoners to guard. Taking all the carriages, wagons and buggies he could find to transport wounded, Duke moved nine miles south to Brookville. The loss of friends in battle is a hard experience for soldiers and there was no joy in the victorious column.

Morgan was sent off to eastern Kentucky to stop the approach of Union general George W. Morgan who was marching to the relief of Ohio River communities. Support for the United States was strong in the east and the Confederate Morgan found it difficult to get information. He had about 1,000 men fit for duty and from these sent reconnaissance and raiding parties to keep him informed and to harass and delay the long Union column. There were times his Union namesake had as much information as John Hunt Morgan did. As the Ranger commander and a few of his officers were watering their horses at a stream, a Union cavalry regiment appeared on a hill above them. Morgan had to bluff his way out and began to shout commands as though he were commanding a large force. Confused, the Union commander ordered his horsemen to fall back.

It rained frequently, and to stay dry Morgan and his men wore oilcloth capes captured from Union soldiers. Fortunately, a cape concealed his uniform when he was stopped on a trail by some Union bushwhackers. Morgan posed as a Union colonel, engaged the men in conversation and listened to them tell of their ambush tactics and the execution of prisoners. He then got the drop on them and took them prisoner. Fighting in the mountains with ambush a constant threat was not the duty Morgan sought, but he believed he was fighting to rid Kentucky of what he saw as a Northern invasion.

In late September 1862, Buell marched his army to Louisville. From there Buell sent detachments to Frankfort and Lawrenceburg. Bragg was aware of the movements, but not of the scope. He could not tell if these were defensive moves or if Buell intended to attack him. While Bragg sat and pondered, Buell marched the bulk of his troops via Bardstown and Springfield to Perryville, thus cutting into Bragg's rear and moving into position to cut Bragg off from his lines of communication and supply. By Wednesday, October 8, 1862, Buell had confused Bragg and had control of

Railroads were a favorite target of Civil War raiders. USAMHI

him. Bragg accused the people of Kentucky of being overly fond of money and ease and came to the conclusion he could not save them for the Confederacy. Parts of each army met at Perryville in a stiff and costly fight that tactically gave slight advantage to Buell, and strategically played havoc with Bragg's mind. Bragg complained of migraine headaches. Although he talked with confidence, he seemed incapable of offensive action. When Morgan's command rode into Lexington it learned that Braxton Bragg had made up his mind to withdraw from Kentucky. Duke wrote, "The movements of Buell had completely mystified General Bragg, and the latter was not only reduced to the defensive, but to a state of mind pitiable in the extreme. He acted like a man whose nerves by some accident or disorder had been crazed."[19] The news of the withdrawal was a hard blow to John Hunt Morgan, Basil Duke and all Confederates of Kentucky. The struggle for their home state was being ended.

On October 10, Morgan's Rangers were on the left flank of the army, performing outpost duty. As they were to provide early warning, Morgan's men had not lighted fires. As darkness and rain fell upon them, the men

could see the long semi-circle of campfires marking the position of the
Union army. Morgan believed that whatever Union units were on picket duty
also would be doing without fire. He sent out a patrol led by Capt. Jacob T.
Cassell to learn the disposition of these Union positions. Despite the darkness, Cassell returned detailing the Union cavalry picket, the infantry regiment that supported it and a cannon that was in support. Prior to sunrise
Morgan attacked the Union picket and found Cassell had given him total
knowledge of what Buell's army had at that location. Cassell had run the perfect patrol.

As Bragg's retreat continued, Morgan's Rangers were given the mission
of rear guard. Thirty miles separated the opposing armies. The Confederates were not heavily pressed by Union troops and Morgan felt he could raid
in the enemy rear and be back into position without affecting his mission.
His corps commander General Smith agreed and Morgan rode off with
1,800 men, marching on October 17 toward Lexington. Part of the route
was over unfamiliar terrain through country with strong Union sentiment.
In the darkness, Morgan secured the services of a guide by posing as a well-
known Union officer. The guide performed his duties skillfully and was
aghast when Morgan, on nearing Lexington, identified himself. Despite difficulties that included his troops mistakenly firing on each other, Morgan
took control of Lexington.

A courier rode in from General Smith countermanding Morgan's
orders. General Bragg wanted Morgan sent to guard a saltworks in Virginia.
The order was given to one of Morgan's staff officers who, having a low
regard for Bragg and an equally low opinion of the order, put the paper in
his pocket and did not tell Morgan.

Order or not, it was time to quit Lexington. Union troops under Gen.
Ebenezer Dumont were dogging Morgan's trail. Morgan hurried to the west
through Lawrenceburg with Dumont thirty minutes behind him. Morgan
continued on a path slightly southwest through Bloomfield and Bardstown.
A patrol riding north toward Louisville captured 150 wagons filled with supplies for the Union army. Taking what they desired, the men of the patrol
burned all of the wagons except for two that belonged to sutlers and were
loaded with merchandise Duke described as ranging from "cavalry boots to
ginger bread."[20]

Morgan's men spent the night at Litchfield then continued moving
southwest and crossed the Green River at Morgantown and Woodbury.
Union troops were in Bowling Green. Basil Duke, who commanded the 2nd
Kentucky under Morgan, decided to set up an ambush along the road
between Bowling Green and Morgantown. His men took up position on one
side of the road and waited. Sure enough a Union column moved out of

town and marched toward them. Much to Duke's amazement the Union soldiers did not pass in front of them, but stopped just short of the Confederate position and set up their own ambush a few hundred yards away. Both the Union and Confederate troops were on the same side of the road waiting for their foes to pass before them. Duke waited till the Union soldiers were in position then slipped away.

Meanwhile Bragg continued to retreat south. The Confederates respected Union general Don Carlos Buell, but his own seniors did not. Lincoln and Halleck felt Buell had allowed Bragg to escape and decided to fire him. Buell was relieved of command on Friday, October 24, 1862, and replaced by Gen. William Rosecrans.

Since they had left Lexington, more than 500 prisoners were taken by Morgan's Rangers. Continuing southwest the column moved on to Hopkinsville, wreaking havoc on the Louisville and Nashville Railroad by burning bridges and destroying equipment. From Hopkinsville they rode southeast into Springfield, Tennessee, then easterly to Gallatin. Now they were back in position to guard Bragg's flank as his army inched its way around Murfreesboro.

Bragg was still moving at a snail's pace and subordinate commanders were restless. Confederate general John C. Breckenridge, who had been vice president of the United States, had information that the Louisville and Nashville Railroad had some 300 railroad cars at the Nashville suburb of Edgefield. The cars were under the protective guns of Union artillery that could fire from Capitol Hill in Nashville. Breckenridge wanted to use two raiding parties. Reinforced with a brigade, Nathan Bedford Forrest would approach Nashville from the southeast and create a diversion. Meanwhile John Hunt Morgan would move by night and make a rapid run in and out, destroying the cars.

The distance would require a night march as daylight travel would reveal their intent. While the guns of Forrest were engaging to their west, Morgan's men made a night ride into Edgefield, approaching from the north. An alert Union picket of forty to fifty men saw them and fought fiercely to prevent their passage. All trees in the area had been cut down and obstacles removed, leaving a clear field of fire for the Union soldiers. Well led, they were difficult to dislodge and retired fighting. The Union garrison responded quickly to their support, moving up infantry and artillery. The best Morgan and his men could do was burn a few cars and get out fast. The raid was a failure.

Upon return to base camp they found another mission waiting for them. The Union Army of the Cumberland, now under General Rosecrans, was on the march from Kentucky toward Nashville. The soldiers in blue were coming southwest on two roads, the Louisville and Nashville Pike and the Scottsville and Gallatin Pike. Rosecrans had General Crittenden's corps serving as his advance guard on each road. At Tyree Springs, Morgan decided to ambush the Union column coming on the Louisville and Nashville road. On the morning of Saturday, November 8, 1862, he put 200 men in ambush including, Basil Duke and Texas Ranger Richard Gano. The Union advance had reached the springs and spent the night there while Morgan was marching to get to them. The Union cavalry scouts rode by, followed by Union infantry who were singing while they marched. The Confederate volley was delivered at seventy-five yards. Men went down, but the reaction was fast. Shocked by the first fire, the ambushed troops opened with artillery on Morgan's position, then the U.S. troops charged.

Morgan pulled his men out, then brought them back against the road farther up. Both sides now had men scattered. Morgan and his chief scout, Lt. Tom Quirk, were capturing Union stragglers when a Union regiment came up and cut them off from the Rangers. Morgan bluffed, claiming he was a Union colonel, but his gray uniform and prisoners did not lend credence to that story. The Union prisoners Morgan had taken were grinning, knowing he was captured. Suddenly acting angry, Morgan said he would prove his case by bringing up his regiment. He jammed his spurs into his horse and with Quirk following, leaped a fence and got away.

The remainder of his men had captured some fifty prisoners. These were paroled and sent to Kentucky by a route that would not put them in contact with the oncoming Union force.

Narrowly avoiding entrapment by the aggressive moves of the oncoming Union army, Morgan moved his total command near Lebanon, east of Nashville and north of Murfreesboro. Rosecrans reached Nashville around November 12 and set a ring of strongly fortified positions around the city. Morgan's men spent much of the month in patrolling and skirmishing. Morgan now had a brigade-sized organization and Lt. Tom Quirk's company of Rangers had been increased to about sixty men.

Beefed up with additional forces, including the troops of his uncle Col. Thomas H. Hunt, Morgan gathered some 1,400 men and soon was off on another raid near Hartsville, Tennessee. The weather was turning wet and bitterly cold. In an effort to rest his men, Morgan allowed his infantry and cavalry to take turns riding. It was not a good move. Both groups of men got their feet wet when marching. While riding, their wet feet quickly froze. Neither infantry nor cavalry were happy with the arrangement. The infantry cursed the cavalry and called them buttermilk Rangers. They wanted to be back on foot. The cavalry called the infantry webfeet and wanted their horses back.

On Sunday, December 7, 1862, Morgan found the Union force he was looking for. He also found that Union commander Col. A. B. Moore was a thousand men stronger than Morgan had expected. Despite a night approach march that had his infantry marching more than thirty miles, Morgan attacked. In an hour-long fight, his men drove Moore's soldiers into a killing zone that brought about surrender. Morgan's casualties were some 165 men while Moore lost nearly 2,100 men, of which 1,700 were taken prisoner. Other Union forces were coming on and Morgan in classic raider style extracted his men and prisoners and returned to camp safely. His mission was not to stay and slug it out, but to hit and run.

Success brought promotion. Morgan was made a brigadier general and given command of a cavalry division consisting of seven regiments organized into two brigades. Basil Duke was promoted to colonel and commanded one of these while Col. Adam Breckinridge held the other. In total the division numbered 3,900 horsemen. Morgan and other cavalry commanders had been assigned to serve under Joseph Wheeler. Neither Morgan nor Nathan Bedford Forrest were pleased with having Joe Wheeler as their commander. Both Morgan and Forrest were raiders who believed in far-ranging operations, striking hard where least expected. Duke wrote that it was often said of Joe Wheeler, "He is not a good raider, but there is no better man to watch the front of an army."[21]

A man who hated the often meaningless paperwork of an army, Morgan had trouble with the Confederate staff officers in Richmond. Duke wrote it was said of one of these men that he would rather have " a neat and formal report of a defeat, than a slovenly account of a victory."[22] Morgan was of little interest to the staff in Richmond and Morgan and his command were frequently ignored.

Despite his many duties, Morgan found time for romance. On December 14, 1862, at Murfreesboro, Tennessee, the thirty-seven-year-old newly promoted brigadier general married seventeen-year-old Martha Ready. Confederate President Jefferson Davis was in attendance as were generals Braxton Bragg, Breckenridge, Cheatham, Hardee and Kirby Smith. Leonidas Polk, an Episcopal bishop from Louisiana, performed the ceremony wearing the full uniform of a lieutenant general of the Confederate States of America. There were many who felt the wartime marriage was a mistake. That the couple loved each other dearly was not the issue. The critics believed the marriage was distraction from the war. The feeling was that while the fighting raged, Morgan's love and attention should be reserved for his men.

Confederate general Braxton Bragg had his army at Murfreesboro, Tennessee. Bragg faced two Union armies commanded by Generals Grant and Rosecrans. Bragg's cavalry force numbered 12,000 horsemen and Gen.

Joseph Wheeler, chief of cavalry, decided to keep nearly half the cavalry to support Bragg while the remainder would be sent raiding. On December 17, 1862, Nathan Bedford Forrest rode out with 3,000 men. His mission was to get behind Grant's army and destroy the railroads that supplied the Union army in western Tennessee and northern Mississippi.

Morgan's men also were eager for battle. The seven regiments each carried pride in unit and were eager to prove themselves to the rest of the division. Each regiment believed it was the best in the division. The surgeon checked the health of each man and each horse was carefully examined and re-shod by the farriers. Morgan was preparing for cold weather campaigning. He made certain each rider carried three days rations, ammunition and water, a half-day forage for his horse, two extra horseshoes and twelve nails, a saddle blanket, an extra blanket and an overcoat or oilcloth.

When all was in readiness, Morgan marched from Alexandria, Tennessee, on December 22. His purpose was to effect a ninety-mile, three-day march to Glasgow, Kentucky, to put himself into position to attack the Louisville and Nashville Railroad. The L&N was running unimpeded and was the principal route of supply and communications of General Rosecrans. Morgan's two brigades were supported by seven pieces of light, wheeled artillery, whose horses were double-teamed for speed,[23] thus earning the title flying artillery. Riding as part of Morgan's 3,900 were 400 men who had entered the army without weapons. They would serve as horse holders until sufficient weapons could be captured.

One of Morgan's favorite officers was not with them. The valiant British officer Col. George St. Ledger Grenfell thought he should have been selected as a brigade commander instead of Col. Adam Breckinridge. Despite the urging of Morgan, Duke and other officers, Grenfell exercised his option as a volunteer and left Morgan's command.

The winter march had begun. Using local guides and traveling over backroads and rough terrain, Morgan's men reached the vicinity of Glasgow at nightfall on December 24. They put out security, bivouacked and Morgan issued orders to continue the march at dawn. The route would be through Glasgow and the next day there would only be one stop when the horses would be unsaddled, rested, curried and fed. As usual the lead element would be Captain Quirk's wide-ranging scouts.

On Christmas morning 1862, the brigade of Col. Adam Breckenridge led the march. Breckenridge sent Captain Jones and some scouts of the 9th Kentucky to check out the town of Glasgow. As they reached the public square, the Confederates came face to face with two companies of the 2nd Michigan Cavalry who were riding through the town. The Union troopers were a foraging party and many had turkeys or chickens strapped to their

saddles. They were riding casually, not suspecting there were any Confederates in the area. Both sides opened fire Captain Jones and Pvt. Will Webb
were killed while the Michigan horsemen had one killed and two wounded.
The element of surprise favored the Confederates and they rounded up
twenty prisoners, including the adjutant of the 2nd Michigan. They also captured chickens and turkeys that now would serve as Christmas dinner for
Morgan's men.

With fifty of Quirk's Rangers a mile in advance, the column marched
on, knowing that word of their presence was now spreading. Ten miles north
of Glasgow, the point men reported that Union troops were waiting in line
of battle to their front. Quirk sent a messenger to the rear and decided to
develop the situation to determine the enemy strength. The Rangers
checked their weapons and ammunition, putting in fresh loads, then rode
forward. Among these was John Wyeth, a Ranger in war who later in life
would become a doctor. Wyeth related that Quirk decided to attack dismounted and called off horse holders, the usual practice being one in every
four men. The remainder Quirk led forward along a lane that had rail fenc-
ing on either side. As they reached the crest of a rise, the Union troops
began shooting. Quirk's men took cover and returned fire.

The Union position had been established as an ambush and now Company C of the 5th Indiana charged Quirk's men from the right rear. Wyeth
noted that the Union troops were at muzzle range. Quirk was hit twice, the
bullets scraping his skull, and several other Rangers were struck. The horses
and horse holders had been following close behind and the noise and confusion terrified the horses who reared and lashed out with their hooves,
finally breaking free and stampeding for the rear with the holders running
after them. Now Quirk's men were left on foot against a larger force. The
Indiana men captured five of the Rangers while Wyeth and the rest of the
men leaped a fence and under fire ran several hundred yards through an
open field for the concealment of a thicket.

What thus far was a difficult situation changed suddenly when Morgan's
lead regiment came into view. Now the preponderance of numbers had
changed and the rescuers brought with them the runaway horses. Swinging
back into the saddle, the Rangers joined the charge that broke the Union
position. Though bleeding from his wound, Captain Quirk killed one Union
soldier and captured two others.

Christmas Day continued with Morgan's command moving to Hammonville, not far from Abraham Lincoln's birthplace. At Hammonville the
Rangers captured sutler wagons loaded with luxury goods that were rapidly
disappearing from life in the South. After marching on they spent the night
bivouacked in a woods near Upton Station on the Louisville and Nashville

Railroad. They had the best Christmas present possible, they had arrived at the objective and it lay open before them.

On the morning of December 26, the work began. At Upton they captured Union soldiers guarding the railroad and began destroying track and railroad facilities. The telegraph line was briefly left operable, and "Lightning" George Ellsworth quickly tapped into the Union communications. At this stage of the war Union commanders tended to believe what came over the wire to them without requiring authentication. Morgan and Ellsworth took advantage of this by working as a team, first listening to Union telegraph traffic and then joining in the traffic. Morgan learned what units were being sent in pursuit of him. He had Ellsworth send messages inflating the number of troops the Confederates had and giving new and false locations of his command. Morgan then sent telegrams countermanding the orders of the troops that had been sent after him. Morgan's messages were not limited to the actions of his own command. He sent messages designed to confuse Union troops in front of Braxton Bragg.

While Morgan and Ellsworth were enjoying themselves at the expense of Union commanders, an L&N train carrying artillery and military supplies came into Upton Station from the North. The quick-witted engineer was suspicious and seeing Confederate uniforms reversed his engine and made a hasty withdrawal. Duke and Breckenridge had their brigades at work and Union guard stockades were destroyed at Bacon Creek Bridge and Nolin. Track was torn up and a bridge was burned.

At Elizabethtown was a Union garrison consisting of eight companies of an Illinois regiment under the command of Lieutenant Colonel Smith. There were 652 Union officers and men at the guard station and they knew Morgan was coming. Smith tried a bluff by sending out a messenger to say he had Morgan surrounded and demanding that the Confederates surrender. Morgan sent back a note that the situation was the reverse and brought up his guns. The Union troops had fortified brick warehouses near the train station but they had no artillery to support them. Morgan pulled his artillery into position and rained shot and shell on the defenders. Having no means of response the garrison surrendered. The 600 rifles provided weapons for men who began the raid unarmed.

At Muldraugh's Hill, the Louisville and Nashville Railroad crossed two wooden trestles, each of which stood nearly seventy-five feet high. The importance of these crossings was demonstrated by their being guarded by an entire regiment of Indiana infantry. The Union soldiers were well armed with recently issued Enfield rifles and occupied two log-and-earth forts that were well situated to guard the approaches to the bridges. Again senior Union commanders had failed to provide their soldiers with artillery support. Morgan pounded the Union guard points with his guns. Having no means of response, the Union troops surrendered and 700 men were taken prisoner. Coal oil was poured on the wooden trestles, then set alight. As flames devoured the two critical spans, Morgan's men divided up the rifles that were the latest addition to their firepower.

Riding onward, Morgan's men reached Rolling Fork River. There most of the men were sent across and marched on Bardstown. Col. Leroy S. Cluke took Quirk's scouts, 500 men and one piece of artillery to attack a bridge guard on the river. Cluke found himself under heavy attack by a Union relief force of some 3,000 men. The Confederates were forced to withdraw with Union colonel John Harlan's troops in hot pursuit.[24] Cluke's brigade commander Basil Duke came across the river with reinforcements and the fight became a stalemate. Harlan's troops had artillery and used it with good effect on the Confederates. A piece of shrapnel ripped Duke's head open and left him unable to continue. Aided by two of his Rangers, Captain Quirk carried Duke over the river, riding double until an ambulance and surgeon could be found.

A pitched battle is to be avoided by a raider and Morgan knew he must strike and move before being pinned down. Seeking to avoid Harlan's command, Morgan pressed on to Bardstown, arriving on the evening of Monday, December 29, 1862. The South was desperate for items that had been readily available before the war. The men promptly began stripping the stores of merchandise, taking shoes, hats, tools and many items for friends and family. With their cumbersome loot tied to their saddles, the Rangers rode on, bending into rain and sleet. They passed through Springfield on December 30, then rode another nine miles to Lebanon, where they halted for the night.

Union Rangers had been encountered in front of pursuing Union troops and the hope was to convince them that a large Confederate force was coming to the assistance of the Rangers. Quirk's men formed the rear guard for Morgan as the command struggled on through a miserable night of cold, sleet and mud. Men, horses and guns mired and an ice coating formed on their hats and oilcloths. Both horses and men were tired from days of hard marching and the tension of combat. Morgan had learned that Union columns were converging to trap his command before it could cross the Cumberland River. Some 8,000 Union infantry and artillery were at Lebanon, eight miles from Morgan and on his intended route. Colonel Harlan and his 3,000 were still behind Morgan and coming on. Confederate sympathizers told Morgan that another Union column was moving from Glasgow to head him off at Lebanon. Morgan had to get around Lebanon without being pinned down. The men were exhausted, but safety lay in movement. Extensive campfires were built by Quirk's scouts within sight of

Lebanon, making it appear that Morgan's command had gone into bivouac. In the darkness the weary men and horses began a night march to bypass Lebanon and its Union garrison. The march was brutal. As exhausted men fell from their saddles Morgan and his officers tried to keep their men awake by having them dismount and lead the equally tired mounts. A constant effort was required to keep men from wandering off and lying down to sleep. Only the great willpower of their leader kept them going.

Around noon on December 31, 1862, they could not go on and paused for one hour's rest. That respite soon over, they pushed on. Safety was now at hand and by nightfall they were in Campbellsville, between Columbia, Kentucky, and the Tennessee line. At this stop much-needed supplies were secured. The Union troops pursuing them had ceased to follow, but as the column rode along they could hear the rumble of cannon fire. Though it seemed impossible that sound could travel so many miles, they were experienced soldiers and knew that somewhere a great battle was taking place.

Seventy-five thousand men under Generals Bragg and Rosecrans were locked in battle along the Stones River at Murfreeboro. The sound Morgan's men heard from more than twenty miles away came largely from the 20,307 rounds that Union artillery fired during the battle. Bragg was employing cavalry under Wheeler and Buford to hit at Rosecrans' rear areas. He had sent a courier after Morgan, ordering him to strike in the rear of the Union army, but the message did not arrive. The Confederates had the best of the battle, but Bragg was indecisive and decided to retreat. Rosecrans held the field, but his army was hurt by the fight. Morgan's and Wheeler's attacks on the Union supply line made it difficult to resupply or reinforce. Morgan's Rangers had destroyed more than sixty miles of railroad from Bacon Creek to Shepherdsville. They had captured some 1,900 Union soldiers, destroyed Union supply dumps and taken a large amount of weapons and ammunition. The 400 men who started without horses were now mounted and many men had extra mounts. All this was achieved at a cost of two men killed, twenty-four wounded, and sixty-four missing.

Morgan's division now went into winter quarters at McMinnville, some forty miles southeast of Murfreesboro. It was a winter of privation. The Southern armies suffered from the hot-headed rhetoric that had inspired a war based on passion without regard to logistics. The Confederate soldier was supporting a government that could not or would not provide the materiel the fighting men needed. As water froze in streams and canteens and as snow blanketed the bivouac area, men exposed to the elements found the Union overcoat or gum cloth they had captured vital to survival. The gum cloth was often stretched over some fence rails, sloped in lean-to fashion with fires built at the open end. If the occupant was also fortunate enough to have a captured Union blanket, they could be reasonably comfortable. Horses were always close at hand for Morgan's Rangers were used as a rapid-reaction force.

Throughout January, February, and March 1863, probing actions were taken and stiff fights occurred in weather that quickly would freeze a disabled man. Union general Rosecrans was running a strong patrolling campaign. Union cavalry detachments would come out of their camps in sufficient number to overcome Confederate patrols. Behind the Union cavalry would be a regiment of infantry. If the cavalry could hold the Confederate horsemen in position, the infantry would finish the job. It was an effective technique. Reconnaissance and combat patrols were abroad day and night and fighting was an almost daily occurrence.

On January 29, 1863, Morgan and fifty Rangers started on a raid to burn the commissary stores at Nashville. They wore blue coats over their Confederate uniforms and had a bogus pass from General Rosecrans. As they were at Stewart's Ferry on Stone River they encountered a Union outpost of Michigan cavalry consisting of a captain and twenty men on the other side. Morgan engaged the officer in conversation, posing as a Captain Johnson from the Union 5th Kentucky Cavalry. The masquerade was working while Morgan was ferrying men over the river and swimming the horses across. Some of the Michigan men noticed that gray cloth showed when Morgan's men bent over. Seeing that the ruse was failing, Morgan captured the Union captain and most of his men. Other Union soldiers got away to give warning of the raiding party and Morgan had to cancel his plans.

There were frequent forays over the Cumberland River and into Kentucky. Capt. Thomas Henry Hines was one of the most daring of the young Ranger officers. Time after time throughout the war, he would prove to be imaginative and capable. Hines proved how effective a small raiding party can be during an expedition in February 1863. Riding north, Hines, with thirteen men and a lieutenant, crossed the Cumberland River at Granville, Tennessee, and rode to near Bowling Green, Kentucky. One of the party, a doctor who was accompanying them, was captured. The raiders dispersed to throw off pursuit then reassembled twelve miles south of Bowling Green. They burned a railroad depot and three cars, then captured a steamboat laden with Union supplies. These were burned. They then rode forty miles and destroyed a train consisting of an engine and twenty-one cars. For twenty-one days and more than 150 miles the small party roamed in the rear of the Union army, causing more than a half-million dollars worth of damage. One man drowned while crossing a swift stream. The remainder came back safely. They demonstrated that once the crust of an opposing army is penetrated, that which is underneath lies exposed and vulnerable to a small raiding party.

It was not only ball and shrapnel that were killing Morgan's Rangers. More than seventeen officers and men died of what doctors of the time called brain fever. Duke wrote, "The patient attacked with it suffered with a terrible pain in the back of the head and along the spine; the extremities soon became cold and the patient sank into a torpor; it was generally fatal in a few hours. I recollect to have heard no recovery from it."[25] The symptoms were those of meningitis. Men also suffered from infection that led to tissue death, gangrene, and blood poisoning.

Raiding in central Kentucky, Col. Leroy S. Cluke, one of Morgan's subordinate commanders, started on February 9, 1863, with 740 men. Effective use was made of scouts dressed in Union uniform. A Union brigade had made its headquarters at Mount Sterling, some thirty miles east of Lexington, Kentucky. One of Cluke's men dressed in Union uniform went into the brigade headquarters, pretended some business and took Union message forms. Cluke then prepared an order that appeared to come from higher headquarters in Lexington. The Union brigade commander was instructed to make a rapid march twenty miles northwest to Paris to stop a raid on the Kentucky Central Railroad. In the interest of speed, the Union brigade commander was told to leave all his baggage at Mount Sterling under a small guard. A Union uniformed, dust-stained courier with sweated horse galloped into Mount Sterling with the message. The Union brigade dashed off on the false mission and the Confederate Rangers rode into Mount Sterling and captured the possessions and stores of the Union brigade.

The climate and hardships the Rangers endured took a toll. So many men were suffering from infections that Cluke had only 300 of the 740 men with which he started. The Union forces were closing in on him and he moved eastward into mountain country where Union bushwhackers were ever-present and dangerous. Cluke made a decision to once again attack Mount Sterling. He and his men made a sixty-mile march in twenty-four hours, then went into the attack in what proved to be house-to-house fighting. He took 428 prisoners, 220 wagon loads of stores and 1,000 weapons and lost three men. Cluke was the definition of audacity. He roamed in the heart of superior forces, striking by surprise, disappearing, then coming back again. Cluke and his men stayed in Kentucky for a month, then crossed the Cumberland River and returned to Tennessee. He had even done some recruiting along the way and came back with eighteen more men than he had when he left base camp.

Leadership is always a challenge, and for the officers of John Hunt Morgan's command the Confederate supply system made it a trial. Often away from the main body of the army, the Rangers frequently were ignored or forgotten when it came to issuance of clothing, shoes and meat. The Confederate logistical system was a disservice to the men who fought for the Confederacy. Under the guise of states' rights, some Confederate states withheld badly needed supplies and kept them warehoused for men of their own state, while soldiers of other Confederate states went lacking. Both Confederate and Union armies foraged and with thousands of hungry men the countryside was blighted no matter which army passed over it. For Morgan's men it was more than a meal, they had to strip houses and take what they could in the way of blankets, coats, clothing and shoes in order to survive the elements.

On March 19, 1863, Morgan was at Liberty, Tennessee, by the Cumberland River, northeast of Murfreesboro. Here he was informed that a combined-arms force of Union infantry, cavalry and artillery had moved out of Murfreesboro heading in his direction. Quirks's scouts were shadowing the enemy and reported the Union command had stopped for the night at Auburn, some fourteen miles to the southwest. Morgan's men were low on ammunition. Requests were in, but supplies were not coming through. Morgan decided to go after the Union column and hope his ammunition would last. He would move at night and attack the next morning.

They rode through the darkness and at first light the plan began to develop. Captain Quirk was sent to attack the rear of the now marching enemy column. Quirk's attack caused the Union command to deploy to defend its rear. This left the Union artillery vulnerable to attack and Morgan went after these guns. The Union soldiers quickly wheeled their artillery about and engaged. Though Union infantry was coming on the run, it was clear the Confederate attack would succeed. Morgan's men were within fifty yards of the guns and victory was in their grasp when they ran out of ammunition. Disgusted, Morgan broke off the attack. He learned that four guns and the ammunition he wanted had arrived at McMinnville. Collecting these he retraced his march and again sought to attack.

The countermarch resulted in his units being strung out and committed piecemeal fashion. Morgan's clothes were pierced with bullets and a number of his company-grade officers were killed leading charges against a determined Union foe. The battle was inconclusive and Morgan withdrew to Liberty. The Union force did not follow.

General Bragg became convinced the Union army planned to leave central Tennessee and Nashville. The belief seems to have started because Union general Rosecrans was sending his sick men and unnecessary baggage to the rear. Morgan thought Bragg had come to the wrong conclusion, that Rosecrans intended to attack. On April 2 the Union army began moving forward. Morgan's command ranged outward, penetrated the Union cavalry screen and identified Union infantry coming on. Morgan's command was positioned to the east of Liberty, intending to take up a defensive posture on a series of sloping ridges called Snow's Hill. There were many things wrong with this position that were not evident at the time it was occupied. The Union attack soon revealed the men were exposed to artillery fire, and advancing Union infantry would have cover in ravines and draws until they closed on the Confederates. A Union column moved to envelop the Confederate flank and came very near in succeeding. The Confederates attempted to withdraw and in so doing regiments became mixed and control was being lost.

Basil Duke had been recovering from wounds and was returning after two months. He was astounded at the lower morale. Confederates were walking and riding quietly for the rear. They did not seem frightened—there was no panic—but they could not be made to fight. Unable to stem the tide of stragglers, Duke rode forward to where the men who would fight were heavily engaged. As the fight went on, some Confederates in blue overcoats came in sight of Morgan's wagon train. The teamsters panicked at the sight, lashed their mules and galloped madly away. Many wagons were overturned and wrecked in the fight.

Confederate soldiers called the Snow's Hill episode a stampede. They fell back eleven miles to Smithville. It was not until they reached McMinnville, nineteen miles farther south, that order was restored. There was much complaint about the leadership. Men said Morgan had not been leading his men, but was at McMinnville with his new wife. Both husband and wife were criticized. Morgan had personally come forward but not in time to be a factor. Duke described Morgan meeting with a straggler and demanding to know why the man was not with his regiment. The response was, "Well, General, I'm scattered."[26] The remark was applicable to Morgan's command.

The Union troops had moved to Alexandria, about five miles north of Liberty. Morgan now moved his men north to Smithville. Given the condition of his command, he was not contemplating attack. The Union advance had stopped and there was little contact. General Joe Wheeler had taken cavalry, including part of Morgan's, and began raiding northward, taking Alexandria. On one raid $40,000 in greenbacks was captured. Wheeler used the money to buy better horses for men who were on the raid. Morgan returned to McMinnville where his wife was staying. He stayed there from April 5 until April 9 when a Union raiding party hit the town and the Confederates were forced to flee. Morgan and some of his officers were hotly pursued. Maj. Dick McCann's horse was shot and McCann stood in front of the charging Union cavalry and shouted, pretending he was Morgan. The blue-coated horsemen were not impressed. They rode over him and slashed him with their sabers before taking him prisoner. McCann was a hard-fighting, hard-drinking man. He asked for a canteen of apple brandy and in consideration of his wounds was granted the boon. He proceeded to outdrink his guard and then dug his way out under the logs of his cabin prison. He soon rejoined Morgan and the rest of the men who had made their escape. The Union raiding party did not remain in McMinnville.

Hoping to trap the Union column, the Confederates concentrated at Smithville. Union movements dictated evacuation and the Confederates pulled out. Rosecrans was concentrating the main body of his army just north of the Cumberland River. Morgan was back in the saddle, seeking to keep the enemy advance from getting south of the Cumberland. The trace of the river was northeast from Tennessee and at Monticello, Kentucky, Morgan began to bring his regiments together. When he assembled his division he found the five regiments he now had with him totaled 800 men and these were short of ammunition. Nonetheless an enemy force was to his front and Morgan intended to attack. As the charge began, the Confederates came under artillery fire which Morgan assumed meant the Union troops had been reinforced. With the agreement of nearly all of his officers, he wanted to break off the battle, but Union troops were charging him.

Morgan began to withdraw. Cluke's two regiments were out of ammunition but withdrew in formation. Morgan brought in Smith's regiment and their fire halted the Union advance. Now Morgan attacked and Union troops withdrew in perfect order. The Union force was a regiment commanded by a colonel named Jacobs who was a skillful fighter. Morgan's division was so under strength that a good Union regiment could fight it evenly.

It was obvious the command needed rest and refitting. Picket duty along the Cumberland allowed time for recruiting, rearming and caring for horses and equipment. There were minor raids, but the main effort was making the division a fighting force again. For a period of six months, Morgan's men were the eyes and ears of the Confederate army, covering a front of more than 150 miles. The mission was well accomplished and while it was being done men on leave or recovered from wounds returned, new recruits were trained and horses well fed.

Still the bloom was gone from the Confederate cause. The rapid victory so many expected had become a seemingly endless time of privation and bloodshed. People did not like those from the North, but they did not like the Southern leadership either. There was dissatisfaction in the army. Basil Duke wrote of the Confederate promotion system, "Cavalry officers, after long and arduous service, and a thorough initiation into all the mysteries of their craft, were rewarded and encouraged by having some staff officer, or officer educated to shoot heavy artillery, run steamships, or mix chemical preparations promoted over their heads."[28]

In an act that was hardly timely, on May 17, 1863, the Confederate Congress passed a resolution of thanks to Morgan and his men for their successful thousand-mile raid in Kentucky in July 1862.

Recruiting went well and Morgan's division numbering 2,800 had its 1st Brigade under Duke headquartered at Alexandria and the 2nd Brigade, now commanded by Texas Ranger Col. Adam Rankin "Stovepipe" Johnson, at Auburn. The regiments were spread out on picket duties, but could be assembled quickly. The horses and men were in good health and the men were well armed. The men had to provide their own horses and weapons, and they were constantly on the lookout for a means to do so. As an encouragement, Maj. Thomas Webber who commanded the 2nd Kentucky Regiment required any man who did not have a weapon to carry a fence rail on his shoulder until he armed himself.[29]

CHAPTER SEVEN

Days of Desperation

The Mississippi River town of Vicksburg was a bastion of Confederate hopes in the west. It was the locked door that prevented the Union from gaining control of the vital waterway. By June 1863, troops were being drained from Braxton Bragg's army to beef up the defense of Vicksburg. Bragg had his army at Tullahoma and found himself being reduced in strength while he faced an impending attack from a larger Union army under Rosecrans coming from Murfreesboro.

Bragg also believed General Burnside would strike from the Ohio River at Simon Buckner who kept Knoxville under the Confederate flag. Bragg was right. Plans were under way for such a Union advance. Union general Henry M. Judah at Glasgow, Kentucky, had 8,000 men of which 5,000 were well-trained cavalry. The Union numbers were vastly superior to the manpower of the Confederates.

Bragg felt he had to withdraw behind the Tennessee River to Chattanooga and force the Union advance into a narrow avenue of approach in mountain country. Given the disparity of forces this was a necessary move, but a hazardous one. If the Union armies attacked while the withdrawal was in progress, Bragg's army would be ground under. Morgan sent a message to Bragg's chief of cavalry Joe Wheeler, proposing a raid on Louisville. Bragg liked the idea and expanded the concept. Morgan was to raise havoc with the L&N Railroad, bring pressure on Louisville and disrupt Rosecrans' rear areas. Bragg hoped this would draw General Burnside's troops in pursuit of Morgan and leave him with only Rosecrans to be concerned about.[1] Morgan thought Bragg's plan lacked the audacity of a great raid and would not have the desired effect. If he stayed in Kentucky he would not be able to draw off Union troops that threatened Bragg. Morgan had foreseen the need for such action and had been gathering intelligence for weeks. Morgan wanted to launch an even greater raid and now proposed going deeper into Union territory, even taking his troops into Indiana and Ohio. Such a raid in Union territory, Morgan argued, would have the Federal armies swarming after him and distract them from Bragg's withdrawal. Bragg needed time to effect his withdrawal, but he felt Morgan's approach too ambitious and would not agree to action beyond Kentucky. Morgan's orders came from Gen. Joe Wheeler. Bragg and Wheeler believed they were clear that Morgan should confine his raid to Kentucky and Wheeler's order said so:

> Headquarters Cavalry Corps
> Near Shelbyville, June 18,1863
> Special Orders
> No 44
>
> I. General Morgan will proceed to Kentucky with a force of 2,000 officers and men, including such artillery as he may deem most expedient. In addition to accomplishing the work which he has proposed, he will as far as possible, break up and destroy the Louisville and Nashville Railroad. He will if practicable, destroy depots of supplies in the State of Kentucky, after which he will return to his present position.
>
> By order of Major-General Wheeler:
> E.S. Burford
> Assistant Adjutant General[2]

Morgan left Burkesville, crossing the Cumberland River on July 2, 1863, with 2,460 men and four guns.[3] The command was organized into two brigades, the 1st Brigade under Basil Duke had 1,460 men and the 2nd Brigade under Stovepipe Johnson had 1,000. The four guns were two 3-inch Parrotts with the 1st Brigade and two 12-pounder howitzers with the 2nd Brigade.[4]

Both Morgan and Forrest had come to doubt Bragg as a commander. When Morgan rode out he already had decided to ignore the orders of his commanding general and follow his own intentions. The battle of Gettysburg was raging. General Lee had a winning record and he was expected to prevail. Morgan felt a daring raid might follow a course through Indiana and Ohio and link up with Lee in Pennsylvania. There was in Indiana and Ohio a pro-Southern movement called the Order of American Knights. They were considered sufficiently serious that Burnside informed Halleck he believed Indiana and Ohio to be more disloyal then Kentucky.[5] In the end these Confederate sympathizers were not a factor, but Morgan may have counted on their help. The sheer audacity of the plan thrilled the men. This was the Morgan in whom they believed, the leader who thought no challenge too difficult and frequently had proven he was right. Why Morgan made the decision to disobey his orders could be only answered by Morgan himself.

Union general Hartstuff had the responsibility to guard the railroads and supply depots of southern Kentucky. The 3rd Division, XXIII Army Corps, under Gen. Henry M. Judah had men guarding the crossings of the Cumberland River. Judah had good intelligence and knew as early as June 18 that a raid was coming his way.[6] The weather did not favor Morgan. The Cumberland River was at flood stage and out of its banks. Judah had his cavalry at Marrowbone, only twelve miles from Morgan's crossing site. He was sure the high water would prevent a crossing for several days and did not put outposts at the river. As usual, Morgan did the unexpected.

Despite the complaints of Union officers in the field, Judah misjudged where the crossing would be made. Union troops were ordered to the wrong positions. Morgan got across the river with Quirk's Rangers leading. The Rangers tangled with 160 men of the 9th Kentucky Cavalry and after a fight with pistols and rifle butts pursued the cavalry for eight miles until they encountered a stiff Union defense.

Morgan broke through after a brisk fight with Judah's troops and headed north. Though successful in the crossing, Morgan's presence in the Union rear was immediately telegraphed to Union commands and a vigorous pursuit organized. Among the horsemen who were tracking Morgan was Theodore F. Allen, a captain in the 7th Ohio Cavalry and one of General Hobson's 3,000 cavalry coming from Somerset, Kentucky. Allen was one of many now on the trail of the Confederate Ranger. The grim intent of the Union leaders was to bottle up Morgan's Rangers and destroy them. To accomplish this, Union home guard militia harassed Morgan's column along the route, Union infantry attempted to block his path and Union cavalry threatened his rear and flanks. Allen wrote they would sometimes lose Morgan's trail during the night, but it was summer and 2,000 riders raise a lot of dust. The scouts would search all possible routes, looking at the grass and shrubs beside the road. When they found those covered with dust they knew Morgan had passed that way and immediately pressed their pursuit.

Confederate Rangers and raiding parties were accustomed to being on friendly territory and having the support of the local populace. This was not the case as Morgan plunged deeper into the Union rear. Now the citizenry were eager to inform on his movements and Union troops were cheered and fed as they rode by. Captain Allen recorded that wherever they went people gathered by the roadside singing the Union song "Rally Round The Flag Boys." They heard the song to the point of distraction and as exhaustion set in began to sleep through the serenades.

Morgan and his men found their march constantly harassed by Union bushwhackers. The Confederates were passing through territory patrolled by the Union guerrilla Dave Beatty, nicknamed "Tinker." Riding with

Morgan's men was Beatty's mortal enemy, the confederate guerrilla Champ Ferguson. Even experienced Rangers found bushwhackers like Beatty and Ferguson dangerous and difficult to understand.[7]

The Union cavalry had started with two days' rations, but they did not miss a meal. Allen found that everywhere they rode, men, women and children turned out to feed the troops. Allen noted, "All the soldier had to do was fill his stomach and his haversack—the enthusiastic citizens did the rest." Allen felt the problem for the Union trooper was lack of menu variety. When he wrote of his experience he entitled his work *Six Hundred Miles of Fried Chicken*. Writing of the experience of one of his companions, George Lloyd, Allen wrote, "having been surfeited with fried chicken and blackberry pie—having it for breakfast, dinner and supper, with a half-dozen lunches of the same between each meal—he one day rode off the line of march hoping to find a farm house where he could get some bacon and cornbread. He soon came to a farm showing every sign of prosperity. He rode up to the house and told the lady of the manor that he was hungry and asked for food. With the greatest alacrity the lady brought him . . . fried chicken and blackberry pie! 'Good Lord, madam,' said Lloyd, 'won't you please give me some bacon and cornbread; the pin feathers are beginning to grow on me, I have eaten so much fried chicken.'[8]

On the morning of July 3, 1863, Morgan pressed on toward Columbia, brushing aside small contingents of Union troops who sought to block his way. There was house-to-house fighting in the town, but few casualties on either side. Capt. J. T. Cassell of Morgan's advance was shot in the thigh and did the rest of the raid while riding in an ambulance. Rumor passed among the Union troops that four soldiers had been shot down after they surrendered to Morgan's troops. Several stores were broken into and looted. Duke wrote that Morgan went to the scene, arrested the marauders and compelled restitution. Morgan's advance encountered a Union scouting party from the 1st Kentucky Cavalry and killed the Union captain commanding; several Confederates also died.

On July 4, Morgan came upon Col. Orlando H. Moore and part of his 25th Michigan Infantry guarding a bridge over Green River. Moore had left his stockade by the bridge and cleverly chosen a blocking position one and a half miles on the Columbia road and south side of the river. This position would prevent access to the bridge.[9] With his flanks protected by thick woods and steep riverbanks, Moore had his 200 men cut trees and build a strong earthwork protected by the sharpened stakes of abatis to stop a cavalry charge. Morgan called on Moore to surrender. The Union officer replied that "the Fourth of July was not a good day to surrender." Colonel Moore added that he had been stationed there to make the Confederates bleed and was ready to do so.[10] Moore was a man of his word. The fight lasted three-and-one-half hours. The Michigan men used aimed shots and though there was not the usual roar of battle, men were being hit. Morgan's attack was beaten back with Duke giving the loss as thirty-six men killed and forty-five wounded. Col. David Walter Canaled of Morgan's 11th Kentucky had his brains blown out while leading an attack. Colonel Moore's report stated he lost six men killed and twenty-three wounded.[11] Basil Duke gave high praise to Colonel Moore writing, "We expected to hear of his promotion."[12]

Leaving his wounded to Union care, Morgan proceeded on to Lebanon, Kentucky, where on July 5 he had another stiff fight. Union Lt. Col. Charles S. Hanson had 360 men of the 20th Kentucky Infantry to defend the place. The town sat in bowl-shaped terrain that allowed it to be dominated by artillery on the hills. Hanson took horses from the local people and sent out scouting parties on all roads, then fought a delaying action in the hills until forced back into town. The Union troops barricaded themselves in the depot and adjoining buildings and hung on for seven hours. Colonel Hanson reported that each of his men fired more than 125 rounds during the fight and Confederates were "killed at a distance of 400 yards and a few as far as 900 yards."[13] Artillery fire and the setting of their buildings on fire brought on the surrender when Morgan's men charged into the town. Morgan lost nine men killed and thirty wounded.[14] He captured medicine, rifles, ammunition and had more than 300 prisoners, but his nineteen-year-old brother Lt. Tom Morgan was among the Confederate dead. John Hunt Morgan's brother Charlton was beside himself with grief and anger. Colonel Hanson reported that Charlton Morgan "seized Captains McLeod and Parrish of the Twentieth Kentucky, and attempted to shoot them, and was with difficulty prevented. Upon my interposition on behalf of those officers, he seized me by the beard, but was prevented from doing me any bodily injury. For the offense to myself he afterward apologized."[15]

Bragg had wanted the Union forces distracted and they were. From his headquarters in Cincinnati, at 4:30 P.M. on July 6, Gen. Ambrose P. Burnside, commanding the Department of the Ohio, informed Brig. Gen. Edward H. Hobson, brigade commander, that Morgan was headed in the direction of Bardstown. He assigned more troops to Hobson and told him to pursue and forage off the countryside. In closing Burnside wrote, "Morgan ought to be broken to pieces before he gets out of the state. Answer at once."[16]

On July 6, 1863, while Lee was withdrawing from Pennsylvania, Morgan was on the march north. As darkness fell, a train from Nashville was captured some thirty miles from Louisville. Tapping into the telegraph line Ellsworth learned Morgan was believed to be heading for Louisville and heated preparations for defense of the town were underway. Morgan's

John Hunt Morgan with his wife. USAMHI

march continued through the night with a three-hour halt after crossing the Salt River.

From Lebanon onward Morgan sought to avoid pitched battles. An advance force headed by Captains Samuel Taylor and Clay Merriwether was sent ahead to capture transport over the Ohio River. Morgan moved by way of Springfield and Bardstown, where he was delayed by twenty-five men of the 4th U.S. Cavalry under the combative Lt. Thomas W. Sullivan. The young officer had fought the Confederates in eight previous engagements and was accustomed to the song of the bullet. He barricaded his small force in a livery stable, shooting from behind a small breastwork of planks and manure. When Morgan's men moved into town they were repulsed. One of the Union soldiers, Pvt. Bartholomew Burke of Company H, 4th U.S. Cavalry, was mortally wounded and as he died his last words were, "Lieutenant, did I fall like a soldier?" Morgan demanded immediate surrender. Sullivan reported Morgan said if he refused he would "blow me to hell with his artillery." Sullivan replied he thought he would trouble Morgan a little longer. He held out until the artillery was clearly in position, then he and his men surrendered while the citizens of Bardstown cheered their courage. Sullivan reported, "Even the marauding chief himself (Morgan) could not help complimenting the twenty-five 'damned Yankees,' who detained him twenty-four hours."[17]

Morgan led his men on to Bradenburg on the Ohio where Taylor and Merriwether had captured two steamboats to make the crossing. It was now July 9, 1863. Despite being fired upon by home guards and an armed river steamer, Morgan got his men across the river. By midnight Morgan's men were in Indiana. Union general Hobson was following, but nearly fifty miles in Morgan's rear and uncertain of the route Morgan planned to take.

The governor of Indiana called out 50,000 home guards to dispute Morgan's passage and they proved effective. Men firing shotguns from bushes and squirrel guns from trees constantly harassed the Confederate column. They could not stop Morgan. but they had to be eliminated or bypassed and either tactic took time.

Morgan's command was well mounted and detachments were sent throughout the countryside, burning bridges, tearing up railroad tracks and taking horses. Everywhere they went, they found the houses deserted as people fled before them. Duke wrote, "At the houses at which I stopped, every thing was just in the condition in which the fugitive owners had left it, an hour or so before."[18] Morgan turned eastward, riding though Corydon, where the home guard fought them and killed or wounded several Confederates. Morgan passed on to Salem, Vienna, Lexington, Paris, Vernon, Dupont, Versailles, Sumansville and into Harrison, Ohio. The governor of Ohio called up his home guard of 50,000 men who, like those in Indiana, were an impediment to the raiders. Morgan made a feint toward Hamilton to throw off his pursuers, then passed by night through the suburbs of Cincinnati. The Confederates rode through prosperous areas that were untouched by war. They burned and looted. One store lost $3,500 worth of goods.[19] The Confederate officers could not or would not control their men. Duke wrote that it seemed a desire to "pay off" all the scores the Federal army had chalked up in the South. He added, "Calico, was the staple article of appropriation—each man (who could get one) tied a bolt of it to his saddle, only to throw it away and get a fresh one at the first opportunity. They did not pillage with any sort of method or reason—it seemed to be a mania, senseless and purposeless. One man carried a bird-cage with three canaries in it, for two days. Another rode with a chafing-dish which looked like a small metallic coffin, on the pummel of his saddle . . . another, still slung seven pairs of skates around his neck."[20]

Though the citizens were outraged, Captain Allen of the 7th Ohio Cavalry took it as part of war. Allen wrote of the cavalry soldier raiding in enemy territory, "the general rule is that 'whatever is outdoors is mine and whatever is indoors belongs to my messmate.'" One Confederate looter with a sense of humor told a storekeeper "he was glad to find the stores so well stocked, that they compared more than favorably with the stores of Dixie, and that he found no occasion whatever to find fault with the prices." Morgan's men took everything that struck their fancy. They shopped not only for themselves, but for their girlfriends, stripping stores of bolts of calico and muslin, shoes, stockings, underwear, corsets and gloves. Watching them loot his business, a disheartened storekeeper noted that the raiders "had left an awful lot of girls behind them or were providing well for a few."[21]

At Salem they burned the railroad depot and several bridges, then went shopping. A hundred members of the home guard were captured and paroled. There were three mills at Salem that were legitimate targets of war. Morgan told the owners he would spare the mills for $1,000 each. One owner handed over a roll of greenbacks that totaled $1,200. Morgan gave the mill owner $200 back and asked, "Do you think I would rob you of a cent?"[22] At Vienna on the Indianapolis and Jeffersonville Railroad, the telegraph operator was captured before he could send a warning. "Lightning" Ellsworth was quickly on the wire learning all he could about the movement of Union troops. The news was not encouraging. They had to keep moving. There were now some 65,000 home guards mobilized and Regular forces were closing on them.

The pursuit force of General Hobson now included the 1st, 8th, 9th, and 12th Kentucky and the 2nd, 5th and 7th Ohio and 8th Michigan cavalry regiments, elements of east Tennessee mounted rifles, artillery and infantry.

More troops were coming in and Union Rangers dressed in Confederate uniforms began to infiltrate Morgan's column.[23] Hobson had good information on Morgan's movements. Hobson's men had been riding for more than weeks. Capt. Henry C. Weaver, Company D of the 16th Kentucky (Mounted) Infantry wrote, "All were completely worn out and exhausted. Horses were staggering and breaking down, men were sleeping in their saddles, and men and horses were dropping asleep by the roadside."[24] Though still ahead, Morgan was now within reach of his pursuers. Gen. Henry Judah had brought his troops up the Ohio by steamboat and joined the chase. Hobson decided to send a flying column ahead of the main body and selected the 2nd and 7th Ohio Cavalry regiments, added two pieces of artillery and put them under the command of Col. August V. Kautz of the 2nd Ohio Cavalry.[25] On the night of July 18, "Boots and Saddles" was sounded and the flying column swung into the saddle. They rode through the night and by the morning of July 19 made contact with Morgan's rear guard.

Duke wrote that Morgan and his men were now averaging twenty-one hours a day in the saddle. Though sleep was scarce, food and forage was plentiful. At Dupont they found a meat-packing plant and every man had a ham slung across his saddle. There were few men to be seen for they were harassing the column from ambush. If a woman was in a house and they asked where her man was she likely would respond, "Oh, you'll see him later on."

Morgan's raid into Indiana and Ohio was answering the question of what Confederate armies would experience if they invaded the North. It would be the same as it was for the Union army in Virginia. The people would resist in every way possible. Union commanders praised the civilians. The women and men who provided food and water also provided information and in many cases took up arms.

Better than any Confederate force before them, Morgan's men were seeing for themselves that the North had enormous power not yet committed to the fight. There were so many people that Duke was astounded. He saw "the dense population, apparently untouched by the demands of the war. The country was full, the towns were full and the ranks of the militia were full. I am satisfied that we saw often as many as ten thousand militia in one day."[26]

Marching through the day and well into the night, Morgan and his men sought to stay ahead of the news of their coming. From Dupont, Morgan's route of march was through Versailles, Pierceville, Milan, Weisburg, Hubbell's Corner, New Alsace, Dover, Logan and on to Harrison which was twenty miles north of Cincinnati. Morgan left Dupont at 4 A.M. on Sunday, July 12, 1863. At 1 P.M., the advance guard of Hobson's cavalry closed on the town.[27] At Versailles the militia was planning its defense when Morgan's advance under Col. J. Warren Grigsby captured them and a herd of fine

horses. At one point they rested near where 2,500 militia waited, not knowing the Confederates were close at hand. Morgan reasoned there would be a
strong Union force at Cincinnati and that this would be his greatest danger.
If he kept moving, the cavalry in pursuit could not catch up. A study of the
railroads helped him plan a route where Union infantry could not be transported easily. Morgan knew he did not have the strength to take Cincinnati,
but felt it was such a logical objective that a threat in that direction would
cause the defenses to draw in and he could bypass the city safely.

From Harrison the route wound through Springdale, Sharon and Montgomery to Williamsburg. Using his trademark tactic, Morgan sent out detachments to harry the countryside in varying directions and hide the movement
of his main body. After covering fifty miles in one day, he moved to the outskirts of Cincinnati as though preparing to attack the city. He had started
with 2,400, but battle losses, illness and fatigue had reduced his ranks to
fewer than 2,000 exhausted men. A long night march now lay ahead to slip
away and bypass the aroused enemy in the city. It was a brutal march made
more difficult by straggling and breaks in the column. Duke's brigade frequently came to crossroads and had no idea which direction the brigade to
their front had taken. They could not tell from hoof prints as there were
many in all directions. By the light of torches they tried to identify the settling
of dust and the slaver on the ground from the horses' mouths. A number of
men could not go on. They crawled off into fields and slept. These men
would be taken prisoner by oncoming Union troops. Dawn came, but the column went on and on until about 4 P.M. when it reached Williamsburg some
twenty-eight miles east of Cincinnati. They had covered more than ninety
miles in thirty-five hours.

In Ohio, they again encountered home-guard militia units who frequently disputed their passage or sniped at them from the roadside. Private
Burks, a lead scout, would ride far in advance posing as a Union soldier. He
would try to locate home-guard defenses and keep them occupied in conversation until the follow-on troops captured them. The only thing the Confederates could do was destroy the weapons and turn the men loose. On July
14 at Camp Denison, Ohio, they encountered stiff resistance from Lt. Col.
George Neff of the 2nd Kentucky (Union) Infantry. Neff blocked their path
with a hastily collected force that included convalescents and militia. He
felled trees across the roads and would not be shelled out of his entrenchments. Morgan was forced to bypass and go ten time-consuming miles off his
route.[28] Morgan's men went riding across southern Ohio on a route that
generally follows the trace of modern-day Route 32. They rode from
Williamsburg to Piketon, to Jackson then to Vinton and Berlin where they
skirmished with home guards. At Wilkesville they stopped for about eight

hours of rest. Meanwhile the home guard was blocking roads and bridges with more felled trees.

On July 18 the weary Confederates were at Pomeroy on the Ohio River. The fighting was constant and worn blue uniforms and stiffened resistance told them they were beginning to meet experienced Union soldiers. Duke compared going through Pomeroy to running the gauntlet. They turned northeast to Chester, but they were in difficulty. No one knew the countryside and a guide could not be found. Morgan halted for an hour and a half to allow the command to close up. It was a bad decision by a tired leader. The wait caused them to arrive at the hamlet of Portland about 8 P.M. on a pitch black night. On the opposite side of the Ohio River was West Virginia. The ford was guarded by an entrenched Union force the Confederates estimated at 300 men with two cannons.

Tension ran high. A critical decision must be made and for leaders in war these decisions often must be made by men who are at the end of their endurance. Portland is a small river town a short distance above Buffington Island. The town is located on a boot-shaped projection of land with the Ohio River on three sides. If they did not get across the river, Morgan's men were in a bottle that easily could be capped, but a night attack over unknown terrain by exhausted men seemed beyond their capability. As his men were not trained in dismounted night attacks and control quickly would be lost, Morgan ruled out a night attack. He also felt the command could not give up its guns and wagons and risk a night march to fords believed to be higher up the river, where only the men would seek to cross. Morgan decided to wait and have Duke's regiments attack at dawn. Pickets were put forward as close as possible to the enemy work, but they were tired and fell asleep.

When Duke attacked at first light, he found the Union troops had rolled their guns into a ravine and pulled out during the night. The river crossing began, but precious hours when the crossing could have been made had been wasted. To his rear, in the direction of Pomeroy, Duke heard firing and moved his two regiments totaling some 500 men into position to stop the Union advance. They clashed with Judah's advance guard and took some forty prisoners and a Union cannon.

Two separate Union columns, one commanded by General Hobson, the other by General Judah, were now on the scene, but neither commander was aware of the presence of the other. The Union gunboat "Moose" had been moored near Buffington Island. It now appeared and added its gunfire to the artillery of Hobson and Judah.

As Morgan tried to lead his men across the Ohio River he found the movement stymied by the gunboat. One Parrott gun and a 12-pounder howitzer tried to cover the crossing, but fire from the gunboat knocked out these two pieces. Morgan was well on his way to safety when he saw trouble behind him and came back. The command had ridden almost without pause and was played out. The sight of the gunboat and the converging Union columns threw the men into confusion and panic. Morgan tried to rally his men and lead them northward up the river to cross higher up. Some were still trying to cross the river; others tried to flee up the road northward. Hobson's column came up as Colonel Kautz led his two regiments of cavalry in a charge that turned the withdrawal of Morgan's raiders into a rout. Morgan's men tried to swim or flee and many drowned. Duke described the scene as "one of incredible confusion" and wrote of Confederates "who were circling about the valley, in a delirium of fright, clinging instinctively in all their terror, to bolts of calico and holding on to led horses, but changing the direction in which they galloped with every shell which whizzed or burst near them . . . wagons and ambulances . . . becoming locked and entangled with each other in their flight, many were upset and terrified horses broke loose from them and plunged wildly through the mass."[29]

Captain Allen of the 7th Ohio took part in the charge on Morgan's men. Allen had been a participant in a number of battles where regimental colors were displayed, but he had never witnessed a battle that saw the color of this mid-July charge. He wrote: "Immediately the stampede began, each one of Morgan's troopers began to unload the 'plunder' carried on his horse—boots, shoes, stockings, bird cages, and skates were scattered to the winds. Then the flying horsemen let loose their bolts of muslin and calico; holding one end, each trooper let the whole hundred yards or more stream out behind him, thus showing under the bright skies, banners galore. In colors these were violet, orange, white and red—embracing every color of the rainbow—and many shades and tints quite impossible to describe. The most kaleidoscopic view imaginable would not serve to describe the retreat of this 'army with banners,' and instantly, though greatly to our surprise we found ourselves to be 'rainbow chasers' in almost the literal sense of the word."[30]

The 7th and part of the 9th Michigan Cavalry charged into this mass, sending it flying. From another direction came more Union cavalry regiments from Ohio and the 1st, 3rd and 8th Kentucky (Union) Cavalry. As they galloped across the fields to gain the road, the fleeing Confederates did not know that to their front a stream flowing from the hills to the river had carved a narrow gorge through woodland. Quick passage of this area by a large contingent of men was not possible. Lashing their horses, Morgan's riders and teamsters galloped into the gorge, only to pile up in a confused heap. Morgan got through with 364 men, but the rest were pinned in position and surrendered.

Johnson and about 350 Confederate officers and men made it across the Ohio River. Some 120 Confederates were shot dead or drowned and 700 captured. Morgan's superb second-in-command, Brig. Gen. Basil Duke surrendered to Sgt. Charles E. Doke of the 9th Michigan Cavalry.[31] Among the captured were Colonels Howard Smith, Richard C. Morgan, John C. Hoffman and seventeen other Confederate officers. Col. Israel Garrard of the 7th Ohio left Captain Allen and a few men to guard the prisoners and galloped after Morgan and those who escaped. A select force of the best mounted men from the 2nd and 45th Ohio, the 3rd East Tennessee and the 1st and 3rd Kentucky went charging off after Morgan.

Morgan took the road from Hanover to West Point and from there was traveling down the Beaver Creek road. He was met by a group of citizens from New Lisbon, Ohio, and the two groups agreed not to fire on each other. The townspeople were anxious that their town not be harmed and Morgan wanting to keep moving. Morgan asked that some of the townspeople ride with him, perhaps as hostage or guides. A civilian named Burbick agreed to be guide with the provision that he could leave when he wanted. In the discussion a local militia officer who was trying to impress Morgan that the civilians were organized called Burbick "Captain." When Morgan saw surrender was necessary he sought to make an arrangement with "Captain Burbick" who was thoroughly confused by the title and his guest/hostage position and agreed to whatever Morgan wanted. Morgan surrendered his men to Burbick on the provision the Confederates would be able to keep all private property and would be paroled as soon as they reached Cincinnati. Maj. George W. Rue of the 9th Kentucky (Union) Cavalry and his command were closing fast and Morgan sent back a flag of truce saying he had already surrendered to Captain Burbick and the terms had been arranged. Rue was a combat-experienced officer and found laughable the notion that Morgan could surrender his command to a civilian whom he was holding prisoner. Major Rue reported, "I therefore treated this absurd claim with no notice whatever and held the prisoners."[32] Thus by the Beaver Creek road near New Lisbon, Ohio, on Sunday, July 26, 1863, Morgan surrendered with 364 officers and men.[33]

Captain Allen of the 7th Ohio Cavalry stood by the bank of the Ohio River looking at his men and their prisoners. The men of both sides had been in the saddle for three weeks with little sleep the entire time. They were covered with the dust of hundreds of miles of dirt roads. So thick was the dust upon their clothes, it was difficult to tell Billy Yank and Johnny Reb apart. Soon both Union and Confederate soldiers came to Allen to request permission to wash their hands and faces in the river.

Allen quickly saw this as a halfway measure. He allowed half the guards and half the prisoners to strip and bathe in the river. The troops were soon frolicking together in the water as though they were companions instead of men recently trying to kill each other. Looking at the nude bodies, a Confederate officer told Allen, "It is difficult to tell 'tother from which." A Confederate soldier said that if Morgan had let them bathe earlier there would have been enough dirt to shoal the river and they could have escaped.

Allen knew he could be in trouble for allowing this fraternization and endured the agony that decision-making often brings, but all went well. When the men finished beating some of the dust from their clothes and bathed, the Union horsemen broke out the food they carried in their haversacks (fried chicken and blackberry pie) and the two sides ate together as at a picnic. Confederate captain Tom Hines gave Captain Allen a small Confederate flag he carried as a memento of the occasion. Much would be heard of the audacious Capt. Thomas Henry Hines in the future.

There were many poor people in the area where Morgan attempted to cross. General Hobson had the plunder gathered and distributed it to them. Basil Duke bemoaned the loss of the division, but felt the raid had accomplished the mission. Duke believed Morgan's raid helped Braxton Bragg by giving him much-needed time. It was not Morgan's fault that Bragg would squander his opportunities. Others were not so kind. North and South, many believed Morgan had become caught up in his own daring and over-reached himself by going into Indiana and Ohio. There was grumbling in the Southern high command that Morgan had exceeded his orders. Bragg had told him not to leave Kentucky and now a much-needed division was eliminated. The world loves a winner and in war a single loss can ruin a reputation. The luster was gone from Morgan's star and he would never again be viewed in that almost legendary light.

The Confederates had not realized that when the North was invaded, the Northern citizens would resist as those in the South did. There were more than 100,000 home guards called out in Indiana and Ohio and they played a major role in slowing Morgan's movement and exhausting his men. The Northern people gave firm support to those who pursued Morgan. The Union defense at Gettysburg and offense at Vicksburg had reversed the tide of Southern victories.

There was great joy in the North now that the man called the Thunderbolt of the Confederacy was taken, and there were calls for retaliation. Nathan Bedford Forrest had captured Col. Abel Streight and his raiders. The rumor had spread that Streight and his men were being mistreated by the Confederate government and people in the North wanted revenge. To the outrage of the Confederacy, General Halleck in Washington had

Morgan and sixty-eight of his officers confined in the state penitentiary at Columbus, Ohio.

Duke and his compatriots were treated well by the Union soldiers who captured them—so well the Confederate officers wrote a letter to Captain Day, who had them in charge, expressing thanks and promising that if the same fate befell him he would be cared for. Duke noted that the combat men, those who fought each other, treated their captives kindly. The rear echelon was another matter. The civilians who had fled now formed a curious mob and the Union soldiers were not hesitant to voice their disgust that those who skedaddled when there was danger and now came to stare and hoot. The captives were taken to Sandusky, then to prison on Johnson's Island. Some of the other prisoners there had been taken at Gettysburg and they provided an account of the battle. Johnson's Island was as good a prison as could be expected, but it was not long before Morgan's officers were transferred to the Ohio penitentiary. The Union wrongly believed that Col. Abel Streight had been imprisoned in the Georgia penitentiary and meant to retaliate. Basil Duke talked to a prisoner who was looking out from a grated cell door. He was astounded to find it was his brother-in-law and commander, John Hunt Morgan.

The prisoners had all their facial hair shaved off. Beards and mustaches that had been worn for years were whisked away. There were sixty-eight officers in the Ohio jail. They were not associated with the convicts, but maintained an equally strict regimen. The gloom of the place was hardest for men accustomed to freedom to bear. Chess, marbles and gymnastics in the prison yard were some entertainment, but prison walls sap the spirit. From time to time officers went to solitary confinement for deeds or suspicion of deeds that were against the rules. It was a terrible experience. Maj. Thomas Webber wrote a letter about the Union use of Negro troops in which he hoped that all such troops and their officers would be hung. Webber went to solitary confinement for that.

It took several months of discussion to come up with a way out. Capt. Tom Hines developed the plan when he heard there was an air chamber. Hines engaged a guard in an architectural discussion and determined the ventilating chamber ran beneath the cells. Small knives from the dining room were purloined. Using these as digging tools they were able to remove the masonry that held cell stones in place and make their way into an air chamber beneath. From there they tunneled under the prison walls. There were many times when obstacles stood in their way, but the prisoners had nothing else to do but plot, and the inspiration of escaping was the mother of solutions. At night they slept with their hands and faces covered so the guards would become accustomed to not seeing their features.

The prison rules allowed a suit of civilian clothes. Morgan and six others had secured these. He paid fifteen dollars for a railroad schedule. Morgan could not reach the tunnel from his cell, but the night of the escape, his brother, Col. Richard Morgan, swapped cells during lockup. Small bits of coal were put on the floor to give early warning of a guard's approach. After the lantern-carrying guard passed, the men quickly arranged dummies in their beds, stamped on the thin covering over the holes in the floor of their cells and dropped into the air chambers beneath. They went through the tunnel then crossed the yard and reached upward with a hook and rope they had contrived to catch the coping of the wall. When they climbed to the top they used the same procedure to lower themselves to the ground. They tried, but could not disconnect the rope. It was left hanging on the wall. Morgan and Captain Hines headed for the depot, bought tickets and boarded a train for Cincinnati. To avoid suspicion the two men sat close to a Union officer and engaged him in light conversation.

As they neared Cincinnati the two set the brakes on the rear car and jumped off as the train slowed. Morgan told Duke there were some Union soldiers sitting on a woodpile and one asked, "What the hell are you jumping off the train for?" Morgan replied, "What the devil is the use of a man going into town when he lives out here? Besides, what matter is it to you?" "Oh, nothing," said the soldier and the two escapees moved on.

It was easy to cross the river to Kentucky where friends helped them with horses, guides and food. His trip though Kentucky was among friends and he got the treatment of a hero. Tennessee was a different matter; they were nearly caught and had to sneak through some Union pickets. Hines was captured but escaped. On December 4 they reached the Cumberland River near Burkesville. There they met some of Morgan's men who had not been involved in the Ohio raid. Morgan was soon back in Confederate uniform.

Duke and the others who remained behind were held in close confinement for three weeks while the escape was investigated and procedures changed. Richard Morgan received no greater punishment than the others. Captains Sheldon and Taylor were recaptured in Louisville and returned to prison. In February 1864, Duke was sent to Camp Chase for parole. He wrote that he and his fellow prisoners were given kind treatment by Colonel Richardson, the camp commandant who had been seriously wounded in battle. Duke's exchange did not come through and he voluntarily returned to be with his comrades in the penitentiary. They had failed at another escape and life was miserable. In March 1864, Duke was sent to Camp Douglas and life improved. While there he began to learn that what the officers experienced was considerably less than what the enlisted men endured. The horrors of Andersonville so frequently described in the Union press were not far different from those found in prison camps in the North.

At Fort Delaware it was announced that Confederate general Samuel Jones, who commanded at Charleston, had taken fifty Union officers and put them into a position where if Union guns fired on the city it would strike them. In retaliation, five Confederate general officers and forty-five field officers were selected to be used in similar fashion. Duke and five other of Morgan's officers were among these. They were sent south to Hilton Head then put in a Union brig, but were not taken where the guns were firing. A group of 600 Confederate officers (called The Immortal 600) were taken. Duke and his companions were exchanged for the fifty Union officers and after a year in prison he was free.

Upon his return to Confederate lines, Morgan asked to have his former command. This request was refused. The policy in Richmond was that all officers who had served with their units and men for three years were to be sent to new commands. The intent of this military idiocy was to bring in new concepts and fresh ideas. What really happened was that men who had fought together, who had forged a bond of trust, were ripped apart. The high level tinkerers had no understanding of morale, of the tradition that is formed in a unit. Basil Duke wrote, "They said that this policy would make the army 'a machine,' and it would be difficult to conceive of a more utterly worthless machine than it would have then been."[35]

In April 1864, after several months of recuperation, Morgan was given command of the Department of Southwest Virginia. In addition to home-guard militia, some 3,000 men were placed under his command. He did not give up and finally arranged that one-third of the troops in his department had been members of his old command. These were men who escaped capture during the Ohio raid and some who had been left behind. The remnants of his former division were organized into two battalions. While Morgan was in prison, Nathan Bedford Forrest was a friend to these men. Only 500 had horses and they were experienced soldiers who could give a good account in battle. However they had been shot up during the years of war and were considerably under strength. When Morgan's men were ordered to be dismounted by General Bragg, Forrest stood up for them and again fought his commander. The men and horses finally ended up in a brigade commanded by Colonel Grigsby. When Bragg retreated after winning at Chickamauga these two battalions of Morgan's men were posted between him and the Union army. They had suffered greatly in protecting Bragg's rear. Now they were back with Morgan.

The Confederacy was having difficulty keeping Union columns from destroying supply and manufacturing facilities. Two critical locations in Morgan's area of command were the leadworks at Wytheville and the appropriately named community of Saltville where much of the salt needed for the Confederate army was produced. In early May 1864, two Union columns moved to attack these works. Gen. George Crook, with infantry and cavalry, moved toward the leadworks and Gen. William Averell led his horse soldiers toward Saltville. A Confederate cavalry brigade under Ranger Col. Albert Gallatin Jenkins was fighting a delaying action against Crook, but Jenkins was badly wounded. Morgan sent 400 of his dismounted troops to Col. John McCausland who had taken command after Jenkins was hit. Morgan's men arrived just in time to turn the tide of battle. The Confederates were able to stop Crook's advance and take a defensive position near the New River Bridge.

Morgan and the rest of his troops were searching for General Averell's force. The route of the Union column convinced Morgan that Averell now planned to attack the leadworks at Wytheville. Taking Henry Litner Giltner's Kentucky cavalry and the two battalions of men from his former division, Morgan moved not to pursue Averell, but to get in front of him. Using superior knowledge of the terrain, Morgan arrived at Wytheville on May 11, 1864. There he found a small Confederate detachment of Grumble Jones' cavalry which had ridden in the day before. These were placed under Col. George B. Crittenden and he was positioned in the mountain gap through which Averell was most likely to attack.

Crittenden had scarcely established his defense when Averell's troops came into the gap and the battle began. Morgan reinforced his defenders and the Northern soldiers withdrew to a ridgeline where they took up a defensive posture. Morgan attacked and after a sharp fight Averell was forced to retreat. The Union general counterattacked and the battle continued with first one side and then the other meeting success. Neither side could gain a decisive victory. At nightfall, Averell withdrew leaving more than 100 prisoners and half that number killed or wounded. Morgan had some sixty casualties.

Though the Confederates had stalled both of the Union efforts, they had not ended the threat. Additional Union commands were available to reinforce those of Averell and Crook, and Morgan knew these soon would be on the march. He did not have sufficient force to stop the Union advance, therefore he had to change his opponents' thinking from offense to defense. Morgan decided to attack.[35] It was a desperate gamble, but Morgan believed it was his only hope.

Toward the end of May 1864, Morgan planned another raid into Kentucky. There were a variety of reasons for wanting to go back. Kentucky was his home state and he never shook the sadness he felt when it did not join the Confederacy. He had many friends there and could recruit men who would be loyal to him. It is likely that he also sought to re-establish his reputation; to wipe out the stain of being captured and losing his command. It

193

was also believed that reinforcements would be coming to Averell and Crook
from the west. Morgan needed to defeat these before a jointure of forces
would create a force to large for him to resist.

Taking 2,000 men, Morgan began a march into Kentucky. To achieve
surprise, his route took him through difficult mountain paths on which he
could not take artillery. They did not encounter resistance, but the effort
was wearing on the horses and there was little food for man or beast. Many
horses broke down—the Kentuckians alone losing 200—but in this rough
terrain, dismounted men managed to keep pace with the column. In seven
days they covered more than 150 miles of mountain paths. Morgan wanted
to reach Mount Sterling, the scene of earlier triumph and a key Union supply depot. Indeed it was the largest in east Tennessee. On June 7 the Kentuckians in the column saw they were back in their beloved bluegrass
country and morale soared. On the eighth they moved into position and on
June 9 they thundered into the town of Mount Sterling and captured vast
quantities of supplies and 380 prisoners. Morgan had not lost his audacity
and victory was his reward.

In order to slow Union reinforcement from Indiana and Ohio, Morgan
had dispatched detachments to destroy bridges on the Louisville and Lexington and the Kentucky Central railroads. Time was a vital consideration in
Morgan's thinking. He had to strike quickly before the superior numbers of
the Union forces could be mobilized against him. Morgan decided to leave
his dismounted men in Mount Sterling to burn the enemy supplies and
equipment he could not use and scour the countryside for horses. Colonel
Giltner was left in command of the dismounted element. Morgan pressed
on toward Lexington.

Meanwhile, as Morgan had expected, Union forces were moving to join
Crook and Averell. Union general Stephen Burbridge, commanding the 5th
Division of the XXIII Corps, was moving on a parallel track with Morgan,
but headed in the opposite direction. Local informants and Union riders
were spreading the word about Morgan's advance and Col. John Mason
Brown, commanding Burbridge's 2nd Brigade gained sufficient information
that he was able to convince his commander to change direction and march
for Mount Sterling to attack Morgan.

Giltner's troops had established an indifferent outpost line and were
enjoying the luxury of their plunder when Colonel Brown's Union soldiers
smashed through the outposts and into the Confederate camp. Taken by
surprise, Giltner's troops could not muster a defense and found themselves
split into two groups under Giltner and Martin. Both officers sought to fight
a delaying action. Col. Richard M. Martin's men were hit hard with Martin
twice wounded and the loss of fourteen officers and some 300 men. Giltner

managed to withdraw toward Lexington with the remainder. After three to four hours of fighting, Martin managed to break contact and, with the few men he had left, rejoined Giltner.

Morgan captured Lexington on June 10 and that night Giltner and what was left of his command came into camp. Morgan had captured a large number of horses at Lexington so all of his command was now mounted. His numbers were dwindling. Men had been detached to destroy bridges, some were needed to guard prisoners and more than 700 had been killed, wounded or captured.

Scouts brought in word that Morgan's former adversary, Union general Edward H. Hobson, who had pursued him so relentlessly through Ohio and Indiana, was at hand. Hobson had 1,500 men and was marching fast toward Cynthiana. Morgan did not wait to be attacked. He sent Giltner with the majority of the men to strike Hobson from the front. With one battalion of his old division, Morgan hit Hobson from the rear. Caught between the two Confederate forces and thinking himself outnumbered, Hobson surrendered. Morgan had never forgotten his imprisoned comrades. He sent one of his brothers with General Hobson to Cincinnati to arrange an exchange. If Hobson failed to make the exchange he was honor-bound to report as a prisoner to Confederate lines.

Taking advantage of his new horseflesh, Morgan left Lexington and marched on Cynthiana. The town was taken after a sharp fight and valuable supplies were captured and destroyed. Morgan's victory was short lived. On June 12, General Burbridge with 5,200 men of his division arrived at Cynthiana and attacked. Morgan fought first a defense, then a delay. He paroled his prisoners, destroyed captured supplies and sought to withdraw in orderly fashion. The battle raged throughout much of the day with Confederate ammunition supplies waning. Morgan's efforts were now devoted to extricating what was left of his command. He lost some 650 men killed, wounded or captured before he could break contact. Moving as rapidly as circumstances would allow, Morgan and his men rode by way of Flemingsburg and West Liberty on through the mountains. They reached Abingdon, Virginia, on June 20.

Morgan's raid had mixed results. It bought the Confederacy several months when it could better organize a defense of southwest Virginia. The cost had been high with fifty percent of Morgan's command casualties. Some of the men on the detached parties, away from supervision, had performed criminal acts. Union leadership was effectively using these crimes to promote support of the Federal government among the local people. There was a feeling in Richmond that Morgan did not take sufficient action against the thieves in his command.[36] One of the reports was that the bank at Mount Sterling had been robbed. Morgan wanted an investigation, but his enemies in Richmond were not interested in finding out what really occurred. Morgan was not in favor and his opponents were more content with rumor. If the Confederate command had evidence that linked Morgan to any wrongdoing it would not share it with the accused man. Before setting out on another raid, Morgan wrote a letter to James A. Seddon, secretary of war of the Confederate States of America. It was a plea for an investigation, a court-martial that Morgan believed would reveal his innocence. Pressed for time, Morgan was unable to mail the letter and carried it with him on the raid.

The brave hopes of the early days of the war had given way to a grim effort to hang on. Basil Duke noticed a change in the Confederate soldier. The man in faded gray or butternut fought on, but he knew the support was not there. His people were tired of war and his government could not support his efforts. He often went without pay, his clothes were in tatters and he did not know when or where his next meal would be. He frequently was sick from living in the elements and eating scraps, but was nevertheless expected to march between twenty and thirty miles a day if infantry and ride fifty to sixty if cavalry, then fight at the end of the march. He was lucky if he had shoes and could find a scrap of blanket. It was a dog-eat-dog existence, his life was on the line and it was likely he was not going to survive. If his government would not or could not look out for him, he would look out for himself. Thus crime increased. Duke found this especially true in cavalry units operating on detached service away from the gaze of senior officers.[37]

Several months passed while Morgan sought to recruit, train and refit his command. The rigors of the campaign and imprisonment had taken their toll. Morgan became seriously ill and for some weeks was confined to bed in Abingdon, Virginia, while his soldiers were in camp at Johnson's Station in eastern Tennessee. Not in numbers or in spirit were they the same men he had led to victory after victory in 1862. A key subordinate, Adam Rankin "Stovepipe" Johnson, had been shot in the face. It was said he was totally blind or at best had lost most of his vision. By August 1864 Morgan's men were reduced to two skeleton brigades under the commands of Smith and Giltner; the whole totaling some 1,200 men. Win or lose, Morgan had achieved the devotion of his men and the command was not the same without him. Hearing about the low morale in camp, Morgan knew that victory was the best medicine. Though his health had not fully returned, Morgan laid plans to raid the Union garrison at Knoxville.

When he rode a train into Johnson Station on August 29, 1864, the word of his arrival spread quickly and the soldiers gathered around him with a tumultuous welcome. They had been fighting defensive battles and they knew Morgan would lead them in the attack.

Camp defensive activity promptly changed to preparations for the raid. Additional troops joined the command and Confederates from east Tennessee came in. Rations were cooked, weapons and forage readied and horses shod. On the afternoon of September 3, 1864, Morgan led his column out on a seventy-two-mile march to Greenville, a railroad stop on the Tennessee and Virginia Railroad. Scouts reported that Union troops under the command of Gen. Alvan C. Gillem were at Bull's Gap, eighteen miles south of Greenville. Gillem was a West Pointer, an aggressive commander and known to be a disciplinarian. On one occasion when he was a colonel, he was reprimanding a soldier who was slightly intoxicated at the time. After Gillem had concluded his rough comments, the soldier remarked, "Yez wuddint have occasion to talk to me so ef I had a pistol." The colonel, much astonished asked, "Well, sir, what would you do if you had a pistol?" The soldier looked pained and said, "Why I'd shoot myself, sir."[38]

Morgan bivouacked his troops for the night several miles from Greenville while he sought to gain more information. What had been a pleasant day showed signs of an approaching storm as Morgan galloped between his brigades. His orders were for the command to be ready to ride at first light to attack the enemy. Morgan normally stayed in camp with his troops, but he was still weak from his illness and with the onset of the storm decided to accept the hospitality of a wealthy Greenville lady named Williams who was an ardent supporter of the Confederacy.

Outposts were established and the command put into positions that guarded the Greenville approaches from Bull's Gap. Smith's brigade, comprised of the veterans from Morgan's old division, was in the center; Giltner's Kentuckians the right and Vaughn's east Tennessee troops on the left. As the storm struck the men hunkered down beneath makeshift rail fence and oilcloth shebangs, or lacking those simply made ready to sleep wet as best they could.

At the Williams house, Morgan was being fed and made comfortable by his hostess. Greenville was a divided community and some were not pleased to see Morgan arrive. Leading citizens who supported the Confederacy came to meet the general and Mrs. Williams had the opportunity to see her son who was a soldier in Morgan's command. All those present were supportive of the Confederacy except one, Lucy Williams, a daughter-in-law. Though her brothers fought for the Confederacy, Lucy Williams strongly believed in the United States and had convinced her husband to do likewise.[39] Duke later wrote that Lucy Williams was angry because Morgan had revoked the parole and sent to prison a wounded Union officer. Morgan believed the man was trying to send a report on Morgan's command to General Gillem. Lucy Williams thought the man's wounds were so serious that he would die.

Only Lucy Williams knew her motive for the actions that followed. Saying she must return to her farm, she left the gathering. She had been born and raised in the area, knew the roads and trails and was an intelligent woman who recognized Morgan was spending the night some distance from his troops. She also knew from the dinner conversation that the Confederates would be moving on the next morning.

Lucy Williams rode through the storm and arrived at the Union camp at Bull's Gap around midnight. Admitted to General Gillem's presence, she convinced the officer that this was an ideal opportunity to kill or capture the Confederate raider. Gillem had "Boots and Saddles" sounded and, with Lucy Williams showing them the way, the cavalry rode for Greenville. She chose a road that entered Greenville from the north, behind the majority of Morgan's men. The Confederates of Vaughn's brigade had pickets on the road, but as they considered themselves in a rear area they had sought shelter and gone to sleep. After a few shots, they were captured with ease.

While Gillem's main force routed Vaughn's brigade, a detachment followed Lucy to the Williams house. Morgan heard the shots and jumped from his bed and began to dress. The Williams house was located on the corner of the two main streets of Greenville. To the rear of the house was a considerable yard with large trees and an ornamental garden with hedges and arbors of vines and flowers. Beyond that was the house of a family named Fry. Like Lucy Williams they strongly supported the United States. The owner of the property had been imprisoned by the Confederates, but his wife was in the house.

Morgan could see Union horsemen approaching the front of the house. Throwing his belt and revolvers over his shoulder he sought to escape through the rear door. He could hear hoofbeats as more cavalry rode to cut off that escape route. The town of Greenville was thoroughly aroused and bedroom windows were thrown up by people peering out to watch the events transpiring beneath them.

Morgan ran for the ornamental garden as he could tell from the firing that his troops were engaged. It was unlikely he could quickly rejoin them as the cavalry was cutting off his escape route. His only option was to hide in the thick vines and flowers in the ornamental garden and hope that when he was not found in the house the cavalry would ride on.

From her bedroom window across the street, Mrs. Fry could see Morgan secreting himself in the garden. Rushing downstairs, she pointed out to the Union soldiers where the Confederate Ranger was hiding. Morgan now attempted to shoot his way clear. It was his last desperate gamble—a losing one.

John Hunt Morgan was shot to death in a Greenville, Tennessee, garden on Sunday, September 4, 1864. Without their leader and struck from behind, Morgan's men were routed.

Morgan's friend and brother-in-law Basil Duke took over the command now reduced to 273 men with scarcely fifty weapons that would function. On September 15, 1864, Basil Duke became a brigadier general. Duke worked hard to round up stragglers, recruit and rebuild the division and fought it well in the fading light of the Confederacy. His missions included actions that must have filled him with grief. Duke had to battle not only Union troops, but organized Confederate turncoats and bushwhackers who had become lawless in the calamity of defeat.

There were few of the old veterans left; the proud Rangers who would have followed Morgan anywhere. Maj. Thomas Webber, who once had men without weapons carry fence rails till they captured one and who endured solitary confinement in the Ohio prison, had resumed command of his regiment. They called it a battalion now. Webber was down to twenty-eight men and fourteen of those were lost in a desperate assault. "Fight, damn you! It's only a scout!" yelled a Union officer to his men as rifles roared. "No, I'll be dammed if it is," shouted one of Morgan's Rangers. "We're all here."[40]

Early's troops had been routed from the Shenandoah Valley by Sheridan and Thomas had smashed John Bell Hood in Tennessee. Basil Duke and his men were traveling with other broken commands, trying to join General Lee. They were somewhere near Danville, Virginia, when the news came that Lee had surrendered. Duke wrote of the other Confederate commands, "Crowds of them threw down their arms and left, and those that remained lost all sense of discipline."[41]

There were 600 men of Morgan's Rangers left and only ten refused to go as Duke marched south to join General Johnston's army. Many of his men were riding wagon mules, often without saddles. They had watched entire brigades quit, but those who could rode on and those that could not ride walked 300 miles southward. Duke wrote, "To command such men was the proudest honor that an officer could obtain."[42]

There was little that remained of the Confederate army. At Charlotte, North Carolina, Duke and his men met a battalion of Mississippi cavalry and the next day Jefferson Davis and his cabinet arrived, escorted by Gen. George G. Dibbrell's division of cavalry. The officers heard of Lincoln's assassination, but they did not believe the news. They heard from General Johnston that he was preparing to surrender. That was believable. The entire party rode on for South Carolina. Duke wrote that an old lady yelled at his men as they were taking forage from her barn.

"You are a gang of thieving, rascally Kentuckians, afraid to go home while our boys are surrendering decently."

"Madam," replied one of the men. "South Carolina had a good deal to say in getting up this war, but we Kentuckians have contracted to finish it out."[43]

Some 2,500 men had rallied to the side of President Jefferson Davis. He wanted them to fight it out, saying they would be a nucleus for thousands more. The officers who had fought the war knew their president could not bring himself to accept the fact that it was over. When they were silent he understood, and the strength and bearing went out of him and he was visibly shaken. It was time to split up with Davis and a small escort trying to make their way to Mexico. Duke and his men had enough of war but did not surrender until they knew Davis had safely left their area. It was time for the killing to end.

After his death, Morgan's body was taken to Abingdon where it was interred, then later removed to Richmond. There is a persistent rumor that he is buried in Richmond, but that is not true. His body was removed to Section C of the Lexington Cemetery in Lexington, Kentucky. The grave lies in a curious family plot where headstones of deceased members are arranged as though forming a perimeter defense. Very near to the grave of John Hunt Morgan is buried his friend, brother-in-law and loyal subordinate Basil Duke. The stones are deteriorating and Morgan's is difficult to read.

PART THREE

Wizard

CHAPTER EIGHT

Once a Ranger, Always a Ranger

In early July 1861, a forty-year-old private soldier walked into the office of Tennessee governor Isham G. Harris. When he walked out of the governor's office, Nathan Bedford Forrest was a colonel ordered to recruit a battalion of mounted Rangers under the authority of the Confederate States. The old adage "It's not what you know, but who you know," seemed to be at work. Governor Harris had no knowledge of the combat ability of the man he had called to his office, but he knew the man.

Nathan Bedford Forrest was born July 13, 1821, in the Duck River settlements of Bedford County (now Marshall County, Tennessee). The oldest of six sons, Forrest became head of the family at age sixteen when his father died. Dawn to dusk farming was a major part of his young life, and opportunities for formal education were limited. Forrest received less than a year of formal schooling. He learned to read and, although his pronunciation often was incorrect, he could express himself with power and persuasion. Forrest did not like to write. He would later say, "I never see a pen but what I think of a snake."[1] His responsibility was to his family and he worked hard to give them a life free from hunger.

At a time when war seemed imminent between the fledgling Republic of Texas and Mexico, twenty-year-old Nathan Bedford Forrest and his next younger brother John became caught up in the fervor and sought to get into the fight. John fought and came home crippled, in need of crutches for the rest of his life. Forrest did not see action. By the time he arrived in Texas, the threat of war had vanished. Forrest missed his first chance at war.[2]

Back in Tennessee after an absence of a few months, he settled south of Memphis, joining his uncle Jonathan Forrest in a livery stable business, boarding horses, trading in grain and hay and livestock. Forrest had grown to be a powerful man, with black hair and gray eyes. He was described as being "six feet two inches in height, with broad shoulders, full chest, long arms and a powerful muscular development, and with an average weight of 180 pounds."[3] In the 1840s, men went armed, and men of the West were

Nathan Bedford Forrest, the "wizard of the saddle." Famed Civil War historian Shelby Foote claimed there were two men of genius in the war: Lincoln and Forrest. LIBRARY OF CONGRESS

quick to settle their disputes with a sword, cane, knife or pistol. On March 20, 1845, Jonathan and Nathan Bedford Forrest were in the town square when the older man was attacked and shot dead by four men. Forrest was twenty-four years old when he drew his pistol and killed his first man. He wounded the other three and they fled.

On September 25, 1845, Forrest married a Presbyterian minister's daughter, Mary Ann Montgomery. His business was prospering and the Forrest family moved to Memphis. Opportunities were better there, and Forrest became involved in buying and selling plantations and slaves. His wealth increased and he became a cotton grower with his own 3,000-acre plantation.

He flirted with politics and twice was elected a Memphis alderman. The youth who had lived in poverty scratched and clawed his way to affluence. He later estimated his pre-war wealth at a million and a half dollars.[4] He was well known to powerful men in Tennessee.

In 1861, the drums of war were sounding. There were different sorts of people in Tennessee. From Knoxville east were German and Scotch-Irish non-slaveholding mountain people. The rest of the state was more involved in the plantation culture, thus favoring enforced servitude. As a result, Tennessee was of two minds; it first voted by a large majority to stay with the Union, then its wily secessionist governor Isham G. Harris maneuvered it toward independence with a view toward forcing the state into the Confederacy. Harris was bald-headed on top with hair like wings on the side of his head and a broad, flowing mustache. No grass grew on the top of his scheming dome. When Lincoln made his call for 75,000 volunteers, it angered border people, and Harris had the tool he needed to press for secession. By June 1861, a divided Tennessee was ostensibly in the Confederate camp. East Tennessee remained strongly pro-Union and talk of secession from Tennessee was rampant.

The pre-Civil War era was a time when communities maintained militia organizations that were frequently gaudily attired social organizations with flowery names. They carried such titles as Guards, Avengers or Hussars. Their drill was a time of community entertainment often accompanied by dances and picnics. Trained and experienced military leaders were rare, and the leading business figures of the community normally held command positions. Nathan Bedford Forrest was busy in his climb from poverty. He devoted no time to military endeavors. Thus despite his wealth, when war seemed imminent, he joined the 7th Tennessee Cavalry as a private.

Whatever success Governor Harris had in Tennessee, the most significant thing he did for the Confederate States of America was to promote Private Nathan Bedford Forrest to a colonel of mounted Rangers. Armed with his new authority, Forrest placed the following advertisement in the Memphis *Daily Appeal:*

A Chance For Active Service—Mounted Rangers

Having been authorized by Governor Harris to raise a battalion of mounted Rangers for the war, I desire to enlist five hundred able-bodied men, mounted and equipped with such arms as they can procure (shot-guns and pistols preferable) suitable to the service. Those who cannot entirely equip themselves will be furnished arms by the State. When mustered in, a valuation of the property in horses and arms, will be made, and the amount credited to the volunteers. Those wishing to enlist are requested to report themselves at the Gayoso House, where quarters will be assigned until such time as the battalion is raised.

N.B. Forrest[5]

Determined to do his part in the defense of his home state, Forrest was searching far afield to enlist men. The first company of his regiment was formed in Kentucky. It consisted of ninety men who called themselves the Boone Rangers and was commanded by Capt. Frank Overton. To get back to Tennessee, they had to take a Louisville and Nashville train. When informed that Union volunteers in larger numbers were prepared to dispute the pas-

sage, Forrest resorted to deception. In sight of another train that was departing southward he assembled his recruits and all their family members. To
onlookers on the train it appeared a vast party had assembled under the Confederate flag. When this train reached the town where the Union supporters
waited, the passengers who had witnessed the gathering greatly exaggerated
the Confederate numbers and this caused the Union supporters to disband.[6]

In August 1861, Forrest led his first company of Ranger recruits to Memphis. There he was joined by a second company of volunteers led by Capt.
Charles May. They called themselves the Forrest Rangers. More companies
comprised of men from Alabama joined and Forrest hurried to complete his
recruiting. The quiet war was about to get noisy. At the time both North and
South were following the unwise practice of electing their officers. There was
no doubt who would command this unit. Forrest was elected lieutenant
colonel.

With these men as a nucleus, Forrest recruited a battalion of eight companies.[7] Experienced Indian fighter and Texas Ranger Adam Rankin Johnson and Robert M. Martin were combat-proven scouts drawn to the power
that seemed to radiate from Forrest. When they first met, Johnson noted of
Forrest, "He was a man to catch the look and hold the attention of the most
casual observer, and as we gazed on each other I felt that he was a born
leader."[8] Superbly mounted on one of his own horses, Forrest was busy
recruiting and purchasing weapons. Rangers normally provided their own
horses and weapons, but there was great competition for war materiel in Tennessee. Forrest traveled into neutral Kentucky and smuggled out weapons,
saddles and other equipment, often disguising it as shipments of potatoes.
His brief venture to Texas and contact with Adam Rankin Johnson had
taught Forrest a military truth. Though skilled with a saber, Forrest understood firepower. He would endeavor to arm his men with six-shooters in the
manner of the Texas Rangers and succeeded in so equipping half of his initial command.

In 1861, rivers and railroads were the key arteries of communication.
The broad Mississippi River was the belt of America's east-west middle. Control of the Mississippi was vital, as it offered easy access to Tennessee and
Kentucky. The Cumberland and Tennessee rivers both flowed northward to
join the Ohio, but they were highways of water that would allow rapid movement of troops and supplies into Tennessee. The ability to move freely on
the Cumberland River would lead to the important communication and factory center of Nashville where the river, the railroads and war production
met. Of equal importance, the Tennessee River rose in east Tennessee and
flowed to Chattanooga where it carved an unnavigable path through ridges
and high mountains, then in a quieter mood ran southwest into Alabama

before turning north again to transverse Tennessee and join the Ohio at Paducah, Kentucky. Control of the Tennessee River would split its namesake state in two. When they crossed into Kentucky, both of these critical rivers were side by side, at one point only twelve miles apart.

Control of the rivers was critical. Both Governor Harris and the commander of the Tennessee state troops, Gen. Gideon Pillow, had more zeal then military experience. Believing that Kentucky would remain neutral, they concentrated their defensive attention on west Tennessee and the Mississippi River. In a tentative effort to forestall river movement on the Tennessee and Cumberland rivers, the Confederates constructed three forts on the border near Kentucky and Tennessee. Fort Henry and Fort Heiman were intended to guard the Tennessee River and Fort Donelson to stand watch over the Cumberland.

Subject to easier interference than the rivers, the railroads were critical to the war effort. Most carried the names of their destinations: the Louisville and Nashville, the Nashville and Ohio, the Mobile and Ohio, and the Memphis and Charleston railroads tied communities and states together with a steel ribbon. Memphis, Nashville and Chattanooga, the key cities of Tennessee, were linked by the steel wheel on the steel rail. Troops and the iron, lead, copper, salt, gunpowder and wheat to sustain the Confederate war effort flowed along these rails. There were more than 100 separate railroads running on 10,000 miles of track in the South. Many were of different gauge, ranging from rails spaced 4 feet $8\frac{1}{2}$ inches apart (a distance which dated back in history to the width of Roman chariot wheels and became the standard gauge of carriages and railroads) to cars that ran on rails 5 feet 6 inches apart. This variance meant that men and materiel often could not travel through to a destination, but had to be transferred along the way to cars that would fit the gauge of a particular railroad.

Clearly evident to Union and Confederate planners alike was the avenue of approach that led from Nashville to Chattanooga to Atlanta. Virginia was a battlefield and was too far forward in the line of fire to provide the production needs of the Confederacy. For the heartland of the Confederacy to be protected, Tennessee must be held.

Kentucky was being wooed by both Union and Confederate agents, but the Southerners made a major mistake. It happened at the Kentucky town of Columbus, a place that would in time be a great Union supply depot called the Gibralter of the West. Columbus was located on a high bluff just a few miles below where the great Ohio River flowed into the Mississippi. On September 3, 1861, Confederates invaded neutral Kentucky and occupied Columbus. The Confederates hoped to block Union passage of the Mississippi, but they had not reckoned the political cost.

Now the Union forces could move freely. Troops under a brigadier general named U.S. Grant occupied Paducah. Union commanders began to occupy positions that would allow them to use the Cumberland and Tennessee rivers. The Confederacy saw the threat and Forest was ordered to the defense of this area. He now had eight companies of mounted troops that initially operated near Fort Henry on the Tennessee and Fort Donelson on the Cumberland River. Forrest found the river forts had been poorly positioned and improperly constructed. He believed the proper place for his command was out front and moved most his men north of the Cumberland River. When they learned a Union gunboat was on the Cumberland, Forrest's men ambushed the heavily armed vessel, firing at its portholes until it was forced to steam away.

On December 28, 1861, Forrest was leading his command west of the Green River when he engaged a Union force near the little Kentucky town of Sacramento. Forrest found the ranks of his Rangers joined by a beautiful Southern girl mounted on a superb horse and eager to fight. What she did in the battle is unknown, but this lassie wanted to fight and she galloped her horse into action beside the men. Forrest later reported, "Her untied tresses, floating in the breeze, infused nerve into my arm and kindled knightly chivalry in my heart."[9]

Forrest divided his force, simultaneously attacking frontally and from the flank. His men were untrained in maneuvers and it was more hell-for-leather than tactics, but the Union troops also were untrained and began to withdraw. A running fight ensued with Forrest leading from the front. In this encounter he personally killed or wounded three Union soldiers.

It was at this fight that the men saw the transformation of Nathan Bedford Forrest when engaged in battle. A Confederate officer wrote, "Forrest seemed in a desperate mood and very much excited. His face was flushed till it looked like a painted warrior, and his eyes, usually mild in expression, glared like those of a panther about to spring on its prey."[10]

Forrest had charged headlong into the enemy and battled two Union cavalry officers and a private soldier. He shot the private and one officer and used his saber on the second officer, then drove his horse into another knocking him to the ground. Adam Rankin Johnson wrote, "Never in any battle did (a) leader play a fiercer individual than Forrest did on this day."[11]

Grant and other Northern commanders had recognized the importance of eliminating the Confederate forts on the Cumberland and Tennessee. Heavy rains had raised the rivers and new Union gunboats under the command of Commodore Andrew Foote plus some 17,000 Union soldiers ready for action. The soldiers of the army of the United States were filled with the confidence that radiated from Grant. Up the Tennessee River came seven gunboats and 23 Union regiments. The battle of Fort Henry began and ended on February 6, 1862. The Confederate flag came down and the surrender opened the water door. Union gunboats now ranged up the Tennessee, destroying Confederate freight-hauling steamboats and supplies waiting for transport.

Confederate hopes were pinned on stopping a Union attack on Fort Donelson. Overall command of Confederate troops in the theater rested with Albert Sydney Johnston, an esteemed soldier who before the Civil War had been Robert E. Lee's commander in the 2nd Cavalry. Johnston had three brigadier generals at Fort Donelson: Gideon J. Pillow, of the Tennessee state troops, a proven soldier from the Mexican War, but a man uncooperative with others; Simon Bolivar Buckner of the Kentucky Confederate state troops, a good man but the junior officer; and John B. Floyd, a political hack who commanded troops from Mississippi and Virginia and was the senior officer. Floyd had been United States secretary of war under President Buchanan and in a clearly traitorous act to his office and oath had used his power to scatter the Regular army of the United States and deprive or shoddily equip Northern militia units while he stocked Southern arsenals and sent the best weapons south.[12]

All available Confederate troops were being sent to Fort Donelson and Lieutenant Colonel Forrest was put in command of the more then 1,000 Confederate cavalry in the area. Pillow wanted all troops kept at the fort, Buckner wanted a large force withheld to flank Grant, and Floyd vacillated from hour to hour. While his three seniors were debating tactics and steadily weakening in resolve, Forrest fought a masterful delaying action against Grant's oncoming force. Several horses were killed under him and his coat was repeatedly torn by bullets. At Fort Donelson, Forrest led his men in a hard-fought struggle to capture two Union guns that had the Confederates stymied. Before the action was concluded Forrest and his men had captured nine guns and nearly 4,000 small arms and had opened a route to Nashville for the Confederates to rejoin General Johnston's army.[13]

Union gunboats were using heavy but ineffective fire on the fort. On February 14 the three brigadier general council decided to evacuate Fort Donelson. Forrest felt his horsemen had now opened several routes on which the army could withdraw. A half-hearted effort to break out was recalled on General Pillow's advice and the troops sent back to the trenches. The weather was terrible, combining winter cold with sleet and ice.

The three Confederate generals were men who at one time or another in their lives had demonstrated courage. They were now taking counsel of their fears. They accepted rumors that vast numbers of Union reinforcements were on the field and they were trapped. The loss of confidence brought on a desire to surrender the fort. If they did, this would be the first large-scale surrender of Confederate forces. There was concern about how the men would be treated. Floyd and Pillow were anxious about their personal safety, fearing if they were captured the Union troops might take reprisal on them. Floyd was under indictment in Washington for his actions in arming people opposed to the United States while serving as secretary of war.[14] Buckner thought that continuing the fight would result in butchery of the troops. Buckner was for surrender.

Forrest spoke for continuing to fight. He told the generals his scouts had been on the site where the Union reinforcements were supposed to be and there was no one there. He told them his horsemen could cover the army as it withdrew. Rank can prevent generals from hearing colonels. They ignored Forrest.

Floyd proposed the surrender of the garrison for others as necessary, but he needed to escape and wanted to take his men with him. Floyd gave up his authority to Buckner. Pillow did not want to surrender, but also wanted to escape and also gave up command to the junior general. Simon Buckner had the responsibility for surrender dumped on him by his two seniors.

Colonel Forrest told his commanders he had not brought his men there to surrender them and that he was going to take his troops out. Generals Floyd and Pillow hurriedly made plans to escape and did so by other means. Floyd took all the water transportation for himself. He tried to get his men out by steamboat, and being primarily concerned with those of his own state, carried off his Virginia troops. He left those from Mississippi standing by the river cursing him. Pillow came out on horseback.

On returning to his men Forrest said, "Boys, these people are talking about surrendering, and I am going out of this place before they do, or bust hell wide open."[15]

Forrest quickly had his exhausted troops on horseback. It took more than physical strength to go forward. It was the power of their commander's will that led these men. There was no enemy encountered, but the danger was always there. The bitter cold of the night sapped men's strength and ice-filled water crossings were torture. At points of difficulty and danger Ranger Colonel Nathan Bedford Forrest led the way.

Behind them, surrender was arranged. In this strange war of intimacies, Simon Oliver Buckner and U.S. Grant were close friends, both West Point graduates and comrades in the Mexican War. If Buckner thought that friendship would help him, he was quickly disabused. Grant clamped a cigar in his mouth and wrote, "No terms except an unconditional and immediate surrender can be accepted."[16] The formal surrender was accepted at Dover Tavern on Sunday, February 16, 1862.

Between 10,000 and 13,000 Confederate troops were surrendered at Fort Donelson. It was the first great Union victory and one of the most significant battles of the war. It kept Kentucky under the stars and stripes and opened Tennessee to the Union army. It was a major step in the Union effort to gain control of the Mississippi River valley and cut the South in two. The Confederates were forced from Kentucky, abandoning their capitol at Bowling Green. From Columbus on the Mississippi to Nashville, most of the west and middle of Tennessee was now under Union control. People said that the U.S. in front of Grant's name stood for Unconditional Surrender. The only aspect of this battle Southerners could point to with pride was the rising star of Ranger Nathan Bedford Forrest.

Forrest took his riders to Charlotte, a town due west of Nashville. The initial Fort Donelson reports sent by the three Confederate generals had been positive, bordering on extravagant. The newspapers and more importantly optimistic reports to Confederate commander Gen. Albert Sydney had given him good reason to believe Southern arms would prevail. Now came the truth about the disaster and middle Tennessee was in a panic. Trains out of Nashville were packed and the roads were clogged with carriages. Confederate troops marched into Nashville, but they marched out heading South. Large amounts of Confederate stores were abandoned by the officers in charge of them and looted or given away by local government.

Forrest rode into the city and pistol-whipped a mob leader, then turned firehoses with icy river water on the mob, freezing their ardor. He next commandeered all transport and used it to get Confederate supplies headed south, before riding out ahead of the oncoming enemy.

While Grant moved troops to take Clarksville, Union general Don Carlos Buell moved his army of 30,000 forward and occupied Nashville. Despite the high-flown oratory of Confederate officers and civic leaders, Nashville rejoined the Union. It would stay that way.

Albert Sidney Johnston had overall command of the Confederate forces in the west. Johnston joined the troops from Nashville with those under the commands of Beauregard, Bragg and Polk and organized them into three corps. Johnston now had command of a unified force. U.S. troops were split between U.S. Grant and Don Carlos Buell and could be coordinated only from Washington. Seeing that the troops of Grant and Buell were separated, Johnston felt each could be defeated in turn.

Over the objections of Beauregard, who was next in command, Johnston attacked Grant's force at Shiloh on April 6, 1862, and was initially successful. The Confederates did not believe General Buell was on the march. Patrols sent out by Forrest found that he was coming to assist Grant, but the fight had begun. The battle of Shiloh was a bloody brawl between untrained civilians thrust into uniforms.

In order to influence the battle, senior commanders had to be in the line of fire. Sherman was wounded twice and had several horses killed under him. Grant had a bullet strike the scabbard of his sword. General Johnston was shot in the leg, and an artery was severed. Intent upon the battle, Johnston did not recognize that life was draining from him and he bled to death. Buell's army arrived and crossed the Tennessee River at Grant's rear, uniting the Union army. On Johnston's death, General Beauregard took command. Beauregard had been opposed to the attack and he ordered the Southern troops to retire.

Forrest and his horsemen covered the retreat with his Ranger force which now included Terry's Texas Rangers and Capt. John Hunt Morgan and his Kentucky Rangers. A Union brigade under Brig. Gen. William T. Sherman moved against Forrest, who drove back the skirmishers of the lead Union infantry regiment by personally leading a charge. When the skirmishers came in running for their lives, the infantry regiment following them broke and ran into the Union cavalry that was following. The whole forward element fell back upon the main body where Sherman could make his considerable presence felt.

William Tecumseh Sherman was a superb commander, a man who knew as much as anyone about war. He knew its horror and was greatly saddened when South Carolinians fired on Fort Sumter. He had a superb understanding of logistics and told a Southern friend that no nation of farmers had ever beaten a nation of mechanics. When the war began many graduates of West Point were clamoring to be promoted to general. Lincoln would have made Sherman a general, but Sherman requested he be made a colonel, given a regiment and allowed to prove himself worthy of star rank. Fellow West Pointer and newly promoted Brig. Gen. Irvin McDowell met Sherman on the street and was aghast that Sherman was only a colonel. "You should have asked for a brigadier-general's rank," said McDowell, "You're just as fit for it as I am." Sherman replied, "I know it."[17]

Sherman had a great sense of priority. Even when he was senior to Grant, he offered to wave his seniority in order to lead his troops to Grant's assistance. Their enemies called Grant a drunk and Sherman crazy, but they were wrong on both counts. Grant and Sherman were men of total dedication with a realistic view of war and the closeness between them is a story of the brotherhood of war. When Forrest's horsemen galloped toward Sherman's steady Union lines they saw the danger and wisely reined in. Carried away with his impetuous charge, Forrest found himself alone in the midst of Union troops who leveled their rifles and pistols on him and blazed away while yelling, "Shoot that man!" "Knock him off his horse!" The number of Union soldiers around him likely proved of assistance as it was difficult to get a clear shot. His horse received a mortal wound as one soldier pushed his musket near Forrest and fired. Forrest also was hit. Struck near the left hip by a bullet that lodged close to his spine, Forrest reeled in the saddle but maintained his seat. Wheeling his horse about, Forrest used his pistol to clear a path and break free to rejoin his men.[18]

Loyal unto death, Forrest's horse carried the badly wounded Ranger leader to a hospital in Corinth before it died. Three weeks later, still carrying the slug near his spine, Forrest was back in action. Leading his men in a reconnaissance, he jumped his horse over a log and the lead ball moved. The pain was terrible, but surgeons now could remove the bullet. He was out of action for a couple more weeks and spent his convalescence recruiting more men.

A practice began that would follow him throughout the war. Time and again Forrest was ordered to take over new command and bring other soldiers to his high standard.

Forrest would be well served by Kentucky Rangers under Capt. John Hunt Morgan and a hard-fighting band of warriors from Texas. Though they carried the numerical designation of 8th Texas Cavalry, they called themselves and were known in Texas and the army as Terry's Texas Rangers. They were initially led by Benjamin F. Terry, an ardent secessionist who had gone east to fight for the Confederacy.

Terry fought at First Manassas (Bull Run), then made campfire talk when he lowered a United States flag by cutting its halyard with one shot.[19] Terry and his sidekick Thomas S. Lubbock then returned to Texas with Confederate authorization to "raise a regiment of mounted Rangers, for service in Virginia."[20] Nearly 1,200 men volunteered and were organized into ten 117-man companies lettered A through K, with the men in the companies grouped according to their home areas. They wore civilian clothing of their own choosing and carried pistols, shotguns and Bowie knives. The Texas Rangers were then sent to serve under Albert Sydney Johnston, who secured prime Kentucky horses for them.

On December 17, 1861, the Rangers went into battle at Woodsonville, Kentucky. It was a brief affair, but Colonel Terry was killed and Maj. Thomas Harrison took command. He was followed by Col. John A. Wharton who commanded these Texas Rangers when they joined Forrest. In tribute to their first commander the men continued the name Terry's Texas Rangers throughout the war.

Lester Fitzhugh, writing about Terry's Texas Rangers, provides an account by "J. K. P.," a Ranger veteran, who wrote that the shotgun played a significant role in Ranger success. Union troops with fixed bayonets would await the Ranger charge in shoulder-to-shoulder lines two men deep. The Rangers would ride within twenty yards, dismount and fire both barrels of shotguns loaded with fifteen to twenty buckshot into the massed men. Then Rangers would then sling the shotguns over their saddle horns, mount, draw pistols and charge. One Ranger described the effect of the shotguns writing, "It reminded me of a large covey of quail bunched on the ground, shot into with a load of bird shot: their squirming and fluttering on the ground would fairly represent that scene in that blue line of soldiers."[21]

As the courage and leadership ability of Nathan Bedford Forrest became known, his rank and responsibility increased. He was given a brigade and more horsemen from various states came under his command. State pride was a hallmark of the Confederate effort and some from Louisiana and Kentucky were reluctant to serve under a man they scorned as a slave trader from Tennessee. Nathan Bedford Forrest demanded excellence and was unsparing of those who served under him. There were many who were repelled by his ferocious temper. The Texas Rangers cared more about his fighting ability and were loyal to him.

Forrest was both a teacher and a student of the art of war. He understood that deception could be more valuable then force. Gen. John T. Morgan related that early in the war, Forrest was watching a regiment changing formations at the sound of a bugle. Forrest asked if in this way the men could be caused to pass in a circle around any given point. When that was accomplished Forrest said, "I will often have need of this maneuver as it will be necessary from time to time to show more men than I actually have on the field."[22]

Guarding the railroad at Murfreesboro was a Union force consisting of the 3rd Minnesota and 9th Michigan Infantry regiments, Companies B, G, L and M of the 7th Pennsylvania Cavalry under Maj. James J. Seibert and four guns of Capt. John Hewitt's Kentucky Field Artillery. The Union troops were scattered in different camps miles apart under the impression they were in secure territory. Bitterness had developed between the Minnesota and Michigan commanders and their troops. The whole Union force comprised about 1,400 men under the command of Brig. Gen. Thomas Crittenden who arrived on July 12 and had not had time to gather his subordinate commanders or their troops. Just returned from two months leave was Col. William Duffield of the 9th Michigan. He had been assigned as commander of the 23rd Brigade and was Crittenden's key subordinate. Union patrols had taken a number of suspect male residents prisoner and were holding them in the Murfreesboro jail. Six of these men had been sentenced to hang.

On July 2 Forrest's men captured two men of the 7th Pennsylvania Cavalry and learned from them of the Union dispositions. Forrest now had some 1,400 men under his command, including Terry's Texas Rangers. Just before dawn on Sunday, July 13, 1862, Forrest culminated a fifty-mile ride by launching an attack on Duffield's men. Many of the Confederates were not experienced and to achieve success. Forrest had to divide his command to attack the separate Union camps. When the Texas Rangers approached the Union pickets they used the advantage gained from their prisoners and identified themselves as a patrol of the 7th Pennsylvania. In this manner they were able to capture the pickets and get into the Union encampment where they overran the Pennsylvania troopers. Those who were not killed or captured hurriedly joined the 9th Michigan.

General Crittenden, who had his headquarters at a house in Murfreesboro, was separate from his troops and captured by 8 A.M. Despite being taken by surprise, the 9th Michigan Infantry fought well, wounding Colonel Wharton and initially fighting off an attack that had the Texans among the Union tents. Supported by Kentucky artillery, the 450 men of the 3rd Minnesota under Col. Henry C. Lester moved as though to assist the Michigan men. The Minnesota regiment moved on line with two guns on each flank. The men were eager for battle, but Lester halted them and they stood waiting, listening to the sounds of Confederate attacks on other Union troops. About noon, with Colonel Duffield wounded and faced with what seemed overwhelming odds, Forrest gave Duffield an ultimatum and the Michigan and Pennsylvania troops surrendered. In the process Forrest killed a Union soldier who fired at him and missed. The Confederate prisoners had been freed from the jail and a large number of prisoners and stores of captured materiel taken. When the Confederate prisoners told Forrest that one Union soldier had mistreated them, he had the man pointed out. When a roll call of Union prisoners was taken later, that man did not answer the call Forrest said, "Pass on, it's all right."[23]

Several attacks were made on the 3rd Minnesota, but were fought off with relative ease. Lester would not move from position. When the Confederates attacked the 3rd Minnesota camp, the camp guards and sick commanded by Cpl. Charles Green repulsed two attacks and were not overwhelmed until Forrest personally led a charge. The action was only a half-mile away yet Lester did not move to assist his own troops.[24] Lester's inaction enabled Forrest to keep the Union commands separated and he was able to concentrate on each in turn.

In the afternoon, a white flag appeared in the distant Confederate positions. Forrest invited Colonel Lester to a parlay in Confederate lines. Lester accepted and rode to meet his adversary. Forrest again was using trickery. Troops paraded to and fro, bodies of cavalry dashes about, orders were dispatched to non-existent units. Forrest's subordinates thought they had done enough and some wanted to break off the action, but Forrest wanted total victory and told them, "I didn't come here to make half a job of it. I'm going to have them all."[25]

In his dealings with Colonels Duffield and Lester and in future demands for surrender Forrest's standard expression was, "I must demand an unconditional surrender of your force as prisoners of war, or I will have every man put to the sword."[26]

Lester was defeated in his mind. He returned to his officers and described the great force against which they were arrayed. The second-in-command, Lt. Col. Chauncey W. Griggs, and others urged that the regiment fight, but Lester prevailed in the vote and surrendered.

Forrest captured 1,565 officers and soldiers, 200 teamsters and clerks, 600 horses, forty wagons, five ambulances, four pieces of artillery, 1,200 rifles and 30,000 sets of uniforms.

The historian of the 7th Pennsylvania Cavalry wrote, "The moral effect of this reverse was great and, for a time demoralized the Union cause in Tennessee. The Seventh felt the consequences in the depression that always follows defeat."[27]

That the Union troops had many factors working against them does not detract from the success of Forrest's Murfreesboro raid. It was not a walkover and Forrest suffered many more than the "about 25" of his soldiers he reported killed. He could justly claim he had as many prisoners as soldiers, and knowing he was in enemy country and must move fast, he paroled the Union enlisted men, earning their cheers. The Nashville and Chattanooga Railroad was cut and a bridge destroyed. The Union commander General Buell was counting on this newly re-opened rail line to supply his advance. For several weeks the operations of the Union Army of the Ohio were hindered by the closing of a major supply route. As soon as repairs were made, Forrest cut the railroad again, dropping three bridges south of Nashville. Blue-coated soldiers went hungry. Buell came under criticism from Washington and was threatened with being removed from command. The officers of the 3rd Minnesota who voted for surrender were dismissed from the service. Forrest had won a significant victory after a string of Confederate defeats in the west. The win was important to Southern morale.

The frustrations of Union commanders were in large part caused by their need to guard the entire length of railroad track. Their lack of cavalry forced them to use infantry as guards. John Hunt Morgan added to Union woes by burning the wooden supports and collapsing a critical railroad tunnel to the north of Nashville. Forrest and Morgan combined daring with the mobility provided by their horses to strike, then vanish to strike again. Union infantry sent in pursuit marched and countermarched, but were easily eluded by the Confederate horsemen.

With Johnston dead, Braxton Bragg commanded the Confederate western army and began to move troops from Mississippi to Chattanooga, Tennessee. Bragg had been born in North Carolina and was living in Louisiana

when the war began. He was a favorite of Jefferson Davis who had nomi-
nated Bragg for promotion to general with date of rank April 6, 1862.[28] The
move of the Confederate army was facilitated by the raiding Forrest was
doing on Union supply and communications centers. Fully 10,000 Union
troops were occupied in the fruitless pursuit of Forrest. Bragg was initially
pleased and Forrest was informed he would be commanding all cavalry.

Promoted to brigadier general on July 21, 1862, Ranger Nathan Bedford Forrest had so proven himself in battle that he was given several more
regiments of cavalry backed up by artillery. Forrest was now making a transi-
tion from Ranger, who is an expert in conducting independent raids, to general, who is more closely confined in operations by his commander. Forrest
kept his command in active service scouting for Bragg's army. In September
1862, he believed it was possible to recapture Nashville. This advice did not
fit the plans of his commander. Bragg believed Forrest was putting his command at unnecessary risk and made a suggestion that Forrest pull back most
of his force—but at the same time Forrest was instructed to "prevent enemy
incursions."

The new brigadier general either did not get the message or was not
familiar with Bragg's manner of giving instructions. Forrest interpreted his
orders as being best followed by taking offensive action. Forrest was fighting
engagement after engagement. He had narrow escapes and Union forces
repeatedly claimed they had beaten him, but he kept showing up for the
next fight. Bragg saw his suggestions as orders and was displeased.

There is an old saying among army officers, "Sooner or later, everyone
meets their bastard." Forrest met his when he came under the command of
Gen. Braxton Bragg. It was a clash of experience and style. Graduation from
the U.S. Military Academy at West Point does not automatically make a man
suited for command. Remarks attributed to Confederate Lt. Gen. Richard
Taylor present a caustic view:

"Take a boy of sixteen from his mother's apron strings, shut him up
under close surveillance for four years at West Point—where half of his time
will be taken up with pure mathematics and chemistry and the humanities
and optical mirage, and all that God-dammed stuff—no use at all to a soldier. Then send him out to a two-company post on the frontier where he
does little but play seven-up and drink whiskey at the sutler's, and by the
time he's forty-five years old he'll furnish the most complete illustration of
suppressed mental development of which human nature is capable."[29]

Some West Point graduates prove to be inflexible men, rigid in their
interpretation of regulations. Deeming themselves possessed of a royal pre-
rogative they are arrogant in their authority and jealous of their reputation.
Such a man was Braxton Bragg.

Gen. U.S. Grant knew Bragg and thought him intelligent and upright, but possessed of an irascible temper and naturally disputatious. Grant said that in the old army Bragg was in frequent trouble. He was always trying to catch his juniors and his seniors in any infraction of the rules.

Grant wrote, "I heard in the old army an anecdote characteristic of General Bragg. On one occasion, when stationed at a post of several companies, commanded by a field officer, he was himself commanding one of the companies and at the same time acting post quartermaster and commissary. He was a first lieutenant at the time, but his captain was detached on other duty. As commander of the company he made a requisition on the quartermaster—himself—for something he wanted. As quartermaster he declined to fill the requisition, and endorsed on the back of it his reason for doing so. As company commander he responded to this, urging that his requisition called for nothing but what he was entitled to, and that it was the duty of the quartermaster to fill it. As quartermaster he still persisted that he was right. In this condition of affairs Bragg referred the whole matter to the commanding officer of the post. The latter when he saw the nature of the matter referred, exclaimed: 'My God, Mr. Bragg, you have quarreled with every officer in the army, and now you are quarreling with yourself.'"[30]

Despite his argumentative nature, Braxton Bragg had a close relationship with President Jefferson Davis who was inclined to believe anything the general told him. Bragg doted on the hatred of his subordinates. He proudly told Col. David Urquhart and other members of his staff that during the Mexican War the men of his battery had placed a shell under his cot which exploded, tearing everything to pieces but not harming him.[31]

Forrest rapidly was coming to the conclusion that Gen. Braxton Bragg was a military cretin. Being a man who spoke his mind, Forrest made uncomplimentary remarks about Bragg that he deemed truthful. These were relayed to their subject. Bragg decided the citizen-soldier Forrest was not the man to head the Confederate cavalry and gave the post to the twenty-six-year-old West Point-trained Joseph Wheeler. Forrest was banished to conduct irregular operations against Union troops in middle Tennessee.

John Hunt Morgan was achieving significant success with his Rangers, but Bragg did not like him either as he was another citizen-soldier and did not fit the conventional mode. Bragg was democratic, his displeasure was not limited to the commanders. He did not think highly of the men the two Rangers had trained.

Forrest and Morgan were Rangers, successful raiders who understood and were eager to learn from each other. Basil Duke, who was Morgan's second in command and a sterling soldier, wrote that he was present at a meeting between the two men when they were comparing experiences they

had during 1862 raids. Each of the leaders expressed more interest in what
the other man had done than in recounting his own exploits. Duke noted
that when General Beauregard passed command to General Bragg he had
recounted a maxim that Napoleon felt was "nearly the gospel of all strategy."
The caution was, "Be careful to move by interior lines and strike the fragments of your enemy's forces with the masses of your own."

Morgan asked Forrest to explain how that at Murfreesboro he was able
to go through a country filled with enemy forces and capture the garrison
and stores. There is no indication that Forrest had ever read Napoleon or
heard of his maxims of war, yet Forrest said it clearer when he responded,
"Oh, I just took the short cut and got there first with the most men."[32] Citizen-soldier Nathan Bedford Forrest was not trained at any military school,
yet he had a genius for war that his West Point-trained commander lacked.

Like the Union general George McClellan, Braxton Bragg could train
an army, but he did not know how to use it. The Confederate commander
moved on Kentucky and, with the considerable aid of Forrest and Morgan,
had Buell's Army of the Ohio cut off from their supplies and in a precarious
position. But Bragg could not bring it off. He frittered away the opportunity
to win the west and the astute Buell recovered. At Perryville on October 8,
1862, Bragg fought an ineffective battle, then departed Kentucky for east
Tennessee.

Bragg also was losing the battle of intelligence. The Union commanders
were well informed of Bragg's moves by slaves eager to help U.S. troops.
Confederate general Daniel H. Hill wrote of Bragg's intelligence problems
at Chickamauga, "The Negroes knew the country well and by dividing the
numbers given by them by three, trustworthy information could be
obtained. The waning fortunes of the Confederacy were developing a large
amount of 'Latent Unionism' in the breasts of the original secessionists—
those fiery zealots who in '61 proclaimed that 'one Southerner could whip
three Yankees.' The Negroes and the fire-eaters with 'changed hearts' were
now the most excellent spies."[33]

Bragg had promised much, delivered nothing and was hated by his
men. A leader can be hard on his men provided he is fair. Bragg's notion of
discipline was cruelty. He had a soldier shot for taking apples from tree. In
time the disgust of his subordinates became evident even to him.

Braxton Bragg reached the pathetic point of writing a letter to his
subordinate generals asking if he should retain command. They recommended he quit. The opinion of his troops was equally negative. Riding near
Tullahoma, Bragg met a Tennessee soldier, dressed in butternut, who was
an astute observer and gave Bragg good information on local roads. Bragg
was impressed and asked the soldier if he belonged to Bragg's army. "Bragg's

army?" was the reply. "He's got none; he shot half of them in Kentucky and the other got killed up at Murfreesboro." The general laughed and rode on.[34]

Unlike Bragg, Forrest could both train troops and lead them to victory. Time and again throughout the war, Nathan Bedford Forrest trained a command only to have it taken from him while he was sent to raise and train another. In time he became known as the Wizard of the Saddle.

Buell's success did him little personal good as his enemies included Andrew Johnson, the Union military governor of Tennessee. Buell was relieved and Union forces placed under command of Gen. William Starke Rosecrans in Nashville who would work with U.S. Grant. The latter was heading south through west Tennessee into Mississippi with the Mississippi River fortress town of Vicksburg as his objective. In December 1862 Grant had his army near the Mississippi town of Oxford and his forward supply point was some twenty-eight miles north at Holly Springs. Most of his supplies were coming south from Columbus, Kentucky, by rail. Forrest was south of Nashville with some 2,000 men, most of whom were new and poorly armed. Half of the troops were armed with shotguns, squirrel rifles and antiquated muskets.[35] Forrest thought Nashville could be taken, but after the battle of Perryville Bragg had withdrawn his army to Murfreesboro. Forrest was called to a meeting with Bragg and over his objections ordered to cross the Tennessee River and operate in west Tennessee in Grant's rear. To no avail Forrest pointed out that his men needed arms and equipment. Bragg would not relent and Forrest moved his command to Columbia, arriving there on December 6, 1862.

Just to get to his assigned area of operations was a major problem. The cruel winter left roads covered with mud or ice and strong Union forces lay ahead. Of initial concern was crossing the three-quarter mile wide Tennessee River. This major obstacle was running with high water that gave advantage to Union gunboats. Forrest had two small flatboats constructed to ferry his troops. He had other problems; supplies were desperately needed and people loyal to the Union were watching and reporting his movements. Disregarding his subordinate's plight, on December 10 Bragg ordered Forrest to begin his campaign. Again Forrest asked for weapons and ammunition, but they were not forthcoming. Near Clifton on December 15, 1862, Forrest began crossing his command. Patrols were sent up and down the river bank with pre-arranged signals to warn the command in the event a gunboat should appear.

Forrest used a variety of strategies to disguise his numbers, including extra campfires and units marching back and forth. Messages were sent to nonexistent subordinate commanders, messages that Union commanders

Nathan Bedford Forrest's prewar home in Hernando, Mississippi. USAMHI

were certain to learn about. Kettledrums were carried and their booming sound seemed to herald the arrival of a large number of Confederate infantry.[36] Through deception, Forrest was making his enemy believe he had numbers five times greater than his actual force. This generated a defensive mentality. Grant's subordinate leaders became obsessed with defending bases. The result was Forrest had greater freedom of movement through the countryside. He could wreck large stretches of railroad and mass his strength when he desired to attack a particular point.

Grant had good information that Forrest was coming, but he also was faced with protecting a long supply line that ran from Columbus, Kentucky, on the Mississippi, through the west Tennessee railroad center of Jackson, then primarily followed a route to Corinth, Mississippi. Based on the exaggerated reports he was getting, Grant was convinced the Confederates under Forrest numbered 5,000 to 10,000 men.

On Thursday, December 18, 1862, east of Jackson and near the little town of Lexington, Forrest engaged the 11th Illinois Cavalry and detachments of the 2nd West Tennessee, 5th Ohio Cavalry, and a battery of the 14th Indiana Artillery, all under the command of Col. Robert G. Ingersoll of the 11th Illinois. There was a brisk fight with numerous casualties on both sides. Forrest used a flanking movement that collapsed the spirit of the blue-uniformed men. Capt. Frank B. Gurley of the 4th Alabama Cavalry was the sparkplug of the attack. With twenty men of his company he managed to get within 100 yards of two of the Union guns, then charged into the muzzles on horseback. The Union gunners went down fighting. At that time Forrest led two regiments in a charge and broke the West Tennessee and Ohio cavalry. After that Ingersoll and the 11th Illinois were isolated and forced to capitulate. Ingersoll and 147 of his men were taken prisoner, but of most importance were the badly needed weapons and horses and the two 3-inch Rodman guns that were captured. After this defeat, the Union command believed they were faced with 10,000 to 20,000 Confederates.[37]

Grant saw his plans being endangered by the threat to his supply route. He sent a message to his subordinate commanders to take offensive action against Forrest. Grant's subordinate commanders had become enamored with defending their positions. Brig. Gen. Jere Sullivan was the Union commander at Jackson. Sullivan had an estimated 10,000 troops and thirty pieces of artillery,[38] but was immobilized by taking counsel of his fears. The prisoner reports, the rumors and the demonstrations at varying locations by elements of Forrest's horsemen all layered in Sullivan's thought. He was convinced he must defend his position. Reinforcements were on the way. A Union brigade that was needed farther south was being sent by rail to help Sullivan.

Forrest had gotten inside the mind of his opponent and used it to his advantage. He faked an attack on Sullivan at Jackson and while freezing him in defense with the 4th Alabama sent two regiments on a destructive rampage. George Dibrill's regiment cut the railroad at Webb's Station, north of Jackson, while Col. A. A. Russell with attached Tennessee troops destroyed railroad bridges to the south. The Union reinforcements had already passed, but wherever Forrest's men cut the railroad, it was done with such totality that repairs could not be made quickly.

The attention being paid to Forrest allowed Confederate troops in Mississippi to raid and destroy Grant's supply depot at Holly Springs on December 20, 1862. That same day Forrest's men ranged wide, capturing Humboldt, the critical junction of the Memphis and Ohio and Mobile and Ohio railroads, while Forrest attacked Trenton where the Federal troops were barricaded in the railroad station. Forrest used his artillery to cause a brave Union garrison that had none to surrender.

Vast quantities of supplies were captured. No thanks to Bragg, the men who rode with Forrest were now fully equipped and well fed. More than 1,000 prisoners had been taken, but these would only delay his movement. Forrest paroled his captives, making a show of it. While the disarmed Union men were signing their paroles, Forrest was busy calling messengers before him. He issued instructions to nonexistent commands in a clear voice that was heard by the prisoners. The messengers then galloped out of sight only to circle back unseen. At night troops left their campfires burning, rode a short distance out of camp then rode back in from another direction and built new fires. To the Union prisoners, this activity appeared to represent a large force. Nathan Bedford Forrest had some 2,000 men. Throughout the campaign his opponents put his strength at 10,000 to 15,000 soldiers.

Sherman was left to do what he could alone against fortress Vicksburg, and at this time Sherman was not enough. Grant had wanted offensive action against Forrest from the beginning and his orders to his subordinates became crisp. Thus inspired, Union forces were converging from varying directions to trap Forrest before he could get back east across the Tennessee River. Blue-coated soldiers were destroying bridges and ferries and gunboats were prowling the Tennessee. It seemed to subordinate Union generals that Forrest was now in a trap from which he could not escape.

After completing his destruction of rail and supply facilities north of Jackson, Humboldt and Trenton, Forrest went to Union City within striking range of the Union's Mississippi River base at Columbus, Kentucky. Another opportunity to trap him was lost when the Union commander adopted a defensive strategy, holding 7,000 men in defense and busying himself moving supplies onto boats instead of going in search of the Confederate Ranger. Forrest had passed westward over the Union line of supply and was sandwiched between Union commands who had the men and materiel to crush him. At Grant's urging, Union columns were sweeping in to close the trap.

The citizen-soldier Forrest seemed to have a better understanding than the professionals of the need to know what the enemy is doing. Forrest kept riders patrolling all points of the compass. As a result he had good information on enemy movement.

Union commanders expected Forrest to move due east to cross the Tennessee River, but Forrest slipped between converging Union forces and headed southeast from Union City to Dresden to McKenzie and then to the little town of McLemoresville. From here his route led to Huntington, but along the way there was a serious obstacle. The heavy winter rains had turned the south fork of Obion Creek into a flooded muck. The only way to cross was an abandoned double bridge. The causeways leading to the bridge were now a morass, filled with sucking mud that grasped at a man, pulling him down. The planks that once covered the bridges were rotted and the supports weak, shaking under weight. Union cavalry had effectively destroyed other bridges, but thought no one could pass over these muck-filled causeways and rotted structures.

Forrest set his men to work cutting forked timber to prop up the supports and young trees and limbs for planking and to provide passage over the causeways. He was among his men swinging an ax and using the force of his personality to inspire men to work. When it was finished the bridge was so ungainly that none of his men would volunteer to drive a wagon across it.

Throughout his campaigns, Nathan Bedford Forrest asked no man to do what he was not willing to do himself. On repeated occasions when his men would not volunteer, Forrest took the risk and proved to troops the challenge could be met. He took the place of a wagon driver, snapped the reins and moved a team and wagon over the rickety bridge. Now the drivers followed, but the next two wagons overturned. Forrest would not relent. His well-known temper exploded at any sign of hesitancy. Scores of men were assigned to push and pull each wagon. When the wagons were over the bridge, the guns were muscled forward and crossed in turn. It was brutal, back-breaking work in cold water, mud and slime.

Union columns were nearby, searching. They did not see the Confederate Rangers at the old bridges, but their information was accurate that Forrest was heading south toward Lexington. After resting his men, Forrest continued on. Four Union columns were hunting him, including three brigades—each of which could exceed or closely match his strength.

At Parker's Cross Roads, some ten miles north of Lexington, Forrest found a Union brigade under Col. Cyrus L. Dunham drawn up in line of battle awaiting him. Forrest engaged Dunham with his artillery and had good results. Dunham incorrectly thought he was vastly outnumbered and saw himself as fighting a delaying action. Forrest accommodated him by flanking the Union commander's position and capturing his guns, wagons and several hundred prisoners. The battle lasted six hours, at which point Dunham's brigade was in a desperate situation and negotiations for the surrender were beginning.

Forrest had dispatched several companies to protect his back while he advanced. Through a misunderstanding or lack of clarity in the orders, this did not happen. Another Union brigade consisting of three Ohio regiments under Col. John Fuller was closing on the rear of the unsuspecting Forrest. Fuller heard the battle and advanced toward the sound of the guns. He was ordered to wait till more forces arrived but, not a man to delay a fight, he disregarded instructions and led his men forward. The seemingly impossible happened when Nathan Bedford Forrest was taken by surprise. Forrest now found the majority of his troops caught between the brigades of Fuller and the re-energized Dunham.

Quick action by subordinates and by Forrest staved off total disaster. The Confederates who had flanked Dunham drove home an attack on his rear and removed that threat. Forrest led a counterattack that slowed, but did not stop, Fuller. Time was gained that allowed Forrest to pull what he could of his force out of the Union pincer. He was able to break contact and continue toward Lexington. After a brief rest halt, Forrest on January 1, 1863, turned his men southeast toward Clifton and the Tennessee River, traveling roads that were bogs that mired men and equipment.[39]

Parker's Cross Roads was a defeat for Nathan Bedford Forrest. Some 300 of his men and six guns had been captured by Colonel Fuller's brigade and Forrest lost all the spoils he had gathered prior to the battle. Confident they had him trapped somewhere among their converging columns, the Union commanders prematurely claimed they had shattered Forrest's command. While they were making bombastic claims, Forrest reached the Western Tennessee River, raised the flatboats he had hidden under water and put the Union pursuers behind him.

Forrest and his men had been on this winter raid for seventeen days, covering some twenty miles a day in snow and rain. They had killed, wounded or captured 1,400 Union soldiers, including four regimental commanders, with a Confederate loss of some 500 men. They began the raid ill-armed and ill-equipped and returned with captured weapons and supplies that would serve them well. Knowing his men needed equipment and his government was not providing the supplies, Forrest kept much of the tools of war he captured. Among these were a fine imported sword of Damascus steel. He had the blade sharpened on both sides and to a fine point and he carried and used it for the rest of the war. His artillery chief John Morton wrote, "It has been stated that he drew his sword with his left hand, but the writer has seen him draw it hundreds of times and always with his right. Instead of being left-handed, the dauntless Ranger Forrest was ambidextrous with a preference for the left hand."[40]

Though not as well known as Confederate cavalryman Jeb Stuart's ride around the Union army, this two-week raid by Nathan Bedford Forrest and his men was far more significant to the Confederate cause than Stuart's flamboyant gesture. Against overwhelming odds, Forrest's men ranged along Grant's line of communication, capturing and destroying his supplies and drawing off men the Union commander needed to continue the attack on Vicksburg. While Forrest was rampaging, his immediate commander Gen. Earl Van Dorn raided Grant's critical supply base at Holly Springs at daylight on December 20. With 3,500 men, Van Dorn captured and paroled 1,500 prisoners and destroyed some $3 million to $5 million worth of supplies.

These two raids brought Grant's Union army to a standstill. In a December 23, 1862, message, he wrote, "Raids made upon the railroad to my rear by Forrest northward from Jackson and by Van Dorn northward from the Tallahatchie, have cut me off from supplies, so that farther advance by this route is perfectly impracticable."[41] Another half year of fighting would be required before the U.S. flag was raised at Vicksburg, Mississippi, and the mighty river became a water road to Union victory.

Forrest received most of the credit in Southern newspapers. Van Dorn was senior and commander of the left wing of Bragg's cavalry, of which Forrest was a part. He did not think Forrest getting the credit for victory was just. As a graduate of the U.S. Military Academy at West Point, Van Dorn knew the rule is that a commander is responsible for all his unit does or fails to do. Subordinates who outshine their commanders are quickly brought to heel. Van Dorn's quartermaster complained that Forrest had not turned in all of the weapons and equipment he had captured. Forrest had turned in the excess, but the rules said it all should be turned in. Forrest did not give a damn about the rules, his men needed equipment, they had captured it and he believed the matter ended there.

The two generals had a falling out over the issue and as the discussion continued, the newspaper publicity must have been in Van Dorn's mind. As usual there are several versions of what followed. Van Dorn said something to the effect of, "I am informed that several articles published in the *Chattanooga Rebel* in which honors for Thompson's Station and Brentwood were claimed for yourself, were written by one of your staff."

On hearing this challenge to his integrity Forrest flew into a rage and snarled at his commander: "I know nothing of the articles you refer to, and I demand from you, your authority for this assertion. I shall hold him responsible and make him eat his words, or run my saber through him; and I say to you as well, that I will hold you personally responsible if you do not produce the author."

This dangerous confrontation was defused by the alert action of Maj. J. Minnick Williams of Van Dorn's staff. He told Van Dorn there was no knowledge of such action and that Van Dorn was doing Forrest an injustice. Van Dorn quickly withdrew his statement. Forrest let his anger cool saying, "General Van Dorn and I have enough to do fighting the enemies of our country without fighting each other."[42] The two men shook hands and parted, not to meet again.

Another version, one purportedly told by Van Dorn to another officer, has Van Dorn openly accusing Forrest of being the instigator of the articles. Tempers flared and both men had swords partially drawn, but Forrest cooled his temper and reminded Van Dorn of the bad example it would set and of the cause that needed their services. Van Dorn was filled with shame and apologized.[43]

Union general William S. Rosecrans moved his army out of Nashville and on December 31, 1862, clashed with Bragg's Confederates in a battle the Confederates called Murfreesboro and the Union troops named Stones

River. Bragg then withdrew to a line along the Duck River. Forrest joined his commander here and was positioned on and in command of Bragg's left.

The right wing would be commanded by Brig. Gen. John A. Wharton from Terry's Texas Rangers. Wharton had taken over leadership of Forrest's former command. Despite the success of Forrest, Bragg chose fellow U.S. Military Academy graduate Joe Wheeler to promote to major general and chief of cavalry. Wheeler was a good general but a better man. He did not have the rough edges of citizen-soldier Nathan Bedford Forrest, under whom Wheeler briefly had served. Bragg was not comfortable with Forrest. There may have been no formal meetings of a West Point Protective Association, but not surprisingly, in the North and South officers developed under the West Point system tended to favor their own kind. Though it did not always work out, it was reasonable to assume that the man best school-trained would be the best leader.

Forrest was given opportunity to rest by being assigned to picket duty guarding the flank of Bragg's army with part of his force. Forrest went off to do that, then had his orders cancelled on January 26, 1863, when he was summoned to Bragg's headquarters. There he was informed that under orders from Bragg, Wheeler had gone raiding to disrupt Union water traffic along the Cumberland River. He had with him Wharton's brigade, including Terry's Texas Rangers. Also by Bragg's orders, Wheeler was taking some of Forrest's command with him. Forrest was naturally concerned about this use of his men and likely complained. Bragg ordered him to follow on and resume command of his own men under Joe Wheeler. Forrest was disgusted to learn that his men had been sent on the mission with far less then their usual basic load of ammunition. They had scarcely enough ammunition to fight a skirmish.

Finding little action on the Cumberland River, Wheeler decided to attack the Union-held Fort Donelson. Forrest saw his men as fast moving Rangers who could raid and disappear. They were not organized to attack a fortified position and there was no purpose to expending men to seize Fort Donelson. It was too far from the Confederate army to be supported and therefore could not be sustained even if taken.

Over strong objections from Forrest and Wharton, Wheeler pursued his plan for the attack. Col. Abner C. Harding commanded the Union troops at Donelson and was not fooled when Wheeler pretended he had two cavalry divisions surrounding the fort. Forrest made a charge on horseback against Illinois troops he thought were retreating. They were just moving to a better position and shot up his men and killed the horse Forrest was riding. He regrouped, got another horse, dismounted his men and led them in a foot attack. This resulted in a temporary, but costly, success. With ammunition almost exhausted and fearing a threat to their horses, the dismounted

Rangers withdrew. The second horse had been shot from under Forrest and he had taken a bad fall. The ill-conceived and ill-coordinated Confederate attack failed and the passionate Forrest was left to mourn the loss of one-quarter of his men. A white flame of anger burned in him.

Later during the Confederate withdrawal, Generals Wheeler, Wharton and Forrest were in a house together. Wheeler was writing his report on the action when the hot-tempered Forrest exploded with rage over the loss of his men. He reminded Wheeler of his objection to the attack, spoke of the valor of his men and his grief at their loss. Then in thunderous tones he told General Wheeler to tell General Bragg, "I will be in my coffin before I will fight again under your command."[44]

Some commanders try to palm off their defeats on others, but Joe Wheeler did not. He kept his temper and as commander of the effort accepted responsibility for the defeat. Though they often fought in the same actions in the future and a mutual and respectful friendship developed, Wheeler never gave another order to Nathan Bedford Forrest.

Mobility is vital to the conduct of war. Prior to 1861, the horse had been vital to the development of the open spaces of the South and West and riding ability was prized. The result was an initial advantage to the South in mounted operations. Confederate units formed as partisan Rangers were combined to form cavalry regiments. These in turn were united into divisions and joined under a single commander. Thus Confederate cavalry was rooted in the Ranger concept of raids. Wars are not won by defensive action. Though outnumbered, the Confederate Ranger strike-and-vanish tactics play-ed havoc with the plans of U.S. Army commanders.

There were many great riders in the North, but the initial Union leader-ship displayed a surprising lack of understanding of the advantage of four-footed mobility. Fighting on terrain they knew less well then their adversary, Union commanders tended to employ their cavalry in defensive tactics of scouting flanks, intelligence- and forage-gathering and mobile reserve. They scattered horsemen on picket duty and used them as orderlies. As the war progressed, Union leadership learned from their defeats and built a power-ful cavalry arm that could meet and defeat the Southern horsemen. Deep penetration raids by Union horsemen began in 1863 and, win or lose, served as a model for later raids. In time and led by dashing, hot spurs such as Wes-ley Merritt and George Armstrong Custer, and under the command of the relentless cavalry leaders of the Phil Sheridan and James Wilson mold, Union cavalry would adopt the Ranger raiding techniques with crushing effect on the South.

In February 1863, Forrest was rebuilding his command. Given two bat-talions of Tennessee partisan Rangers, he began to mold them into a single unit of his command. These Rangers would fight well under Forrest, but they greatly resented giving up unit pride. When they complained, Forrest arrested the Ranger officers of these battalions and it took the intervention of the new cavalry commander, Gen. Earl Van Dorn, to get them released. General Bragg was seeking to mass the 6,000-man cavalry he had available and Forrest was now one of Van Dorn's five brigade commanders.

Though they repeatedly knew the thrill of winning battles, Confederate leaders constantly were faced with new threats. The columns of men in Union blue uniforms kept coming on. One such column of 2,500 Northern troops was led by a hard-fighting colonel named John Coburn. He was marching from Franklin, south of Nashville, to unite with another column under Phil Sheridan. Coburn was somewhat hampered by escorting a long train of forage wagons. Van Dorn met the smaller Union force with the full weight of his cavalry and Coburn was forced into a fighting withdrawal.

Forrest led his men on an envelopment of the Union left flank. His favorite horse, Roderick, was badly wounded under him and Forrest took still another mount. Being a horse under Nathan Bedford Forrest was a dangerous occupation. Again Forrest flanked the Union defense and when Colonel Coburn attempted to break out from between Van Dorn and Forrest, the Confederate Ranger led his men in a dismounted action with both sides meeting in a charge. Coburn was held in the trap and he and some 1,200 men taken prisoner.

Forrest continued to lead his men into the enemy rear on raids to disrupt Union supplies. In late March 1863 he captured a Union supply point at Brentwood, just south of Nashville. He took some 500 prisoners there and destroyed a key railroad bridge. At a nearby Union garrison he captured another 300. On each of these operations he continued his practice of personally leading the attack and seeking to strike the enemy from the flank. Forrest proved he could control his command while they attacked in two different directions. When a Union force got in his rear, he would sidestep and attack from the enemy rear.

CHAPTER NINE

Abel Streight and the Jackass Raid

Union general Ulysses S. Grant was again moving his army to take Vicksburg and open the Mississippi River. To facilitate this move, two Union columns were sent on deep penetration raids to disrupt Confederate communications and supply routes. A force of Union cavalry under Col. Benjamin H. Grierson rode forth from a base near Memphis. His mission was to cut across Mississippi and tear up railroads and bridges, forcing the Confederates to draw off men who otherwise would oppose Grant's movement. Grierson's men would ride through Mississippi to Baton Rouge, Louisiana, which was now in Union hands. A second party of raiders under Col. Abel Streight would be sent on the more difficult task of moving from Nashville to penetrate into Georgia and cut the Western and Atlantic Railroad. This line came north from Atlanta to Rome, Georgia, and supplied the Confederate stronghold of Chattanooga. In Georgia, Streight would be in position to attack the factories that were furnishing war materiel to the South. Both Grierson and Streight were fighters, but Grierson had the option to go directly through enemy territory. Streight was expected to go there and come back.

Streight's four regiments were primarily infantry and the decision was made to mount them on army mules. Horses were in short supply and the mules were thought to be hardier and more able to sustain themselves. It was expected that horses could be captured along the route. This was wishful thinking. Abel Streight was overeager, he was a natural born fighter, brimming with confidence and eager to get off and conduct a raid. It was poor planning. From the outset the mules proved to be more of a hindrance than an asset.

Streight's infantry men were not skilled riders and the mules Streight was given were in large part unbroken and wild. Many of them were diseased. The army mule was an institution in itself and totally unsuited as mounts for raiders. No mule worthy of the name considers itself a subordinate and the best that can be arrived at between man and mule is an understanding.

In *Hardtack and Coffee*, John Billings told the story of a Negro mule driver who approached his mules to hitch them to a wagon. A mule kicked the man and knocked him flat. The mule driver regained his feet, calmly walked to the wagon and got a club the size of his arm, walked slowly back and hit the mule over the head, felling the beast to the ground. The man then slowly walked back to the wagon and put away his club. After a moment the mule arose and shook his head. Mule and man now understood each other and a truce was declared.[1]

To the opposition the idea of raiding on mules was ridiculous. John Morton, Forrest's chief of artillery wrote: "From the beginning the mules gave no end of trouble. Being hard to manage, they caused endless confusion, and the appearance of the 'Jackass Cavalry' caused amusement wherever they went. The mules kept the whole countryside informed of their presence morning, noon and night. The idea of conducting a raid mounted on a thousand noisy mules filled the whole country with laughter."[2]

Streight's plan was to travel from Nashville by steamboat and mule to Eastport, Mississippi, where he would meet and work in conjunction with a force under Brig. Gen. Grenville Dodge. General Dodge was coming out of Corinth, Mississippi, for the purpose of leading an attack designed to cover Streight's movements. The attack would be made eastward in northern Alabama toward the Florence/Muscle Shoals area. Streight's men would appear to be part of the Dodge attack, then break off and move south and east across Alabama with their initial objective being Rome, Georgia. Ranging from this area they could slice the Confederate supply artery to Chattanooga. Forrest and his men were south of Nashville, operating as part of the force engaging Dodge. It was standard operating procedure for Forrest to have scouts ranging the countryside for information. One of these spotted Colonel Streight's column near Mount Hope in Lawrence County heading toward Moulton, southwest of Decatur, Alabama. This meant they were moving past the Confederates. Forrest now suspected the attack by Dodge was a feint and Streight posed the primary threat. Taking no chances, he left part of his troops to keep Dodge occupied and drove the remainder of his men in pursuit of Streight. Forrest had men who were enured to the saddle. Colonel Streight was a skilled fighter and had good men, but they were primarily mounted infantry on mules. It takes some time to harden the body to a saddle.

Streight believed Dodge would be continuing to demonstrate against the Confederates, holding any Confederate pursuit at bay. When Streight left him, Dodge believed his mission accomplished and withdrew to Corinth. Now Forrest could give his full attention to Colonel Streight and his raiding party.

Streight had a head start and was covering thirty-five miles a day. Forrest pushed his men to ride fifty miles a day and on April 30, 1863, made contact. Then began a series of fights.

Streight would set an ambush to delay Forrest, then push on with Union outriders scouring the countryside to bring in fresh horses, mules and supplies. Not only were the soldiers in blue being well supplied, they were keeping much-needed mounts and supplies from Forrest. Streight's first ambush had caught the aggressive Forrest by surprise. Forrest kept his artillery well forward. A successful ambush followed by a Union attack resulted in the loss of two Confederate guns. The guns were under the command of the brave. Lt. A. Wills Gould. Forrest would not tolerate the loss of a gun no matter the circumstance. He humiliated Gould and later relieved him with tragic result.

Colonel Streight continued to delay the onrushing Forrest with skillfully deployed ambushes. Forrest quickly made adjustments. Themselves experts at ambush technique, Forrest and his scouts could identify terrain where danger threatened. The horse Forrest rode and those ridden by many of his men were animals trained to war. Their enhanced senses often could detect a concealed enemy position. Forrest then brought his artillery to the front and fired into the ambush site, routing its occupants.

The pressure on Colonel Streight was relentless. Forrest told his command, "Whenever you see anything blue, shoot at it, and do all you can to keep up the scare."[3] Forrest kept a forward force constantly nipping at the Union commander's heels. With advantage of being the aggressor, Forrest could choose when his force would attack, thus he was able to give his men a few hours rest. It was more difficult for Colonel Streight to rest his command as it was under constant harassment that at any moment could be a major attack. Forrest was fury in action, his temper terrifying brave men. When one of his scouts brought him information Forrest knew to be wrong, the general seized the man by the throat and repeatedly banged his head against a tree. "Now, damn you," snarled Forrest, "If you ever come to me again with such a pack of lies you won't get off so easily!" Concussed and with a bloodied skull, the dazed scout was left to ponder the meaning of the word easy.

Both sides were pushed to the limit, but the fury of Forrest carried his soldiers onward. Streight's men were exhausted when the two sides clashed at the small community of Blountsville. Beyond the town at Big Will's Creek, Streight's men had an opportunity for advantage. The creek was believed unfordable. Streight's men burned the bridge, then used accurate gunfire from a rear guard to keep the pursuing Confederates from extinguishing the flames. Streight pushed his weary men onward, hoping to be able to rest them at Gadsden, Alabama.

Forrest found a ford across the creek thanks to sixteen-year-old Emma Sanson, a local girl who scrambled up on the saddle behind Forrest and rode with him to point out the ford location. Several bullets passed through Miss Sanson's skirts in the process. When they dismounted Forrest stood between Emma Sanson and the Union positions and said, "I am willing to have you as a pilot but not as a breastworks."[4]

Forrest was so impressed with the courage of this young woman that he took time to write her a note with an interesting beginning.

> Hed Quaters in Sadle
> May 2 1863
>
> My highest regardes to Miss
> Emma Sansom for hir gallant
> conduct while my posse was skirmishing with the Federals
> a cross Black Creek near Gadsen Allabama
>
> N. B. Forrest
> Brig Genl
> Comding N. Ala—[5]

Reflecting sour grapes, the Northern view was less romantic. They believed a local prisoner they released on parole had violated his word of honor and revealed the site to the Confederates, but Emma Sanson was the genuine article and thanks to her, Forrest and his riders soon were across the creek and again in hot pursuit of Abel Streight.

Streight found no rest at Gadsden and pushed eastward. He hoped to cross the Oostenaula River at Rome, burn his bridges behind him and fight Forrest until Union reinforcements could come south from Chickamauga, near Chattanooga. Streight sent a 200-man reconnaissance party under Capt. Milton Russell to take the Rome bridges.

Meanwhile, a Southern Paul Revere named John Wisdom was riding ahead of Russell to warn the citizens of Rome "the Yankees are coming." Panic ensued and people fled or buried valuables. Some men of more stern backbone threw up cotton-bale barricades near the bridges. These were manned by boys, old men and wounded soldiers carrying antiquated weapons or shotguns. A few old cannons that had been used for decoration where muscled into the firing line. The defense looked far more formidable than it was, and the image that appeared in Captain Russell's telescope was greater than the reality. He questioned locals including slaves. Not having seen defensive works before, they thought the preparations were awe inspiring. Russell was convinced that Rome would be hard to capture and so reported to Colonel Streight. Now Streight was in bad straits. His men were so exhausted they were asleep in their saddles or, if on outpost duty, sleeping on watch. Given the negative report from Captain Russell, the Union officers believed their mission was hopeless.

Forrest called upon Streight to surrender, but the tough colonel was not willing to oblige unless he knew he faced an overwhelming force. Streight wanted to see the number of men Forrest had, but Forrest said he would not humiliate his men by having them appear before a force they had driven and beaten for the past three days.[6]

Once again Forrest used his trick of having his subordinate commanders march their men this way and that with false commands being issued, messengers galloping off and guns being drawn in and out of sight.

Forrest and Streight were talking while two guns were being made to seem like many. Forrest noted that Streight kept looking over Forrest's shoulder. Streight asked how many guns he had. Forrest replied "Enough to destroy your command in thirty minutes."[7]

Another account is that finally the Union colonel burst out, "Name of God! How many guns have you got? That's fifteen I've counted already!" Forrest responded, "I reckon that's all that has kept up."[8]

Forrest badly needed Streight to surrender and granted generous terms that allowed officers to retain their side arms. Some twenty miles from Rome, Georgia, Streight surrendered on the basis that all were to be held as prisoners of war and that officers should retain side arms and baggage. He was allowed to address his men and lead them in three cheers for the United States.[9]

It was not till he had given up his fighting capability that Colonel Streight found he had surrendered 1,700 men to 600. He was so angry he demanded his weapons back in a ludicrous "Fight like a man!" tirade. A laughing Forrest reminded him that all is fair in love and war. Colonel Streight and his men saw Rome, Georgia, as prisoners.

Abel Streight was a courageous man. At the time of the surrender he and his men were exhausted, but so were those of Forrest. Colonel Streight made the error of asking tired subordinates what should be done. Councils of war seldom opt for offensive action and tired counselors frequently give up. Forrest proved at Fort Donelson that surrender was not a Ranger word. Abel Streight had courage, but he did not have the will of Nathan Bedford Forrest, a power of will that is rare in any generation.

With only a short pause to look after men, mounts and equipment, Forrest was back in the saddle leading his men. He soon was ordered back to Tennessee. Gen. Earl Van Dorn had been shot by a jealous husband and

Forrest was ordered to take over Van Dorn's command. Now it was Forrest's turn to face unexpected danger.

Though his fellows thought Lt. A. Wills Gould fought bravely at Streight's first ambush, he had lost two guns. That was unforgivable under any circumstance to Forrest, who relieved Gould and ordered him to another command. He would not explain his reasons to the young officer. Gould rightly saw his honor and reputation for the rest of his life at stake. Seething with anger at what he considered injustice, he went after Forrest carrying a pistol in the pocket of a duster, a light linen coat worn to protect the uniform from soil. Gould had his hand thrust into the duster pocket. Forrest was unarmed save for a small penknife he was twirling in his fingers.

Gould's pleas were rejected and the discussion turned into a heated argument which Forrest brought to a close by turning his back to walk away. Gould put his hand around the pistol in the duster pocket, pushed it against Forrest's side and fired into the left hip of his commander. Possessed of enormous physical strength, Forrest used one hand to seize Gould's gun hand and pin it against the lieutenant's side. With his other hand and his teeth he opened the pen knife and stabbed Gould in the chest.

Gould broke away and ran while the wounded Forrest went in search of a gun.

Forrest thought his wound was mortal. Enraged, he took a revolver from a holster strapped on a saddled horse. Now armed, Forrest went in search of Gould and found him being treated by doctors. The young officer tried to escape again with Forrest firing at him and missing. The doctors and bystanders pleaded with Forrest that Gould had already been given a serious wound. Forrest yelled, "Get out of my way; he has mortally wounded me, and I intend to kill him before I die."[10] The doctors stalled and examined him, then stated that Forrest was not seriously wounded. When Forrest was told that Gould was dying, his anger cooled. Forrest quickly recovered from his gunshot, but Gould died in a few days. The two men were reconciled before Gould's death. The incident put a scar on Forrest's heart. It was said he wept, but he could not change for his was not a forgiving nature.

In early June Forrest led two brigades north from Spring Hill toward Franklin. Some three miles from the town, he encountered Union pickets and drove them into their fortifications. The 85th Indiana Infantry was in town and began an active attempt to communicate with its higher headquarters by signal flag. Forrest saw a white flag and thought Union troops wanted a truce to talk about surrendering. Acting on this belief he rode forward toward the Union positions. One Union officer correctly recognized the situation and came running toward him calling out, "General Forrest, go back! Go back! There is no truce. That is a signal-flag." Forrest raised his hat in salute and gratitude and retired.[11] He then proceeded to shell and shoot his way into Franklin, freeing prisoners from the jail and capturing sutler and commissary supplies. This accomplished, Forrest then returned to Spring Hill.

Military skill was a family trait. Nathan Bedford's youngest brother, Maj. Jeffery Forrest, also had a flair for raiding and captured a large herd of beef cattle that was much needed by the Confederates. Jeffery was some fifteen years younger and as he was born after the death of their father was as much like a son as a brother to Nathan Bedford Forrest.

Forrest had become superhuman in the eyes of the Southern civilian. Many could not comprehend that any significant war involves cycles of advancing and retreating and could not imagine Forrest pulling back from a fight. At the mountain town of Cowan, Forrest was seeking to escape from Union cavalry when an old woman yelled at him, "You great big coward, you, why don't you turn and fight, instead of running like a cur? If old Bedford Forrest was here, he'd make you fight."[12]

In early July 1863 the Confederate Army of Tennessee was withdrawing while Forrest and his men covered the flanks and rear. Grant took Vicksburg on July 4 and that, coupled with news of the Union victory at Gettysburg, had Braxton Bragg in a defensive mood. Bragg knew that Chattanooga was the doorway to Atlanta and the Deep South. Nature helped the defense of the area. Chattanooga was surrounded by the Cumberland Mountains, and rolling forest and the Tennessee River was the natural barrier to Rosecrans' Union army. Flowing into the Tennessee just above Chattanooga was a stream that passed between Lookout and Pigeon mountains. It was called Chickamauga, an Indian name meaning River of Blood. Writer Andrew Lytle claimed the name came from a furious day-long battle Indians fought among themselves long before the Civil War.[13]

By the third week of August, Bragg's opponent General Rosecrans had men positioned across the Tennessee River from Chattanooga. There Rosecrans initiated an elaborate sham, simulating boat building in preparation for a river crossing. With Bragg fooled, Rosecrans crossed the Tennessee more than one hundred miles away in Alabama, moving east and flanking Bragg. In making his move, Rosecrans had split his forces. Bragg had the opportunity to consolidate his command and fall on lesser numbers, crushing the separate elements of his opponent each in turn. Instead, he wasted the energy and time of his troops in aimless marching. Bragg was not a coward, but he was overly wary of the mountains in the vicinity of Chattanooga. He saw these heights as places behind which an enemy army could lurk, then suddenly appear through gaps or on rivers to attack him. Bragg compared these mountains to a house full of rat holes, a place where a rat could

Union general Samuel D. Sturgis, whom
Forrest routed at Brice's Crossroad, driving Sturgis more than fifty miles in one
of the most complete victories of the
war. USAMHI

pop out at any time.[14] A prisoner of his own mind, Braxton Bragg surrendered the initiative to his opponent.

Forrest was adept at using subterfuge in battle, but utterly devoid of it in
personal relations. He could not tolerate inefficiency in his subordinates or
his superiors. Forrest believed that the only measure of an army officer was
success in battle. He was not impressed by what military school a man
attended, or what peacetime assignments a man had held. These often came
by way of the old boy network. The practice of reading off a laundry list of
peacetime staff and command assignments to show an officer's accomplishments is an eternal measuring stick of regular armies.

When Nathan Bedford Forrest looked at his fellow officers, he found
that being a West Point graduate was no guarantee of success. West Pointers
frequently were losing battles and Forrest was winning them. He had proven
that the battlefield is not complicated, that battles are won by offensive
action, properly delivered. Forrest attacked and his attacks came home on
the flank of the enemy. His assault was delivered with speed, creating shock
and unnerving his opponent. Though Forrest is touted as a great leader of
cavalry, he learned at Shiloh the difficulty of controlling mounted men in
broken country and the ease with which a horse could be killed. Forrest
used the horse as transportation to the battlefield, but after Shiloh, in many
of his actions, his troops fought on foot. Confederate general Daniel Harvey
Hill had a low opinion of cavalry and had made the remark, "He never saw a

dead soldier wearing spurs." Hill changed his mind when he saw Forrest and his men making a dismounted attack.

When professional soldiers were equipping their cavalry units with sabers, Forrest continued to follow the Texas Ranger concept of using revolvers. On one occasion when Union cavalry executed a mounted charge with sabers against the dismounted horsemen of Forrest, the Confederates stood their ground and shot their opponents from the saddle or killed the horses and then shot the men thrown to the ground. Unhampered by years of Regular army standard operating procedure, citizen-soldier Nathan Bedford Forrest used the best current battlefield technique he could develop.

The relations between Forrest and his commanding general Braxton Bragg had soured to the point that even if it meant leaving his beloved brigade, Forrest wanted out of Bragg's command. On August 9, 1863, he sent a letter through Bragg's headquarters to the adjutant general in Richmond. It soon became clear that his letter was in a dead file. On August 19, in a serious breach of military protocol, he sent a copy of the letter directly to President Jefferson Davis.

Forrest told Davis he wanted to leave Bragg's command, taking 400 picked men, well-equipped and mounted, and four pieces of artillery. Forrest proposed going into Union-controlled territory between Vicksburg and Cairo and taking command of all Confederates he could raise from the occupied region. He also asked permission to assemble volunteers from northern Mississippi, west Tennessee and any who wanted to join him from Arkansas and southern Kentucky. The volunteers Forrest wanted to recruit were primarily behind enemy lines and could not otherwise be brought into Confederate service. Forrest had frequently traveled the proposed area of operation as a pre-war slave trader. He knew the territory and had many friends behind enemy lines. Many of the officers and men he would be taking with him were local to his destination. Forrest wrote, "There are thousands of men where I propose to go that I am satisfied will join me." Without taking any significant numbers of men from General Bragg's command, Nathan Bedford Forrest intended to raise an army from behind enemy lines and close the Mississippi River to Union traffic.[15]

Jefferson Davis was intrigued by the idea, but was himself Old Army and recognized that Braxton Bragg had not endorsed the proposal. Davis asked Bragg for comment and Bragg replied that to remove Forrest from command would take away one of his "greatest elements of strength." From this it has often been assumed that Bragg genuinely liked Forrest, or at least recognized his ability.

Some who have made a career of the army might recognize another agenda. From time to time senior officers who dislike a subordinate will not allow him to transfer out, but will do all in their power to hold him under their thumb, frustrating the subordinate officer's desires. Without the consent of Bragg, Davis would not act on the proposal and a great opportunity died.

Had Davis approved the request, Forrest would have been turned loose to range the hundred of miles of Mississippi shore, raiding communications, supplies and isolated commands. River traffic would have been ambushed until it was shut down. The western states of the Confederacy could have been reunited in commerce with those in the east. As John Singleton Mosby, Harry Gilmore, and the McNeills proved in Virginia, such Ranger tactics as Forrest proposed would force the North to have thousands upon thousands of troops tied down in guard duty instead of at the front.

Part of Longstreet's corps had arrived from Virginia as reinforcements and after much vacillation, Bragg determined to attack Rosecrans' army. His record of retreats had not inspired confidence in his officers or men and there was little hope that Braxton Bragg would change his ways. Southeast of Chattanooga, on September 19, 1863, the two armies clashed. The dismounted men of Forrest's command opened the fight, clashing with soldiers under the skilled Virginia-born Union general George H. "Pap" Thomas. More of Longstreet's men arrived and the Union forces increased. A pile-on battle erupted with each side committing more troops. The problem for both sides was lack of knowledge of what the enemy had and where he was. Rosecrans was attacking with an army that was divided and he thought Bragg was retreating. Bragg was attacking and had an excellent opportunity to defeat the scattered forces of Rosecrans.

But Bragg was uncertain in his efforts, fearful that the enemy would pop out of the mountains at him. When he got scouting reports, he denied them and then issued impossible orders that subordinate commanders began to disregard. Bragg had not made a terrain study and did not understand the field. Union cavalry supported by infantry kept Bragg's cavalry from developing the location of Rosecran's scattered forces. When Rosecrans learned that Bragg had been reinforced he hurried to bring his army together. Alexander McCook's Union corps made an incredible fifty-seven-mile forced march to join George Thomas.[16]

Bragg had golden opportunities in the preliminaries to defeat the pieces of Rosecrans' army, but on the twentieth when he finally ordered a major attack, he was four days late and Rosecrans had brought much of his army together. Forrest was ordered by Bragg to the extreme right of the Confederate line, told to attack and to uncover the Union positions. If he encountered problems he would be supported. Forrest did as told, but encountered heavy resistance and was not supported as promised. In hours of charge and countercharge, Forrest had another horse killed under him. The Confederate attack on the Union left forced Thomas to withdraw, but he established a good position and would not be driven out.

Bragg later blamed General Polk for failing to carry out his orders and said, "I found Polk after sunrise, sitting down reading a newspaper at Alexander's Bridge, two miles from the line of battle, where he ought to have been fighting."[17] Bragg's statement was not true. Later investigation showed Polk was up with his troops, it was Bragg who was not.

Longstreet found a gap in the Union center where a division had been mistakenly withdrawn, and smashed through. One hungry Irish Confederate was heard to yell, "Charge them boys, they have cheese in their haversacks!"[18] Longstreet forced a hurried Union retreat, all except for George Thomas. The man who was affectionately called Pap was beloved by his troops. Thomas shared their hardships and a sketch of him sleeping on the ground without shelter as his troops did is worth a thousand words about leadership.[19] When his troops ran low on ammunition and asked for more Thomas said, "Use your bayonets." After the fighting ended on September 20, the 19th U.S. Infantry had only four officers and fifty-one enlisted men left for duty and was commanded by a second lieutenant, but they held their ground.[20] A new nickname was added this day both to George Thomas and the 19th U.S. Infantry which treasures the motto "The Rock of Chickamauga."

Elsewhere there was high excitement in the Confederate ranks. Officers and men sensed victory was in their grasp. Cheers rang out along the line, cheers that Longstreet thought Bragg must be hearing and following up the success. But Bragg wasn't on the battlefield and he thought the battle was lost. Forrest and his men had chased the Union troops they faced almost to the suburbs of Chattanooga. Forrest sent couriers to Bragg telling him that the Union army was demoralized and to press the attack. Getting no response, Forrest rode back to Bragg's headquarters and found the commander sleeping. When he pointed out the opportunity, Bragg said his army was without supplies. Forrest told him, "General Bragg, we can get all the supplies we need in Chattanooga." Bragg did not respond and Forrest rode away disgusted.[21]

On September 21 Thomas withdrew and joined the rest of the army in hastily constructing positions at Chattanooga. Confederate casualties were 18,454 while the Union suffered 16,170. The Confederates had the momentum. Union general Burnside was ordered by President Lincoln to march from east Tennessee to assist Rosecrans. It was critical that Bragg smash Rosecrans before Burnsides arrived. Bragg ordered a dawn attack, then cancelled the orders and ordered his troops into positions to besiege the Union army. Forrest took his men on the high ground and secured the roads to Missionary Ridge and Lookout Mountain, thus giving Bragg critical terrain. The men of Forrest's command are credited with firing the opening and closing shots of the battle of Chickamauga.

On September 30th, Forrest received the following order from General Bragg:

> Missionary Ridge, September 28 1863
> *Brigadier-General Forrest, near Athens:*
>
> General,—The general commanding desires that you will without delay turn over the troops of your command, previously ordered, to Major General Wheeler.[22]

Forrest was furious at being relieved. He dictated to Maj. Charles W. Anderson, his assistant adjutant, a stinging letter of rebuke to General Bragg, charging his commander with duplicity and lying and saying the he would call on the commanding general in a few days to say to him in person what he had written. En route to keep his promise Forrest picked up Dr. J.B. Cowan, his chief surgeon, who was returning to the command from hospital duty. For reasons unknown, Cowan accompanied Forrest on his trip to see General Bragg. Cowan had no knowledge of why Forrest was making the visit, but noted that Forrest was obviously displeased. When they arrived at Bragg's tent, Cowan noted that Forrest did not return the salute of the sentry, an action unusual for Forrest. Forrest did not tell Cowan to remain outside and strangely Cowan took it upon himself to be party to the meeting between the two generals. Cowan wrote that Bragg rose and stretched out his hand, but Forrest refused it and said:

> I am not here to pass civilities or compliments with you, but on other business. You commenced your cowardly and contemptible persecution of me soon after the battle of Shiloh, and you have kept it up ever since. You did it because I reported to Richmond facts, while you reported damned lies. You robbed me of my command while I was in Kentucky, and gave it to one of your favorites—men that I armed and equipped from the enemies of our country. In a spirit of revenge and spite, because I would not fawn upon you as others did, you drove me into West Tennessee in the winter of 1862 with a second brigade I had organized, with improper arms and without sufficient ammunition, although I had made repeated applications for the same. You did it to ruin me and my career.

When in spite of all this I returned with my command, well equipped by captures, you began again your work of spite and persecution, and have kept it up; and now this second brigade, organized and equipped without thanks to you or the government, a brigade which has won a reputation for successful fighting second to none in the army, taking advantage of your position as the commanding general in order to further humiliate me, you have taken these brave men from me.

I have stood your meanness as long as I intend to. You have played the part of a damned scoundrel, and are a coward, and if you were any part of a man I would slap your jaws and force you to resent it. You may as well not issue any more orders to me, for I will not obey them and I will hold you personally responsible for any further indignities you endeavor to inflict on me. You have threatened to arrest me for not obeying your orders promptly. I dare you to do it, and I say to you that if you ever again try to interfere with me or cross my path it will be at the peril of your life.[23]

This is astounding, both in the tone of the speech and the remarkable ability of Cowan, who was in attendance for no particular reason and did not know what Forrest was going to say, to remember word for word such a lengthy diatribe. But Major Anderson had sent Forrest's letter to Bragg and was witness to its content. Forrest lashed out at Bragg and whatever words he used were clear and complete. Forrest had been shaking his finger in Bragg's face and now gave him no time to respond, but turned on his heel and stalked away.

Outside, Cowan said, "Well you are in for it now!"

Forrest responded "He'll never say a word about it; he'll be the last man to mention it; and mark my word he'll take no action in the matter. I will asked to be relieved and transferred to a different field, and he will not oppose it."[24]

Forrest was correct. Bragg never took disciplinary action or mentioned the letter or confrontation in any known instance. That Bragg intensely disliked Forrest is clear in Bragg's future actions while serving as military advisor to President Davis. Forrest was right about Bragg but, if as Grant said, Bragg was disputatious, Nathan Bedford Forrest was hardly less so, he quarreled with any commander who did not agree with him or give him a free hand. Forrest expected total obedience, but would not give it.

Although not present when Forrest visited Bragg, President Jefferson Davis was at the headquarters. He did not mention the incident directly but set up a meeting with Forrest at Montgomery. At that meeting Davis promised Forrest an independent command.[25] The best way for Bragg to gracefully exit the situation was to go back to the August request of Forrest and let him go west. On October 13, 1863, Bragg wrote to President Davis saying that Forrest's request could now be granted. Davis on October 29 wrote Forrest, giving him his new assignment. Bragg managed to cut the number of troops Forrest could take. He was a brigadier general but was given only 271 men. Forrest was allowed his eight-man staff, a sixty-five man escort, a 139-man battalion and an artillery battery of sixty-seven men and four guns. This was not much of a force to close the Mississippi River to Union forces, but if his commander did not recognize his worth, his enemies did. As soon as the Union commanders learned that Forrest was to take command in west Tennessee, the telegraph wires began to hum. From Memphis on November 3, 1863, General Hurlbut sent a message to Grant, "It is currently believed that Forrest has been assigned to this department. If so there will be more dash in their attacks."[26]

Forrest now marched west into territory he knew well. He moved to Okalona where he hoped Col. Robert Vinkler Richardson would join him with a brigade. Richardson had organized the 1st Tennessee Partisan Rangers in early 1863. He had ten companies and was building, but they were roughly handled by the 6th Illinois Cavalry and recruiting fell off. Unloved by Union or their fellow Confederate troops, they were reorganized as the 12th Tennessee Cavalry later in the year. Richardson had only 250 troops to offer Forrest. Other men came in, but of those who arrived many were without weapons or had ancient or civilian shotguns or squirrel guns. They were often in wretched clothing, without shoes or blankets. They had no food and what horses they could bring often were broken down.

Forrest had been a wealthy man when the war started. He spent $20,000 of his own money to help improve the lot of his men. In a typical action, Forrest boldly moved his headquarters into Union-occupied territory at Jackson and started recruiting volunteers and conscripting citizens by whatever means it took. The volunteers guarded the conscripts. By December 1863 he had three regiments organized though he had yet to equip them. He planned to make war pay for itself by getting the weapons and materiel he needed from the enemy. As he began this it also was reported that Forrest was taking all Negroes fit for soldiers.[27] If true it was not to put weapons in their hands. Forrest may well have wanted an engineer element to be employed in a variety of ways, from building bridges to tearing up railroad, thus sparing his troops except for guards for offensive action. Forrest practiced eternal vigilance. His scouts constantly patrolled the countryside, keeping him well informed of enemy movements.

On December 13, 1863, Forrest was promoted to major general. On the twenty-eighth Maj. Gen. William Sooy Smith set out from Nashville. Union raider Benjamin Grierson was coming out from Nashville and the two Union generals hoped to catch Forrest between them and give him a promotion party. They were bringing gifts of shells from Parrott guns and Minie balls. Near the Hatchie River at Bolivar, Tennessee, Forrest's new command had its first skirmish with Benjamin Grierson's Union cavalry. It was inconclusive, but held promise of better things.

Forrest quickly began moving his untrained men and the materiel he had collected south to Mississippi to avoid the trap. Forrest fought a skillful delaying action when required, but the key to his successful escape was doing the unexpected. He went by hard routes instead of taking the easy paths that were expected and he found a bridge that was mistakenly thought destroyed by Union commanders. Forrest recruited en route. He took some 400 men into enemy-occupied territory and when he arrived safe at Holly Springs, Mississippi, he had 3,000. Given authority to organize this diverse group, Forrest created regiments of cavalry that would allow him to look for more recruits. By rounding up fragments of Confederate regiments scattered about the country, Forrest could raise his number to 4,000 and he planned to use that to conscript a cavalry force of 10,000 men.

Although they did not discount his prowess, Union commanders believed Forrest did not have the strength to disturb their next offensive move. The centerpiece of this effort would be under Gen. William Sherman who would move eastward from Vicksburg with 26,000 troops. Sherman's objective was to destroy the important rail center of Meridian in eastern Mississippi. When that was accomplished, the intention was to press toward the supply bastion of the Confederacy at Selma, Alabama. Sherman intended to freeze the main Confederate forces in a defensive posture while freeing 20,000 Union troops from Mississippi garrisons for attacks eastward. He intended to use superior numbers of cavalry to destroy Nathan Bedford Forrest. Sherman's men were primarily infantry, therefore the attack on Meridian was to be made in conjunction with a force of 7,600 horseman under Gen. William Sooy Smith who would move from Memphis.

The Confederates who had to face this challenge were under Lt. Gen. Leonidas Polk, a warrior-bishop of the Episcopal Church whose headquarters was at Meridian. Polk had more then 20,000 men to oppose the Union troops, but they were located at various points throughout the state and an effective command relationship for consolidating the troops was not in place. Polk sought to fight a delaying action. Sherman, as was his custom, moved with dispatch from Vicksburg on February 3, 1864. After skirmishing with

Polk across Mississippi, Sherman captured Meridian on February 14 and set about the destruction of one of the key links in Confederate transportation.

Sherman had given General Smith specific orders regarding Forrest. Sherman wrote in his memoirs, "I explained to him personally the nature of Forrest as a man, and of his peculiar force; told him that in his route he was sure to encounter Forrest, who always attacked with a vehemence for which he must be prepared, and that after he had repelled the first attack, he must in turn assume the most determined offensive, overwhelm him and utterly destroy his whole force."[28]

Smith was supposed to move from Memphis on the first, but to the disgust of Sherman was delayed waiting for George Waring's 2,000-man brigade which was off on another mission. Smith did not leave Memphis until the eleventh. Until they were united at Meridian, the Union cavalry and infantry would be operating separately, unable to support each other. Smith would be further delayed by orders that en route to join Sherman he was to arrest known secessionists and lay waste to all crops, leaving nothing on which a Confederate army could subsist. Houses were not to be burned unless they were inhabited by the enemy.

On February 18, 1864, Polk ordered Forrest to attack Smith's cavalry as it moved to join Sherman. Among the blue-coated troopers sweeping across eastern Mississippi was the dashing Col. George Waring, commander of the 4th Missouri Cavalry. Waring loved his work and years later would write of it:

> It is a very pleasant thing to be a colonel of cavalry in active field service. There are circumstances of authority and responsibility that fan the latent spark of barbarism which, however dull, glows in all our breasts, and which generations of republican civilization have been powerless to quench. We may not have confessed it even to ourselves; but on looking back to the years of the war, we must recognize many things that patted our vanity greatly on the back.[29]

Since 1861 retribution had followed retribution. By 1864, hatreds had become deeper, savagery more prevalent and destruction routine. Waring wrote:

> It was an important incident of our mission to destroy everything which directly or indirectly could afford subsistence to the Rebel forces. . . . The sky was red with the flames of burning corn and cotton . . . no sooner was its light seen at the plantation houses than hundreds of Negroes, who swarmed from their quarters to join our column, fired the rail cribs in which the remaining nine-tenths of

the crop was stored. Driven wild with the infection, they set the
torch to mansion house, stables, cotton gin and quarters until the
whole village-like settlement was blazing. . . . As we marched, the
Negroes came en masse from every plantation to join our column,
leaving only fire and absolute destruction behind them.

Delicate women and children, whom the morning had found in
peace and plenty, and glowing with pride in the valor of southern
arms and the certainty of an early independence for their beloved
half-country, found themselves before nightfall, homeless, penniless
and alone, in the midst of a desolate land.[30]

Resistance brought death. Waring recounted:

Captain Frank Moore, the Cossack of our brigade, went at night to
an outlying plantation, of which the showy mansion-house stood on
a gentle acclivity in the edge of a fine grove. Here lived alone with
an only daughter, a beautiful girl, a man who had been conspicuous
in his aid to the Rebellion, and whose arrest had been ordered. The
squadron drew up in front of the house and summoned its owner to
come forth. He came armed, sullen, stolid and determined, but
obviously unnerved by the force confronting him. Behind him followed his daughter, dressed in white, and with her long light hair
falling over her shoulders. The sight of the hated "Yanks" crazed
her with rage, and before her father could reply to the question
with which he had been accosted, she called to him wildly, " Don't
speak to the villains! Shoot! Shoot them down, shoot them down!"
wringing her hands and screaming with rage. The excitement was
too much for his judgement and he fired wildly on the troops. He
was riddled through and through with bullets; and as Moore turned
away he left the fine house blazing in the black night and lighting
up the figure of the crazy girl as she wandered desolate and beautiful, to and fro before her burning home, unheeded by the Negroes
who ran with their hastily made bundles to join the band of their
deliverers.

Col. George Waring thought this "the most vivid picture we had seen of
the unmitigated horror and badness of war."[31]

Many Southern plantation owners were fleeing the land. Wherever
Union forces went, slaves were attaching themselves to the columns. It was
not only slaves who were leaving. Reporter Albert Richardson wrote that it
was the slave who had always been a runaway. When Union forces were clos-

ing in it was the plantation owner who was hightailing it down the road and the slave would say "mass'r run away from me!"

Richardson noted that the lines of "Kingdom Coming" exactly depicted the feelings of the slaves:

Say, darkies hab you seen de mass'r
Wid de muffstach on his face,
Go 'long de road some time dis morning,
Like he's gwine to leave de place?
He seen de smoke way up de ribber
Where de Linkum gunboats lay;
He took his hat and left berry sudden
And I s'pose he runned away.
De mass'r run, ha ! ha!
De darkey stay, ho! ho!
It must be now de kingdom comin',
An de year of Jubilo[32]

By the twentieth Sherman still had not been joined by Smith and knew well that he would need cavalry to attack Selma. At Meridian, Sherman destroyed twenty locomotives, more than sixty bridges, well over a hundred miles of railroad track, and dozens of buildings and warehouses loaded with supplies for the Confederate army. Turning his back on smoke and flame, he slow-marched back toward Vicksburg. Sherman was Polk's job; Forrest intended to bring an end to Smith's activities. While he was gathering his force, he sent his youngest brother, Col. Jeffery Forrest, riding ahead with a flying column of about 1,000 men to delay and distract Smith. The Union commander was hampered by hundreds of escaped slaves who clung to his column. On February 21, Smith was stung repeatedly by assaults that put him on the defensive and put an end to his plan to join Sherman.

On Monday, February 22, Forrest united his command of some 2,500 men. Despite being heavily outnumbered, Forrest opened a fierce, running fight in which he would know the personal tragedy of the death of his brother Jeffrey. His 9 P.M. report reads: "We have had severe fighting all day with the enemy. The engagement closed about dark. We have killed about 40 of the enemy and captured about 100. Our loss not known, but not so heavy as the enemy. The prisoners captured report 2 Colonels and 1 Lieutenant Colonel killed this evening. Colonel Forrest was killed this evening, Colonel Barksdale badly wounded in the breast, Colonel McCullough was wounded in the hand." Three days later, he amplified this report, writing:

We met them on Sunday morning last at Ellis' Bridge or Saka-tonchee Creek, 3 miles south of West Point in front of which Colonel Forrest's brigade was posted to prevent the enemy from crossing. After a brisk engagement the enemy retired toward West Point. . . . I moved forward with my escort and a portion of Faulkner's Kentucky regiment and found the enemy had begun a systematic retreat, and being unwilling they should leave the country without a fight, ordered the advance of my column. . . . It is sufficient for me to say here that with 2,500 men the enemy numbering from 6,000 to 7,000 strong were driven from West Point to within ten miles of Pontotoc in two days. All his efforts to check our advance failed, and his forces at last fled utterly defeated and demoralized leaving 6 pieces of artillery, 100 killed, over 100 prisoners, and wounded estimated at 300 . . . our loss is about 25 killed, 75 wounded and possibly 8 or 10 captured.[33]

The official report of a battle deals in numbers that cloak the ache of tragedy. Forrest held his brother in his arms as young Jeffery, who had been shot through the neck, died.[34]

General Sooey Smith found Nathan Bedford Forrest wherever he went and wherever he found Forrest he tried to avoid him. Forrest kept breaking up Smith's force into smaller elements and hitting them hard. In his after-action report, Smith blamed the pack mules, the Negroes, the better armament of the Confederates, the mistrust of his men and the imperfect gun carriages of his artillery and sought to make his withdrawal sound as though he lured Forrest after him. About his mission to join Sherman, Smith wrote only, "Attempting to cut through to Sherman, I would have lost my entire command and of course would have rendered him no assistance."

Col. George Waring was unsparing in criticism of his commander, Gen. William Sooy Smith, writing, "Our commander evidently had no stomach for a close approach to the enemy." Waring understood what was at stake : "There lay before us a fair opportunity for dispersing the most successful body of cavalry in the Rebel service and could we effect a junction with Sherman, we should enable him to divide the Confederacy from Vicksburg to Atlanta."[35]

Sherman lost all confidence in Smith as a soldier and long after the war would not relieve him from censure, answering Smith's plea by writing that to do so would falsify history.[36]

Life was not smooth in Forrest's command. On Saturday, March 12, 1864, Major General Forrest reported, relieving brigadier generals Chalmers and Richardson and sending them to Lieutenant General Polk. Chalmers was an experienced and capable officer new to serving under the mercurial Forrest. He had watched in shock as Forrest nearly beat to death a man he saw running from the fight. Seizing a tree limb Forrest administered a severe thrashing then faced the man toward the battlefront and said, "Now go back to the fight, sir! I'll kill you if you run away again, and you might as well get killed there as here." Chalmers did not like serving under Forrest and wrote him a letter saying so.[37] In time they would overcome their differences and James R. Chalmers became like the left arm of Forrest. This was better than the right arm as Forrest preferred to fight left-handed.

In the army and out the realization that the war was being lost was beginning to reveal itself in a breakdown of resolve and discipline. Confederate Brig. Gen. Wirt Adams reported that disloyal men on the Yazoo River were ginning cotton and selling it to the enemy and complained of men under the command of Lieutenant Baker abusing women they were supposed to be escorting, writing "Tucker and Allen were sent with two ladies, Mrs. Askew and Miss Askew, to headquarters at Canton. They detained these ladies all night in a camp on the road, offered them every indignity and are supposed to have violated one or both of them." Judge Hudson of the 5th District of Mississippi wrote to Jefferson Davis complaining, "The State is now under the tacit rule of deserters, thieves and disloyal men . . . Many of our soldiers who remain in or along with the service are as destructive to property as the Yankees; they steal, destroy, and appropriate without restraint . . . Open-day and midnight robbery is practiced every day and night in every neighborhood . . . Officers in command are much to blame for this."[38]

Mr. Goodman, the president of the Mississippi Central Railroad, complained to General Polk that he could not keep his railroad running unless he had supplies from the North and sought permission to send cotton north to trade for parts to keep the railroad running for the Confederacy.[39]

With the difficulties between Forrest and Brig. Gen. James R. Chalmers resolved, on March 29 Chalmers was ordered to take his division to LaGrange. On March 24, Col. William L. Duckworth with 800 men of Forrest's command captured Union City, Tennessee. The Confederates were faced by a 500-man Union garrison that was getting the best of the fight but Duckworth sent in a demand for surrender in a message using Forrest's name. Union colonel Isaac R. Hawkins lost his nerve and, over the objections of his officers and the indignation of his men, surrendered his command.[40]

On March 25, 1864, Forrest approached the Union defenses at Paducah, Kentucky. The Union patrols fell back under heavy pressure and took up position at Fort Anderson. Forrest sent in a flag of truce demanding that Col. Steven G. Hicks of the 40th Illinois Infantry surrender his garrison. The message included, "If you surrender, you shall be treated as prisoners of war; but if I have to storm your works, you may expect no quarter."[41] Colonel Hicks refused the demand, noting that while the flag of truce was in effect, Forrest was moving his men into position close to the fort. The Confederates denied this, but the purpose of the truce was to gain advantage and Forrest was not one to stand on protocol. On Union refusal, three attacks by Forrest were fought off and Confederate general Albert P. Thompson was killed. Confederate sharpshooters in nearby houses were picking off Union gunners with head shots. Hicks sent out a detachment of Kentucky cavalry to burn the buildings. Forrest proposed a prisoner exchange on the basis of equal rank. Hicks learned that the Union troops Forrest was willing to exchange were with one exception men too sick to be anything but a burden to the defense. Forrest burned the dry-dock but his passion for Paducah cooled when he learned of an outbreak of smallpox there. When the Union gunboats, *Peosta, Captain Smith* and *Paw Paw,* came steaming up and added the fire of their cannon to Hick's defense, Forrest withdrew, leaving on the morning of the twenty-sixth.

Forrest had sent part of his command under Col. James Jackson Neely to Bolivar, Tennessee, where it encountered troops of the 6th Tennessee (Union) Cavalry under the command of Lt. Col. Fielding Hurst. This Union officer was known for a "take no prisoners" policy. He hated secessionists with a brutal passion and his burnings and killings were often accompanied by torture. Near Bolivar, Neely soundly defeated Hurst, taking thirty prisoners, five wagons with teams and two ambulances. The Confederates were short of ammunition and were delighted to find 50,000 rounds they could use.[42]

Forrest next turned his eyes toward Fort Pillow, Tennessee, fifty miles above Memphis on the Mississippi River. Union commanders where aware Forrest might move to strike the fort. On March 28, 1864, Maj. Gen. Stephen A. Hurlbut had ordered Maj. Lionel F. Booth, commanding officer of 1st Battalion, 1st Alabama Siege Artillery (Colored) to move his command to Fort Pillow.

Maj. William F. Bradford of 1st Battalion, 13th Tennessee Cavalry was already at the post. The 13th Tennessee Cavalry was forming and had enlisted four companies. The men of a fifth company were present but had not yet been mustered into service. General Hurlbut thought Bradford a good man, but like his men, he was inexperienced, thus Major Booth would be in command.

Booth arrived at Fort Pillow and on April 3, reported to Hurlbut that all seemed to be quiet within a radius of thirty to forty miles, and the place was "perfectly safe." Now reinforced, Fort Pillow had four companies of the 1st Battalion, 1st Alabama Siege Artillery (Colored) under Booth and some 250 recruits of the 13th Tennessee Cavalry under Bradford. There were 557 men in the garrison—295 white and 262 black troops.

The artillery consisted of two 10-pounder Parrotts, two 6-pounder field guns and two 12-pounder howitzers. The U.S. gunboat *New Era*, with Captain Marshall in command, was on the river, but Fort Pillow was on high bluffs so to achieve the trajectory needed to support the fort, the gunboat had to fire at long range.

At 5:30 on the morning of Tuesday, April 12, 1864, Forrest's advance drove in the 13th Tennessee pickets and came on like a gray wave. Major Booth deployed companies D and E of the 13th Tennessee as skirmishers and attempted to delay the onslaught. By 8 A.M. the Union troops were driven back into the fort. Casualties to the two companies of the 13th Tennessee had been heavy, but the men in the fort were well positioned and took a toll in lives as the Confederates closed to within rifle range of the fort. At 9 A.M. Forrest assaulted the fort proper, but heavy fire from the fort's guns repulsed the assault. Forrest next employed sharpshooters to good effect. Shooting from behind stumps and brush piles the Confederates took a heavy toll of Union officers, many of whom were killed by head shots. Major Booth was shot in the chest and killed instantly. Now command rested upon the inexperienced Major Bradford.

About 11 A.M. Forrest again attacked. This effort also was beaten back, but the Confederates took control of two barracks that were parallel to the south side of the fort and only 150 yards distant. The Union troops had tried to burn these to prevent their capture, but were driven back by heavy fire. Now the Confederates had surrounded the fort and on the south side were beneath the angle of which the guns of Fort Pillow could be depressed. Heavy firing continued from both sides.

At 3:30 P.M., a white flag appeared in the Confederate lines and both sides ceased firing. A Confederate truce party appeared 150 yards away. Three Union officers were ordered out receive the message, including Lt. Mack J. Leaming, adjutant of the 13th Tennessee Cavalry. Leaming later wrote that Forrest demanded unconditional surrender, but assured them that the garrison would be treated as prisoners of war. Forrest also warned that he could take the works by assault and the Union troops would have to bear the consequences. Major Bradford sought to delay and asked for one hour to consult with his officers and the officers of the gunboat. In order to conceal his death, the name of Major Booth was signed to the bottom of the message.[43]

Forrest quickly responded that he was not seeking the surrender of the gunboat. He gave the garrison twenty minutes to come out of the fort and lay down their arms. If not he intended to assault and again warned the garrison that it must bear the consequences. Forrest used that time to make a personal reconnaissance. Two horses were killed under him and a third wounded, but Forrest found a ravine which enabled him to move troops close to the fort.[44] This was done. The response of Bradford, again over Major Booth's name, was, "I will not surrender."[45] When the negative answer came, Forrest was in position to assault and promptly did so.

Much historical argument has raged over weather it was fair play for Forrest to move troops during a truce. Forrest was not playing. It was his intent to take Fort Pillow with as little loss as possible to his own men and he was too practical to care about the chivalry of war. Lieutenant Leaming later reported "the Rebel charge was immediately sounded; when, as if rising from out the very earth on the center and north, within 20 yards of our works, the Rebels received our first fire, wavered, rallied again and finally succeeded in breaking our lines, and in thus gaining possession of our fort."[46]

What followed would become one of the great controversies of the war. Lieutenant Leaming wrote, "The enemy carried our works at about 4 P.M., and from that time until dark, and at intervals throughout the night, our men were shot down without mercy and almost without regard to color. This horrid butchery did not cease even with the night of murder, but was renewed again the next morning, when numbers of our wounded were basely murdered."[47]

Union lieutenants James A. Smith and William Cleary of the 13th Tennessee Cavalry reported of Forrest's attack, "The Rebels came pouring in solid masses right over the breast-works. . . . The moment they reached the top of the walls and commenced firing as they descended, the colored troops were panic-stricken, threw down their arms, and ran down the bluff, pursued sharply, begging for life, but escape was impossible . . . The whites, as soon as they perceived they were also to be butchered inside the fort also ran down. They had previously thrown down their arms and submitted. In many instances the men begged for life at the hands of the enemy, even on their knees. They were only made to stand on their feet, and then summarily shot down."[48]

The survivors of Fort Pillow told a consistent account of seeing Union soldiers both black and white shot down after they surrendered. Some thirty sick black soldiers in the hospital were sabered to death; prisoners were hanged or shot. There was a particular anger among the Confederates that the whites of the North would arm blacks and send them into battle against the South. The white officers of black units were executed at Fort Pillow with their men.

To most Southern minds of the period, blacks were not people but property. The great fear of the pre-war South was an uprising of the slaves. The economy, the political system, indeed the Southern way of life depended on slavery and slavery depended on total control. To arm blacks against Southern whites was reprehensible to the South. Thus a mindless fury seized the troops of Nathan Bedford Forrest at Fort Pillow. Despite the objections of some of their officers and men, they were merciless. Major Bradford was taken prisoner, but while being marched away was shot.

According to the Union reports, Bradford was taken about fifty yards from a road and executed. The Confederates claimed he violated parole and was shot trying to escape. A series of heated written exchanges followed between Northern and Southern officials and commanders. The Southern response was that their men did not know the garrison had surrendered. Lt. Gen. Stephen D. Lee wrote, "Your colors were never lowered, and your garrison never surrendered, but retreated from the fort to the cover of a gunboat with arms in their hands and constantly using them." Lee complained, "You had a servile race armed against their masters" and added "I do not think many of them are killed. They are yet wandering, over the country, attempting to return to their masters."

Forrest lost twenty killed and sixty wounded. He wrote, "I regard captured Negroes as I do other captured property and not as captured soldiers."[49] He responded to charges of atrocities by writing, "I slaughter no man except in open warfare," but that statement echoed hollow on the grounds of Fort Pillow. Of the 557-man garrison, some 400 were killed, wounded, or captured. The Confederates said they captured 237. Among these were seventy-five Negro troops and forty Negro women and children who were returned to slavery. The percentage of killed at Fort Pillow greatly exceeded the norm.

The massacre at Fort Pillow was not an isolated example, but a common occurrence. A paper read at a gathering of Matthew C. Butler's Confederate cavalry after the war contains the following:

> Comrades did you ever fight Negroes in the war. Well, if so did you notice that your guns would shoot faster and straighter than ever before? Did you ever see a comrade after he surrendered to a Negro soldier, and if so where? And did you ever take a Negro soldier prisoner, and if so, what did you do with him? I never saw one captured nor one after he was captured. General Sherman says "war's hell," and we found race prejudice to be strong there.[50]

Combat experience gave white Southern leaders a new opinion of the fighting ability of the black American. As the strength of their army dwindled, Southern generals including Robert E. Lee would call for the recruitment of slaves to fight for the Confederacy. The freedom that was promised as reward did not extend to the black soldier's family. The idea of blacks fighting for the South was a hot topic of discussion. A Southern officer said to one of his slaves: "Now Bob, we have concluded to put all of the able-bodied slaves in the war and give them their freedom when it is over. What do you think of it?" Old Bob looked at him and scratched his head and said:

Union colonel Abel Streight, the redoubtable warrior who led a deep penetration into Confederate territory with Forrest on his trail. Forrest tricked Streight into surrender, but Streight later made a daring escape from Libby Prison in Richmond and would fight Forrest again. USAMHI

"Boss, just let me tell you. Did you ever see a bone do anything when two dogs was a fighting over it?"[51]

The killings at Fort Pillow brought cries for retaliation and advanced the cause of the abolitionists. Only the fact that the endless retribution of executing prisoners would result prevented the United States from officially taking action. Had war crimes trials been in vogue at the close of the Civil War, Nathan Bedford Forrest, being on the losing side, would have been indicted. Forrest was quick to point to the depredations of Col. Fielding Hurst who butchered Confederates. Some Union officers, including General Sherman, commented that Forrest had always treated prisoners fairly and it is likely Forrest while in command of the action was not on the scene at the point of the killings. Others contended that a commander is responsible for what his men do and although Forrest might regret the economic loss, coming from his background he likely felt no more compunction over killing a black man then squashing a fly. Fort Pillow was but a larger scale example of the common savagery that was the truthful face of a war that often is falsely portrayed as romantic.

Lt. Gen. Leonidas Polk was not aware Forrest was at Fort Pillow. Indeed he did not know where he was, and that disturbed him. On April 14 he wrote from Columbus, "I have been disappointed in not being frequently advised of your movements, and am therefore at a loss as to the proper orders to give you. I have not heard from you in two weeks." Polk gave Forrest discretion to move as he saw fit, "remembering that your command will be required against the movements of Sherman on North Alabama and Georgia so soon as they shall have commenced."[52]

Forrest sent press gangs about the countryside conscripting every man they could take between the ages of eighteen and forty-five. Forrest then moved to Jackson where he remained until May 2, 1864, when he set out for Tupelo via the Bolivar, Tennessee, and Ripley, Mississippi, road. At Bolivar his scouts reported they were engaged with skirmishers of an enemy battalion. Forrest rode to the front and with a casual disregard for his safety attacked the Union troops with only his escort to back him up. His impetuous charge drove back the Union skirmish line on the main body.

CHAPTER TEN

Brice's Crossroads and Beyond

With the departure of General Grant to the east to assume overall command of Union armies, Sherman now held command in the west. With these assignments the North found relentless leaders. U. S. Grant was a no-nonsense man whose aggressive streak matched that of Robert E. Lee. Grant did not care about pomp and circumstance. Gen. Rufus Ingalls was quartermaster general of the Army of the Potomac when Grant took command. The fastidious Ingalls arrived to visit his commander in a double-seated top-wagon drawn by four fine dapple gray horses with four handsomely uniformed and mounted orderlies as body guard. Ingalls had on a new uniform with polished boots and spurs. When Ingalls rode up in his conveyance and said he would like to talk to Grant, the army commander was simply dressed and standing in the mud. Grant looked over Ingalls and his party and softly suggested that the two men walk while they conversed.

Grant proceeded to walk Ingalls up and down through the mud as cavalry and couriers cantered past spraying the dandy general with muck. When Ingalls looked like a mud-covered soldier of the line, Grant walked him to his wagon and said, "That is all; good-by General." Ingalls was a competent quartermaster, a fine officer who thereafter dressed plainly and eased off on the spit and polish for his men.[1]

Grant intended to attack everywhere, sink his military teeth into the Confederate armies and not let go. Since the beginning of the war the North had seen the military advantage of controlling the Mississippi to split the Confederacy in two. That objective had been obtained. Now Sherman was in position to destroy or render ineffective Joseph E. Johnston's Confederate army, take Atlanta and make a sweeping envelopment across Georgia, then move northward to strike at Robert E. Lee from the rear while Grant held him from the front. Opposed by Gen. John Bell Hood, Gen. George Thomas would guard Tennessee; if Hood followed Sherman, Thomas would follow Hood.[2]

The Confederates understood the Union intent. It was the hope of President Jefferson Davis that when Sherman made his move, attacks on his supply line would force Sherman to cancel his plans. The South counted on Nathan Bedford Forrest to play a major role in frustrating Union intentions.

Sherman did not fear Forrest. For a commander to fear his opponent is a certain path to defeat. Sherman respected the military ability of Forrest. By June 1864 it was known that Forrest was a military genius. But Sherman was brilliant and Sherman had 60,000 troops. Sherman intended to live off the fat land of Georgia, but armies need some supplies and Sherman wanted to keep the shining rails of the one-track Cumberland, Nashville and Chattanooga Railroad open at his rear. To do this it was necessary to keep Forrest in western Tennessee. To that end, Sherman ordered a Union column to move from White's Station near Memphis on June 1, 1864, to threaten the Confederate railroad system at Corinth and Tupelo.

On May 29, Forrest received a dispatch requesting that he join his 2,000 men with another Confederate column of 1,000 Alabama cavalry of Brig. Gen. Philip Roddey's command. Like Forrest, Roddey was a citizen-soldier skilled in Ranger tactics. He was known as the Swamp Fox of the Tennessee Valley. On June 1, Forrest moved north for an attack on Sherman's lines of communication and supply. His march was halted by a dispatch from Maj. Gen. Stephen. D. Lee, commander of cavalry, stating that a Union column was coming out of Memphis en route to northern Mississippi. This was the Union advance initiated by Sherman to keep Forrest in the west.

On June 2 a column that was the distraction in blue was put under the command of Brig. Gen. Samuel D. Sturgis, an 1846 graduate of the U.S. Military Academy at West Point where he was a classmate of Stonewall Jackson. Sturgis had followed a typical cavalry career of the time that included service in the Mexican War and Indian campaigns. He set a new standard for criticism of commanders while serving under Gen. John Pope, remarking, "I do not give a pinch of owl dung for John Pope." Sturgis was a pudgy-faced man who had built a respectable career and done well in actions in Missouri. He had a not unusual favor for liquor and women and was the author of the Sturgis Principle defined as, "Sooner or later a man will not live up to his pronouncements."

Sturgis had his troops in pursuit after Forrest took Fort Pillow, but could not catch him. This led Sturgis to send bombastic messages that Nathan Bedford Forrest would not fight him. These statements were premature.

Sturgis had with him two brigades of cavalry under the astute Col. Benjamin Grierson and an infantry division of three brigades commanded by Col. William McMillen. McMillen's 3rd Brigade contained two regiments, the 55th and 59th that were U.S. Colored Troops. The total Union force numbered some 9,000 men. Forrest would have 3,500 troops in opposition. Sturgis was ordered to bring Forrest to battle. To accomplish that his intent was to move by Corinth to Tupelo and then if necessary to Okolona, tearing up railroads along the way.[3]

By June 8, Sturgis had moved eighty miles and was at the town of Ripley. Southern women of the town vocally abused the men as they marched by. Although he had not encountered the enemy, Sturgis was having second thoughts about the wisdom of the expedition. Rain had been falling in torrents and the wagons and artillery were constantly being mired, exhausting the horses and mules that drew them. A Union chaplain passed by a teamster whose wagon and mules were mired in the mud. True to his calling the teamster was ripping the air with profanity. The chaplain remarked, "My friend, do you know who died for sinners?" "Damn your conundrums," snarled the teamster. "Can't you see I'm stuck in the mud!"[4]

Operating away from a supply line, Sturgis had a train of some 250 wagons that carried eleven days of rations for the troops, ammunition and other supplies, but not forage for the horses and mules. Colonel McMillen estimated that including those of the cavalry there were 4,600 animals with the column. The route of march Sturgis was ordered to take had been fought over previously, so the countryside was used up and forage was scarce. Discouraged by the weather and lack of food for the animals, Sturgis considered turning back and discussed a withdrawal with his key subordinates. Grierson felt the command was too much encumbered by wagons and the road would not sustain the movement. He recommended calling off the operation. Sturgis was dissuaded from Grierson's advice by Colonel McMillen, who reminded Sturgis that he had turned back from another expedition and could be subject to ridicule, if not dismissal, if he did it again. Sturgis lacked confidence. He wrote in his after-action report "with a sad foreboding of the consequences, I determined to move forward."[5]

On June 9, the Union column covered fourteen miles, marching southeast on a road that would lead through an isolated country crossroads where a man named Brice had his house. Sturgis lacked information about the enemy and did not think any Confederate force was nearby.

The Confederates were operating on friendly soil and had the advantage of being well informed of Union movement. On the ninth Forrest learned of the direction in which Sturgis was traveling. He had the area scouted well and after consideration of his mission, the enemy, the terrain and the troops he had available, he determined that Brice's Crossroads would be a good place to fight a battle. Forrest knew that terrain and inclement weather would keep his enemy in linear formation at that point. He reasoned that the Union cavalry would lead and be somewhat separated. Forrest believed the road conditions were so bad that he could defeat the Union cavalry before the infantry came up, then he could isolate and destroy the foot soldiers. He began to move his troops toward Brice's Crossroads with the intention of getting there first.

On the evening of June 9, Sturgis halted his troops for the night at Stubb's farm, some nine miles short of Brice's Crossroads. Grierson's cavalry would lead out on the morning of the tenth and Grierson gave Col. George Waring, formerly of the Fremont Hussars and now the commander of a brigade, his orders. Waring would have with him his old regiment, the 4th Missouri, plus the 2nd New Jersey and the 7th Indiana Cavalry regiments. Out front as skirmishers Waring had 200 men of the 3rd and 9th Illinois Cavalry. His artillery was two rifled guns and four small howitzers. He had a total of 1,600 men.

Waring wrote, "We breakfasted at three in the morning and marched at half past four. My command had the advance. The enemy allowed himself to be easily driven until half past eight when he made some show of resistance. At this time the last of our regiments could hardly have left the camping ground."[6] Waring was followed by Edward Winslow's 1,800-man cavalry brigade. Waring's 4:30 A.M. march was unknown to Sturgis who thought he was starting at 5:30. Sturgis had calculated it would take an hour and a half for the cavalry to clear the road for the infantry to move, and issued his orders accordingly.[7] Thus the Union infantry regiments did not complete breakfast and begin to march until 7 A.M., two and one half hours after the cavalry had moved. A gap developed between the cavalry and the infantry.

Initially Waring's men marched through farmland where many of the trees were cleared away. Some three-quarters of a mile short of Brice's Crossroads the land was low-lying, wet and swampy and densely forested. Tishomingo Creek flowed through this area and the water was running high beneath a crude wooden bridge. The terrain would restrict movement to the road for nearly a mile.

Before Waring reached Tishomingo Creek his troops began to skirmish with a company of the 7th Tennessee Cavalry under Lt. Robert Black. The small Confederate force slowed Waring, but could not prevent his advance. Black quickly found Forrest and reported the situation. Two companies of the 12th Kentucky Cavalry under Capt. H. A. Tyler were committed and stiffened the Confederate resistance.

Grierson's command had been moving southeast on the road that led past Brice's house. Continuing on would have taken them to the hamlet of Guntown six miles distant. From there the road led to the larger community of Fulton. At Brice's the Guntown Road was bisected by a road that ran from Baldwin in the northeast to Pontotoc in the southwest. Baldwin was seven miles distant and the general direction from which Forrest was coming. Tyler's companies fell backward before Waring's advance and turned left at

Brice's Crossroads. They then took the road toward Baldwin, falling back upon the main body of Confederates. The route of the Union advance was toward Guntown and Fulton so Waring did not pursue the Confederates, but took up position at the crossroads. Grierson came on the scene and ordered patrols sent forward in the three directions of Baldwin, Guntown/Fulton and Pontontoc. The patrol that took the Baldwin road soon encountered a Confederate force it estimated at a brigade. Grierson ordered Waring's brigade to attack down the Baldwin road and Waring made contact about a mile east of Brice's Crossroads.

Forrest had been foiled in his effort to be the first to reach the crossroads, but aggressive action by two regiments of Lyon's brigade stopped the Union cavalry at the place Forrest wanted to fight. Lyon had the 3rd, 7th 8th and 12th Kentucky Cavalry regiments totaling about 800 men. Lyon would form the right of the Confederate line straddling the Baldwin-Pontotoc Road. Rucker's brigade, consisting of the 7th Tennessee and the 18th and 19th Mississippi Cavalry, would be tied in with Lyon's left and would extend across the Guntown/Fulton road. The 8th Mississippi Cavalry under Col. William L. Duff was put to the extreme left to prevent an attempt to flank the Confederates. Forrest was content to keep up probing attacks and a heavy fire while General Buford closed with the rest of the troops and the artillery.

With the roar of gunfire building, Grierson dismounted Waring's cavalry and put them into defensive position. He moved Edward Winslow's brigade forward through the crossroad and directly ahead on the Guntown/Fulton road, then spread them left so Winslow's left flank would tie in with Waring's right in the defense.

As Union and Confederate units came onto the battlefield the lines began to form a half-circle with most of the troops to the left or east and southeast of Brice's Crossroads. The battle would begin with Grierson's and Lyon's cavalry fighting dismounted against each other. The terrain was slightly rolling and heavily wooded with thick undergrowth in full foliage that deprived mounted men of mobility. Owing to the dense woods, Union artillery was not being employed and Forrest's guns were not yet present. Grierson had the advantage of numbers, but did not know this as the woods concealed the Confederate troops. Forrest was content to keep up a steady and aggressive skirmishing posture. Colonel Waring reported, "Here, for four mortal hours, or until half past twelve, we carried on a tolerably equal warfare, both sides blazing away at each other with little effect across the six hundred yards of cleared valley that lay between two skirts of wood."[8]

By one o'clock, Gen. Abraham Buford, Gen. Tyree Bell's brigade and the Confederate artillery had arrived. Forrest determined to attack. Both sides now had artillery in action with the Union guns firing from Brice's

Crossroads at the only targets they could see: Troops they thought were Confederate reserves. Forrest's artillery opened a counter-battery fire with their shells bursting over and among the Union guns.

His observation hampered by the trees, Grierson was cautious. At the opening of the action, he had sent word to Sturgis to bring on the infantry. Instead of attacking with his cavalry over bad terrain into what he thought was a larger force, Grierson waited for the infantry to come up. Meanwhile his ammunition was being exhausted and the wagon train carrying ammunition reserves was behind the infantry. As the battle increased it was apparent that the Union cavalry could not sustain its position.

Sturgis got involved in clearing a blockage in the road and did not immediately go forward to see the situation for himself. When he received Grierson's request for support, Sturgis ordered Colonel McMillen to send the infantry forward. In the after-action report, Sturgis later would claim that his orders to McMillen were, "Move as rapidly as possible without distressing his troops." McMillen said he was ordered to move "as rapidly as possible" and so ordered his men. In their after-action reports infantry regimental commanders wrote of advancing their columns at the double-quick for two to four miles. The thick mud of the road and the hot sun exhausted the men; many fell from heat stroke and were unable to continue.

In the meantime Forest ordered Brig. Gen. Tyree H. Bell's brigade to attack Winslow on the Guntown/Fulton road. The trees were so thick that Bell's men were within thirty yards before the two sides saw each other. Forrest had ordered Abraham Buford and Col. Edmund W. Rucker to strike on the Union center and right at the sound of Bell's guns. This Confederate attack would come in on Waring's brigade and the junction of Waring's and Winslow's lines. Forrest rode to Buford and personally made certain all Confederate artillery was engaged.[9]

The battle raged for more than two hours. Waring was down to five rounds of ammunition per man and had exhausted the ammunition for his artillery. As Forrest continued his pressure, Waring's center began to waver, and his brigade was forced back to the crossroads, creating a gap between Waring and Winslow. Sturgis arrived on the battlefield about noon.[10] Forrest had flanking fire coming from both the left and right sides of the Union position. The Confederate artillery of eight guns was up and in action. Forrest brought his guns within sixty yards of the Union line just as Union troops began to attack. Firing double-shotted canister, the Confederate guns cut a swath through their opponents.[11]

Meanwhile Winslow was being struck from the flank where Waring's men had withdrawn. Winslow was sending urgent messages that made Sturgis distrustful his cavalry brigade commander would stay in position until relieved. Sturgis committed his escort, 100 men of the 19th Pennsylvania Cavalry, to help hold the line until the infantry came up. About 1:30 the Union infantry was coming on line. One by one the tired Union infantry regiments reached the battle area to be hastily thrown into position to relieve the cavalry. Waring's brigade withdrew through the infantry and began to assemble to their rear, frantically seeking a resupply of ammunition. Colonel McMillen got two brigades of infantry committed to action and Winslow was withdrawing through them. The 3rd Brigade which contained the U.S. Colored Troops was still protecting the wagon trains.

Confederate colonel Clark Barteau had brought a 250-man detachment into action and succeeded in getting behind the Union left flank. McMillen was calling for reinforcements in the center, but Sturgis had little to give as he was trying to get the third brigade to meet Barteau's threat to his left flank. One regiment of black troops was able to support McMillen and did well, earning praise from Sturgis. With ammunition exhausted, the Union cavalry was trying to fight on the flanks or pulling out. Meanwhile the wagon train had continued to follow the column, jamming the roadway. The terrain over which Union soldiers had to withdraw was low, mud-filled ground severed by a swift creek. The Union soldiers began to mill about, seeking a way to escape. Discipline began to break in the face of fear. Sturgis wrote, "Orders soon gave way to confusion and confusion to panic."[12]

By 5 P.M. Sturgis's troops were drifting toward the rear and out of control. Sturgis wrote, "The road became crowded and jammed with troops, the wagons and artillery sinking into the deep mud, became inextricable, and added to the general confusion that now prevailed. No power could now check or control the panic stricken mass as it swept toward the rear."[13]

Six Union guns had been captured at the crossroads. The Confederates turned these on what was now a mob of men. The rest of the Confederate artillery came up and sixteen guns opened fire, tearing apart flesh and bone. The bridge over Tishomingo Creek was jammed, blocked with wagons whose teams had been killed. Men plunged into the high water, but those who got across the stream had to run a gauntlet of artillery fire. Forrest briefly halted his cavalry to reorganize. He put four guns near the head of the column. Within minutes they were in pursuit, constantly hammering the Union troops who were too panicked to establish a defense or counterattack and were unable to maneuver off the muck-filled road. Two miles from the crossroads an effort at defense was made, but the artillery being well forward smashed the effort and the rout was on. Most of the wagons were taken or destroyed.[14]

Col. Edward Bouton was commander of the 59th U.S. Colored Infantry. Bouton wanted to make a stand at Hatchie Bottom during the retreat and asked Sturgis for a white regiment to help get the wagons and the artillery clear. Bouton said Sturgis replied, "For God's sake, if Mr. Forrest will let me alone I will let him alone. You have done all you could and more than was expected of you, and now all you can do is save yourselves."[15]

The Union retreat began around 4 P.M. on June 10, 1864, and some twenty-four hours later, after frequent one-sided battles, the soldiers of the United States had been driven fifty-eight miles. The Confederates reported the capture of nineteen pieces of artillery, twenty-one caissons, more than 200 wagons, thirty ambulances, and vast quantities of ammunition and materiel. They claimed 2,000 prisoners and 1,900 Union dead.[16] The Union put its total loss at fourteen guns, 250 wagons, twenty-three officers, and 594 men killed or wounded and fifty-two officers and 1,571 men captured for a total loss of 2,240.[17]

Brice's Crossroads (Forrest called it Tishomingo Creek) was a classic battle. The men of both sides had courage and by 1864 mostly were experienced soldiers. It was leadership that decided this fight. Forrest had studied the terrain, the weather and the enemy and knew he could fight and win at Brice's Crossroads. He knew what the rains and limitation on routes of withdrawal would do to a defeated enemy. Union Col. George Waring said, "It seemed always Forrest's plan to select his own fighting-ground and the plan of our commanders to gratify him."[18]

Sturgis did not have the knowledge of his opponent that Forrest did. Sturgis did not familiarize himself with the terrain and did not arrive on the battlefield in time to know or control the field. He exhausted his men trying to rush them forward and brought his wagons forward to the point they blocked his withdrawal. All this was true, but the battle was decided by Nathan Bedford Forrest's will to win and his unrelenting philosophy of attack. A slang expression of the time was frequently used to express getting the advantage on your opponent. The word used was bulge. Forrest got the bulge on Sturgis.[19]

Union general Washburn sent a telegram to Sherman on June 14: "Our troops were badly handled from the moment they left here. They were nine days in going out and thirty-six hours in returning."[20]

General Sherman, in writing General McPherson included, "Forrest is the very devil, and I think he has got some of our troops under cower. There will never be peace in Tennessee till Forrest is dead."[21]

In his after-action report Forrest truthfully wrote, "This victory may be justly considered one of the most complete of the war."[22] He told his men, "You stand before the world an unconquerable band of heroes."[23]

All this was true. Forrest had won a great battle, but when Forrest moved to attack Sturgis, Gen. William T. Sherman achieved his goal. Voices that should have been important had been seeking to put all the Confederate cavalry in the west under the command of Nathan Bedford Forrest and have him operate in Sherman's rear. To that end Gen. Joseph Johnston frequently wrote to General Bragg and twice in July proposed this to President Jefferson Davis.[24] Gov. Joseph Brown of Georgia wanted Forrest in command of the cavalry and at Sherman's rear. Jefferson Davis disliked both Johnston and Brown and refused their requests. Davis planned to relieve Joe Johnston and sent an angry response to Governor Brown: "Your telegram received. Your dicta cannot control the distribution of troops in different parts of the Confederate States. Most men in your position would not assume to decide on the value of the services to be rendered by troops in distant positions."[25] As Jefferson Davis did not like General Johnston and Governor Brown, and General Bragg did not like Forrest, personalities played a major role in a bad decision by the Confederates.

Sherman was disappointed in the failure of Sturgis but took it in stride. Punching the Army of the United States only led to another commander marching south. The victory by Forrest delayed him from going after Sherman's railroad. Within a short time word came that Gen. Andrew J. Smith had brought his Union troops over from Red River. At La Grange, Tennessee, fifty miles east of Memphis, another large Union force began to form. Two infantry divisions, a cavalry division commanded by Brig. Gen. Benjamin Grierson and twenty guns comprising a 14,000-man force had come together. On July 1, they marched south through Pontotoc, Mississippi. Smith was an astute general who intended to bring Forrest to battle and keep him from interfering with Sherman. To do this Smith intended to seize Tupelo and its railroad and force Forrest to attack him on ground of Smith's choosing. Grierson led off, taking his division of horsemen toward Tupelo.

Forrest, who was suffering from boils, had been joined by Gen. Stephen D. Lee. The two Confederate commands numbered about 8,000 men. On July 11 near Pontotoc the advance of both armies made initial contact and intermittent fighting began. Stephen Lee was now the senior officer. With characteristic daring Forrest and Lt. Samuel Donelson of his staff made a night reconnaissance of the Union position. They were challenged by a Union picket and Forrest confused the enemy by shouting, "What do you mean by halting your commanding officer!" The two Confederates escaped under fire.[26]

Stephen Lee knew that three-quarters of the Confederate troops belonged to Forrest and felt he should give up command. Forrest declined, saying that Lee was senior. They both agreed it was necessary to attack. Both generals knew the Union troops had a good position and they tried to lure General Smith into making an attack. Smith knew warfare and would not take the bait. Around 7 A.M. on July 14, 1864, the Confederate lines moved forward. With Grierson's cavalry at Tupelo, Smith had settled into a defensive position at a crossroads hamlet called Harrisburg, on a broad knoll with a clear field of fire. The only woods was 200 yards distant from the Union lines. With Smith's command in the open, Forrest could not get to him without greatly exposing his men. The aggressive Forrest took that chance and attacked about 6 P.M. The Confederates marched into the massed fire of 4,000 rifles and were shot down in rows. In Hinchie P. Mabry's Mississippi brigade, every regimental commander fell and the 2nd Tennessee had only one commissioned officer left.[27]

Beaten back, Forrest attacked again and again and again. Each of the four assaults were defeated. He employed his artillery with skill, but the Union guns were equally well served. Union sergeant Brown stood to his guns though three times wounded. When Union artillery became a torment, Col. Edward Crossland's Kentuckians charged the guns and were mowed down. Col. William W. Faulkner of Kentucky was at the front of an effort to capture the Union artillery, but regiments from Illinois, Indiana and Missouri struck his troops in the flank and sent the Confederates in retreat. Faulkner had his horse shot from under him and was wounded twice before he was killed.

Forrest kept trying, his men coming dismounted as they usually fought and attacking the Union position from another direction. It was to no avail. Smith had chosen his ground well, his troops were combat experienced and would not be routed. Forrest said his force did not exceed 5,000 men and he had 210 dead and 1,116 wounded. His loss was compounded by the loss of key officers. All colonels were either killed or wounded and three brigade commanders—Rucker, McCulloch and Crossland—severely wounded.[28] At this stage of the war, these men were almost impossible to replace. The blame for the severe Confederate losses at Harrisburg tended to fall on Maj. Gen. Stephen D. Lee. He was relieved and Maj. Gen. Dabney H. Maury made chief of cavalry.

Union general Smith had 650 casualties and eighty-two killed—a heavy toll but losses he could sustain.[29] The next morning, July 15, Forrest tried again, but his command had enough of this fight and the attack was quickly beaten back. Both sides threw parting shots of artillery at each other and the battle ended. Smith claimed his men were short of rations and that he had but one day of bread left. Grierson returned after tearing up the railroad at Tupelo and the Union column made an easy march back to Memphis. Some Confederates felt Smith's departure made Harrisburg a victory for the South. If so a few more such victories would have left the Confederate ranks empty. Some of Smith's detractors claimed there was plenty of food in the area for the Union troops to remain, others complained that Smith laid waste to everything before he departed. Smith made a rapid withdrawal to Memphis. His withdrawal was too rapid in the eyes of his seniors.

General Smith did not have to worry about what the Confederates said about him, but what Grant and Sherman said was another matter. Grant led off with a chastising message and Sherman quickly followed suit. It was made clear to Smith that he should get on the trail of Nathan Bedford Forrest and stay there. Sherman had learned that Jefferson Davis had relieved Joe Johnston in favor of John Bell Hood. Sherman was delighted by this and believed he would profit by the change. Sherman wrote, "Hood though not deemed much of a scholar, or of great mental capacity was undoubtedly a brave, determined and rash man."[30] Johnston had been fighting a wily campaign of delay, stretching the war out while the people of the North grew ever more eager to end the bloodshed. Hood would come and fight and that was to Sherman's advantage. Hood's troops knew he was a fighter, but had a lesser opinion of his generalship. He was known to the ranks as Old Wooden Head.

Smarting under sharp words, Smith hastened to cover his posterior by informing his seniors that he had returned to Memphis only to get supplies and soon would be marching after Forrest. The Union army had the troops and, fully understanding the pile-on concept so critical in war, they continued to build the size and power of Smith's command. Jefferson Davis had passed on the opportunity to put Forrest in Sherman's rear with 10,000 horsemen. Now Sherman had made certain Forrest would not interfere.

Trying to follow Smith, Forrest was up front seeking to clear an ambush when he received a painful wound in the foot. Taken to Okolona for recovery, Forrest could not return to action until early August. Forrest had suffered from numerous wounds, but the shot in his foot caused excruciating pain. Unable to ride a horse, he procured a buggy and continued to command, riding about with his foot propped up on the dash-board.

At a time when he needed the support of his government, Forrest came under criticism from Richmond because he had appointed officers proven on the field of battle to key positions instead of allowing the men to elect their leaders. Gen. Braxton Bragg was now the military adviser to President Jefferson Davis. Bragg could have stopped this foolishness, but did not and may well have had a hand in it. Popular officers are frequently not the best officers and men serving under incompetents gave up and went home or died in battle due to the wrong men being in command.

Forrest could not meet Smith's large force in frontal attack. He opted to strike oncoming Union columns at their flanks and rear while delaying them with strong fortifications. Still suffering from his wound, Forrest while at his headquarters at Pontotoc studied likely enemy avenues of approach and ordered the impressment of slaves to construct the defensive works that would impede a Union advance.

As Smith's command advanced, one of Forrest's divisions, that of Brig. Gen. James Chalmers, fought the delaying action, burning bridges behind it while Forrest gathered men and materiel for offensive action. Union troops made considerable effort to repair the Mississippi Central and Mobile and Ohio railroads to supply movements south. The Confederate defenses were spread thin. There was too much territory and too few men. On August 8 a Union attack over the Tallahatchie River forced the defenders from position. It was now clear the axis of advance was via Holly Spring, Abbeville and Oxford along the Mississippi Central Railroad. Forrest and his men reached Oxford on the night of August 10 and Forrest brought the scattered Confederate defenders in the region under his command.

The opposing forces skirmished for two days. On August 13, the Union column launched a determined attack that ended in a grudging and brief withdrawal by the Confederates. Two more days of skirmishing saw brief attack and counterattack. The Union advance was not pressed and the Confederates did not have the means to defeat their opponents. Reviewing his limited options, Forrest decided that the most likely way to force his enemy to withdraw was to raid their rear area.

The objective would be Union headquarters at Memphis. Onlookers on the Mississippi River bluffs had cried when on June 6, 1862, Union gunboats and rams destroyed a makeshift Confederate fleet and the city was forced to surrender. Memphis was well known in the North as a hotbed of secession. Among those present when Memphis surrendered was the roving reporter of the *New York Tribune,* Albert D. Richardson.

In the deserted office of the Memphis secessionist newspaper *The Appeal,* Richardson found the following manuscript.

A Challenge

Where as the wicked policy of the president————making war upon the south for refusing to submit to wrong too palpable for Southerners to do. And where it has become necessary for the young Men of our country, My Brother in the number To enlist to do the dirty work of Driving the Mercenarys from our sunny south. Whose soil is too holy for such wretches to tramp And whose atmosphere is to pure for them to breath

For such an indignity afford to Civilization I merely challenge any abolition or Black Republican lady of character if there can be such a one found among the Negro equality tribe. To Meet Me at Masons and dixon line. With a pair of Colt's repeaters or any other weapon they May Choose, That I may receive satisfaction for the insult.

Victoria E. Goodwin

Spring Dale, Miss., April 27 1861[31]

Nathan Bedford Forrest knew he could count on the support of much of the population of the city. A successful raid on Memphis would cause a furor in Northern newspapers and embarrass Union commanders and the Lincoln administration. If some generals could be captured, the Union army would be shamed.

Forrest left some 2,000 men under Brigadier General Chalmers in front of Smith's army of 20,000. It was Chalmers' mission to threaten Smith, to make numerous demonstrations that would make the Union commander believe a Confederate attack was impending. Forrest needed several days of uninterrupted movement and it was up to Chalmers to provide that. After a rigid inspection that separated out the sick and the lame horses and men, Forrest had a force of some 1,500 officers and men and four guns to begin his march. The weather favored a raid. It was terrible. Incessant storms had flooded streams, the ground was soaked and roads were channels of mud. Shortly after 5 P.M., on August 18, 1864, Forrest's raiders put foot to stirrup, swung into the saddle and set forth in a pelting rain.

Even in the worst of conditions, morale is better when offensive action is being taken. Despite the ordeal of the mud-march the men held up well. In the black of night under a torrential rain, flooded streams had to be crossed and men, horses and guns pulled from bogs or dragged up hills. The route was so difficult that it required a forty-mile detour to find passage. Forrest reached Panola at 7 A.M. and found that some 100 men and many of the artillery horses could not continue. They rested for a few hours, then continued on and made another twenty-three miles before exhaustion compelled a halt. Ahead lay Hickahala Creek—fully sixty feet wide, with steep banks and at flood stage. Forrest had no engineers, bridging equipment or pontoons. He sent tired men throughout the countryside collecting everything from telegraph poles and grapevines, to the flooring from mills and houses. Telegraph poles were tied together with grapevines and used as pontoons. Other poles were laid across the pontoons and the flooring laid across. In one hour the bridge was built that carried Forrest and his men across the raging stream.[32] Some seven miles farther on they were forced to repeat their bridge construction to cross Cold Water River. This construction was completed in three hours. Before dark, Forrest and his men were within twenty-five miles of Memphis and had not been discovered. They pressed on, reaching the city about 3 A.M. on Sunday, August 21, 1864.

Scouts and friendly locals provided information on the location of Union outposts and the disposition of troop units. It was believed some 5,000 Union soldiers were in the city and some of their units were comprised of hundred-day men, untrained and likely to panic. Forrest held a commanders' call and assigned mission to each. Men were sent to cut telegraph wires at key places, severing Union communications. Bedford Forrest's son, the youthful Capt. William H. Forrest, was given the point with forty men to eliminate the Union pickets. William Forrest was then to press on and raid the Gayoso House, a hotel where Maj. Gen. Stephen Hurlbut and other senior Union officers were known to stay. Forrest's brother, Lt. Col. Jesse Forrest, led a detachment to the headquarters of Maj. Gen. Cadwallader Colden Washburn, commanding general of the District of West Tennessee. Another team went after Gen. Ralph P. Buckland, Memphis District commander. Some of the raiding force occupied blocking positions, one was sent to control the steamboat landing and still another to attack the Union hundred-day men. A rallying point was established for reassembly on completion of the missions.

Fog rolled in off the river and combined with the blackness of night served to disguise the presence of the raiders. Much depended on the ability of Capt. William Forrest and his men to capture the picket. Knowing that the Union 12th Missouri Cavalry was with Smith's army near Oxford, Captain Forrest answered the picket challenge by saying he was a member of the 12th Missouri bringing in Rebel prisoners. With that ruse he was able to get close to the picket and fell him with his pistol butt. His men closed on the remainder of the Union outpost and captured them with but one shot fired in the process. That shot however, alerted other outposts and when Nathan Bedford Forrest rode forward, he and his escort were fired upon.

Secrecy was lost, but an element of surprise was available. As the first light appeared in the sky, Nathan Bedford Forrest ordered his buglers to sound the charge. The Confederate riders raced into the city yelling at the top of their lungs and sweeping away the hasty defenses that stood in their path.

Captain Forrest and his detachment shot their way through an artillery detachment and reached the Gayoso Hotel. The youthful Forrest and several of his men did not dismount, but rode their horses into the hotel lobby. Once inside, his men leaped from their saddles, fanned out and engaged newly awakened Union officers in a shootout, killing one and forcing the others to surrender. Confederate colonel Aleck Chalmers found General

Emma Sanson, the teenage girl
who rode with Forrest and showed
him a ford, allowing him to catch
Abel Streight and his Union
raiders. USAMHI

Hurlbut's room and kicked in the door. Hurlbut was not there, but a beautiful woman was. She threw her arms around Chalmers' neck and begged him for protection. With masterful wit, Chalmers told her he would protect her provided she would not take up arms until regularly exchanged as a prisoner of war.[33]

Throughout the city, the raid was breaking down into a series of street fights often done before the open windows and eyes of the townspeople. Some of the men of Forrest's command were from Memphis and they were cheered by family and friends.

Forrest wanted the hide of Major General Washburn. Washburn was from Wisconsin, one of the wealthiest men in the United States and the rare combination of a brilliant and thoroughly honest businessman. He also was a dedicated soldier who hated slavery. The killings at Fort Pillow had ignited an exchange of correspondence between the two men which despite all the "I have the honor of" and "your obedient servant" salutations was Washburn telling Forrest he was a murderer and Forrest responding with fury at the challenge to his reputation. Lt. Col. Jesse Forrest went after the Union general. Washburn had a fine officer in Col. Matthew H. Starr of the 6th Illinois Cavalry among the forefront of the defenders. Starr sent Washburn a galloper warning him of the attack. Washburn had to run for safety in his nightshirt, but got out a back door of his house and made a half-mile sprint to safety at Fort Pickering.[34] General Buckland was also warned and being close to Colonel Starr's men, joined them and evaded capture.

Now fully awake, the Union forces were beginning to stiffen. Holed up in a brick building of the State Female College, a group of dismounted Union cavalrymen played a hot fire on Forrest and would not be dislodged by his artillery. Forrest now had men scattered throughout the city, often fighting as individuals or small groups rather than as a unified effort. Forrest turned his attention to consolidating his units. No Union generals had been captured, but the city and the Union forces therein were in an uproar. Union cavalry under Colonel Starr was already in pursuit, chasing Confederate stragglers and those who were lost out of town. Nathan Bedford Forrest led his 2nd Missouri against the Union soldiers and repulsed them with Forrest personally giving Colonel Starr a serious wound.

More than 400 prisoners had been taken, many pulled from their beds and without boots or clothes. Forrest sent a captured officer offering to exchange the Union prisoners for those of his men who had been captured. If that was not acceptable, clothing and food should be sent for the Union prisoners. General Washburn felt he did not have the authority to release Confederate prisoners so clothing and rations were sent that would last the prisoners for some time. Washburn thus unwittingly did Forrest a favor. Sufficient rations were given prisoners by the Confederates to feed them for two days, the rest was used to feed Forrest's command.[35] As soon as the cut telegraph wires were spliced Washburn sent a message to General Smith ordering that Smith's cavalry cut off Forrest's escape. Some of Forrest's men found it difficult to break contact. Lieutenant Sale was in charge of two pieces of artillery, 3-inch steel Rodmans that had been captured at Lexington in 1862. Unable to get away with his guns, Sale buried them in the middle of the road. The Confederates escaped and later sent a detail back to dig up their artillery.[36]

To Washburn's anger, Smith did not seal the routes and Forrest came out safely. Among his prizes was General Washburn's uniform. Forrest thought enough of this incident to put it in his report. Either as a courtesy or in a mocking fashion, Washburn's uniform was returned by Forrest under a flag of truce. Washburn had possession of Forrest's hometown of Memphis and that was where the pre-war tailor of Nathan Bedford Forrest lived. Washburn sent Forrest a tailor-made uniform. Only the participants knew if this was courtesy or a game of one-upmanship. Men take their amusements where they can in war.

Forrest, the one leader who could have done the most to disrupt the Union Atlanta-to-the-sea march, was in western Tennessee. Sherman was delighted that Forrest was where he wanted him and sent a message to Washburn, "If you get a chance send word to Forrest that I admire his dash, but not his judgement."[37] But it was by decision of Jefferson Davis, likely influenced by Braxton Bragg, that Forrest was withheld from Sherman's rear. That decision hurt the South. Abraham Lincoln was in serious political trouble and likely would not have been reelected president but for Sherman's capture of Atlanta. The summer of discontent in the North was followed after Atlanta by a winter of hope and resolution and a revitalized leadership power for Lincoln. A string of critical Union victories was led by the Atlanta success of the red-headed angel of destruction, William Tecumseh Sherman.

Gen. James Chalmers had carried out his orders to demonstrate in front of the Union army and the combination of his efforts and the raid on Memphis caused Union general Smith to cease his advance. Forrest withdrew to Hernando from where it would seem he was still threatening the Union rear. He paroled his prisoners and sent men he had borrowed back to their commands.

General Sherman had left Atlanta, turned his back on John Bell Hood's army and was marching through Georgia toward Savannah and the sea. The crops were high and the army lived easy, cutting a fifty-mile wide swath and making Georgia governor Brown hurry his family to safety. The Confederacy's war within a war continued with Governor Brown among many castigating Jefferson Davis and in turn being criticized by Davis. Brown felt he could not support the call for more Georgia men to go to Hood's army. The Union army was on Georgia soil and state rights dictated that a governor could say where troops from his state were needed. Brown was seeking other governors to join in his resentment of central authority and in varying degrees others did. The in-fighting would continue with Brown being called down by Secretary of War Seddon and Florida governor John Milton. General Sherman held out an olive branch to Governor Brown, suggesting it was possible for Georgia to leave the Confederacy and return to the fold of the United States.

Lt. Gen. Richard Taylor, five years younger than Forrest, was now his commanding officer. In early September 1864, the two men met at Meridian, Mississippi. Forrest had been ordered previously to assist in fending off an anticipated attack on Mobile, Alabama, and was en route ahead of his troops for that purpose. Taylor had determined the threat to Mobile was not valid and had a change of plans for his subordinate. Taylor described the meeting as follows:

> [T]he General whom I had never seen, came to report. He was a tall, stalwart man, with grayish hair, mild countenance, and slow and homely speech. In few words he was informed that I considered Mobile safe for the present, and that all our energies must be

directed to the relief of Hood's army, then west of Atlanta. The only way to accomplish this was to worry Sherman's communications north of the Tennessee river, and he must move his cavalry in that direction at the earliest moment.

To my surprise Forrest suggested many difficulties and asked numerous questions: how was he to get back over the Tennessee; how was he to get back if pressed by the enemy; how he was to be supplied; what would be his line of retreat in certain contingencies; what he was to do with prisoners if any were taken, etc. I began to think he had no stomach for the work; but at last, having isolated the chances for success from causes of failure . . . he rose and asked for Fleming, the superintendent of the railway . . . Fleming appeared . . . and at once stated what he could do in the way of moving supplies on his line . . . Forrest's whole manner now changed. In a dozen sharp sentences he told his wants . . . informed me he would march with the dawn, and hoped to give a good account of himself.[38]

Forrest turned to his new mission with zeal. He made certain the sick and the lame were weeded out, that his men had ammunition and food and those who did not have horses were organized as a foot battalion until horses could be captured. He was very careful to have the Memphis and Charleston Railroad repaired and organized as his lifeline of supply. Forty rounds of ammunition were in the cartridge boxes, but they were backed up with another sixty rounds per man close at hand on the rail cars.

On September 16, 1864, Forrest set out from Verona, Mississippi, with 3,542 men. On September 18 the command arrived at Cherokee Station, Alabama, the eastern end of the Memphis and Charleston Railroad. He had used rail to get his supplies to this point, now his most critical backup supplies would be transferred to wagons. By September 21 Forrest was over the Tennessee River and the next day he marched on Athens, Alabama. En route, additional Confederate troops from Gen. Philip D. Roddey's command and under Col. William Johnson joined Forrest, bringing his strength to 4,500 men, of which some 400 were dismounted.[39] On the evening of September 23, Forrest reached Athens and prepared to attack its Union garrison. Railroad tracks and telegraph wires were torn up to isolate the Union soldiers. The town, fort and blockhouses were invested and artillery rolled into position.

In opposition was Col. Wallace Campbell of the 110th U.S. Colored Infantry with 469 men and two guns. He occupied a fort 1,350 feet in circumference, seventeen feet from the bottom of the encircling ditch to the parapet, with all encircled by a palisade and an abatis of felled trees.[40] The fort was well-supplied with food, water and ammunition and, with the exception of the commander, was ready to fight. Forrest drove in Campbell's pickets and fired some artillery into the fort. Knowing he faced a bloody assault he sent in a demand for surrender. Campbell refused, but the refusal was done with such hesitancy that Forrest believed he had the "skeer" on Campbell. At about 7 A.M. on the twenty-fourth Forrest again opened fire with his artillery, dropping some fifty-five or sixty about the fort with twenty-four rounds landing inside. One non-combatant was killed and one soldier wounded. At 9 A.M. Forrest sent in another demand for surrender: "[S]hould you, however accept the terms, all white soldiers shall be treated as prisoners of war, and the Negroes returned to their masters." Forrest used a carrot and stick approach, he offered the officers prompt parole, seeking to separate them from their men. Forrest felt so confident that he had mental dominance on his opponent that he invited Campbell to come tour his lines. Campbell did this and his imagination ran away with him. Campbell would later write that Forrest "had 10,000 men and nine pieces of artillery."[41] Campbell claimed he returned to the fort and consulted with his officers who felt he should surrender. Later thirty-two of the fort's officers, ranging from second lieutenant to major and from platoon to company and surgeon to quartermaster, would write that they were not consulted and were opposed to surrender. The enlisted men wanted to fight. The white soldiers knew that surrender meant the hell of Andersonville or Salisbury prisons. The black soldiers knew they would be forced back into slavery. These men wanted to fight and reinforcements were on the way, but their commander said, "The jig is up; pull down the flag." Soldiers both black and white wept at being ordered to surrender. Forrest ordered the fort destroyed and then wrecked or burned two locomotives and three cars while taking thirty-eight wagons, two guns, two ambulances and 300 horses.

Detachments of the 18th Michigan and 102nd Ohio under Lt. Col. Jonas D. Elliott were close at hand and marching to reinforce the fort.[42] Forrest attacked the Union troops whom he said "fought with great gallantry and desperation." Forrest's brother Lt. Col. Jesse Forrest was severely wounded in this fight. With no resistance from the fort, Forrest was able to throw the weight of his command on the column and these men surrendered. Forrest then moved his command on the road to Pulaski. The bridges and key railroad installation were guarded by blockhouses that were sufficient to protect against infantry, but helpless in the face of artillery. Forrest captured thirty men from one of these, destroyed the railroad bridge it protected and pressed onward toward the Sulphur Springs trestle. It was seventy-two feet high and 300 feet long and defended by two large blockhouses.[43] The fighting here was bloody with Forrest pounding the block-houses with eight pieces of artillery firing from all four directions. Union commander Col. William H. Lathrop was killed and second-in-command Lieutenant Colonel Minnis knocked unconscious in the shelling. Riddled with shrapnel, the blockhouses surrendered about 11 A.M. on September 25, 1864. Forrest added two more guns to his artillery and now had some 973 prisoners and 300 more horses.

With his command now fully mounted, Forrest marched to Elkton. His troops destroyed the blockhouse and bridge there and not far distant found some 2,000 Negroes living in hovels that he termed a "government corral." Forrest described them as "ragged and dirty" and in "absolute want."[44] The captives were ordered to take their clothes and bedding from their "miser-able hovels" and the structures—nearly 200 in number—were burned. No report was made on the disposition of the people Forrest said were mostly old men, women and children.

Forrest moved on and at Richland Creek took another blockhouse and fifty prisoners. After resting for a night he continued marching toward Pulaski. The Union defense made a determined stand and seven hours of constant fighting ensued. By nightfall progress was not made and Forrest was frustrated and angry. Though he could be mild mannered, Forrest was fierce when aroused. At such times his temper was legendary and his lan-guage profane. Few men ever saw Nathan Bedford Forrest run for his own safety, but on one occasion he did.

A captured Union caisson that had been carrying gunpowder was stuck in the mud and as Capt. Andrew McGregor and his men struggled to free it, Forrest rode up.

"Who has charge here?" Forrest demanded.

"I have, sir," responded McGregor.

"Then why in hell don't you do something?" Forrest shouted and began to curse Captain McGregor.

McGregor also had a temper. "I'll not be cursed by anyone, even a supe-rior officer!" he roared. Seizing a lighted torch, he rammed it into the ammunition chest.

Horrified, Forrest jammed his spurs into his horse and bolted away, yelling warnings for men to run. "What infernal lunatic is that just out of the asylum down there?" he shouted at his staff. "He came near blowing himself and me up with a whole caisson of powder."

What Forrest did not know was the powder had been removed in the efforts to free the caisson. When he learned he had been foxed, he joined his staff in laughter. Forrest was known to knock down officers who disputed him, shot and killed one who tried to assassinate him, and cursed many of them, but he never cursed Andrew McGregor again.[45]

Forrest went into camp and ordered numerous campfires lit to deceive the enemy. Pulaski was too difficult to capture so Forrest bypassed the town and moved on to Fayetteville. His scouting parties were constantly in motion across the countryside, cutting telegraph wires and tearing up railroad tracks.

The raid was running out of momentum. Forrest had 100 rounds of ammunition per artillery piece left and did not consider that sufficient. He also had detached a large number of men to escort prisoners. Concerned that the gathering forces of the Union army were larger than he deemed wise to fight, Forrest changed his direction and moved toward the line of the Tennessee and Alabama Railroad. He reached Lewisburg at noon on September 30, then moved on to Spring Hill and the road to Columbia. Twelve miles from the town he found a series of railroad bridges guarded by blockhouses defended by the 7th Pennsylvania Cavalry. Forrest had no artillery with him at these blockhouses and used a bluff to get one to surrender. Fortunately for the Confederates, this fortification was commanded by Lt. Edward F. Nixon of Company E, 7th Pennsylvania Cavalry. Nixon surrendered without firing a shot and then ordered the three other blockhouses under his command to give up. Sgt. William H. Rhinemiller of the 7th Pennsylvania Cavalry refused the order three times and Nixon threatened his sergeant with arrest and fired on the blockhouse and its United States flag. Not understanding what his commander was doing, Rhinemiller surrendered his fortification. Nixon, in company with Forrest's adjutant, then rode to blockhouse number six, bridge number five. This was commanded by 1st Lt. Jonas F. Long of Company B, 7th Pennsylvania Cavalry. Long was furious about Nixon's cowardice and ordered the two officers away from his position.[46] Long fought Forrest from 2 P.M. until midnight. As Forrest did not have artillery the attacks were made by infantry and ten Confederates were killed and others wounded. Under the cover of darkness a Confederate patrol moved along the railroad bank, poured turpentine on Lieutenant Long's bridge and burned it. Forrest destroyed all he could and moved on. One blockhouse was still standing. It was occupied by Lieutenant Long and his brave men.

On October 2, Forrest was within six miles of Columbia. The defenses were strong and Forrest did not make a serious attempt to take the town. After making a demonstration and gathering information he hoped to use in future, Forrest withdrew and began the trek home. By October 5 he was at Florence where he found the river running extremely high and the enemy pressing after him. Unable to ferry his command with sufficient speed to clear the north bank before the enemy came up, Forrest had all the men that remained, except Colonel Wilson's regiment, mount up and swim their horses about seventy yards across a slough to a large island. Here they had security until they could be ferried to the south bank. Wilson fought a brilliant delaying action, constantly making demonstrations and attacks and living off what his command captured. When all the Confederates were across the river, Wilson's regiment crossed to safety.

Forrest was back at Cherokee on October 6. Anticipating the Union would use its control of the Tennessee River to advantage, he sent Colonel Kelley with a brigade of infantry and two guns to an ambush position on the river bank. Two Union gunboats and three transports came up the stream. Kelly let the lead brigade and some guns land, then opened fire on them. The transports attempted to withdraw but were shelled. About thirty prisoners and three guns were taken.

The raid was at an end. Forrest reported the capture of eighty-six commissioned officers, sixty-seven government employees, 1,274 noncommissioned officers and privates, 933 Negroes and 800 horses. He estimated enemy killed and wounded at 1,000 more.[47] His unstinting efforts and wounds had worn upon him and he asked General Taylor for a twenty- to thirty-day leave to rest and recruit. He had captured thirty-nine guns by Union count and these were organized into a formidable artillery. While he was absent Forrest asked that Brig. Gen. James Chalmers be in charge.

War has its own schedule and Taylor badly needed Forrest to go out again. General Sherman had established another supply route with the main base at Johnsonville on the Tennessee River west of Nashville. Taylor wanted Forrest to destroy these stores and interfere with the Union's navigation on the river. There was an urgency to this as the main Confederate army in the west was on the move. The long-awaited action was an attempt to get Sherman to withdraw from Georgia.

On July 17, 1864, Jefferson Davis had relieved Joe Johnston and given Gen. John Bell Hood command of the Confederate Army of the Tennessee. A long-faced, sad-eyed man, Hood had given much to the secessionist cause. An arm was rendered useless at Gettysburg and a leg was lost at Chickamauga. He knew much physical pain and the use of drugs to forestall that pain likely affected his reason. He had conspired to high command, deriding Joe Johnston to President Jefferson Davis, who had a personal dislike for Johnston. Hood got the command by promising the offensive action Davis felt Johnston was not taking. This was good news to Sherman who wrote, "The Confederate government rendered us a valuable service."[48]

Johnston had fought a wily delaying action, making Sherman pay a bloody price for ground gained while Atlanta was ringed with fortifications. At Kennesaw Mountain on June 27, Sherman had lost 3,000 men to 630 of Joe Johnston's Confederates. Sherman knew Hood would slug it out. To meet the Southern army in open country was what Sherman wanted.

On July 20, Hood attacked and lost 4,796 men to Sherman's 1,710. Not satisfied, Hood attempted to flank Sherman on July 22 and lost 8,499 men to

Sherman's 3,641. On July 28, Hood again attempted to flank Sherman and lost 4,632 men to Sherman's 700.[49] An excess of manpower was not a Confederate luxury. Hood learned he could not whip Sherman from the front. The Confederate strategy now became to operate on Sherman's rear. Hood moved his army to Lovejoy's Station some thirty miles southeast of Atlanta.

On Friday, September 2, 1864, Sherman took Atlanta. It was a critical victory, and insurance that President Lincoln would be reelected and the war would continue. But on the battlefield much remained to be accomplished. From the time Grant took command, the Union strategy was clear. Through the application of superior manpower and logistics in unrelenting pressure, the destruction of the Confederate armies would be accomplished. It was not the mere occupation of land. Grant must beat Lee. Sherman must win in the west and Sheridan must beat Early in the Shenandoah Valley. On all fronts this pressure was applied. As they defeated the Confederate armies they would move to help each other in a pile-on concept. If Grant beat Lee first he would move to help Sherman at Atlanta. If Sherman were successful first he would lead his army to help Grant.

By September 21, Hood moved his army to Palmetto Station, twenty-five miles southwest of Atlanta. It was the opening move to get to the rear of Sherman. President Jefferson Davis visited Hood and made an exuberant and foolish speech in which he publicly announced that the Confederates would make Sherman's retreat more disastrous than Napoleon's retreat from Moscow. The speech was widely reported and Sherman took immediate steps to strengthen his stay-behind forces, putting General Thomas in charge.

George H. Thomas was born in Southampton County, Virginia, and graduated from West Point in 1840. He had commanded a section in Capt. Braxton Bragg's battery of artillery in the Mexican War and was known for his coolness under fire. At the onset of the war, Lincoln was concerned about the loyalty of Virginia born-Thomas but Sherman, certain of Thomas's devotion to the United States, pressed for his promotion to brigadier general. When he saw Thomas, Sherman asked what the Virginian intended to do. "I'm going South," was the response. Sherman was dumbfounded until Thomas grinned and said, "At the head of my men." Thomas had a reputation for being slow, but could read a battlefield like a book. In the early part of the Civil War troops were firing furiously at a wood where the Confederates were believed to be. A fellow officer said, "The brigade on the right seems to be hotly engaged." Thomas replied, "I hear no return shots."[50] Thomas was scorned by his sisters for remaining loyal to the United States, but he would not give up the flag of his fathers. He was a patient man who would not move until he was ready. When he fought, he was among the best generals of the war.

Sherman saw the opportunity to make a bold and decisive move. He would not take the bait and follow Hood, but would leave sufficient strength behind to allow Thomas to deal with that threat. Sherman would cut loose from his base of supply and for a time live off the land and captured supplies that had been gathered for Confederate armies. Sherman knew his troops could not survive indefinitely in that fashion. He wrote, "No army dependent on wagons can operate more than a hundred miles from its base, because the teams going and returning consume the contents of their wagons."[51]

Savannah, on the Atlantic coast, was but 300 miles from Atlanta and the skilled logistician Sherman knew he needed a seaport to supply his troops. He decided to cut a path across Georgia, resupply at Savannah and march north to strike against the rear of the main Confederate army under Robert E. Lee. The plan seemed to justify the claim that Sherman was insane. To cut an army of 50,000 men loose from its lifelines of supply and communication deep in enemy territory was an invitation to disaster. Lincoln doubted it would work. Generals from the North and South predicted failure. Only Grant and Sherman believed the move would succeed.

Happily laboring under the delusion he would bring Sherman back from Georgia, John Bell Hood began moving his army through northern Alabama to Decatur and Florence, then across the Tennessee toward Franklin and Nashville. The Confederates believed Hood would gain control of middle Tennessee. As Union forces left western Tennessee to fight Hood, Nathan Bedford Forrest saw the opportunity to fill that vacuum and defeat the stay-behind Union troops. Then Forrest could join forces with Hood for a move into Kentucky, the Mississippi River could again be closed and the Confederacy reunited.

Putting aside his need for rest, Forrest began organizing an attack into west Tennessee. His objective would be Fort Heiman on the Tennessee River below the Union supply dump at Johnsonville. He would shut off the Union flow of supplies on the river. Forrest also planned to round up the numerous deserters and absentees who roamed the countryside and conscript others. The conscription teams freely used in the Confederacy in 1864 differed little from the press gangs once used by the English navy. Forrest recommended that the men he rounded up be put in the infantry, telling General Taylor, "The facilities of these men for running away is much greater in the cavalry service."[52]

On October 16, 1864, Forrest moved his lead brigade, then brought together his command from their scattered positions. He made a feint toward Memphis that confused the Union generals. By October 29, Forrest had his men at Fort Heiman and Paris Landing on the Tennessee River and his artillery controlled the waters. Unaware that Forrest was nearby, Union commanders continued to send freight-hauling transports into a skillfully established Confederate ambush on the river.

The steamer *Mazeppa* and two barges came under the Confederate guns and were allowed to steam well into the trap before being fired upon. The steamer was run toward the opposite shore and, with the exception of the captain, the crew deserted the ship. Hungry eyes looked toward the prize, but no means existed to get there. A daring young private named W. C. West, of the 2nd Tennessee, hung his revolver around his neck and used a log and a makeshift paddle to cross the cold waters and make the capture. The steamer captain brought his vessel and cargo to the Confederate side and Forrest's men found a wealth of supplies they desperately needed.

The ambush created a dilemma for Union commanders, who promptly dispatched gunboats to the scene. Then began a series of ship and shore fights, with transports trying to run the ambush gauntlet. Despite enormous difficulty in getting guns into position, Forrest and his commanders were able to make use of thick underbrush and canes to conceal both guns and riflemen along the river bank. Once deep in the ambush, the Union vessels were taken under heavy fire. The steamer *J.W. Cheeseman* was disabled as was the gunboat *Undine*. The steamer *Venus* was captured. The *Cheeseman* was a wreck but the *Venus* and the *Undine* were in good condition and the *Undine* carried eight 24-pounder brass howitzers. Forrest now decided to launch an attack on Johnsonville by both land and water. American Rangers were making amphibious attacks in New England in the 1740s, but in 1864 the horsemen under Forrest were landsmen uncertain what fodder a steamboat required. Though Forrest was serious and those chosen to be sailors tried hard, men on the shore found much merriment in the predicament of their comrades. Lt. Col. William A. Dawson was made the unwilling commodore of Forrest's two-ship navy. Dawson was a landsman and complained until he was assured that Forrest would not reprimand him if things went wrong in the Ranger fleet.

For two days the water and land forces moved within sight of each other, but as the crews became more confident the steamboats began pulling ahead. The transport *Venus* was leading when it rounded a bend in the river and met two Union gunboats. The sailors of the U.S. Navy made short work of the *Venus* and sent the *Undine* hurrying back to the protection of Forrest's land artillery. Supplies, two pieces of artillery and much of the loot Confederates had taken from the *Mazeppa* were recaptured . The Union gunboats came on firing and wrecked the *Undine*, forcing Colonel Dawson to take to the shore and hide out, then raft his men back across the river. Dawson was delighted to give up the naval career he never wanted.

Though deprived of his navy, Forrest pressed on and by November 3 was on the opposite side of the river from the little village of Johnsonville. He found the river here about 800 yards wide. A steamboat landing and a railroad depot enabled Union forces to consolidate their supply lines. Warehouses and sheds stocked with supplies could be seen. On high ground was an extensive fortification flanked by rifle pits that ran west and south. The redoubt overlooked the supply storage area and the shore where transports and gunboats were moored.

On personal reconnaissance, Forrest saw that his guns could reach these targets with accuracy. There were within Forrest's command a number of skilled artillerymen. Aided by infantry labor they constructed cane-and-brush screens that concealed them from observation. They worked throughout the day and into the darkness, building emplacements which gave protection for the guns yet brought them close to the enemy. So well was this performed that the Union defenders and dockworkers did not know Forrest and his men were on them until shell and shrapnel began the terrible work among them. John Morton wrote that when his guns opened fire, "The scene changed as if a magician's wand had been suddenly waved over it. Spurts of steam and smoke broke from the boats, showing that the range had been gauged with pretty fair accuracy; the crews dropped their washing, hauling and packing and jumped into the water like rats deserting a sinking ship; the passengers who had been sauntering around in the neighborhood of the wharf rushed wildly up the hill, and everybody made for shelter."[53]

Soon flame began to appear and spread among the buildings and stacked supplies. By darkness on November 4 a wall of fire ran two miles of riverfront as buildings, boats and supplies were consumed by hungry flames. Union officers estimated the damage at $2,200,000.[54]

Forrest was having such a good time that he took over a gun and with Generals Bell and Buford and Major Allison serving as his crew, tried his hand at being a gunner. Morton wrote that when his shot fell short, Forrest would exclaim, "A rickety-shay! A rickety-shay! I'll hit her next time." And when ordering a range change Forrest commanded, "Elevate the breech a little lower." Each time the gun recoiled Bell and Buford would push it back into position.[55]

To Union generals, Forrest seemed to be a phantom who was here, there and everywhere. Sherman sent a November 1, 1864, message to Grant that "Forrest seems to be scattered from Eastport to Jackson, Paris and the lower Tennessee." There was a report Forrest was going about Chicago, Michigan City and Canada in disguise, had raised 14,000 men and planned on November 7 to seize Chicago and shoot all Union soldiers. The reputation of Nathan Bedford Forrest had put the "skeer" into a number of people. That feeling did not extend to George Thomas or William Sherman. They were friends of long standing, classmates at West Point and had served together as lieutenants in Florida, hunting Seminole Indians in the 1840s. Although they did not fear Forrest, they respected his ability. General William "Cump" Sherman had a clear, complete and concise usage of the English language. Sherman defined war as "hell" and Forrest as "that devil."

Though he still was not well, there would be no leave of recuperation for Maj. Gen. Nathan Bedford Forrest. On October 30, Forrest was ordered to move his command to middle Tennessee where he would join General Hood and become cavalry commander of the Army of Tennessee. The rains were incessant and bottomless roads made travel exhausting. Starting from Johnsonville on November 5, Forrest and his command arrived at Florence, Alabama, on the eighteenth.

Two western armies that had long opposed each other were now moving in different directions. On November 17, General William Sherman began his eastward march through Georgia to the sea.

CHAPTER ELEVEN

Gray Twilight

John Bell Hood was moving north to Nashville. Hood placed Forrest in command of all cavalry of the Army of the Tennessee, some 5,000 men. Forrest was ordered forward to serve as the advance of army. Through rain and snow he went to his mission with characteristic vigor, skirmishing with Union cavalry through northern Alabama. Union general George Thomas was expecting Hood and was assembling his army at Nashville. In advance, seventy-five miles south of Nashville at Pulaski, Thomas had Gen. John Schofield with one corps and a division totaling 23,000 men. Schofield had the mission of delaying Hood until Thomas had his forces gathered. Hood moved his main army on November 21, seeking to drive between Schofield at Pulaski and Thomas at Nashville. With Forrest leading the way, Hood marched northeast from Florence toward Columbia, thirty miles to the north of Pulaski. Out front Forrest was engaged with four brigades of Union cavalry under Brig. Gen. Edward Hatch. Forrest had a slight numerical advantage and was on the attack. Hatch had the job of screening General Schofield's army. Recognizing his exposed position, Schofield had begun withdrawing toward Nashville. Columbia was a critical point where the turnpike, railroad and Duck River joined. If Hood beat Schofield to Columbia, Thomas' army would be separated. As Forrest drove Hatch's horsemen before him he was on the verge of reaching Columbia when a Union infantry division under Brig. Gen. Jacob Cox came up in support and stalled the attack. In this action Lieutenant Colonel Dawson, who had tried his best to head Forrest's navy, was killed trying to seize Union colors.

Schofield reached Columbia first and began fortifying the town. On November 27 Hood's army arrived and began making preparations to attack. Schofield looked at the ground he would need to defend and concluded that Hood could flank him. As Hood's army was completing its move, Schofield left Columbia, moved north of the Duck River to ground he liked and began digging in. Hood called a commanders' meeting on the night of the twenty-seventh and ordered Forrest to cross the river to the north bank and cover the construction of pontoon bridges that would move the infantry across.[1] In the early morning hours of the twenty-eighth, the bridge was put in some three miles above Columbia. Forrest had a cavalry division across the river before noon and was pushing back James Wilson's Union cavalry. Wilson had come west from Sheridan's army to head up Sherman's cavalry.

Still hoping to isolate and destroy Schofield, Hood hurried two of his three corps across the river. Both commanders knew that to rejoin Thomas, Schofield needed to follow the route of Spring Hill and Franklin to Nashville. Possession of the turnpike that ran north was critical to success. Schofield gave Maj. Gen. David Stanley the mission of keeping the road open. As Stanley approached Spring Hill he was met by a frightened cavalry soldier who told him that Buford's division of Forrest's cavalry was approaching from the east. Stanley moved his three brigades on the double into the town and managed to beat back the attack.[2]

Stanley's division was isolated, seven miles from Union support, while Hood's army with Maj. Gen. Benjamin Franklin Cheatham in the lead closed on Spring Hill. Any Confederate force of size thrown across the turnpike would have cut off Schofield. Hood later would claim he had the turnpike in sight, could see the withdrawing Union soldiers and that he ordered Cheatham and division commander Maj. Gen. Patrick R. Cleburne to "take possession of and hold that pike at or near Spring Hill." Cheatham later denied Hood's claim and said that from Hood's position the only way he could have seen the turnpike was from a mirage.[3]

On the twenty-ninth Forrest was fighting a running battle with Wilson's cavalry, pushing the blue-coated riders before him while Union horsemen sought to establish barricaded positions to limit the advance. What Forrest planned to do was hold Wilson in the front while he sent Chalmers' division on a flanking movement, to strike his flank and rear. That plan failed. When Chalmers' attack struck home he met well-armed and experienced Union horseman who beat back the attack. Despite this Wilson was greatly concerned that Forrest had gotten by him and was headed for Nashville. Forrest had achieved his goal of taking Wilson out of the action. While Wilson was thinking of defense and being flanked, Forrest disengaged all but a holding force and headed for Spring Hill.[4] A dispatch from Hood ordered Forrest to attempt to block Schofield at Spring Hill. Forrest attacked, but ran into a determined defense that included some Illinois, Tennessee, and Michigan cavalry. A message came from Hood that infantry was on the way to assist.

It appeared Schofield was trapped. Hood's army was consolidated and could break Schofield's line of withdrawal. To join Thomas, Schofield would have to string his army out over ten miles of threatened road. Schofield had 800 supply wagons to protect and there was no mounted screening force. Schofield was out of contact with his cavalry commander, James Wilson.

Forrest had come close to blocking the road, but supply problems arose. Chalmers' and Buford's divisions were without sufficient ammunition to continue the attack. Only William H. "Red" Jackson's division had enough ammunition to continue. Forrest knew that if Union troops managed to pass through Spring Hill they must cross the Harpath River. He dispatched Jackson to Thompson's Station north of Spring Hill to destroy two bridges. Jackson found one bridge over the Harpath down. He burned the other, a railroad bridge, then withdrew because he lacked strength to hold the road. Forrest tried unsuccessfully to get ammunition while waiting for Hood's infantry.

Hood had advanced boldly, but now became cautious. Marching fast to cut the Union road of withdrawal, he became concerned Schofield might strike him in the left flank. Hood sent orders to Gen. Alexander P. Stewart's corps to perform flank security. This would require coordination with Gen. Benjamin F. Cheatham's corps, but Cheatham was not present when Hood's orders were issued and confusion arose over what missions were assigned. Stewart and Cheatham were uncertain if they should attack or wait. Forrest and Patrick Cleburne, who headed one of Cheatham's divisions, moved forward and were having success. Forrest was in dire need of ammunition, darkness was coming on and he needed to pull out to resupply. Cheatham felt he needed to wait until his forces were linked with those of Stewart. He ordered the aggressive Cleburne to not proceed with his attack until additional Confederate divisions came up. Stewart was confused. He had been ordered to seize the road and yet occupy a position away from it.

About 9 P.M. Stewart's corps moved near Forrest's position. When the two generals conferred they found their orders were in conflict. They rode together to Hood's headquarters. En route Forrest saw that Cleburne's division, which he had believed was blocking the road, actually was some 600 yards from it—cooking rations. Hood was surprised when he was told the road was not blocked, but did not go forward to see for himself. He ordered Forrest to block the road north of Spring Hill. Forrest sent Jackson to do that.

Now in nail-biting anxiety over his predicament, Schofield was astounded that his road of escape was still open. Though he had few choices, his action was reasoned and daring. Knowing he needed the supplies, Schofield kept his wagons with him and prepared to march his strung-out divisions across the front of Hood's army as though it were passing in review. Schofield issued orders for excess gear to be discarded and units do all that was possible to eliminate noise and began his night march. While Schofield's men marched past they could see the Confederate lines, the campfires and men cooking and eating. Many of Hood's soldiers saw the

Hard-charging Union cavalry general James H. Wilson, who pursued Forrest to the finish. USAMHI

Union troops marching by. The Confederate men in ranks and their junior commanders were aghast and disgusted at the lack of action, but senior commanders had no orders to attack.

Hood was exhausted and went to bed. His wounds were troublesome and the pain-relieving opium in laudanum may well have drugged his reason. Several times throughout the night men came to wake him to tell him the Union army was marching by. He told his subordinates that Schofield was trapped and would be taken in the morning.

North of Spring Hill, Forrest's division under Red Jackson blocked the road and fought a fierce battle to prevent the Union passage. Schofield threw several divisions into the contest, drove Jackson from his path and continued the march that would cover twenty-five miles that night. Forrest was still trying unsuccessfully to get ammunition for Buford and Chalmers, but Confederate supply trains had not come up.

When he awoke on the morning of November 30, 1864, Hood learned the Union army had escaped him. His fury was remarkable. He now recognized that one of the greatest opportunities of the war had slipped from his grasp. The escape of Schofield's army was of such military significance that many men could describe it only as an act of God. Hood preferred to blame it on his subordinate commanders. He complained, "Had my instructions been carried out there is no doubt that we should have possessed ourselves of this road."[5]

The town of Franklin had 1,000 residents and was located in a bend on the south side of the Harpath River, twelve miles from Spring Hill. When Schofield arrived at Franklin he found the bridges over the Harpath were down and would need to be repaired or another constructed before he could cross with his wagon train and continue north. The uneven U-shape of the bend was open to the south, the direction from which Hood's army would be approaching. There were existing defensive positions across the mouth of the U that had been constructed during 1863. Schofield ordered these strengthened. He intended to keep Hood at bay until he rebuilt the bridges and extricated his army and trains. The Union soldiers stripped nearby buildings of planks and boards and built forms they filled with dirt. Logs on top were elevated to provide a firing slit without exposing a man's head over the breastwork. Tying his flanks to the river, Schofield had the town of Franklin and the Harpath River at his back, but his half-circle defense was strongly rooted and for the first time in days, Schofield felt a sense of confidence.

Hood pressed on after Schofield with Forrest leading the way. Forrest struck repeatedly at the Union rear guard until it was under the protection of fortifications at Franklin. He then scouted the Union positions and found the Confederates could cross the Harpath River farther to the right and flank the Union entrenchments. Hood had captured dispatches to Schofield from Thomas that made him believe Schofield would try to hold Franklin until Thomas came up. Hood thought it best to try to defeat Schofield before the Union forces united. He knew the bend of the river prevented his making an attack on the flanks, but Hood believed Schofield could be whipped in position and that it was easier to drive him from his works than try cross the river elsewhere and try a flanking movement. Hood decided to attack "In front and without delay."[6] With the Harpath River at Schofield's back there would be a great opportunity to deny the Union a second escape and to crush it. Hood intended to attack Schofield head on and told Forrest to dispose his cavalry on each flank and be prepared to take up the pursuit when Schofield's lines were broken.[7]

Hood decided to send his 20,000 men into battle with Cheatham's corps on the left, Stewart on the right and Stephen Lee in reserve. Forrest would have Chalmers' division of 2,000 men on the left flank of the army and Buford's and Jackson's divisions totaling 3,000 men on the right. At a tense and angry breakfast in a small dining room at the Cheairs house beside the Columbia-Franklin Pike, General Hood tongue-lashed his commanders with much of his fury falling on Cheatham. His subordinates sought to explain and counseled against a frontal attack, but Hood was adamant. About 1 P.M. on the thirtieth, Forrest completed a full reconnaissance. General Chalmers was impressed with the disregard Forrest had for danger while leading his command and the impact this had on subordinate commanders being willing to take risks. Chalmers said, "near Franklin I witnessed Forrest with two division and three brigade commanders all on the skirmish line."[8]

Forrest never let rank stand in the way of military success. He had unleashed his temper on Generals Wheeler, Van Dorn and Bragg when he felt they were wrong and did not hesitate to speak his mind to Hood. Forrest met Hood and told him a frontal attack was mistake. Forrest was the only general Hood thought was doing his job, but he did not listen to him.

South of Franklin, flanking the Columbia-Franklin Pike, were the Winstead Hills. They were not close enough to the battlelines to be significant but they served as the point of the grand entrance of the Confederate army. Coming over the hills over two miles of open slopes that led to Franklin this vast army suddenly appeared, flowing downward toward the Union defenders. They marched with fixed bayonets in rank upon rank with colors flying and bands playing, their officers waving swords and urging them onward.

Armies moving across country and into battle frequently put wildlife to flight. Seeing a rabbit run for safety made many soldiers think of the wisdom of the rabbit. Earlier in the war at Malvern Hill one Confederate yelled at a running rabbit, "Go it, Molly Cottontail! I wish I could go with you!" One of his comrades nearby caught up the refrain, and answered: "Yes and, 'y golly Jim, I'd go with Molly, too, if it wasn't for my character."[9] On another occasion a Confederate yelled at a fleeing rabbit, "Run old hare. I'd run too if it wasn't for my reputation." These expressions had become standard and were used by Confederates at Franklin as the wildlife fled.

If the massive Confederate army was an awesome sight to the Union defenders, the entrenchments of the Union command were a sobering sight to the men in butternut and gray. Hood had decided not to give his men artillery support, reporting, "During the day I was restrained from using my artillery on account of the women and children remaining in the town."[10] Among the officers and enlisted men, there was a sense of desperate valor. Many felt they were going to a slaughter, but orders had to be obeyed.

Skirmishers had been thrown forward of the Union lines where 13,000 men, many of them veterans, waited. Designed to provide early warning and to force the enemy to deploy, the thin line of skirmishers normally would allow themselves time to withdraw within the entrenchments before the enemy closed upon them. Division commander George D. Wagner had two brigades out front as skirmishers and for reasons historians have attributed to factors from blind courage to alcohol, Wagner intended to fight it out with Hood's army in front of the main line. He would not allow his men to withdraw. One fire staggered the Confederate front, but before Wagner's men could reload, Hood's army bowled over the skirmishers and forced them to flee. In the process the Union soldiers and the Confederates were mixed together. Now the Union defenders were hesitant, unwilling to fire into their own men as the advance came forward.

When they could wait no longer, a sheet of flame erupted from the Union lines. The sound was the ripping of a giant canvas blended with the roll of a thousand thunders. Union cannon firing canister tore great swaths through the Confederate ranks. Entire companies were obliterated amid the sound of breaking bones and the screams of men. Into the shot and shell the Confederates came, bending forward as though to protect themselves from rain. Had it not been for Wagner's blunder it is doubtful the Confederates would have reached the works. They managed to make an entry at a few points, but the blood was up in the Union soldiers. They charged and in hand-to-hand combat with bayonet, rifle butts and camp axes smashed the Confederate advance and sent it reeling.

While Hood's center was torn to pieces by Union fire, Forrest's horsemen were attacking on the flanks. Chalmers was on the left of Cheatham's corps, he advanced and engaged Union infantry but was not able to dislodge them. On the right, Forrest got Jackson's division across the river and engaged Wilson's cavalry. Buford crossed and the two divisions steadily pushed forward against stiff resistance. As night fell Hood withdrew. On learning this, Forrest and his men re-crossed the Harpath River and rejoined the bloodied Confederate army.

Fortune had embraced Gen. John McAllister Schofield. He had escaped a certain trap by the blundering of his enemies and had won a battle he had not sought. Schofield's purpose now was to link up with Gen. George Thomas. Under cover of night, Schofield left campfires burning, withdrew his army across the river and marched north. He left behind his dead and many of his wounded. During the night Hood moved his cannon closer to the Union works in evidence that he intended to try again. When he learned he had possession of the field, Hood claimed a victory.

Hood's dead refuted his claim. About half—or 16,000 men—of Hood's army made the assault at Franklin. The bloodletting was so severe that an accurate count of casualties was never made. Estimates of between 6,000 and 7,000 killed, wounded or taken captive are realistic. Six Confederate generals were killed, the bodies of four of them laid side by side on a porch. Six other Confederate generals were wounded. The combat-experienced majors and colonels died in numbers the Confederacy could not replace. Hood's army would never recover from the battle of Franklin. The combative spirit was no longer there. Men will risk their lives in battle but they will not accept having their lives wasted by incompetence. Schofield's army suffered 2,326 casualties—189 killed, 1,033 wounded and 1,104 missing, most of whom were taken prisoner.[11]

On learning Schofield was gone, Hood pressed north with Forrest leading and began to invest Thomas and his army at Nashville. It would not be a meeting of strangers. The two generals had served together. Prior to the war George H. Thomas had been the junior major in the 2nd Cavalry when Hood was a second lieutenant.[12] Chalmers' division of Forrest's cavalry followed Union horsemen to within four miles of Nashville. Forrest, with Buford's and Jackson's divisions, skirmished with the enemy at Wilson's Crossroads and pressed on toward Nashville. Forrest began to strike at blockhouses guarding key bridges and railroads and to attack commerce on the Cumberland River. Using their artillery well, his subordinate commanders were taking a heavy toll on the isolated Union blockhouses that were designed to protect against infantry and few of which had artillery to defend themselves. A steady flow of prisoners, horses and supplies was achieved. Commerce on the Cumberland River was shut down for eleven days.

Hood reasoned that if he made attacks elsewhere he would draw Thomas out of his Nashville emplacements. He believed that the Union command at Murfreesboro, southeast of Nashville, was a target of opportunity. Commanded by Maj. Gen. Lovell Rousseau, Murfreesboro was reported to have 8,000 Union troops. Though his numbers had been greatly depleted, Hood decided to split his force. He gave Forrest an infantry division and ordered him to attack with a force of some 6,500 and eliminate the Union command at Murfreesboro. The slaughter at Franklin had severely harmed Confederate morale. When troops from the Union garrison at Murfreesboro advanced on them, Forrest knew that if the infantry could stop the attack he could strike the rear of the Union force with his cavalry. To his surprise the Confederate infantry division broke and ran. Forrest tried desperately to stem the retreat, even seizing a color and advancing toward the enemy. When he could not stop the rout, he sent Buford against the town. This brought about the withdrawal of the Union force into its fortifications and took the pressure off the Confederate infantry. Forrest went so near to the Union works that the bugler riding beside him had his horn pierced by several bullets. This was the second time this occurred.[13] Despite his audacity, the effort on Murfreesboro was a failure. Forrest went back to raiding Union outposts.

Having squandered thousands of his army, Hood did not have the strength to make an attack on Nashville. General George Thomas was taking his time, waiting until his army and the weather favored attack. As the days passed, both armies settled into fixed lines. Gen. U.S. Grant was urging Thomas to take the offensive and becoming increasingly disturbed that he was not. It was beginning to appear Grant would relieve Thomas. In a remarkable display of character, Thomas held to his course. The weather was below zero and he was not yet ready. When Thomas felt the time was right he intended to bring Hood to one final battle and crush him. To have the options of protecting his flanks and enveloping Hood's position, Thomas needed a strong force of cavalry. Much effort went into giving James Wilson 12,500 horsemen, of which some 9,000 were well mounted.[14] These Union horsemen were organized into five divisions.

On December 13, General Sherman reached the sea and had the city of Savannah in a noose. At Nashville the weather was improving and the ice melting. Hood's sending of troops to attack elsewhere in order to draw Thomas out would work to his disadvantage. Thomas had prepared well. He now had approximately 50,000 men. On Thursday, December 15, 1864, George Thomas came out of his entrenchments and began to pummel John Bell Hood.

Thomas feinted against the Confederate left and struck Hood's right a massive blow that drove the Confederates from their prepared position. Hood shortened his lines, but on the sixteenth Wilson's cavalry got behind the Confederate left flank and began to collapse the position. Chalmers' cavalry division was cut off and lost its headquarters. Chalmers and the remainder of his men fought their way back to Hood and tried unsuccessfully to stem the attack. Thomas pounded the Confederates with artillery, then about 4 P.M. on the sixteenth drove home another attack that completely broke Hood's defense.

Forrest was not present—he had been east of Stone River seeking to ambush a Union supply column. Initially Forrest received a warning order from Hood to be prepared to come to the aid of the army. But Forrest and the two cavalry divisions and infantry he had with him were not recalled until he was informed of Hood's defeat. Union cavalry commander James Wilson called Hood's detachment of Forrest and these divisions "a fatal mistake."[15] Hood was driven in retreat.

On the seventeenth, Forrest joined Hood at Columbia and was assigned the mission of covering the withdrawal of the Confederate army. A message from Hood to Chalmers was captured by Union horsemen and Wilson learned of Hood's plans.

Hood's army had lost its will to fight. They were men who had fought valiantly and suffered from want of food and clothing. Many of them had been without shoes in one of coldest winters of the time, marching barefoot through ice and slush. Now all their suffering seemed useless. Totally demoralized, their only thought was self preservation. They ignored officers who tried to stop them, threw away their weapons and ran. Thomas reported "We have captured 13,189 prisoners of war including 7 general officers and nearly 1,000 other officers of all grades and 72 pieces of serviceable artillery and battle flags. During the same period over two-thousand deserters were received, to whom the oath was administered."[16] Hood was distraught, pulling his beard and weeping.

One of the Union officers greatly enjoying the Confederate rout was Forrest's one-time foe Col. Abel Streight. After capture by Forrest, the gallant colonel of the ill-fated Jackass Raid had been sent off to Libby Prison in Richmond. Most captives want to get out of prison. Commanded by General Winder, Libby was one of the many jails on both sides that a man had better get out of, or he would likely die of maltreatment or starvation. The prisoners at Libby had a poem that went:

> Our Father who art in Washington
> Abraham Lincoln is thy name;
> Thy will be done in the South as it is in the North,
> Give us this day our daily rations of hardtack and salt horse,
> Forgive our Quartermasters as we forgive our commissaries.
> Lead us not into battles or rivers.
> But deliver us from General Winder.
> For thine is the power of the soldiers and the Negroes,
> for the term of three years or sooner shot.
> Amen

On February 9, 1864, 109 Union officers made a daring escape from Libby. Fifty-nine of them made it back to Union lines and among them was Abel Streight who got a horse and weapons and was back in battle. The fighter Forrest bluffed was now commanding the 1st Brigade of the 3rd Division of the IV Army Corps and was enjoying the knowledge that it was the Confederates who were on the run.

Hood relied on Nathan Bedford Forrest to fight the rear-guard action while Hood sought to get the remnants of his army over the Tennessee River. Forrest agreed to the mission on the proviso that he be able to pick the troops and commanders of his rear-guard force. In addition to his 3,000 cavalry, Forrest wanted 4,000 select infantry. As commander of these foot soldiers, Forrest sought and received the services of Maj. Gen. Edward C. Walthall, a fighting division commander of Alexander Stewart's corps.

General Thomas, in his after-action report, wrote, "With the exception of this rear-guard, his [Hood's] army had become a disheartened and disorganized rabble of half-armed and barefooted men, who sought every opportunity to fall out by the wayside and desert their cause, to put an end to their sufferings. The rear-guard however was undaunted and firm, and did its work bravely to the last."[17]

When an army is routed, those who are running and those who are chasing exhaust themselves. Both Union and Confederate forces became scattered and control was difficult. The weather grew increasingly bad as freezing rain was followed by snow. Many of General Walthall's infantry were without shoes. They wrapped rags around their feet and tied them with thongs. On both sides, rations for men were exhausted and the countryside offered no forage for horses. Forrest used abandoned wagons and teams to transport the infantry when possible. As his horses gave out, he took oxen from local farmers to pull his wagons.[18] As Forrest fought his delaying action he destroyed bridges behind him. On December 19, during a fierce winter rain-storm, Wilson's cavalry arrived at Rutherford Creek. The bridge had been destroyed and the sizable stream was running full. While supply trains were hurried forward, Wilson's men worked through the night building a floating bridge that they used to cross the river. Forrest had bought time for Hood's army to cross and for him to destroy the bridges over the Duck River. Thomas' engineers with their horse-drawn pontoons were pressing forward, but having difficulty catching up with the cavalry. When Wilson reached the Duck River he was unable to cross until the pontoons could come up. War is not a perfect endeavor. While coming forward, the pontoon train took the wrong road. This mistake resulted in a twenty-four hour delay in bridge building. It was not until the evening of December 23 that Wilson was able to get his riders across the river.[19] Forrest used this time to evacuate Confederate wagons and artillery.

The destruction of bridges by Forrest and Walthall at a time of adverse winter weather and high water contributed greatly to the escape of what was left of Hood's army. Trying to make up for time lost, Wilson's cavalry was pushing on hard, their impetus making them ripe for an ambush. Wilson wrote, "Hood's reorganized rear-guard under the redoubtable Forrest, was soon encountered by the cavalry advanced guard, and he was a leader not to be attacked by a handful of men, however bold."[20]

Forrest fought a series of delays. These were small skirmishes which required Wilson to deploy. Like Forrest, Wilson fought with his troops dismounted. Wilson would write, "[H]orses were used . . . mainly for the transportation of men."[21] Each time Forrest and Walthall forced Wilson to dismount, deploy his men and position his artillery. John Bell Hood had more time to get away and try to establish control over his shattered army.

These skirmishes required a quick getaway and not all were successful. At Richland Creek on December 24, Forrest positioned six pieces of artillery supported by a brigade to cover the turnpike. He put Chalmers and Buford to the left of the artillery and Ross' brigade on the right. Wilson's 5th Cavalry Division under Brig. Gen. Edward Hatch engaged Chalmers and Buford's divisions, forcing them rearward. Forrest committed Jackson's division to their support. Wilson then struck from the flank with Brigadier General Croxton's 1st Brigade of the 1st Cavalry Division. Combat lasted nearly thirty-six hours before Forrest withdrew, losing prisoners, a set of colors and with Gen. Abraham Buford badly wounded. Forrest withdrew to Pulaski where he destroyed railroad equipment and supplies that could not be evacuated. With their leader out of action, Buford's command was consolidated with that of Chalmers.

Near sundown on December 25, 1864, Forrest set an ambush at Anthony's Hill. Here the road passed through a valley so narrow as to be described as a ravine. The hillsides were heavily wooded, making envelopment difficult. Forrest put his well-concealed guns in position to deliver fire down this narrow opening while his infantry and dismounted cavalry were concealed on the flanks. Wilson's lead brigade under Col. Thomas Harrison rode into the ravine and was hit hard with 150 men killed or wounded and fifty prisoners taken. The Confederates captured one piece of artillery that had belonged to Battery I, 4th U.S. Artillery. Wilson's men flanked the hills and the withdrawal continued.

At Sugar Creek on the twenty-sixth, Forrest and Walthall came up with the rear of what was left of Hood's ordnance train. Taking position on the south side of the waist-deep creek, the Confederates constructed hasty emplacements and waited in a fog so thick that men could scarcely see. Wilson's advance crossed the stream, the sound of its passage giving notice to the defenders. Though unable to see the Union soldiers, the Confederates could hear their approach. At approximately thirty yards a savage fire raked Wilson's troopers and the Confederates charged, following the Union soldiers through the creek and driving them rearward on the main body. It was difficult in the fog to determine the number of killed and wounded, but 150 officers and men were taken prisoner.

Sugar Creek was the last significant action of the withdrawal. Forrest followed Hood, crossing the Tennessee River on December 27, 1864. A flying column of the 12th Tennessee reached the river on the twenty-eighth, but the Confederates had crossed over and burned bridges behind them. Hood began to disperse what was left of his army, granting leave to those who lived close by. He ordered his pontoon and supply trains to Columbus, Mississippi, under the guard of General Roddey's cavalry. Wilson's 15th Pennsylvania Cavalry rode this force down and captured eighty-three pontoons, 150 wagons and 400 mules.[22] The Union troopers found the pontoons were state-of-the-art, well-painted and bore the names of Confederate females such as Lady Davis, and Lady Bragg. When Hood reached Tupelo he had an army of some 21,000 men remaining, but it was an army in name only. Some troops went to Mobile, Alabama. The majority marched to join General Johnston in North Carolina. Hood said that 9,000 men left the ranks (deserted) en route and 5,000 men of the once proud Army of the Tennessee reached General Johnston. Forrest did not go east, he was crucial to whatever effort the Confederate army could muster in the west.[23]

On January 13, 1865, Hood sent a message to Secretary of War Seddon requesting that he be relieved. His request was granted and on January 23, 1865, Hood was replaced by Lt. Gen. Richard Taylor, who became the commander of Nathan Bedford Forrest. Taylor was one of Forrest's favorite commanders as he gave mission-type orders then concentrated on supplying his hard-charging subordinate, giving Forrest a free tactical hand.

On January 24, 1865, Nathan Bedford Forrest was made commander of the Cavalry Department of Alabama, Mississippi and East Louisiana. Four days later he published a circular that showed his disgust with the disintegration of Confederate commands. It included, "The rights and property of citizens must be respected and protected, and the illegal organizations of cavalry, prowling through the country, must be placed regularly and properly in the service or driven from the country. They are in many instances nothing more or less than roving bands of deserters, absentees, stragglers, horse-thieves and robbers . . . and whose acts of lawlessness and crime demand a remedy, which I shall not hesitate to apply even to extermination. The maxim 'that kindness to bad men is cruelty to the good,' is peculiarly applicable to soldiers."[24]

In February 1865, Nathan Bedford Forrest was promoted to lieutenant general. He had come a long way from his brief stint as a soldier in ranks. Indeed no Confederate lieutenant general could rival his meteoric rise. Nathan Bedford Forrest did not have the West Point education, the army training or the combat experience in the Mexican War that Stonewall Jackson and others had. Forrest never was given the opportunity to command the large numbers of men that Confederate corps or department commanders had under them, but he accomplished as much and in most cases more than any of them. According to John Watson Morton, who commanded his artillery, Forrest held in contempt the idea that only West Pointers were fitted to command and on one occasion said, "Whenever I meet one of them fellers that fit by note, I generally whipped hell out of him before he got his tune pitched."[25] Forrest was the essence of the citizen-soldier, caring only about excellence in battle. He led from the front and his courage was beyond compare. He is reputed to have had twenty-nine horses killed under him in battle and to have personally killed thirty-one men.[26]

On March 9, 1865, General Beauregard wrote General Taylor, and his message contained his distress at the demoralization of the Confederate army. "I regret to hear that the furloughed men are so slow in returning . . . desertion from the army is now an epidemic. They deserted by the hundreds from the cars on the way here. The same complaint reaches us from Lee's Army."[27] On March 13, Lt. Gen. Nathan Bedford Forrest sent a message to his brother, Col. Jesse A. Forrest, that included, "While en route for Oxford you will spread out your men as much as possible to gather up all deserters, absentees and stragglers from the army. When caught, dismount, disarm and forward them to General Wright at Grenada. . . . While on your rounds you will collect all companies and parts of companies or soldiers that you may find. . . . Any officer thus found refusing to obey your orders you will arrest and send in irons to Brigadier General Wright."[28] On March 15 a message from Forrest to Captain W.F. Bullock, assistant adjutant general, includes, "Colonel Scott telegraphs me that ninety of his men ran away night before last."[29]

Desperation in the Confederate government in Richmond led to the issuance of commissions to those who would agree to raise units behind Union lines. Men used this authority to avoid active service and in some cases to raise bands that raided their own people. In a March 18 letter to Secretary of War Breckinridge, Forrest complained that his three Kentucky regiments numbered about 300 men and wrote, "They have deserted and attached themselves to roving bands of guerrillas, jayhawkers and plunderers . . . preying upon the people, robbing them of their horses and other property." He found the same problems in Tennessee and along the Mississippi River.[30] Many of the final days of the military career of Nathan Bedford Forrest were spent hunting down his fellow Southerners who recognized the war was lost and were looking for profit and to save their own skin.

On March 22, 1865, the expected knock-out punch began. The blow came south in the form of Maj. Gen. James Wilson who marched with 12,500 horsemen and 1,500 foot soldiers on what would become known as Wilson's Selma raid. Forrest tried to interfere, but the very action of trying to move against Wilson's powerful force caused some of his troops desert. Men feared they would be taken into North Carolina and forced to leave the vicinity of their homes. Forrest had two men, one young, one older, shot for desertion. For Forrest to do this was a sign of the desperation of a losing cause.

Nathan Bedford Forrest had given everything but his life to his cause, and his survival was little short of a miracle. When the end of the war came and Forrest was ordered to surrender, he did it with grace. He would not be a part of the hot-headed rhetoric that encouraged Southerners to go to Mexico or South America to continue to fight. He would not stoop to the tactic that some commanders, including John Singleton Mosby, used of disbanding their units so they could make the empty boast that they had never surrendered. With the remarkable honesty that was a hallmark of his life, Forrest in his May 9, 1865, farewell address to his troops included words that told the simple truths and reached out for healing.

> That we are beaten is a self-evident fact, and any further rashness on our part would be regarded as the very height of folly and rashness. . . . The cause for which you have so long and manfully struggled, and for which you have braved dangers, endured privations and sufferings, and made so many sacrifices is to-day hopeless. . . . Civil War such as you have just passed through, naturally engenders feelings of animosity, hatred and revenge. It is our duty to divest ourselves of all such feelings, and so far as it is in our power to do so, to cultivate friendly feelings towards, those with whom we have so long contested and heretofore so widely but honestly differed. . . . You have been good soldiers, you can be good citizens. Obey the laws, preserve your honor, and the government to which you have surrendered can afford to be and will be magnanimous.[31]

Forrest returned to his Memphis home and tried to rebuild his plantation. Many of his former slaves choose to remain as free workers. For two years he labored and success was returning. Eager to improve his fortune he put his money and energy into the construction of a railroad from Selma, Alabama, to the Mississippi River. His dream fell victim to one of the recurrent financial crises and valor was not a substitute for money.

His railroad went bankrupt, leaving him with debts that would plague him for the rest of his life. His nerves were frayed by money worries and he fell into an argument with a former officer, Colonel Shepherd, who was now a contractor. Forrest lost his temper and abused Colonel Shepherd to the point that Shepherd challenged Forrest to a duel. As the challenged party Forrest had the choice of weapons and chose Navy Colt revolvers at ten paces to fire, on signal, and advance until one or the other was killed. The duel never took place. When his temper cooled Forrest realized he had behaved badly and went to Colonel Shepherd and apologized.[32]

The assassination of President Abraham Lincoln was a more devastating blow to the South than the North. Without Lincoln's prestige, without his wisdom and desire for healing, the South, laid waste by the war it had initiated, now was beset by a reign of terror from without and within. Blacks who had never had the opportunity to be educated were in positions of power. They were skillfully manipulated by white scoundrels primarily from the North, but also from the South. In early Reconstruction days, political offices in the South were used more for monetary gain than for rebuilding society. There were men in Washington who wanted vengeance on the South and men who sought a genuine rebuilding. The former outnumbered the latter. There were many men in the South who had no intention of treating blacks as equal citizens. They worked to gain control of politics and law and shamefully used their position for repression.

Even if a war had not been fought, a sudden transformation from a slave-based economy to one based on individual worth would have been volcanic in the South. To make the transformation with the economy, the political structure and the countryside in ruins was hell. Reconstruction was a shameful period in American history.

Organizations such as the Loyal League and the Freedmans' Bureau were intended to give former slaves opportunity in the South and it was help that was desperately needed. In some case these worthy organizations were infiltrated by profit-seekers who made a mockery of the law. Counter-organizations sprang up that appealed to white Southerners who felt oppressed. The Order of the White Rose, the Knights of the White Camellia and the Ku Klux Klan were among these. For generations the two races had been separated; one as one master, one as slave. Some now saw it as "bottom rail on top," and Southern whites would not accept such an arrangement.

In 1866 these white associations turned violent. Bloody riots erupted at various points in the South. One of the worst clashes was in New Orleans where more than eighty blacks were killed. It made news, but no action was taken. The North was tired of war, slavery was finished and someone else's civil rights were not their concern.

Nathan Bedford Forrest was a member and because of his fame was selected as grand dragon of the Klu Klux Klan. The organization had been put together by college students and was filled with mystical names such as hydra and cyclops. The names and the spooky rituals likely would have confused the uneducated but straightforward Forrest. The mission would not confuse him. He would accept the black slave being free, but he would not be governed by a black man. Terror was the initial aim of the Klu Klux Klan, a terror that kept blacks from the polls and made certain the officials and the lawmen who were elected were white. A White southern government must be in power to keep the black man down.

Terror was a weapon with which Forrest was familiar. To put the "skeer" on his opponent was a favored tactic. But in his sense of honor, violence was not a solution to the racial problems of the South. When members of the Klan began to use torture and murder to keep blacks in what was considered "their place," Nathan Bedford Forrest ordered the organization disbanded and left its membership. In the light of present thinking, Forrest held other human beings in bondage and many condemn him for it. But Forrest did not live in the present. He was a man of his time and his culture. He had been raised in a society that thought of blacks as property, valuable property. Before the Civil War he had been a slave dealer and slavery contributed much to his pre-war wealth. He was not out of step with his time and locale. Most wealthy Southern men were slave owners. The indications are that he would not split up families, did not believe in whips and shackles and fed and cared for those he enslaved as he would a good hound, horse or hog. In his time he would have been considered by his associates and even by slaves as a good master. General Sherman and other Union officers who fought against him believed he treated prisoners fairly and although a massacre did occur at Fort Pillow, Forrest did not order it and was not on the scene when it occurred. This could hardly excuse him. He was the commander and shared the rage of Southerners that the North would arm what they considered a servile race and send them against white people. The attitude of a military commander is reflected in the actions of his command.

In war and in peace Nathan Bedford Forrest traveled a hard road. While many of his wartime opponents knew financial security and ease, his last years were spent in money woes and constant struggle. Still, Forrest kept working, kept trying. When he lost his land to debts, he managed to lease other property and begin to make it profitable. He had never been a religious man, but age and the hopes of his wife Mary turned his thoughts to prayer. In November 1875 he became a member of the Presbyterian branch of the Christian belief. Less than two years later Forrest began to lose weight. It likely was a cancer that gnawed at him, drawing away his strength. He wasted away until he was a mere shadow of his once-vibrant self. On the evening of October 29, 1877, at age 56, Nathan Bedford Forrest died at his home on Union Street in Memphis. The following day, his remains were taken to Elmwood Cemetery. More than 2,000 people marched in his funeral procession. While many thousands lined the sidewalks, bells mournfully tolled and the still air cracked as guns were fired in salute.

His life was over, but the memory of him will not fade from American history. Forrest had fought for his cause with a brilliance few men have ever shown. When the fight was over, Forrest had the character to put it behind him and look to the future. Many in the North felt that gatherings of Southern veterans were but a prelude to another rebellion. At a September 21, 1876, reunion of the 7th Tennessee Cavalry, Forrest defended the gatherings and said, "We will show our countrymen by our conduct and dignity that brave soldiers are always good citizens and law-abiding and loyal people." Nathan Bedford Forrest was not one of "the South will rise again" clique, he was an American and he was proud to be a citizen of the United States.

APPENDIX ONE

Mosby's Rules for Ranger Operations

Remember that the weakest point of any army is its rear.

Weaken the enemy front by making him guard everything in his rear.

Do not depend on friendly supply channels. Make war support war by using captured enemy equipment.

War is not chivalry—don't give the enemy an even break.

Know the terrain better than your enemy, reconnoiter carefully.

Gain the support of the local people; they are a vital intelligence and early-warning source.

Choose the time and place you want to fight. Go for the weakest spots. Always seek the advantage.

Be audacious. Use shock action. Hit the enemy hard and quickly clear the area.

Seek better mobility and firepower than your enemy.

Use dispersion as a tool to protect your unit and communications and mobility to reassemble it.

Men expect action and dislike routine camp duty.

Let "ability" be the only criteria in the selection of leaders.

Have no tolerance for the malcontent and the shirker. Recruit only volunteers.

The survival of the guerrilla requires eternal vigilance.

Use offensive action in extreme weather conditions and difficult terrain.

Be loyal to your men as well as your commanders, be willing to stand up for your men.

War According to
Nathan Bedford Forrest

1. "I just took the shortcut and got there first with the most men." (A plain English application of Napoleon's maxim, "Move by interior lines and strike the fragments of the enemy forces with the masses of your own.")
2. "Kindness to bad men is cruelty to the good."
3. "War means fighting and fighting means killing."
4. "Five minutes of bulge is better than a week of tactics."
5. "Whenever you see anything blue, shoot at it, and do all you can to keep up the scare."

Notes

PROLOGUE

1. Theodore F. Lang, *Loyal West Virginia* (Baltimore, Md: The Deutsch Publishing Co., 1895), 17–21.
2. *The Picket Line and Camp Fire Stories: A Collection of War Anecdotes, Both Grave and Gay, Illustrative of the Trials and Triumphs of Soldier Life* (New York: Hurst, n.d.), 45 (hereafter cited as *Picket Line and Camp Fire Stories*).
3. William Tecumseh Sherman, *Memoirs of W. T. Sherman* (New York: Library of American, 1990), 360–63.

CHAPTER ONE: THE GRAY GHOST

1. *Dictionary of American Biography* (New York: Scribner, 1981), Vol. 3, 272.
2. John Singleton Mosby, *The Memoirs of Colonel John S. Mosby* (Boston: Little, Brown, and Company, 1917), 2 (hereafter cited as Mosby, *Memoirs*).
3. Richard Taylor, *Destruction and Reconstruction: Personal Experiences of the Late War* (New York: D. Appleton and Co., 1879), 234.
4. Mosby, *Memoirs*, 367.
5. John Singleton Mosby, *Mosby's War Reminiscences and Stuart's Cavalry Campaigns* (Boston: G.A. Jones & Co., 1887), 7 (hereafter cited as Mosby, *War Reminiscences*).
6. Ibid., 9.
7. Ibid., 205.
8. Mosby, *Memoirs*, 30.
9. Mosby, *Memoirs*, 32; *The Letters of John S. Mosby* (Richmond, Va: Stuart-Mosby Society, 1986), 7.
10. *The Letters of John S. Mosby*, 11.
11. Ibid., 14.
12. Mosby, *Memoirs*, 89.
13. Mosby, *War Reminiscences*, 22, 23.
14. Ibid., 22.

15. Mosby would fight for Stuart and Stuart's reputation all his life. In *Memoirs*, Mosby devotes fifty-seven pages to his defense of Stuart's conduct during the Gettysburg campaign. He refutes Lee's and Longstreet's comments and attacks Lee's staff. It is unlikely that J. E. B. Stuart had a better friend than John S. Mosby.

16. William Harrison Beach, *The First New York (Lincoln) Cavalry, from April 19, 1861, to July 7, 1865* (New York: The Lincoln Cavalry Association, 1902), 123 (hereafter cited as Beach, *First New York Cavalry*).

17. Mosby, *Memoirs*, 111.

18. *The Letters of John S. Mosby*, 24.

19. Mosby, *Memoirs*, 144.

20. Mosby, *War Reminiscences*, 233.

21. Mosby, *Memoirs*, 147.

22. Mosby, *War Reminiscences*, 29.

23. Ibid., 29. Mosby claimed he began with six men, Mosby, *Memoirs*, 148. In *War Reminiscences* he put the number at nine men, Mosby, *War Reminiscences*, 29. John Scott, who wrote the Mosby-approved history of Mosby's Rangers, put the number at nine. John Scott, *Partisan Life with Col. John S. Mosby* (New York: Harper & Brothers, 1867), 21. Nine is the accepted number.

24. Scott, *Partisan Life*, 21.

25. Louis N. Boudrye, *Historic Records of the Fifth New York Cavalry, First Ira Harris Guard: Its Organization, Marches, Raids, Scout Engagements, and General Services, during the Rebellion of 1861–1865* (Albany, N.Y.: S. R. Gray, 1865), 47–48 (hereafter cited as Beaudry, *Fifth New York Cavalry*).

26. George Grenville Benedict, *Vermont in the Civil War* (Burlington, VT: The Free Press Association, 1886), 582.

27. *Dictionary of American Biography*, Vol. 3, 272.

28. Boudrye, *Fifth New York Cavalry*, 48.

29. Ibid.

30. Scott, *Partisan Life*, 22.

31. Mosby, *War Reminiscences*, 30.

32. Ibid., 31–32.

33. Ibid., 22–23.

34. *History of the Eighteenth Regiment of Cavalry, Pennsylvania Volunteers (163rd Regiment of the Line), 1862–1865* (New York: Wynkoop Hallenbeck Crawford Co., 1909), 35.

35. Ibid.

36. Boudrye, *Fifth New York Cavalry*, 49.

37. Mosby, *Memoirs*, 151.

38. Scott, *Partisan Life*, 26; *The Letters of John S. Mosby*, 29.

39. Mosby, *War Reminiscences*, 32.
40. Ibid., 41.
41. Scott, *Partisan Life*, 20.
42. Mosby, *War Reminiscences*, 39.
43. Ibid., 44.
44. Boudrye, *Fifth New York Cavalry*, 53.
45. Scott, *Partisan Life*, 33.
46. *Annual Report of the Adjutant-General of the State of New York for the Year 1894, Register of the 5th, 6th, 7th, and 8th Regiments of Cavalry, N.Y. Vols., in the War of the Rebellion* (Albany, N.Y.: James B. Lyon, 1894), 4.
47. James J. Williamson, *Mosby's Rangers: A Record of the Operations of the Forty-Third Battalion of Virginia Cavalry from Its Organization to the Surrender* (New York: Sturgis & Walton, 1909), 38.
48. Ibid., 34–46.
49. Ibid., 46.
50. Mosby also reported in the "History of the United States Secret Service" as, "I'm sorry for that. I can make new Brigadier Generals, but I can't make horses." *Memoirs*, 181.
51. Scott, *Partisan Life*, 76.
52. Ibid.
53. Mosby's willingness to challenge General Lee's desires was critical. Had Mosby not done so, the success of the Rangers is doubtful.
54. O.R., Vol. 51, 688; O.R., Vol. 25, 857.
55. William H. Rauch, *History of the "Bucktails," Kane Rifle Regiment of the Pennsylvania Reserve Corps (13th Pennsylvania Reserves, 42nd of the Line)* (Philadelphia: Electric Printing Company, 1906), 247–48.
56. Williamson, *Mosby's Rangers*, 50.
57. Boudrye, *Historic Records of the Fifth New York Cavalry*, 53.
58. Mosby, *Memoirs*, 193.
59. Boudrye, *Historic Records of the Fifth New York Cavalry*, 53.
60. Mosby, *Memoirs*, 193.
61. Ibid., 195.
62. Mosby, *War Reminiscences*, 264.
63. Williamson, *Mosby's Rangers*, 52.
64. Benedict, *Vermont in the Civil War*, 587.
65. Williamson, *Mosby's Rangers*, 56.
66. Mosby, *War Reminiscences*, 122.
67. Scott, *Partisan Life*, 78–83.
68. John S. Mosby, "A Bit of Partisan Service" in *Battles and Leaders of the Civil War*, Vol. 3 (New York: Yoseloff, 1956), 148.
69. Williamson states ninety-eight men reported.

70. Mosby, *War Reminiscences,* 131.
71. Ibid., 133.
72. Ibid.
73. John W. Munson, *Reminiscences of a Mosby Guerrilla* (New York: Moffat, Yard, 1906), 66 (hereafter cited as Munson, *Reminiscences*).
74. Williamson, *Mosby's Rangers,* 56–60.
75. Ibid.
76. Beach, *First New York Cavalry,* 222–23.
77. Ibid., 319–20.
78. Mosby, *War Reminiscences,* 139.

CHAPTER TWO: MOSBY AND THE GUN
1. Letter, Sergeant Michael J. Coleman, Company B, 5th N.Y. Cavalry, in *The Artilleryman* 22 (Fall 2001).
2. Benedict, *Vermont in the Civil War,* 589–91.
3. The captured Mosby cannon would be a salute gun for General Stahel, a war trophy of the 5th New York Cavalry veterans. It presently resides at the 45th Infantry Division Museum at Oklahoma City.
4. Williamson, *Mosby's Rangers,* 65–67.
5. Beach, *First New York Cavalry,* 228.
6. Mosby, *War Reminiscences,* 145.
7. Ibid., 80
8. Williamson, *Mosby's Rangers,* 70.
9. Ibid., 71–72.
10. Report of Mosby to Stuart from Fauquier County, Va., July 28, 1863; Williamson, *Mosby's Rangers,* 85.
11. Williamson, *Mosby's Rangers,* 87.
12. Mosby, *Memoirs,* 261.
13. Aristides Monteiro, *War Reminiscences by the Surgeon of Mosby's Command* (Richmond, Va.: E. Waddey, 1890), 34 (hereafter cited as Monteiro, *Reminiscences*).
14. O.R., Series I, Vol. 29, 90.
15. Mosby, *Memoirs,* 264.
16. O.R., Series I, Vol. 29, 80–81.
17. *The Letters of John S. Mosby,* 34.
18. J. Marshall Crawford, *Mosby and His Men: A Record of the Adventures of That Renowned Partisan Ranger, John S. Mosby* (New York: G. W. Carleton & Co., 1867), 113.
19. Ibid., 126.
20. Munson, *Reminiscences,* 171–72.
21. Mosby, *Memoirs,* 263.

22. *History of the Third Pennsylvania Cavalry, Sixtieth Regiment Pennsylvania Volunteers, in the American Civil War, 1861–1865* (Philadelphia: Franklin Printing Company, 1905), 338–39 (hereafter cited as *History of the Third Pennsylvania Cavalry*).

23. Williamson, *Mosby's Rangers*, 110–11.

24. Ibid., 113–14.

25. Crawford, *Mosby and his Men*, 145.

26. Ibid., 152–53.

27. Christopher A. Newcomer, *Cole's Cavalry* (Baltimore: Cushing and Co., 1895), 10.

28. Williamson, *Mosby's Rangers*, 126.

29. Ibid., 126.

30. Crawford, *Mosby and His Men*, 159.

31. Newcomer, *Cole's Cavalry*, 95.

32. Ibid.

33. Lt. Thomas Turner took five days to die. He was buried at Hillsboro Cemetery some ten miles from Harpers Ferry.

34. Mosby, *Memoirs*, 268.

35. Crawford, *Mosby and His Men*, 159.

36. Ibid., 269.

37. Ibid., 270.

38. Crawford, *Mosby and His Men*, 168.

39. Ibid., 168–69.

40. Ibid., 171.

41. *History of the Third Pennsylvania Cavalry*, 402.

42. Ibid., 402–3.

43. Ibid., 403.

44. Chauncey Norton, *"The Red Neck Ties;" or History of the Fifteenth New York Volunteer Cavalry* (Ithaca, N.Y.: Journal Book and Job Printing House, 1891), 21–22.

45. Ibid., 21–24.

46. Williamson, *Mosby's Rangers*, 137–41 Williamson claimed the action included men of the Union 2nd Battalion Maryland cavalry. The records do not indicate that to be true. Three-fourths of Cole's Maryland had reenlisted on February 13, 1864, and were granted thirty days of leave. *The History of Cole's Maryland Cavalry* makes no mention of this action.

47. *Loyal Order of the Legion*, Vol. 60, 53.

48. Williamson, *Mosby's Rangers*, 142–47.

49. Francis Trevelyan Miller, *The Photographic History of the Civil War* (New York: The Review of Reviews Co., 1911), chapter 1.

50. Mosby, *War Reminiscences*, 213.
51. U. R. Brooks, *Butler and His Cavalry in the War of Secession, 1861–1865* (Columbia, S.C.: The State Company, 1909), 315.
52. Scott, *Partisan Life*, 209.
53. Williamson, *Mosby's Rangers*, 161.
54. Ibid., 165.
55. *The New England Quarterly* V (Jan–Oct 1932): 328
56. Williamson, *Mosby's Rangers*, 175.
57. Ibid., 180.
58. Ibid., 183.

CHAPTER THREE: THE SWEET TASTE OF VICTORY

1. Munson, *Reminiscences*, 238.
2. Briscoe Goodhart, *History of the Independent Loudoun Virginia Rangers* (Washington, D.C.: Press of McGill & Wallace, 1896), 132 (hereafter cited as *Loudoun Rangers*). Scott reported the name as Ellen Fisher, *Partisan Life*, 245.
3. Goodhart, *Loudoun Rangers*, 133.
4. Williamson, *Mosby's Rangers*, 187.
5. Munson, *Reminiscences*, 97.
6. Williamson, *Mosby's Rangers*, 188.
7. Munson, *Reminiscences*, 97.
8. Nearly preventing the writing of this book. The Confederate regiment that included the author's Southern great-grandfather, Sgt. John Wesley Black, had been positioned over the area in which the mine exploded. Temporarily relieved, they were sent back on line but to a position on the flank where the crater would be.
9. Brooks, *Butler and His Cavalry in the War of Secession*, 503.
10. Alexander, *Mosby's Men*, 99.
11. Ibid., 102.
12. Williamson, *Mosby's Rangers*, 200.
13. Munson, *Reminiscences*, 82.
14. Alexander, *Mosby's Men*, 200.
15. Munson, *Reminiscences*, 102.
16. Munson, *Reminiscences*, 102–4.
17. Mosby, *Memoirs*, 290.
18. Alexander, *Mosby's Men*, 208.
19. Williamson, *Mosby's Rangers*, 434.
20. Mosby, *Memoirs*, 292.
21. Munson, *Reminiscences*, 105.
22. Williamson, *Mosby's Rangers*, 209–10.

23. Beach, *First New York Cavalry,* 413–14.
24. O.R., Series I, Vol. 43, 811.
25. Henry P. Moyer, *History of the Seventeenth Regiment Pennsylvania Volunteer Cavalry* (Lebanon, Pa: Sowers Printing Company, 1911), 211.
26. O.R., Series 1, Vol. 43, 822.
27. Josiah William Ware, "Springfield during the Civil War," *http:www.bigballoonmusic.com/goddardreagan/josiahware.htm* (accessed on 31 August 2007)
28. Williamson, *Mosby's Rangers,* appendix 11.
29. *New York Times,* Thursday, August 25, 1864.
30. Alexander, *Mosby's Men,* 218.
31. O.R., Series 1, Vol. 43, 901.
32. Ibid., 942.
33. Ibid., 27–28.
34. Ibid., 860.
35. Ibid., 22.
36. Ibid., 145–46; Williamson, *Mosby's Rangers,* 234.

CHAPTER FOUR: HANG THEM HIGH

1. O.R., Vol. 43, 428.
2. Francis B. Heitman's Historical Register and Dictionary of the U.S. Army, 1789–1903, National Archives Microfilm Publication M233.
3. Theodore F. Rodenbaugh, *Everglades to Canon with the Second Dragoons, Second United States Cavalry* (New York: D. Van Nostrand, 1875), 358–59.
4. Nominal List of Casualties for the 2nd Regiment U.S. Cavalry during the month of September 1864.
5. Rodenbough, *Everglades to Canon,* 358–59.
6. Williamson, *Mosby's Rangers,* 240.
7. Conrad Schmidt Pension File, National Archives.
8. James B. Tryon Pension File, National Archives.
9. Rodenbough, *Everglades to Canon,* 358–59.
10. James Henry Avery, *Under Custer's Command: The Civil War Journal of James Henry Avery,* compiled by Karla Jean Husby and edited by Eric J. Wittenberg, with a forward by Gregory J. W. Urwin (Washington, D.C.: Brassey's, 2000), 109–10.
11. Avery, 109–10; "5th Michigan Cavalry" in *Record of Service of Michigan Volunteers in the Civil War, 1861–1865* (n.p., n.d.).
12. "Hanging of Mosby's Men" *Warrenton Virginian* 24 (1864): 108–10.
13. D. Mark Katz, *Custer in Photographs* (Gettysburg, Pa.: Yo-Mark Production Co., 1985), 31.
14. Mosby, *Memoirs,* 300–302.

15. R. C. Wallace, *A Few Memories of a Long Life,* ed. John M. Carroll (Fairfield, Wash.: Ye Galleon Press, 1988), 31–32, 64–66.

16. O.R., Vol. 43, 428.

17. Ibid., 441.

18. Ibid., 490.

19. Ibid.

20. Williamson, *Mosby's Rangers,* 250–51.

21. Ibid., 255.

22. Samuel P. Bates' History of the Pennsylvania Volunteers, 1861–1865, *http: //www.pacivilwar.com/bates.html* (accessed on 31 August 2007).

23. Thomas J. Evans and James M. Moyer, *Mosby's Confederacy: A Guide to the Roads and Sites of Colonel John Singleton Mosby* (Shippensburg, Pa.: White Mane Publishing Co., 1991), 105; Edward J. Stackpole, *Sheridan in the Shenandoah: Jubal Early's Nemesis* (Harrisburg, Pa.: Stackpole Co., 1961), 373. Ames is believed to be buried by the spring at Yew Hill. Evans and Moyer wrote that a grave marker for him is beside the tall Confederate monument at Richmond's Hollywood Cemetery.

24. Robert U. Johnson and Clarence C. Buell, eds., *Battles and Leaders of the Civil War,* Vol. 3 (New York: The Century Co., 1887), 149.

25. O.R., Series I, Vol. 43, 335.

26. Williamson, *Mosby's Rangers,* 25.

27. O.R., Vol. 43, 509.

28. Williamson, *Mosby's Rangers,* 289.

29. Ibid.

30. Ibid., 477.

31. Crawford, *Mosby and His Men,* 271–72.

32. Mosby, *Memoirs,* 313.

33. Alexander, *Mosby's Men,* 109.

34. Ibid.

35. Crawford, *Mosby and His Men,* 271–72.

36. Mosby, *Memoirs,* 316.

37. Alexander, *Mosby's Men,* 113.

38. Munson, *Reminiscences,* 26–27.

39. Williamson, *Mosby's Rangers,* 263.

40. O.R., Series I, Vol. 43, 918.

41. Ibid., 368–69.

42. Ibid., 373.

43. Ibid.

44. Ibid.

45. Ibid.

46. Williamson, *Mosby's Rangers,* 266–69.

47. Evans and Moyer, *Mosby's Confederacy*, 63.
48. Beach, *First New York Cavalry*, 477.
49. Williamson, *Mosby's Rangers*, 273.
50. Ibid., 277.
51. Beach, *First New York Cavalry*, 441.
52. Ibid., 399.
53. O.R., Series I, Vol. 43, 355.
54. Williamson, *Mosby's Rangers*, 283.
55. Ibid., 284. John Mosby did at times remain as an observer when there was a small action such as the capture of General Duffie. It seems out of character that he would accept a subordinate role in a stiff fight against a proven enemy. His name is not mentioned again in the action by Williamson, Alexander, or Munson. The accounts of these three men are combined in the relating of this fight.
56. Alexander, *Mosby's Men*, 136.
57. Munson, *Reminiscences*, 168.
58. Ibid., 170.
59. Ibid., 166.
60. "Rosters in Records of Service" in *Record of Service of Michigan Volunteers in the Civil War, 1861–1865.*
61. Military Order of the Loyal Legion of the United States, *War Papers and Personal Reminiscences, 1861–1865* (St. Louis: Becktold & Co., 1892), 75–88 (hereafter cited as MOLLUS, *War Papers and Personal Reminiscences*).
62. Ibid., 88.
63. *Annual Report of the Adjutant-General of the State of New York for the Year 1896, Register of the 5th, 6th, 7th, and 8th Regiments of Cavalry, N.Y. Vols., in the War of the Rebellion* (Albany, N.Y.: James B. Lyon, 1896), 160.
64. Williamson, *Mosby's Rangers*, 288–94.
65. MOLLUS, *War Papers and Personal Reminiscences*, 89.
66. Ibid., 95.
67. Alexander, *Mosby's Men*, 148.
68. *New York Times*, 12 November 1864; *Washington Post*, 6 September 1891; Williamson, *Mosby's Rangers*, 452–58.
69. Evans and Moyer, *Mosby's Confederacy*, 63.
70. *New York Times*, 12 November 1864.
71. Ibid.
72. *Annual Report of the Adjutant-General of the State of New York for the Year 1904, Register of the 5th, 6th, 7th, and 8th Regiments of Cavalry, N.Y. Vols., in the War of the Rebellion* (Albany, N.Y.: James B. Lyon, 1904), 1,001.
73. John O. Casler, *Four Years in the Stonewall Brigade* (Girard, Kan.: Appeal Publishing Company, 1906), 242.

74. The report of the monument dedication and the controversy that fol-
    lowed is recorded in *Southern Historical Society Papers* 27, 250–83

75. Marguerite Merington, *The Custer Story: The Life and Intimate Letters of
    General George A. Custer and His Wife Elizabeth* (Lincoln: University of
    Nebraska Press, 1987), 89.

CHAPTER FIVE: END OF A DREAM

1. Williamson, *Mosby's Rangers*, 301.

2. Crawford, *Mosby and His Men*, 285–86.

3. Monteiro, *Reminiscences*, 59–60.

4. Mosby, *Memoirs*, 320.

5. After exchange Blazer returned to the 91st Ohio. After the war, he lived
   in Gallipolis, Ohio. He died of yellow fever in 1878.

6. In time McDonough would be trapped in a wood by Union cavalry.
   Knowing he faced a rope, he committed suicide.

7. Williamson, *Mosby's Rangers*, 311–13; Goodhart, *Loudoun Rangers*,
   172–73. Montjoy is buried in the Warrenton, Virginia, cemetery, not far
   from Mosby.

8. Carl Sandburg, *Lincoln: The War Years* (New York: Harcourt, Brace &
   Company, 1939), Vol 3., 235.

9. E. A. Pollard, *The Lost Cause* (New York: Gramercy Books, 1994), 603.

10. Mosby, *Memoirs*, 334.

11. Williamson, *Mosby's Rangers*, 319.

12. Crawford, *Mosby and His Men*, 308.

13. Williamson, *Mosby's Rangers*, 39.

14. Crawford, *Mosby and His Men*, 309.

15. Scott, *Partisan Life*, 376.

16. Williamson, *Mosby's Rangers*, 322.

17. Ibid., 323.

18. Mosby, *Memoirs*, 333–34.

19. Philip Henry Sheridan, *Personal Memoirs of Philip Henry Sheridan, General,
    United States Army* (New York: D. Appleton and Company, 1902), 100.

20. Williamson, *Mosby's Rangers*, 324.

21. Monteiro, *Reminiscences*, 10.

22. Mosby, *Memoirs*, 334.

23. Monteiro, *Reminiscences*, 17.

24. Monteiro, *Reminiscences*, 29.

25. Ibid., 30.

26. Williamson, *Mosby's Rangers*, 330.

27. Mosby, *Memoirs*, 338–39.

28. Williamson, *Mosby's Rangers*, 335.

29. Mosby, *Memoirs*, 341.

30. Scott, *Partisan Life,* 262.
31. Monteiro, *Reminiscences,* 67.
32. Ibid., 79–80.
33. Ibid., 91.
34. Peter G. Tsouras, ed., *The Greenhill Dictionary of Military Quotations* (London: Greenhill Books, 2000), 179.
35. Goodhart, *Loudoun Rangers,* 191.
36. J. G. Wiltshire, *The Confederate Veteran* 8 (January 1900): 74.
37. Williamson, *Mosby's Rangers,* 356.
38. Wiltshire, *The Confederate Veteran* 8 (January 1900): 74.
39. Goodhart, *Loudoun Rangers,* 192.
40. Ibid., 193–94
41. *Massachusetts, Soldiers, Sailors and Marines in the Civil War* (Boston: Wright & Potter, 1937).
42. James L. Bowen, *Massachusetts in the War, 1861–1865* (Springfield, Mass.: Bowen and Son, 1893), 451–63.
43. Scott, *Partisan Life,* 460–61; Williamson, *Mosby's Rangers,* 361–62.
44. Wiltshire, *The Confederate Veteran* 8 (January 1900): 74.
45. Williamson, *Mosby's Rangers,* 366.
46. Monteiro, *Reminiscences,* 126–30.
47. W. C. King and W. P. Derby, *Camp-Fire Sketches and Battle-field Echoes of the Rebellion* (Springfield, Mass.: W. C. King & Co., 1887), 229–32.
48. O.R.
49. Monteiro, *Reminiscences,* 148.
50. Ibid., 150.
51. Monteiro, *Reminiscences,* 159–74.
52. Ibid., 181–82.
53. Scott, *Partisan Life,* 473.
54. Williamson, *Mosby's Rangers,* 393.
55. Scott, *Partisan Life,* 476; Williamson, *Mosby's Rangers,* 393–94; Monteiro, *Reminiscences,* 207–8.
56. Mosby, *War Reminiscences,* 23.
57. Mosby, *Memoirs,* 388.
58. Ulysses S. Grant, *Personal Memoirs of U. S. Grant* (New York: The Century Co., 1895), 67.
59. Sheridan, *Memoirs,* 499.
60. Mosby, *Memoirs,* 399.

CHAPTER SIX: THE THUNDERBOLT OF THE CONFEDERACY

1. *Dictionary of American Biography,* Vol. 7, 174.
2. Basil W. Duke, *History of Morgan's Cavalry* (Cincinnati, Ohio: Miami Printing and Publishing Company, 1867), 19.

3. Ibid., 86.
4. Ibid., 24.
5. William B. Sipes, *The Seventh Pennsylvania Volunteer Cavalry* (Pottsville, Pa.: Miners Journal Print, 1905), 20.
6. Duke, *History of Morgan's Cavalry*, 105.
7. Ibid., 140.
8. Ibid., 146.
9. Major Coffee was paroled on his word that he would not fight again until exchanged. The Union was no longer accepting these paroles, and Coffee was ordered to his unit. He would not break his word and made his way through the lines to Knoxville and turned himself in to the Confederates as a prisoner of Morgan until properly exchanged. Basil W. Duke, *Reminiscences of General Basil W. Duke* (Garden City, N.Y.: Doubleday, Page & Company, 1911), 88–89 (hereafter cited as Duke, *Reminiscences*).
10. Duke, *History of Morgan's Cavalry*, 166–67.
11. Ibid., 180.
12. Duke, *Reminiscences*, 154.
13. Thurman Sensing, *Champ Ferguson, Confederate Guerrilla* (Nashville, Tenn.: Vanderbilt University Press, 1942).
14. Duke, *History of Morgan's Cavalry*, 194.
15. Ibid., 198.
16. *Picket Line and Camp Fire Stories*, 35.
17. *Duke, History of Morgan's Cavalry*, 207.
18. Ibid., 232.
19. Ibid., 261.
20. Ibid., 289.
21. Ibid., 344–46.
22. Ibid., 320.
23. Miller, *Photographic History of the Civil War*, Vol. 4, 144.
24. Later in life, Harlan would become an associate justice of the U.S. Supreme Court.
25. Duke, *History of Morgan's Cavalry*, 363.
26. Ibid., 387.
27. Ibid., 397.
28. Ibid.
29. Ibid., 405.

CHAPTER SEVEN: DAYS OF DESPERATION

1. Richard W. Surby, *Two Great Raids* (Washington, D.C.: The National Tribune, 1897), 139.

2. O.R., Vol. 33, Pt. 1., 817.
3. Johnson and Buell, eds., *Battles and Leaders of the Civil War,* Vol. 3, 634.
4. Surby, *Two Great Raids,* 14.
5. Ibid., 150.
6. *Sketches of War History,* Vol. 4 (Cincinnati, Ohio: Robert Clark & Co., 1896).
7. Duke, *History of Morgan's Cavalry,* 416–18.
8. Theodore F. Allen, "Six Hundred Miles of Fried Chicken" in *JUSCA* 12 (1899): 166.
9. O.R., Vol. 33, Pt. 1, 645.
10. Allen, "Six Hundred Miles of Fried Chicken," 164.
11. O.R., Vol. 33, Pt. 1, 646.
12. Duke, *History of Morgan's Cavalry,* 423.
13. O.R., Vol. 33, Pt. 1, 648, 649.
14. Surby, *Two Great Raids,* 145.
15. O.R., Vol. 33, Pt. 1, 649.
16. *Sketches of War History,* 290.
17. O.R., Vol. 33, Pt. 1, 652–53.
18. Duke, *History of Morgan's Cavalry,* 435.
19. Surby, *Two Great Raids,* 153.
20. Duke, *History of Morgan's Cavalry,* 437.
21. Allen, "Six Hundred Miles of Fried Chicken," 170.
22. Surby, *Two Great Raids,* 153–54.
23. *Sketches of War History,* 292.
24. Ibid., 301.
25. O.R., Vol. 33, Pt. 1, 660.
26. Duke, *History of Morgan's Cavalry,* 439.
27. Surby, *Two Great Raids,* 156.
28. O.R., Vol. 33, Pt. 1, 671.
29. Duke, *History of Morgan's Cavalry,* 451.
30. Allen, "Six Hundred Miles of Fried Chicken," 172.
31. O.R., Vol. 33, Pt. 1, 661.
32. O.R., Vol. 33, Pt. 1, 669.
33. Johnson and Buell, eds., *Battles and Leaders of the Civil War,* Vol. 3, 635.
34. Duke, *History of Morgan's Cavalry,* 513–14.
35. Johnson and Buell, eds., *Battles and Leaders of the Civil War,* Vol. 4, 423–24.
36. *Dictionary of American Biography,* Vol. 7, 174.
37. Duke, *History of Morgan's Cavalry,* 529.
38. Frank Moore, *Anecdotes, Poetry and Incidents of the War North and South, 1860–1865* (New York: The Arundel Print, 1882), 288.

39. King and Derby, *Camp-Fire Sketches and Battle-field Echoes*, 581–82.
40. Duke, *History of Morgan's Cavalry*, 555.
41. Ibid., 570.
42. Ibid., 571.
43. Ibid., 575.

CHAPTER EIGHT: ONCE A RANGER, ALWAYS A RANGER
1. John Allen Wyeth, *Life of General Nathan Bedford Forrest* (New York: Harper & Brothers Publishers, 1899), 626.
2. Ibid., 6.
3. Ibid., 628.
4. Ku Klux Report of 1872, 2nd Session, 42nd Congress, Senate Document No. 41, Vol. 13, 24.
5. Wyeth, *Life of General Nathan Bedford Forrest*, 24.
6. Robert S. Henry, *"First with the Most:" Forrest* (Westport, Conn.: Greenwood Press, 1974), 34.
7. Thomas Jordan and J. P. Pryor, *The Campaigns of Lieut.-Gen. N. B. Forrest, and of Forrest's Cavalry* (New York: Da Capo Press, 1996), 41–43 (hereafter cited as Jordan and Pryor, *Campaigns of Forrest*).
8. Adam R. Johnson, *Partisan Rangers of the Confederate States Army* (Louisville, Ky.: G. G. Fetter Company, 1904), 39.
9. Wyeth, *Life of General Nathan Bedford Forrest*, 30.
10. Ibid., 32.
11. Johnson, *Partisan Rangers*, 42.
12. Johnson and Buell, eds., *Battles and Leaders of the Civil War*, Vol. 1, 401; Grant, *Personal Memoirs*, 206.
13. Wyeth, *Life of General Nathan Bedford Forrest*, 67.
14. Johnson and Buell, eds., *Battles and Leaders of the Civil War*, Vol. 1, 426.
15. Johnson, *Partisan Rangers*, 67.
16. Johnson and Buell, eds., *Battles and Leaders of the Civil War*, Vol. 1, 427.
17. Sandburg, *Abraham Lincoln: The War Years*, Vol. 1, 289.
18. Wyeth, *Life of General Nathan Bedford Forrest*, 79.
19. Lester N. Fitzhugh, *Terry's Texas Rangers: 8th Texas Cavalry, CSA* (Houston: Civil War Round Table, 1958), 76.
20. Ibid., 77.
21. Fitzhugh, *Terry's Texas Rangers*, 85.
22. Wyeth, *Life of General Nathan Bedford Forrest*, 639–40.
23. Ibid., 92.
24. MOLLUS, *War Papers and Personal Reminiscences*, 358.
25. Henry, *"First with the Most,"* 88–89.
26. Wyeth, *Life of General Nathan Bedford Forrest*, 89.

27. Sipes, *Seventh Pennsylvania Volunteer Cavalry*, 29.

28. James Richardson, *Messages and Papers of the Confederacy* (Nashville, Tenn.: U.S. Publishing Company, 1905).

29. Eric William Sheppard, *Captain Bedford Forrest* (London: The Dial Press, 1930), 316. Remarks attributed to Confederate lieutenant general Richard Taylor.

30. Johnson and Buell, eds., *Battles and Leaders of the Civil War*, Vol. 4, 710; Grant, *Personal Memoirs*, 449–50.

31. Johnson and Buell, eds., *Battles and Leaders of the Civil War*, Vol. 3, 604. The murder or attempted murder of unpopular officers became known as fragging in Vietnam. It is a subject rarely examined by the Army.

32. Duke, *Reminiscences*, 345–46.

33. Johnson and Buell, *Battles and Leaders of the Civil War*, Vol. 4, 644.

34. Ibid., 609.

35. Wyeth, *Life of General Nathan Bedford Forrest*, 106.

36. Ibid., 109.

37. Ibid.

38. Harvey J. Mathers, *General Forrest* (New York: D. Appleton & Co., 1902), 85.

39. On this date President Abraham Lincoln issued the Emancipation Proclamation.

40. John Watson Morton, The Artillery of Nathan Bedford Forrest's Cavalry (Nashville, Tenn.: M.S. Church, 1909), 60.

41. O.R., Vol. 17, Pt. 1, 463.

42. Wyeth, *Life of General Nathan Bedford Forrest*, 176–77.

43. Henry, *"First with the Most,"* 143.

44. Wyeth, *Life of General Nathan Bedford Forrest*, 151.

CHAPTER NINE: ABEL STREIGHT AND THE JACKASS RAID

1. John Billings, *Hardtack and Coffee* (Boston: G. M. Smith & Co., 1887), 318.

2. Morton, *The Artillery of Nathan Bedford Forrest's Cavalry*, 91.

3. Wyeth, *Life of General Nathan Bedford Forrest*, 201.

4. Wyeth, *Life of General Nathan Bedford Forrest*, 189; Jordan and Pryor, *Campaigns of Forrest*, 268.

5. Wyeth, *Life of General Nathan Bedford Forrest*, 208–12.

6. Jordan and Pryor, *Campaigns of Forrest*, 273.

7. Ibid.

8. Dabney H. Maury, *Recollections of a Virginian* (New York: Scribner's Sons, 1894), 209.

9. Jordan and Pryor, *Campaigns of Forrest*, 273.
10. Wyeth, *Life of General Nathan Bedford Forrest*, 202.
11. Ibid., 227; Morton, *The Artillery of Nathan Bedford Forrest's Cavalry*, 105.
12. Morton, *The Artillery of Nathan Bedford Forrest's Cavalry*, 110.
13. Andrew N. Lytle, *Bedford Forrest and His Critter Company* (Nashville, Tenn.: J. S. Sanders, 1992), 187.
14. Johnson and Buell, *Battles and Leaders of the Civil War*, Vol. 3, 641.
15. Wyeth, *Life of General Nathan Bedford Forrest*, 268–70.
16. Johnson and Buell, *Battles and Leaders of the Civil War*, Vol. 3, 645.
17. Ibid., 653.
18. Ibid., 660.
19. Ibid., 654.
20. John K. Mahon and Romana Danysh, *The Army Lineage Series: Infantry* (Washington D.C.: Office of the Chief of Military History, 1972), 413.
21. Wyeth, *Life of General Nathan Bedford Forrest*, 267.
22. Ibid., 264; O.R., Vol. 30, Pt. 4, 710.
23. Wyeth, *Life of General Nathan Bedford Forrest*, 242–43.
24. Ibid., 264–67.
25. Morton, *The Artillery of Nathan Bedford Forrest's Cavalry*, 133.
26. Wyeth, *Life of General Nathan Bedford Forrest*, 268.
27. Ibid., 276–77.
28. Sherman, *Memoirs*, 419.
29. George E. Waring, Jr., *Whip and Spur* (New York: Doubleday and McClure, 1897), 67.
30. Ibid., 111–13.
31. Ibid., 113–14.
32. Richardson, *Messages and Papers of the Confederacy*, 176.
33. O.R., Vol. 32, 350.
34. Jordan and Pryor, *Campaigns of Forrest*, 397.
35. Waring, *Whip and Spur*, 115–16.
36. Sherman, *Memoirs*, 423.
37. O.R., Vol. 32, 616; Morton, *The Artillery of Nathan Bedford Forrest's Cavalry*, 148–49.
38. O.R., Vol. 32, 624–27.
39. Ibid., 710.
40. Ibid., 545.
41. Ibid., 547.
42. Jordan and Pryor, *Campaigns of Forrest*, 419.
43. O.R., Vol. 32, 560.
44. Jordan and Pryor, *Campaigns of Forrest*, 429.
45. O.R., Vol. 32, 559–61.

46. Ibid., 561.
47. Ibid., 562–63.
48. Ibid., 564.
49. Ibid., 590.
50. Brooks, *Butler and His Cavalry,* 363–64.
51. Ibid., 487.
52. Ibid., 782.

CHAPTER TEN: BRICE'S CROSSROADS AND BEYOND

1. John Parker, *The History of the Twenty-second Massachusetts Infantry* (Boston: Rand Avery Company, 1887), 408–9.
2. O.R., Vol. 45, Pt. 1, 32.
3. Johnson and Buell, eds., *Battles and Leaders of the Civil War,* Vol. 4, 420.
4. Moore, *Anecdotes, Poetry and Incidents of the War North and South,* 179.
5. O.R., Vol. 39, 91.
6. Waring, *Whip and Spur,* 129.
7. O.R., Vol. 39, 92.
8. Waring, *Whip and Spur,* 129–30.
9. O.R., Vol. 39, 323.
10. Johnson and Buell, eds., *Battles and Leaders of the Civil War,* Vol. 4, 420.
11. Jordan and Prior, *Campaigns of Forrest,* 473.
12. O.R., Vol. 39, 93.
13. Ibid., 94.
14. Johnson and Buell, eds., *Battles and Leaders of the Civil War,* Vol. 4, 420; Jordan and Pryor, *Campaigns of Forrest,* 474–78.
15. O.R., Vol. 39, 214.
16. Jordan and Pryor, *Campaigns of Forrest,* 480.
17. Johnson and Buell, eds., *Battles and Leaders of the Civil War,* 421.
18. Waring, *Whip and Spur,* 129.
19. Samuel Sturgis was shelved for the remainder of the war but still held a Regular army commission. Grant did not hold the defeat against him. After the war Sturgis would become colonel of the 7th Cavalry and the commander of Lt. Col. George Armstrong Custer.
20. O.R., Vol. 31, 118.
21. Ibid., 121.
22. O.R., Vol. 39, 224.
23. Ibid., 229.
24. Johnson and Buell, eds., *Battles and Leaders of the Civil War,* Vol. 4, 276.
25. Wyeth, *Life of General Nathan Bedford Forrest,* 433.
26. Ibid., 440.
27. Ibid., 447–48.

28. Ibid., 454.

29. Johnson and Buell, eds., *Battles and Leaders of the Civil War*, 422.

30. Sherman, *Memoirs*, 549.

31. Richardson, *Messages and Papers of the Confederacy*, 266–67.

32. Jordan and Pryor, *Campaigns of Forrest*, 535–36.

33. Wyeth, *Life of General Nathan Bedford Forrest*, 473.

34. Ibid., 474; *Dictionary of American Biography*, Vol. 10, 495–96.

35. Jordan and Pryor, *Campaigns of Forrest*, 547.

36. Morton, *The Artillery of Nathan Bedford Forrest's Cavalry*, 219–20.

37. Wyeth, *Life of General Nathan Bedford Forrest*, 477.

38. Taylor, *Destruction and Reconstruction*, 198–99.

39. O.R., Vol. 39, 542.

40. Ibid., 523.

41. Ibid., 522.

42. Elliott would die of wounds received on September 24, 1864.

43. O.R., Vol. 39, 545; Wyeth, *Life of General Nathan Bedford Forrest*, 496.

44. O.R., Vol. 39, 544.

45. Morton, *The Artillery of Nathan Bedford Forrest's Cavalry*, 239–40.

46. According to the history of the 7th Pennsylvania Cavalry, Nixon was a former commissary sergeant made a second lieutenant on May 4, 1863. He was discharged on December 7, 1864, and killed in a railroad accident on the Philadelphia and Erie Railroad on January 21, 1880. Sergeant Rhinemiller was later commissioned and became a captain, as did Lieutenant Long.

47. O.R., Vol. 39, 548.

48. Johnson and Buell, eds., *Battles and Leaders of the Civil War*, Vol. 4, 253.

49. Ibid., 253–54.

50. George F. Price, *Across the Continent with the Fifth Cavalry* (New York: Noble Offset Printers, Inc., 1883), 200.

51. Johnson and Buell, eds., *Battles and Leaders of the Civil War*, 255.

52. Wyeth, *Life of General Nathan Bedford Forrest*, 517.

53. Morton, *The Artillery of Nathan Bedford Forrest's Cavalry*, 255.

54. O.R., Vol. 39, 860.

55. Morton, *The Artillery of Nathan Bedford Forrest's Cavalry*, 255–56.

CHAPTER ELEVEN: GRAY TWILIGHT

1. Jordan and Pryor, *Campaigns of Forrest*, 618.

2. Wyeth, *Life of General Nathan Bedford Forrest*, 541.

3. Johnson and Buell, eds., *Battles and Leaders of the Civil War*, Vol. 4, 429.

4. Jordan and Pryor, *Campaigns of Forrest*, 621.

5. O.R., Vol. 45, 652.

6. Ibid., 653.
7. Mathers, *General Forrest,* 311.
8. Wyeth, *Life of General Nathan Bedford Forrest,* 544.
9. John B. Gordon, *General Reminiscences of the Civil War* (New York: Charles Scribner's Sons, 1904), 76.
10. O.R., Vol. 45, 653–54.
11. Ibid., 35.
12. Price, *Across the Continent with the Fifth Cavalry,* 24.
13. Mathers, *General Forrest,* 317.
14. Ibid., 321.
15. Johnson and Buell, eds., *Battles and Leaders of the Civil War,* Vol. 4, 466.
16. O.R., Vol. 45, 46.
17. Ibid., 42.
18. Wyeth, *Life of General Nathan Bedford Forrest,* 568–69.
19. Johnson and Buell, eds., *Battles and Leaders of the Civil War,* Vol. 4, 470.
20. Ibid.
21. Ibid., 471.
22. Mathers, *General Forrest,* 334.
23. Johnson and Buell, eds., *Battles and Leaders of the Civil War,* Vol. 4, 471.
24. Wyeth, *Life of General Nathan Bedford Forrest,* 513.
25. Morton, *The Artillery of Nathan Bedford Forrest's Cavalry,* 13.
26. Wyeth, *Life of General Nathan Bedford Forrest,* 605.
27. O.R., Vol. 49, 1,042.
28. Ibid., 1,058.
29. Ibid., 1,060.
30. Wyeth, *Life of General Nathan Bedford Forrest,* 582.
31. Ibid., 613–14.
32. Ibid., 618.

Bibliography

Alexander, Edward P. *Military Memoirs of a Confederate.* New York: Charles Scribner's Sons, 1907.

Alexander, John H. *Mosby's Men.* New York: The Neale Publishing Company, 1907.

Ashby, Thomas A. *Life of Turner Ashby.* New York: The Neal Publishing Company, 1914.

Avirett, Rev. James B. *The Memoirs of General Turner Ashby and His Compeers.* Baltimore: Selby & Dulany, 1867.

Auman, William Thomas. *Neighbor against Neighbor: The Inner Civil War in the Central Counties of Confederate North Carolina.* Unpublished doctoral dissertation, University of North Carolina, Chapel Hill, 1988.

Barrett, John G. *The Civil War in North Carolina.* Chapel Hill: University of North Carolina, Press, 1963.

Beymer, William Gilmore. *On Hazardous Service.* New York: Harper & Brothers, 1912.

Billings, John D. *Hardtack and Coffee.* Boston: George M. Smith & Company, 1887.

Boatner, Lt. Col. Mark Mayo. *The Civil War Dictionary.* New York: David McKay Company, 1959.

Burch, John P. *Charles W. Quantrill.* Vega, TX: n.p., 1923.

Bushong, Millard K. *General Turner Ashby and Stonewall's Valley Campaign.* Varona, VA: McClure Printing Company, 1980.

Butler, Lorine Letcher. *John Morgan and His Men.* Philadelphia: Dorrance & Company, 1960.

Brewer, James D. *The Raiders of 1862.* Westport, Conn.: Praeger, 1997.

Brandt, Nat. *The Man Who Tried to Burn New York.* Syracuse, NY: Syracuse University Press, 1986.

Breihan, Carl W. *Quantrill and His Civil War Guerrillas.* New York: Promontory Press, 1959.

Brooks, U. R. *Butler and His Cavalry.* Columbia, SC: The State Company, n.d.

Casler, John O. *Four Years in the Stonewall Brigade.* Guthrie, OK: n.p., 1906.

Collins, Darrell L. *General William Averell's Salem Raid*. Shippensburg, PA: White Mane, 1999.

Connelley, William Elsey. *Quantrill and the Border Wars*. Cedar Rapids, Iowa: The Torch Press, 1910.

Crawford, Marshall. *Mosby and His Men*. New York: G. W. Carleton & Company, n.d.

Crook, George. *General George Crook: His Autobiography*. Edited by Martin F. Schmitt. Norman, OK: University of Oklahoma Press, 1946.

Crouch, Richard E. *Rough-Riding Scout*. Arlington, VA: Elden Editions, 1994.

Delauter, Roger U. *McNeill's Rangers*. Lynchburg, VA: H. E. Howard, 1986.

Divine, John E., et al. *To Talk Is Treason*. Waterford, VA: Waterford Foundation, 1996.

Dodson, W. C. *Campaigns of Wheeler and His Cavalry*. Atlanta: Hudgins Publishing Company, 1899.

Downs, Edward C. *Four Years a Scout and Spy*. Zanevill, OH: Dunne, 1866.

Duke, Basil W. *A History of Morgan's Cavalry*. Bloomington, IN: Indiana University Press, n.d.

Duke, Basil W. *Reminiscences of General Basil W. Duke, C.S.A.* New York: Doubleday, Page & Company, 1911.

Dupuy, R. Ernest, and Trevor N. Dupuy. *Brave Men and Great Captains*. McLean, VA: Nova Publications, 1993.

Dyer, Frederick H. *A Compendium of the War of the Rebellion*. Dayton, OH: Press of the Morningside Bookshop, 1979.

Eckart, Edward K., and Nicholas J. Amato, eds. *Ten Years in the Saddle*. San Rafael, Calif.: Presidio Press, 1978.

Eddy, T. M. *The Patriotism of Illinois*. 2 vols. Chicago: Clarke & Company, 1865.

Edwards, John N. *Noted Guerrillas of the Warfare of the Border*. St. Louis, MO: Bryan, Brand & Company, 1877.

Emerson, Edward W. *Life and Letters of Charles Russell Lowell*. Reprint edition. New York: Kennikat Press, 1971.

Evans, Thomas J., and James M. Moyer. *Mosby's Confederacy: A Guide to the Roads and Sites of Colonel John Singleton Mosby*. Shippensburg, PA: White Mane, 1991.

Fay, John B. *Capture of Generals Crook and Kelly by the McNeill Rnagers*. Cumberland, MD: Laney Souvenir Company, 1865.

Freeman, Douglas Southall. *Lee's Lieutenants: A Study in Command*. 3 vols. New York: Charles Scribner's Sons, 1943.

Frost, Lawrence A. *Custer Legends*. Bowling Green: Popular Press, 1981.

Gilmore, Col. Harry. *Four Years in the Saddle*. New York: Harper & Brothers, 1866.

Goodhart, Briscoe. *History of the Independent Loudoun Virginia Rangers.* Washington, D.C.: Press of Mcgill & Wallace, 1896.

Gordon, John B. *General Reminiscences of the Civil War.* New York: Charles Scribner's Sons, 1904.

Grant, Ulysses S. *Personal Memoirs of U.S. Grant.* 2 vols. New York: The Century Company, 1895.

Haislip, Joan. *The Crown of Mexico.* New York: Holt, Rinehart and Winston, 1971.

Hakenson, Donald C. *This Forgotten Land.* N.p.: n.p., 2002.

Headley, John W. *Confederate Operations in Canada and New York.* New York: The Neale Publishing Company. 1906.

Henry, Robert Selph. *"First with the Most."* New York: Mallard Press, 1991.

Herr, Pamela, and Mary Lee Spence. *The Letters of Jessie Benton Fremont.* Chicago: University of Illinois Press, 1993.

Holland, Cecil Fletcher. *Morgan and His Raiders.* New York: The Macmillian Company, 1943.

Hunter, David. *Report of the Military Services of Gen. David Hunter, U.S.A.* New York: D. Van Nostrand, 1873.

Husby, Karla Jean, comp., and Eric J. Wittenberg, ed. *Under Custer's Command.* Washington, D.C.: Brassey's, 2000.

Johnson, Adam Rankin. *The Partisan Rangers (of the Confederate States Army).* Louisville, KY: George G. Fetter Company, 1904.

Johnston, Milus E. *The Sword of Bushwhacker Johnson.* Edited and annotated by Charles S. Rice. Huntsville, AL: Flint River Press, 1992.

Jones, Virgil Carrington. *Gray Ghosts and Rebel Raiders.* New York: Henry Holt & Company, 1956.

Jones, Virgil Carrington. *Ranger Mosby.* Chapel Hill, NC: University of North Carolina Press, 1944.

Jones, William J. Rev. *Southern Historical Society Papers.* Vol. 7. Dayton, OH: Broadfoot Publishing Company, 1990.

Jordan, Thomas, and J. P. Pryor. *The Campaigns of General Nathan Bedford Forrest (and of Forrest's Cavalry).* Reprint edition. New York: Da Capo Press, 1996.

Katz, D. Mark. *Custer in Photographs* Gettysburg, PA: Yo-Mark Production Company, 1985.

Lang, Theodore F. *Loyal West Virginia from 1861–1865.* Baltimore: The Deutsch Publishing Company, 1895.

Long, E. B. *The Civil War Day by Day: An Almanac, 1861–1865.* Garden City, NY: Doubleday & Company, 1971.

Lonn, Ella. *Desertion during the Civil War.* New York: Century Company, 1928.

Osborne, Randall, and Jeffrey C. Weaver. *The Virginia State Rangers and State Line.* Lynchburg, VA: H. E. Howard, 1994.

Pollard, E. A. *The Lost Cause.* Facsimile edition. New York: Gramercy Books, 1994.

Pond, George E. *The Shenandoah Valley.* New York: Charles Scribner's Sons, n.d.

Porter, Gen. Horace. *Campaigning with Grant.* New York: The Century Company, 1897.

Mathers, Capt. Harvey J. *General Forrest.* New York: D. Appleton & Company, 1902.

Merington, Marguerite, ed. *The Custer Story.* New York: Barnes and Noble, 1950.

McClure, Alexander K. *Lincoln's Yarns and Stories.* Chicago: The John Winston Company, n.d.

McClure, J. B., ed. *Anecdotes of Abraham Lincoln.* Chicago: Rhodes & McClure, 1884.

McDonald, William N. *History of the Laurel Brigade.* Reprint edition. Gaithersburg, MD: Old Soldier Books, 1987.

McElroy, John. *The Struggle for Missouri.* Washington, D.C.: The National Tribune Company, 1909.

McPherson, James M. *Battle Cry of Freedom.* New York: Oxford University Press, 1988.

Miller, Francis Trevelyan. *The Photographic History of the Civil War.* Vol. 4. New York: The Review of Reviews Company, 1911.

Miller, Rex. *Croxton's Raid.* Depew, NY: Patrex Press, 1992.

Monaghan, Jay. *Custer.* Lincoln, NE: University of Nebraska Press, 1959.

Monteiro, Aristides. *War Reminiscences (by the Surgeon of Mosby's Command).* Reprint edition. Gaithersburg, MD: Butternut Press, 1979.

Moore, Frank. *Anecdotes, Poetry and Incidents of the War North and South, 1860–1865.* New York: The Arundel Printing Company, 1882.

Morton, John Watson. *The Artillery of Nathan Bedford Forrest's Cavalry.* Nashville, Tenn.: M. E. Church, 1909.

Morton, Joseph W., ed. *Sparks from the Camp Fire.* Philadelphia: Keystone Publishing Company, 1891.

Mosby, John S. *Mosby's Memoirs.* New York: Little, Brown and Company, 1917.

Mosby, John S. *War Reminiscences, Stuart's Cavalry Campaigns.* New York: Dodd, Mead and Company, 1898.

Munson, John W. *Reminiscences of a Mosby Guerrilla.* New York: Moffat, Yard and Company, 1906.

Myers, Frank M. *The Comanches (A History of White's Battalion, Virginia Cavalry).* Baltimore: Kelly, Piet & Company, 1871.

Ness, George T. *The Regular Army on the Eve of the Civil War.* Baltimore: Toomey Press, 1990.

Ramsdell, Charles W. *Behind the Lines in the Southern Confederacy.* Baton Rouge: Lousiana State University Press, 1944.

Rice, Allen Thorndike. *Reminiscences of Abraham Lincoln.* New York: North American Publishing Company, 1886.

Sandburg, Carl. *Abraham Lincoln.* 3 vols. New York: Dell, 1959.

Sandburg, Carl. *Abraham Lincoln: The War Years.* 4 vols. New York: Harcourt, Brace & Company, 1939.

Scott, H. L. *Military Dictionary.* New York: D. Van Nostrand, 1862.

Sheppard, Eric William. *Bedford Forrest.* New York: The Dial Press, 1930.

Sheridan, Philip H. *Personal Memoirs of Philip Henry Sheridan.* 2 vols. Edited by Michael V. Sheridan. New York: D. Appleton and Company, 1904.

Sherman, William Tecumseh. *Memoirs of General W. T. Sherman.* 2 vols. New York: Charles L. Webster & Company, 1892.

Sifakis, Stewart. *Who Was Who in the Civil War.* New York: Facts on File Publications, 1988.

Simon, John Y., ed. *The Papers of Ulysses S. Grant.* 12 vols. Carbondale, Ill.: Southern Illinois University Press, 1984.

Rice, Otis K. *The Hatfields and the McCoys.* Louisville, KY: University Press of Kentucky, 1982.

Richardson, Albert D. *Secret Service.* Hartford, Conn.: American Publishing Company, 1865.

Sensing, Thurman. *Champ Ferguson, Confederate Guerilla.* Nashville, Tenn.: Vanderbilt University Press, 1942.

Siepel, Kevin H. *Rebel: The Life and Times of John Singleton Mosby.* New York: St. Martin's Press, 1983.

Simpson, Col. Harold B. *Soldiers of Texas.* Waco, TX: n.p., 1973.

Strother, David Hunter. *A Virginia Yankee in the Civil War.* Chapel Hill, NC: University of North Carolina Press, 1961.

Surby, R. W. *Grierson's Raid.* Washington D.C.: The National Tribune, McElroy, Shoppell & Andrews, 1897.

Swiggett, Howard. *The Rebel Raider: A Life of John Hunt Morgan.* Garden City, New York: The Garden City Publishing Company, 1937.

Tarbell, Ida M. *The Life of Abraham Lincoln.* New York: McClure, Phillips & Company, 1895.

Taylor, Richard. *Destruction and Reconstruction.* New York: D. Appleton and Company, 1879.

Thomason, John W. Jr. *Jeb Stuart.* New York: Charles Scribner's Sons, 1930.

Vasvary, Edmund. *Lincoln's Hungarian Heroes.* Washington D.C.: The Hungarian Reformed Federation of America, 1939

Vale, Joseph G. *Minty and the Cavalry: A History of the Cavalry Campaigns in the Western Armies.* Harrisburg, PA: Edwin K Meyers, 1886.

Van Noppen, Ina. *Stoneman's Last Raid.* Raleigh, NC: North Carolina State Print Shop, 1961.

Veil, Charles Henry. *The Memoirs of Charles Henry Veil.* Edited by Herman J. Viola. New York: Orion Books, 1993.

Wallace, R. C. *A Few Memories of a Long Life.* Helena, MT: n.p., 1916.

Waller, Altina L. *Feud: Hatfields, McCoys and Social Change in Appalachia, 1860–1890.* Chapel Hill, NC: University of North Carolina Press, 1988.

Waring, George. *Whip and Spur.* New York: Doubleday and McClure, 1897.

Warner, Ezra J. *Generals in Blue.* Baton Rouge, LA: Lousiana State University Press, 1964.

Wert, Jeffry D. *Custer: The Controversial Life of George Armstrong Custer.* New York: Simon & Shuster, 1966.

Williamson, James J. *Mosby's Rangers.* New York: Ralph B. Kenyon, 1896.

Woodward, Harold R. *Defender of the Valley: Brigadier General John Daniel Imboden, C.S.A.* Berryville, VA: Rockbridge Publishing Company, 1966.

Wyeth, John Allen. *Life of General Nathan Bedford Forrest.* New York: Harper & Brothers, 1899.

REGIMENTAL HISTORIES

Armstrong, Richard L. *7th Virginia Cavalry.* Lynchburg, VA: H. E. Howard, 1992.

Armstrong, Richard L. *19th and 20th Virginia Cavalry.* Lynchburg, VA: H. E. Howard, 1994.

Beach, William H. *The First New York Lincoln Cavalry.* New York: The Lincoln Cavalry Association, 1902.

Benedict, George Grenville. *Vermont in the Civil War.* 2 vols. Burlington, VT: The Free Press Association, 1881. (Includes history of the 1st Vermont Cavalry.)

Boudrye, Louis N. *Historic Records of the Fifth New York Cavalry, First Ira Harris Guard.* Albany, New York: J. Munsell, 1868.

Delauter, Roger U. *18th Virginia Cavalry.* Lynchburg, VA: H. E. Howard, 1985.

Divine, John E. *35th Battalion Virginia Cavalry.* Lynchburg, VA: H. E. Howard, 1985.

Elwood, John W. *Elwood's Stories of the Old Ringgold Cavalry.* Coal Center, PA: self-published, 1914.

Farrar, Samuel Clark. *The Twenty-Second Pennsylvania Cavalry and the Ringgold Battalion, 1861–1865.* N.p.: The Twenty-Second Pennsylvania Cavalry Assocation, 1911.

Hard, Abner. *History of the Eighth Cavalry Regiment, Illinois Volunteers.* Aurora, Ill.: n.p., 1868.

History of the Eighteenth Regiment of Cavalry, Pennsylvania Volunteers. New York: Wynkoop-Hallenbeck Crawford Company, 1909.

Lee, William O. *Seventh Regiment, Michigan Volunteer Cavalry, 1862–1865.* N.p.: 7th Michigan Cavalry Association, n.d.

Loyal Legion of the United States. *War Papers and Personal Reminiscences, 1861–1865.* 60 vols. St. Louis, MO: Becktold & Company, 1892.

Kirk, Charles H. *History of the Fifteenth Pennsylvania Volunteer Cavalry.* Philadelphia: n.p., 1906.

Moyer, H. P. *History of the Seventeenth Regiment Pennsylvania Volunteer Cavalry.* Lebanon, PA: Sowers Printing Company, 1911.

Newcomer, C. Armour *Cole's Cavalry, or Three Years in the Saddle.* Baltimore: Cushing & Company, 1895.

Norton, Chauncey S. *History of the Fifteenth New York Volunteer Cavalry.* Ithaca, NY: Journal Book and Job Printing House, 1891.

Parker, John L. *History of the Twenty-second Massachusetts Infantry.* Boston: Rand Avery Company, 1887.

Price, George F. *Across the Continent with the Fifth Cavalry.* New York: Noble Offset Printers, 1883.

Rauch, William H. *History of the Bucktails.* Philadelphia: Electric Printing Company, 1906.

Ripley, William Y. W. *Vermont Riflemen in the War for the Union.* Rutland, VT: Tuttle & Company Printers, 1883.

Rodenbough, Theo F. *Everglade to Cannon with the Second Dragoons, Second U.S. Cavalry.* New York: D. Van Nostrand, 1875.

Stevenson, Thomas M. *History of the 78th O.V.V.I.* Zanesville, OH: Hugh Dunne, 1865.

3rd Pennsylvania Cavalry Association. *History of the Third Pennsylvania Cavalry.* Philadelphia: Franklin Printing Company, 1905.

Todd, Glenda McWhirter. *First Alabama Cavalry, U.S.A.* Bowie, MD: Heritage Books, 1999.

Weaver, Jeffrey C. *45th Battalion Virginia Infantry, Smith and Count's Battalions of Partisan Rangers.* Lynchburg, VA: H. E. Howard, 1994.

Weaver Jeffrey C. *Thurmond's Partisan Rangers and Swann's Battalion of Virginia Cavalry.* Lynchburg, VA: H. E. Howard, 1993.

Wood, D. W. *20th O.V.V.I. Regiment.* Columbus, OH: Paul & Thrall Book and Job Printers, 1876.

Young, J. P. *The Seventh Tennessee Cavalry (Confederate).* Nashville, Tenn.: M. E. Church, 1890.

NEWSPAPERS
Charleston (SC) Mercury
Harper's Illustrated
Leslies Illustrated Weekly
Nashville Dispatch
New York Herald
New York Times
Richmond (VA) Examiner
Washington Post

MANUSCRIPTS
Curry, Capt. William L., 1st Ohio Volunteer Cavalry of Columbus, Ohio.
"Raid of the Confederate Cavalry through Central Tennessee." Read before the Ohio Commandery of the Loyal Legion, 1 April 1908. Republished as part of the Birmingham Public Library's "Eyewitness Accounts of the Civil War" Series, 1987.

Acknowledgments

First and foremost, my thanks to my best friend, travel companion, advisor, publicity director, proofreader, critic, lover, and wife, Carolyn Black, without whom I would be a ship without a rudder. Thanks also to my pal and editor, Chris Evans, the alchemist who puts it all together, and to all my long time friends at the U.S. Army Military History Institute at Carlisle Barracks, Pennsylvania: Dr. Richard "Dick" Sommers, Randy Hackenburg, Richard Baker, Jay Graybeal, Kathy Olsen, and JoAnna McDonald, my friend who went to California. They have always been willing to show the path to that elusive document or volume.

Thanks to Martha Steiger and Julia Scott at Virginia tourism, to Patty Rogers and the staff of the Leesburg Virginia Convention and Visitors Bureau, and to Corporal Gerald G. Crosson of the Berryville, Virginia, Police Department, who helped me greatly in finding the site where Union soldiers were hung on Mosby's orders. My deep appreciation to my friend Mosby tour guide Dave Goetz and to Tom Evans, Don Haakenson, and other fellow members of The Stuart-Mosby Historical Society. Thanks are due to John and Bronwen Souders, who shared their time and knowledge about the Loudoun Rangers in that beautiful village of Waterford, Virginia. Thanks to my daughter, April Black Croft, and my wife for their help at the National Archives and the Library of Congress. Thanks to the staff at the West Virginia Archives and the University of West Virginia Library as well as to the research staff of Dickinson College, Carlisle, Pennsylvania, and the Pennsylvania State Library in Harrisburg. As one who knows joy when sitting in the stacks and uncovering some pearl of historical beauty, my thanks to all archivists and librarians. They are the great guardians of our experience.

Index

Page numbers in italics indicate photographs

Stackpole Military History Series

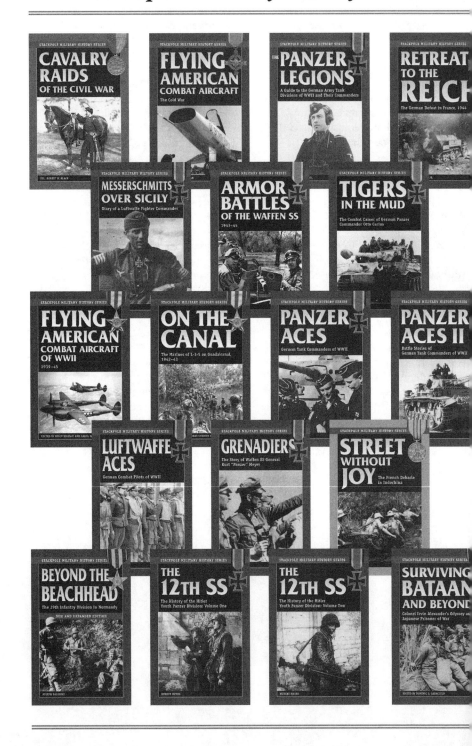

Real battles. Real soldiers. Real stories.

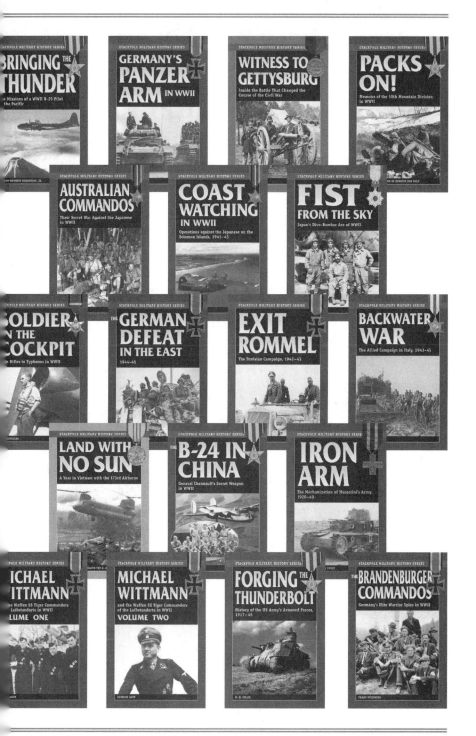

Stackpole Military History Series

Real battles. Real soldiers. Real stories.

STACKPOLE MILITARY HISTORY SERIES

THE BATTLE OF SICILY
How the Allies Lost Their Chance for Total Victory

STACKPOLE MILITARY HISTORY SERIES

FORTRESS FRANCE
The Maginot Line and French Defenses in WWII

STACKPOLE MILITARY HISTORY SERIES

CARRIERS IN COMBAT
The Air War at Sea

STACKPOLE MILITARY HISTORY SERIES

EAGLES OF THE THIRD REICH
Men of the Luftwaffe in WWII

STACKPOLE MILITARY HISTORY SERIES

SURVIVING BATAAN AND BEYOND
Colonel Irvin Alexander's Odyssey as a Japanese Prisoner of War

STACKPOLE MILITARY HISTORY SERIES

THE BRANDENBURGER COMMANDOS
Germany's Elite Warrior Spies in WWII

STACKPOLE MILITARY HISTORY SERIES

COLOSSAL CRACKS
Montgomery's 21st Army Group in Northwest Europe, 1944–45

STACKPOLE MILITARY HISTORY SERIES

DIVE BOMBER!
Aircraft, Technology, and Tactics in WWII

STACKPOLE MILITARY HISTORY SERIES

PANZERS IN WINTER
Hitler's Army and the Battle of the Bulge

STACKPOLE MILITARY HISTORY SERIES

GI INGENUITY
Improvisation, Technology, and Winning WWII

STACKPOLE MILITARY HISTORY SERIES

THE PATH TO BLITZKRIEG
Doctrine and Training in the German Army, 1920–39

STACKPOLE MILITARY HISTORY SERIES

ROMMEL'S DESERT WAR
The Life and Death of the Afrika Korps

STACKPOLE MILITARY HISTORY SERIES

GHOST, THUNDERBOLT, AND WIZARD
Mosby, Morgan, and Forrest in the Civil War

STACKPOLE MILITARY HISTORY SERIES

EASTERN FRONT COMBAT
The German Soldier in Battle from Stalingrad to Berlin

STACKPOLE MILITARY HISTORY SERIES

SOVIET BLITZKRIEG
Battle for White Russia, 1944

STACKPOLE MILITARY HISTORY SERIES

T-34 IN ACTION
Soviet Tank Troops in WWII

STACKPOLE MILITARY HISTORY SERIES

THE WAR AGAINST ROMMEL'S SUPPLY LINES
1942–43

STACKPOLE MILITARY HISTORY SERIES

MOUNTAIN WARRIORS
Moroccan Goums in WWII

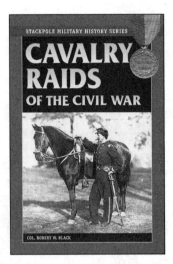

Stackpole Military History Series

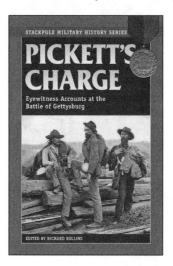

PICKETT'S CHARGE

EYEWITNESS ACCOUNTS AT THE
BATTLE OF GETTYSBURG

Edited by Richard Rollins

On the final day of the battle of Gettysburg, Robert E. Lee
ordered one of the most famous infantry assaults of all time:
Pickett's Charge. Following a thundering artillery barrage,
thousands of Confederates launched a daring frontal attack on
the Union line. From their entrenched positions, Federal
soldiers decimated the charging Rebels, leaving the field
littered with the fallen and several Southern divisions in tatters.
Written by generals, officers, and enlisted men on both sides,
these firsthand accounts offer an up-close look at Civil War
combat and a panoramic view of the carnage of July 3, 1863.

$19.95 • Paperback • 6 x 9 • 432 pages • 11 maps

WWW.STACKPOLEBOOKS.COM
1-800-732-3669

Stackpole Military History Series

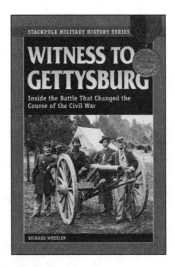

WITNESS TO GETTYSBURG
INSIDE THE BATTLE THAT CHANGED THE
COURSE OF THE CIVIL WAR
Richard Wheeler

In the summer of 1863, the gray tide of Robert E. Lee's Confederate army swept north in a grand offensive to end the war. Union forces under new commander George Meade pursued, and amid the rolling hills and green fields of Gettysburg, Pennsylvania, the two sides clashed in one of the Civil War's most pivotal battles. Combining eyewitness accounts with dramatic narration, Richard Wheeler relates these events as they unfolded, from Lee's strategic planning to Meade's failure to deliver a deathblow to the battered Rebels. The result is a startlingly vivid tapestry of war that brings the battle of Gettysburg to life.

$19.95 • Paperback • 6 x 9 • 432 pages • 48 b/w illustration, 9 maps

WWW.STACKPOLEBOOKS.COM
1-800-732-3669

Stackpole Military History Series

D-DAY TO BERLIN
THE NORTHWEST EUROPE CAMPAIGN, 1944–45
Alan J. Levine

The liberation of Western Europe in World War II required eleven months of hard fighting, from the beaches of Normandy to Berlin and the Baltic Sea. In this crisp, comprehensive account, Alan J. Levine describes the Allied campaign to defeat Nazi Germany in the West: D-Day, the hedgerow battles in France during the summer of 1944, the combined airborne-ground assault of Operation Market-Garden in September, Hitler's winter offensive at the Battle of the Bulge, and the final drive across the Rhine that culminated in Germany's surrender in May 1945.

$16.95 • Paperback • 6 x 9 • 240 pages

WWW.STACKPOLEBOOKS.COM
1-800-732-3669

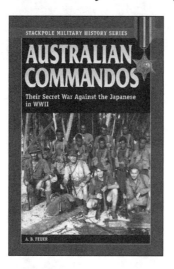

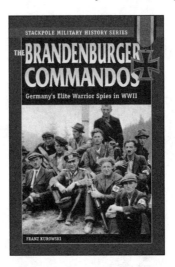

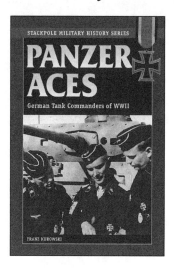

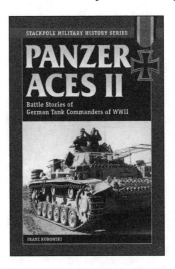

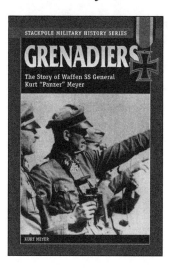

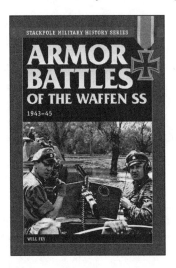

Stackpole Military History Series

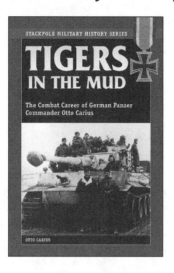

TIGERS IN THE MUD
THE COMBAT CAREER OF GERMAN PANZER COMMANDER OTTO CARIUS

Otto Carius,
translated by Robert J. Edwards

World War II began with a metallic roar as the
German Blitzkrieg raced across Europe, spearheaded
by the most dreadful weapon of the twentieth century:
the Panzer. Tank commander Otto Carius thrusts the
reader into the thick of battle, replete with the
blood, smoke, mud, and gunpowder so common
to the elite German fighting units.

$19.95 • Paperback • 6 x 9 • 368 pages
51 photos • 48 illustrations • 3 maps

WWW.STACKPOLEBOOKS.COM
1-800-732-3669

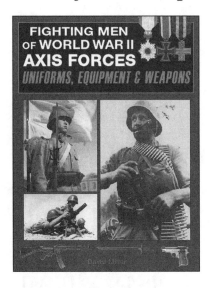